Collaborative Intimacies in Music and Dance

DANCE AND PERFORMANCE STUDIES

General Editors:
Helena Wulff, *Stockholm University* and **Jonathan Skinner**, *University of Roehampton*

Advisory Board:
Alexandra Carter, Marion Kant, Tim Scholl

In all cultures, and across time, people have danced. For performers and spectators, the expressive nature of dance opens up spaces where social and political circumstances are creatively negotiated. Grounded in ethnography, this series explores dance, music and bodily movement in cultural contexts at the juncture of history, ritual and performance in an interconnected world.

Volume 1
Dancing at the Crossroads: Memory and Mobility in Ireland
Helena Wulff

Volume 2
Embodied Communities: Dance Traditions and Change in Java
Felicia Hughes-Freeland

Volume 3
Turning the Tune: Traditional Music, Tourism and Change in an Irish Village
Adam Kaul

Volume 4
Dancing Cultures: Globalization, Tourism and Identity in the Anthropology of Dance
Edited by Hélène Neveu Kringelbach and Jonathan Skinner

Volume 5
Dance Circles: Movement, Morality and Self-Fashioning in Urban Senegal
Hélène Neveu Kringelbach

Volume 6
Learning Senegalese Sabar: Dancers and Embodiment in New York and Dakar
Eleni Bizas

Volume 7
In Search of Legitimacy: How Outsiders Become Part of the Afro-Brazilian Capoeira Tradition
Lauren Miller Griffith

Volume 8
Choreographies of Landscape: Signs of Performance in Yosemite National Park
Sally Ann Ness

Volume 9
Languid Bodies, Grounded Stances: The Curving Pathway of Neoclassical Odissi Dance
Nandini Sikand

Volume 10
Collaborative Intimacies in Music and Dance: Anthropologies of Sound and Movement
Edited by Evangelos Chrysagis and Panas Karampampas

Collaborative Intimacies in Music and Dance

Anthropologies of Sound and Movement

Edited by

Evangelos Chrysagis and
Panas Karampampas

First published in 2017 by
Berghahn Books
www.berghahnbooks.com

© 2017, 2020 Evangelos Chrysagis and Panas Karampampas
First paperback edition published in 2020

All rights reserved. Except for the quotation of short passages
for the purposes of criticism and review, no part of this book
may be reproduced in any form or by any means, electronic or
mechanical, including photocopying, recording, or any information
storage and retrieval system now known or to be invented,
without written permission of the publisher.

Library of Congress Cataloging-in-Publication Data
Names: Chrysagis, Evangelos, editor. | Karampampas, Panas, editor.
Title: Collaborative intimacies in music and dance : anthropologies of
sound and movement / edited by Evangelos Chrysagis and Pana Karampampas.
Description: New York : Berghahn Books, 2017. | Series: Dance and performance studies ; Volume 10 | Includes bibliographical references and index.
Identifiers: LCCN 2016053587 (print) | LCCN 2017005992 (ebook) |
ISBN 9781785334535 (hardback : alk. paper) | ISBN 9781785334542
(eBook)
Subjects: LCSH: Music and dance. | Music--Social aspects. | Dance--
Anthropological aspects.
Classification: LCC ML3916 .C56 2017 (print) | LCC ML3916 (ebook) |
DDC 306.4/84--dc23
LC record available at https://lccn.loc.gov/2016053587

British Library Cataloguing in Publication Data
A catalogue record for this book is available from the British Library

ISBN: 978-1-78533-453-5 Hardback
ISBN 978-1-78920-838-2 Paperback
ISBN: 978-1-78533-454-2 Ebook

Contents

List of Illustrations and Table	vii
Preface	ix
Introduction: Collaborative Intimacies *Evangelos Chrysagis and Panas Karampampas*	1

PART I   SOUND, MEANING AND SELF-AWARENESS

1. Being in Sound: Reflections on Recording while Practising Aikido and Shakuhachi — *Tamara Kohn and Richard Chenhall* — 27

2. Performing and Narrating Selves in and through Classical Music: Being 'Japanese' and Being a Professional Musician in London — *Yuki Imoto* — 44

PART II   PEDAGOGIES OF BODILY MOVEMENT

3. Kinaesthetic Intimacy in a Choreographic Practice — *Brenda Farnell and Robert N. Wood* — 65

4. The Presentation of Self in Participatory Dance Settings: Data Collecting with Erving Goffman — *Bethany Whiteside* — 96

PART III   MUSIC PRACTICES AND ETHICAL SELFHOOD

5. The *Animador* as Ethical Mediator: Stage Talk and Subject Formation at Peruvian *Huayno* Music Spectacles — *James Butterworth* — 121

6. A Sense of Togetherness: Music Promotion and Ethics in Glasgow — *Evangelos Chrysagis* — 139

PART IV BODIES DANCING IN TIME AND ACROSS SPACE

7. Rumba: Heritage, Tourism and the 'Authentic' Afro-Cuban Experience   163
   Ruxandra Ana

8. Cinematic Dance as a Local Critical Commentary on the 'Economic Crisis': Exploring Dance in Korydallos, Attica, Greece   187
   Mimina Pateraki

PART V MOTION, IRONY AND THE MAKING OF LIFEWORLDS

9. Performing Irony on the Dance Floor: The Many Faces of Goth Irony in the Athenian Goth Scene   209
   Panas Karampampas

10. The Intoxicating Intimacy of Drum Strokes, Sung Verses and Dancing Steps in the All-Night Ceremonies of Ambonwari (Papua New Guinea)   234
    Borut Telban

Index   259

Illustrations and Table

Illustrations

3.1	An onsite movement exploration for the camera, near Te Anau	69
3.2	Kelly Slough enters a visceral foray in *Reverence*	76
3.3	'I no longer "perform" – I'm walking through time'	81
3.4	Robert Wood and Margie Gillis in *Devotion*	86
6.1	'Bye Parrot' poster	156
7.1	Participants in the Cuban Experience Project	164
7.2	Rumba dancers and members of the public at Callejon de Hamel	173
7.3	Rumba rehearsal in Santiago de Las Vegas, Havana	182
9.1	Alex and Luna's Facebook discussion	216
9.2	Cybergoth	219
9.3	Screenshot of Nikos's Facebook post	223
9.4	Female goth dances industrial on a table	224
9.5	Greek Carnival (*Apókries*) at Seven Sins club	225
10.1	The first stanza of the first song-cycle of *yamin siria*	239
10.2	The leading dancers with their specific decoration	244
10.3	Painted faces of the dancers	245
10.4	Painted faces of the dancers	246

Table

4.1	Participant observer roles adopted	103

Preface

This edited volume is the culmination of a discussion that began in 2013 when we first met in Edinburgh. Panas had a long-standing interest in human movement and corporeality, and Evangelos was looking to expand his research focus beyond music practices and ethics to include the anthropological exploration of sound and space. The catalyst was our second meeting, this time at the EASA2014 conference in Tallinn, where we convened a panel on the collaborative dimensions of music and dance. Following a suggestion by the series editors, we decided to submit a proposal to the Dance and Performance Studies series, and we invited a number of scholars working on related topics to write chapters specifically for this volume. Several panel participants also contributed to this book. The resulting collection of texts serves a key purpose: to provide an account of the nexus between sound and movement that is intrinsically ethnographic. Similarly, the contributions to this volume were chosen based on their capacity to attend to a particular configuration of themes: space, ethics and the body. While the authors underscore anthropology's potential to address such themes, the range of theoretical standpoints, methodological frameworks and ethnographic settings that the reader will come across in the book highlights its interdisciplinary appeal.

The editing process has depended upon the assistance and generosity of many people. In particular, we wish to take this opportunity to thank our contributors for being so receptive to our editorial feedback and for their patience during the volume's long gestation. Without them, this book would never have happened. In addition, we would like to pay tribute to the editors of the series, and especially Helena Wulff for her inspiration and guidance. Thanks also go to the two anonymous reviewers for their extensive and constructive comments, and everyone at Berghahn for their help throughout the publication process. Finally, Evangelos is immensely grateful to Alexandra Chrysagi and Maria Stathopoulou for their unconditional support and ongoing encouragement, while Panas wants to express his profound gratitude to Vasilios Karampampas, Zoi Vasilaki and Eleni Moutesidi for providing him with unfailing support in all his endeavours and wholeheartedly believing in him.

Evangelos Chrysagis and Panas Karampampas

Introduction

Collaborative Intimacies

Evangelos Chrysagis and Panas Karampampas

> Since the practice of the performing arts can be an important factor in social change, study of the anthropology of the performing arts can, and in my opinion should, be directed toward changing, as well as understanding, the world.
>
> —J. Blacking, Introduction to *The Performing Arts: Music and Dance*

This book considers the spatial, bodily and ethical dimensions of sound and movement, as well as their methodological significance in anthropological research. In exploring forms of sonic practice and expressive movement across multiple registers, we seek to examine ethnographically their distinctive importance in everyday life. Patterns of sound and movement sequences are intrinsic elements of the ways we live and conduct ourselves in different contexts. For example, as Stokes (1994a) argues and as DeNora (2000) has demonstrated, it would be hard to imagine our everyday lives without the presence of musical sound. Similarly, dance, which is sometimes presented as art on stage, as leisure in dance halls or as part of religious rituals, is used to create intimate relations between individuals and to enhance the solidarity of a group, thus becoming an inseparable part of human sociality (Kaeppler 1978; Reed 1998). While we do not postulate a homological view of music, dance and society, we find Blacking's proposition in the opening quote attractive because of his framing of the performing arts as resolutely and primarily social in nature. Therefore, the accounts included in this collection begin from the premise that sound and movement comprise prima facie social practices and processes. These may convey the activities of performers or of subjects whom we do not designate as 'musicians' or 'dancers'. In addition, the lack of thematic and geographical foci that would neatly map onto musical and dance categorizations allows for greater conceptual heterogeneity and methodological open-endedness, while underscoring the volume's ethnographic diversity.

The latter element relates to the fact that various conceptions of music and dance cross-culturally do not necessarily correspond with the assumption that they are interrelated but essentially separate entities. Nevertheless, we do not propose to treat dance as 'simply a part of music' (Kaeppler 1978: 33) or vice versa. Rather, we think that there is a lot to be gained by focusing empirically on the specificities of these different domains of creative practice. Yet we believe that highlighting the mutually constitutive nature of sound and movement and their diverse uses in particular contexts will be equally beneficial. In short, we do not presume that 'acoustemology' (Feld 1996), 'sounded anthropology' (Samuels et al. 2010) and the 'primacy of movement' (Farnell 2012) are a priori distinctive spheres. Having said that, we do not suggest that all sound is 'music' and that all movement is 'dance', but we do embrace the need for a plural and expansive understanding of music and sound, dance and movement and their role in social life.

After all, the realms of music and dance cannot be disentangled from their multiple social functions, while it would be inappropriate to approach music and dance based on definitions that disregard native categories. Rather, our interpretations should depend not so much upon the formal properties of sound and movement and their systematization, but on how people perceive and make use of them. By focusing upon specific genres, then, many of the chapters grapple primarily with modes of conduct and practical arrangements relevant to the enactment of music and dance, but also with discursive attitudes and explicit debates about their enactment. In doing so, the authors aim to explore the intimate ways in which places, selves and bodies coalesce through sound and movement. As a result, in adapting Blacking's suggestion (1979b: 10), our task here is to explore music and dance with reference to sound and movement, but *in terms of* their spatial, corporeal and ethical features.

It is the capacity of sound and movement to engender, evoke, inform, transform, contest and negotiate a sense of place and thus locate subjects in space that exemplifies their inherently social nature. As such, our initial premise should be complemented by the conviction that they also represent spatial practices. What is more, sound and movement engage and envelop the body in its totality. For instance, music and dance 'move' us. By this we do not only mean that they have an emotional effect, but also that they orchestrate bodies. Music, specifically, demands attention: the body cannot escape it because sound vibrates and penetrates it – sound affects bodies. Thus, sound and movement also emerge as fundamentally bodily practices. Anthropologists have further suggested that the somatic investments that underpin ethical projects within specific traditions of disciplinary practice highlight the idea that vocal sounds and bodily movements may facilitate or impede processes of self-fashioning (e.g., Mahmood 2005; Hirschkind 2006). It follows that, in specific contexts, music and dance, too, can be conceived of as ethical practices that encourage the formation of particular subjects.

In addition to the aforementioned themes, we also intend to address methodological questions that stem from intimate fieldwork collaborations between ethnographer and participants and to problematize the relation between motion, sound and the fieldworker's body. In doing so, we emphasize the sheer physicality of the ethnographic encounter and the forms of sociality that gradually emerge between self and other. Researchers' immersion in sonic events and the flow of movement induces bodily responses that render fieldwork an intensely visceral experience. By employing their bodies as tools of research, ethnographers find themselves in spaces of sonic and kinetic intimacy and reciprocity with their informants, which articulate what Rouch called 'shared anthropology' (*anthropologie partagée*) (2003). In turn, this plurosensory emplacement reflects the nexus between bodies, space and relational self-becoming.

It is worth noting that several contributors to this edited volume are music and dance practitioners affiliated with relevant institutions. Yet, as we discuss later on, the expectation that this would be so may reflect disciplinary biases about privileged forms of ethnographic participation. This reinforces ethnocentric assumptions regarding the 'special' nature of music and dance practices, seen as detached from everyday life. However, we hold musical and dance 'knowledge' to be yet another instance of the personal qualities and skills of each researcher, which to various degrees may or may not have facilitated the collection of specific kinds of ethnographic data. Therefore, we would like to underscore the fact that musical and dance training, or lack thereof, is of secondary importance in appreciating the arguments put forward in this book.

Similarly, we do not attempt to trace disciplinary genealogies or solve the conundrums relating to the place of music and dance within anthropology. We do claim, however, that an exclusive and narrow focus on music and dance per se would deprive us of the opportunity to tackle certain pressing ethnographic questions. As Bigenho explains when discussing the divergent approaches of anthropologists and ethnomusicologists, making music our object of analysis would result in 'many compelling anthropological and theoretical questions' being 'swept to the sidelines' (2008: 28). Perhaps unsurprisingly, we find similar disciplinary boundaries in the case of dance. Thus, it has been argued that what makes movement studies either dance-anthropological or ethnochoreological is how researchers try to locate meaning in the dance or its social evaluation (Grau 1993: 21; Kaeppler 2000: 120). Yet dance events do not restrict the focus only upon dance; they also comprise the social circumstances in which it is both practised and performed (Thomas 2003: 179). Therefore, as Giurchescu suggests (2001: 109), the two approaches should not necessarily be kept separate.

In highlighting the diverse social character of music and dance, we also aspire to transcend certain ambiguous classifications, such as 'the popular' (e.g., Dodds and Cook 2013). Moreover, this volume builds on previous ethnographically informed collections on sound and music, dance and movement (e.g., Spencer 1985; Keil and Feld 1994; Stokes 1994b; Farnell 1995; Desmond 1997; Thomas 1997; Buckland 1999; Davida 2011; Born 2013; Dankworth and David 2014), but also differs from them in that it mainly foregrounds not the role of performers but that of individuals and groups that make music and dance possible. In particular, we place under ethnographic scrutiny the invaluable but rarely considered efforts of music promoters, *animadores*, choreographers and audiences, among other actors, vis-à-vis musicians and dancers. The aforementioned works consider in great depth some of this book's individual themes and questions and, therefore, have informed various parts of the analyses presented here. Yet a third contribution of this essay collection lies in the convergence of music and dance practices at the crossroads of space, ethics and the body, while providing an associated commentary on certain methodological implications of doing ethnography in sound and movement. For the purpose of clarity, however, we have separated the remainder of this Introduction into four sections that explicitly deal with the book's main themes, followed by a fifth section that provides an overview of the chapters.

Making Place, Forging Pathways

> Imagine gentle currents of energy, flowing freely through and beyond your body, forming warm pools of movement in the space just around you.
> —S.A. Ness, *Body, Movement, and Culture*

The musicologist Sheila Whiteley states that '[a]s well as providing the sociocultural backdrop for distinctive musical practices and innovations, urban and rural spaces also provide the rich experiential settings in which music is consumed' (2004: 2). Likewise, the dance floor and the extension of it, the dance event, is a space where people come together to dance and socialize. The range of spaces employed for music and dance performances is remarkable and this volume attests to the fact that everyday dancing and music-making are framed by an array of contexts, ranging from urban sites and rural places to cinematic spaces and digital environments. Of course, this is not a novel proposition (see e.g., Williams 1991; Bennett and Peterson 2004), but instead of taking these spaces for granted or considering them merely as blank canvases, one of our main aims is to interrogate the processes through which space interacts with sonic modalities and moving bodies.

As Lefebvre points out in *The Production of Space* (1991), we should attend not to the 'givenness' of space but to the ways in which it is produced, lived and transformed. Therefore, we need to take into account the ways in which music and dance contribute to such processes by observing how they convert spaces into places, as the former are progressively experienced and endowed with value, thus acquiring 'definition and meaning' (Tuan 1977: 136). Stokes argues for attention to how places are musically constructed and delineated (1994a), and he writes that music itself can be 'considered as a "context" in which other events happen, and without which they cannot' (idem 1997: 674). Along similar lines, Cowan notes that the dance event is a 'temporally, spatially, and conceptually "bounded" sphere of interaction' (1990: 4), while Born (2013) highlights the powerful potential of sonic events to change the spaces within and through which they occur. By drawing and building on these insightful contributions, we seek to tackle questions regarding the configuration and mediation of music and dance practices as they blend with what Born calls '"exterior" spatialities' (ibid.: 16); that is, their physical, virtual and social settings.

The musical and choreographic rendering of spatial territories through performance and other related activities underpins feelings of belonging, while imposing boundaries between different groups. Consequently, by constituting spaces of access and exclusion, sound and movement become political tools. Pipyrou (2015) has revealed how the dance performances of 'Ndrangheta Mafiosi in Reggio Calabria in southern Italy can become a vehicle for public engagement, territorial patronage and embodied governance during important religious city celebrations. Correspondingly, Sara Cohen maintains that '[t]he production of place through music is always a political and contested process and music has been shown to be implicated in the politics of place, the struggle for identity and belonging, power and prestige' (1995: 445). Nevertheless, contested places should not necessarily be perceived as sites of direct conflict, opposition or resistance (Low and Lawrence-Zúñiga 2003: 18), but as concrete examples of people's sustained efforts to negotiate on their own terms and alter from within the spaces they inhabit.

Music not only creates the necessary space for its enactment but 'it also *fills* it', writes Finnegan (1989: 336), while dance instils new meanings in space and at the same time is transformed by it (see Royce 2004). Thus, in addition to marking a particular area, sound and movement infuse spaces with particular sensations, feelings and experiential qualities. This further underscores their potential to elicit particular 'capacities' and become the context of agentive action (see Corsín-Jiménez 2003). In focusing upon the inherently transient but distinctive spatial faculties of music and dance practices (Chapters 3, 4, 7, 8 and 10), we approach places not as bounded geographical entities but as a series of '*spatio-temporal events*' (Massey 2005: 130).[1]

The conjunction of space and time in sound and movement highlights the usefulness of Finnegan's notion of 'pathways' (1989: 305–7), which alludes to a sense of place characterized by 'routes rather than roots' (Cresswell 2004: 53). Nevertheless, as Finnegan notes, pathways do provide a sense of spatio-temporal structure in people's lives through the repetitive enactment of music practices taking place across the city (1989: 317). What the idea of pathways captures so well is that music has first and foremost an important *value* in people's lives. By extending the concept of pathways to include dance practices and an array of different contexts, we suggest that sound and movement produce and constitute spatial settings as assortments of activities with their own intrinsic temporalities (see also Telban 1998).

Our ethnographic examination of the ways in which particular locations impinge upon music and dance and, in turn, are sonically and kinetically constructed and experienced, offers a lens into processes of place-making and self-fashioning. As Appadurai observes, anthropologists 'have taken locality as a ground not figure, recognizing neither its fragility nor its ethos *as a property of social life*' (1995: 207). This calls for a reconsideration of space as a generative modality and not as contextual ground, and begs the question of how spatial practices produce specific kinds of subjects. To return to Lefebvre (1991), music and dance not only provide us with ways to examine how subjects cultivate themselves in space – or with space – but also how the production of space brings into focus the manifold ways in which people strive to realize an ethical self (Baxstrom 2008).

Sound and Movement as Ethical Resources

> The sense of music always exceeds whatever is or can be expressed by its means, and it is here that we can trace a specific musical or sonic ethics.
> —M. Cobussen and N. Nielsen, *Music and Ethics*

To say that there has been a recent resurgence of interest in ethics and morality within anthropology would be an understatement (e.g., Zigon 2008; Lambek 2010; Faubion 2011; Fassin 2012; Laidlaw 2014; Keane 2015). However, with few exceptions, ethnographic data explicitly on the constitutive role of music and dance in ethical life is lacking, both within and outside of anthropology.

Among the scholars who have addressed the topic is the sociologist Tia DeNora (1999, 2013), who has explored music as a 'technology of the self' and more recently has elaborated on the therapeutic capacities of music-making and its potential to create ethical spaces or 'asylums'. In addition, Duranti and Burrell (2004) have examined the nexus between jazz improvisation and the quest for an ethical self underpinned by honesty and modesty, and Wilf (2015) has tackled questions of self-making in relation to the development of particular sensory skills in the context of jazz music education. Furthermore, Chrysagis (2013, 2016) has drawn attention to the plural ethical dimensions of 'do-it-yourself' (DiY) music-making in Glasgow, while Butterworth (2014a, 2014b) has focused on processes of subject formation among commercial *huayno* pop stars in Peru. Finally, Bramwell (2015) has considered the relationship between ethical values and the aesthetic features of rap music in London, Skinner (2015) has coined the term 'Afropolitan ethics' to capture the ways in which professional musicians in Mali employ music as a form of moral expression, and Senay (2015) has scrutinized the ethical significance of verbal instruction in the practice of *ney* (reed flute) learning in Turkey. Dance scholars have also considered ideas relating to ethics and morality. Kringelbach's ethnography in urban Senegal (2013), for example, describes how dance is intimately tied up with processes of Dakarois self-making and social mobility and the ways in which dance performance becomes a medium for the embodiment of gendered moral norms and social hierarchies. Similarly, Wulff's examination of Irish dancing (2007) highlights the historical conjunction of bodily attributes and moral virtue. According to Wulff, in the Irish context, appropriate bodily postures in dance performance signified a virtuous self, thus foregrounding the dancing body as a site for the simultaneous embodiment and acting out of social values. Anthropologists working outside of the fields of music and dance have also provided important insights, by focusing on the interface between affective audition and ethical self-formation (Hirschkind 2006) and between bodily movement, self-constitution and the active acquisition of a pious habitus (Mahmood 2005).

While existing ethnographies on music and dance focus on performers, the ethical role of other actors is seldom considered. We endeavour to address this lacuna by delving into the ethics of subjects that are neither musicians nor dancers, but are nevertheless essential to the organization and successful execution of events and performances. We shall argue that practices such as reflecting on the ways in which a music event should be set up and promoted, consuming alcohol, or simply 'being in sound', can be powerful ethical techniques in specific contexts. Although certain contributors focus on particular figures, such as the choreographer (Chapter 3), the *animador* (Chapter 5), the music promoter (Chapter 6) or the anthropologist herself (Chapters 1, 2 and 4), the common underlying objective is to underscore the relational characteristics of ethical trajectories. As Pandian observes in his evocative ethnographic portrait of a single individual, ethical selfhood 'highlights the relationship between personal biographies and shared collective histories' (2010: 66).

The authors approach the ethical as an everyday mode of conduct and a form of self-fashioning and personhood. In doing so, our ethnographic examples emphasize sonic and corporeal practices that encompass the role of affect and emotion in ethical life, but also stress the salience of reflection, judgement and exemplars. By illuminating the pedagogies of self-making as an integral aspect of music and dance, they also point to the internalization of virtuous dispositions, capacities and sensibilities through external practices and comportment. Finally, the authors avoid the association of ethical action with moral obligation and notions of 'right' or 'wrong', by highlighting the idea that ethics is the object of continuous formation and reformation. In other words, we remain cautious towards the Durkheimian conflation of morality with society that, until recently, hindered the development of a concerted anthropological approach to ethics (see Laidlaw 2002). Notably, we have not confined our empirical descriptions within instances, acts and utterances that our informants explicitly framed in terms of 'ethics' or 'morality'. This would dramatically diminish ethnography's potential to elucidate the ethical pluralism and ambivalence of sound and movement. It would further inhibit us from tracing the complex interrelationships and encounters that pervaded ethical discourse and practice in our informants' effort to occupy, negotiate and expand specific 'subject positions' (Faubion 2011).

Exploring the nexus between music, dance and ethics might seem counter-intuitive in the sense that we normally search for the ethical in other domains, such as religion and its associated practices and beliefs. Yet we suspect we are not alone in taking for granted that music and dance are forms of human activity that bring plenitude and have self-evident benefits for musicians, dancers and audiences alike, to such an extent that they normally go without saying. In other words, music and dance practices are so attached to our experience of everyday life and so close to our definition of 'the good' (Robbins 2013) that we tend to forget or disregard their ethical value and that, when playing or listening or dancing to music for its own sake, this value is internal to these practices (MacIntyre 1981). Yet there is nothing inherently ethical (or, for that matter, unethical) in music qua music or dance qua dance, waiting to be revealed by the ethnographer.

In contributing to the emergent anthropology of ethics and morality, we intend to trace how sound and movement can distinctively contribute to our understanding of ethical personhood and projects of self-constitution. As Born writes, music materializes identities, although 'musical sound is non-representational, non-artefactual and alogogenic' (2011: 377). This is because identity is not conferred through music in a visceral, prereflective manner. Rather, sonic encounters index an active self. Thus, as Frith contends, the musical experience 'is best understood as an experience of this *self-in-process*' (1996: 109).

Kinaesthesia and the Resounding Body

> As I dance I feel the shifting of my weight and the changing shapes of my body. I see my surroundings and I sense the rush of air past my skin; I hear, and I feel, the percussive rhythms of my footfalls.
> —C.J.C. Bull, *Sense, Meaning, and Perception in Three Dance Cultures*

Understanding the ways in which music and dance activities bring about particular selves and contribute to the formation of certain kinds of persons also requires consideration of the embodied dispositions actively cultivated through various practices. For example, Farnell asserts that there is a need to attend to the '*moving* body – to the person as physical actor in the social world – so that an anthropology or sociology of the body develops which truly transcends Cartesian limitations' (1994: 931).

An influential contribution at the nexus between music, body and dance is Blacking's work (e.g., 1977). Blacking examined the corporeal qualities that underpin musical ability and performance within an analytical framework that integrated body and mind, thought and practice. As Grau (1993) has established, his writings have been instrumental in the emergence of the anthropology of dance. By contrast, as Grau further remarks, ethnochoreologists view 'the dancer's body as an instrument moving in time and space, in some ways separated from the dancer's mind' (ibid.: 21). Echoing the need to abolish such a dichotomy, Finnegan (2003) suggests that the study of musical experiences should cut across a mind–body dualism, in order to encompass emotional, affective and expressive registers, and convey how these come into play in different socio-cultural contexts.

In resorting to the body's capacity to be affected by sound and movement, the contributors to this volume endeavour to substantiate the convergence of corporeal registers, sensuous articulations and mental processes. Because of the multisensory ways in which individuals relate to sound and movement and to the world as such, music and dance should first and foremost be conceived of as bodily practices. These consist of instances in which haptic, aural, visual and kinaesthetic elements, among others (see e.g., Potter 2008), merge in what is a profoundly visceral experience. Nevertheless, this physicality is not distinguished from social interaction or personal reflection. In the dance event, for example, 'individuals publicly present themselves in and through celebratory practices – eating, drinking, singing, and talking, as well as dancing – and are evaluated by others' (Cowan 1990: 4). The hyper-density and intensity of physical intimacy that music and dance events afford may also facilitate a sense of unity, community or 'communitas' (Turner 1969) among members of the audience, as well as between audiences and performers. Keil (1966: 137) has elegantly documented the interaction between blues performers and audiences, by revealing how the expression of common problems through elaborate gestural, oral, aural and visual symbols promotes a catharsis, a sensuous resolution that fosters solidarity.

Music and dance essentially become aesthetic experiences, in the sense that they elicit a particular 'aesthesis' – a sensual involvement (Mazzarella 2009: 293). Among jazz students, for instance, embodied practical mastery and the acquisition of particular sensory capacities become open-ended processes informed by an aesthetics of differentiation, in addition to normative dimensions (see Wilf 2010). Also, Hirschkind (2001: 628–29; 2006: 101) draws on Collingwood's classic *The Principles of Art* (1938) to argue for a synaesthetic understanding of bodily affects in the nonmusical context of sermon listening. In dance contexts, the term 'kinaesthesia' is frequently employed to convey such sensory pluralism (e.g., Bull 1997; Sklar 2000, 2008; Farnell and Varela 2008; Foster 2011; Sheets-Johnstone 2011). Kinaesthesia, according to Sklar, is 'the reception of stimuli produced within one's own body' (2000: 72). For example, the Anlo-Ewe-speaking people in southeastern Ghana give importance to 'kinaesthetic sensations' and there is a 'clear connection, or association, between bodily sensations and who you are or who you become' (Geurts 2002: 76). In general, it has been suggested that dancers are able to 'read' each other by employing their dance skills and 'kinaesthetic empathy' (Parviainen 2002: 20), because individuals who focus on disciplined bodily training and awareness are more proficient in deciphering their own and others' corporeal traits and movements (Ness 1996: 135, 136; Kohn 2008: 108–10; Skinner 2010: 117–18; Bizas 2014: 11).

Various forms of sensory 'interplay' (Classen 1993: 136) find ethnographic expression in subsequent chapters of this book (Chapters 1, 2, 3, 5, 8, 9 and 10). In most cases, the ethnographer's body emerged as a methodological tool and the means to attain cultural knowledge. Such awareness was at least partly gained *through* sound and movement, but we cannot disregard that our particular positioning in the field, among other factors, conditioned and largely determined the ways in which we listened or put our bodies into motion. Nevertheless, cultural information passed down as embodied knowledge by virtue of our mere presence and participation in unfolding events should not be deemed irrelevant or misleading. Rather, important questions can be put into perspective by paying attention to our own bodily responses. Although many of the authors do not explicitly address the tacit knowledge obtained through their resonating and moving bodies, somatic appreciation and conscious reflection following their exposure to intense field experiences have largely shaped their accounts (see also Kohn 2010). Therefore, we can only agree with Csordas (1993: 138) and his injunction to attend '"with"' and '"to" the body' and explore how this can enrich our ethnographic analyses. The felt dimensions of fieldwork deserve at least an implicit recognition, especially when the subject matter directly relates to the sensorium. As one of Chrysagis's interlocutors put it when the former was describing why his presence in music events was important, an anthropologist had to 'get the *feel* for it' in order to be able to write about it.

Between Participation and Collaboration

> It was almost always in singing that I forgot my place as an anthropologist.
> —M. Engelke, *A Problem of Presence*

One can feel the sound and go through the motions, but how does one write about it? As Rice notes, 'while recognizing the sound might be easy, describing it is evidently more difficult' (2010: S45). And what if even the sound recorder is not enough (see Chapter 1)? Issues of sonic representation have been dealt with exhaustively elsewhere (e.g., Erlmann 2004; Feld and Brenneis 2004; Samuels et al. 2010), but the problematic nature of the trope of sonic 'immersion' and its subsequent transduction into written form remains (Helmreich 2007). Dance anthropologists have confronted similar issues (see Chapter 3). This is partly because movement-notation systems are quite complex, while relevant training is rare and time consuming (Royce 1977). Video recordings provide an accessible alternative, but ultimately they raise additional methodological and ethical issues (see e.g., Dodds 2001; Pink 2007).

If sound and movement raise issues of representation they also exemplify processes of fieldwork collaboration. There is a tendency nowadays to conceive of ethnographers and research subjects as collaborators (e.g., Marcus 1997; Lassiter 2005; Holmes and Marcus 2008; Konrad 2012). However, in contrast to collaboration as an explicit and deliberate form of coproduction of ethnographic knowledge, the collaborative dimension of the relationship between researchers and their informants explored in this book is a direct, pragmatic response to the contributors' fieldwork experience: a process that has fostered a genuine, mutual interest in each other's work (Chapters 3, 6, 8, 9 and 10). This emergent collaboration has taken many forms. For example, several informants actively contributed to our research by introducing us to or contacting potential interviewees on our behalf; they invited us to specific events that they thought were related to our fieldwork; they made suggestions on relevant readings and offered friendly advice on what to include (or not) in our fieldnotes; they were keen to engage in dialogue with us, to debate and learn from what we had to say about their practice; they relied upon our cultural knowledge in the absence of readily available information; they offered insightful comments on our research reports and also expressed their interest in reading our published outputs; last but not least, they shared with us the experience of moving together in space and listening to sounds we had collectively produced.

It would not be far from the mark to claim that collaboration, in its many facets, has become a sine qua non of anthropological research. This is especially true for dance and music ethnographies because it is rarely the case that a comprehensive account of any performance could be based exclusively on observations and fieldnotes, except if the anthropologist has the opportunity to repeatedly witness the same event (see Wulff 1998). Nevertheless, the objective here is not accuracy in the sense of measurable outcomes in representation or, for that matter, in execution (Farnell and Wood 2011). Rather, embodied collaboration, such as dance, can become an important vehicle for the researcher's introduction into the field (Skinner 2010: 114; Paterak01 and Karampampas 2014: 155–56), but it can also act as a space of knowledge exchange with research participants by creating a shared experience. Therefore, through dance, anthropologists are able to build rapport and foster relations that are vital to ethnographic research (Skinner 2010: 117–18).

Central to this process is participation. A participant observer – or observant participant (see Chapter 4) – oscillates between the two poles of participation and observation, while most anthropologists would situate themselves somewhat ambiguously in the middle of the spectrum. However, participation is frequently restricted due to issues of access. Yet lack of physical access is only one factor that determines accessibility and thus opportunities for participation in music and dance activities (see Eisentraut 2013). This problem is further exacerbated by the unavoidable unevenness in the distribution of ethnographic attention in our effort to account for at least some of the diverse practices we encounter while in the field.

What is more, although dance and music knowledge can ease ethnographic participation, it is also fraught with ambivalence. Koutsouba (1999) discusses the issues that emerge when the fieldworker is already a 'dance expert'. While this clearly has benefits, Koutsouba professes that her status as a dance teacher had the potential to disrupt local hierarchies between teachers and dancers and, therefore, she decided to place her role as a researcher before that of a dance teacher. By contrast, Karampampas (see Chapter 9), a goth specialist and DJ, was repeatedly approached by other Athenian goths during his six-year field research for advice relating to various goth-related topics. Consequently, he opted to share his knowledge with other members of the goth scene. Finally, in her discussion about employing dance notation for research purposes, Van Zile (1999: 91–92) addresses several advantages and disadvantages of the different positionalities of dance ethnographers.

Bigenho (2008) further stresses the implications of a singular focus on participation during fieldwork and offers a compelling argument that disavows privileging music participation over other forms of ethnographic engagement. Notably, she resists a narrow definition of the role of music ethnographers as participating musicians and thus as complete insiders. After all, it is rarely the case that one is either an insider or an outsider. As Narayan (1993) has forcefully argued, the insider/outsider distinction should be rather perceived as a complex continuum. We have already alluded to the idea that musical or dance training is not a prerequisite for anthropological research in music and dance or participation in relevant events and performances. Therefore, we approach participation in actual music and dance events in the sense of 'participatory performance' (Turino 2008: 26), which undercuts a sharp distinction between audience and performers. In doing so, however, this book also seeks to capture the palpable characteristics of sound and movement that conjure up expansive and eventful forms of ethnographic participation and collaboration.

The Chapters

The volume is organized into five parts. Part I is devoted to musicians' narratives and the autoethnographic examination of sonic practices. The ways in which they exemplify issues pertinent to self-awareness and corporeality raise particular methodological implications, among others. Part II shifts the focus from sound to movement and from music to dance. In particular, the contributions in this section explore the collaborative dimensions of choreography and ethnography through an intimate look into the creative ideas and everyday routines of dance practitioners, as well as the ethnographer's own mode of conduct in dance spaces. Part III returns to sonic territory, with an explicit focus upon social actors who organize and facilitate music events and performances. By considering the ethical value of their practices, the authors advance the proposition that ethical self-formation is often an integral component of music-making processes. Part IV describes the crafting of particular experiences and identities within dance contexts. Specifically, the authors scrutinize local and cinematic dance spaces as sites for the articulation of national(ist) discourses, authenticating narratives and tourist imaginaries. This is not a straightforward process, however, because dancing bodies moving in heterogeneous space-time continua may produce, resist or mediate between competing points of view. Finally, Part V conveys the idea not only that song and dance enable people to fashion themselves and their lifeworlds in relation to the spaces they inhabit, but also that there is a profound sense of irony in the manner that sound and movement engender relationships, express sociality and cherish what it means to be human.

Part I: Sound, Meaning and Self-Awareness

In their contribution, Tamara Kohn and Richard Chenhall examine the distinctive sonic and kinetic elements that constitute one's experience of 'being in sound' in the practice of aikido and shakuhachi respectively. By drawing upon their own bodily and sensory experiences and the digitally recorded sounds of their training sessions in Japan, they provide two compelling autoethnographic narratives that interrogate the limits of sonic knowledge and understanding. Their analysis begins from the premise that sound is the outcome of social interaction rather than an object of passive reception on the part of the listener. By expanding the notion of 'aural sensibility' to include the manifold ways in which the ethnographer's body participates in sonic production, Kohn and Chenhall raise important methodological questions. They contend that sonic representation should refer not only to the experience of the *other*, but also to one's own capacity to fully immerse oneself, feel and reflect upon the complex nature of sound-making processes. Such an approach challenges the objectivity of recorded sound, as opposed to the subjective nature of sonic experience and embodied memory, qualifies the use of recording media for sonic representation and underscores the participatory qualities and somatic dimensions of doing fieldwork in sound and music. According to the authors, listening with one's whole being versus searching for 'meaning' reflects the basic difference between 'being in sound' and after-the-fact sonic analysis. This begs the fundamental question: can we really 'listen' without the need to 'understand'?

In a similar vein, Yuki Imoto draws on autobiographical and reflective techniques, as well as interviews, in order to account for different modes of self-conception among Japanese classical musicians in London. Having spent several years studying music and anthropology in the U.K., the author embarks on a close examination of how 'Japaneseness' is played out in the musicians' narrations of their migration experiences. Through a concerted critique of simplistic models that enforce a sharp dichotomy between 'collectivist' Japan and the 'individualist' West, her analysis raises more questions than it answers. As Imoto exclaims: 'So what then *can* be represented and analysed?' The answer is that looking into Japanese senses of identity and how they are mediated through 'language about music' provides useful insight into pluralistic ideas regarding 'national character'. For example, her interviewees perceived the characteristics of sensitivity and perfectionism, strict forms of discipline and education, a sense of lyricism and the passivity of audiences to be quintessentially Japanese. Yet, while classical musicians mobilized a series of elaborate oppositions to convey the distinctiveness of the Japanese self, these were ultimately intertwined with Western-influenced and diffused notions of creativity and musicianship. Their narratives further attest to a process of 'self-orientalism' as a response to their migrant status – the appropriation of Zen philosophy and practice is telling. Far from being embedded within rigid cultural schemata, therefore, the contours of Japanese identity are being assembled within a 'cultural supermarket' offering a range of lifestyle choices.

Part II: Pedagogies of Bodily Movement

Brenda Farnell and Robert Wood skilfully demonstrate how processes of collaboration that induce 'kinaesthetic intimacy' can be reversed through a 'hypervisceral' exploration of choreographic practice. Their chapter outlines Wood's artistic vision by tracing his diverse influences, ranging from New Zealand's landscapes and Japanese butoh to New York City in the 1980s and his relationship with Merce Cunningham and John Cage. By placing emphasis on Wood's oral narratives, the analysis outlines his multifaceted choreographic ethos, revolving around procedures of spatial and temporal manipulation, a profound sensuousness and an intense physicality that obliterates dualistic ontologies. Wood's 'movement explorations' constitute a wordless pedagogy through a sharp focus on kinaesthetic awareness and an ongoing affective feedback between choreographer and dancers. Against an array of techniques that privilege the authoritative voice of the choreographer-master, Wood's approach to his dancers as people and as 'fundamentally *moving beings*' transcends a narrow conception of the dancing body as the means to predefined ends. Rather, choreographer and dancer become mutually attuned to one another, seeking artistic excellence through reciprocal participation and self-discovery. Such values accomplish a particular mode of being and animate choreographies even in the absence of material or other external rewards, such as status or prestige. Farnell and Wood point out that dancers' embodied understanding of their craft results in the lack of verbal articulation about their practice in public contexts. However, as movements and sensations are transduced into words for the anthropologist, interesting repercussions emerge for ethnographic representation.

Bethany Whiteside examines another important dimension of dance ethnography by exploring the dual role of researcher/participant in a range of contexts across the city of Glasgow, U.K. By adapting Goffman's model of dramaturgy (1990 [1959]) she orchestrates an interdisciplinary critique of the notion of participant observation par excellence. Her account tackles uneasy realities about ethnographic access and participation in dance educational contexts and addresses issues of collaboration and 'reflexivity', etiquette and comportment. The author employed her classically trained dancing body as a data collection tool. She says: 'I was able to, willing and happy to dance'. In certain contexts, however, such as the salsa club, she ended up dancing 'on the periphery'. In focusing upon dance knowledge transmission and embodiment through pedagogical instruction, her analysis also offers a glimpse into the the role of the dance teacher as an authority figure and the enforcer of discipline. According to Whiteside, dance pedagogues and performers alike make use of 'dramaturgical discipline' in order to assert their authority, regardless of any errors that may occur during a class or performance. Ethnographers-cum-dancers, too, stand in a pedagogical relationship to their informants, but in a mutual and much more nuanced manner than what the seemingly unquestioned authority of dance instructors might suggest. Consequently, while dancing one's way through the field may provide valuable insights, it appears that when dance pedagogy is pervaded by the teacher's authority it cannot provide a model for doing ethnographic research.

Part III: Music Practices and Ethical Selfhood

James Butterworth takes up the theme of subject formation among Andean working-class migrants in his examination of *huayno* music spectacles in Lima, Peru, to explain how audience experiences are ethically framed and mediated by the figure of the *animador*, a type of compere. A flamboyant, quasi-pedagogical character, the *animador* ensures a continuous flow of alcohol and his theatrics play a decisive role in eliciting audience responses. As Jaime Ponce, an *animador*, explains: 'An artist without an *animador* does not have much to deploy on stage'. Butterworth persuasively argues that for many audience members the meta-identity of being an Andean migrant encompasses various other subject positions that they come to inhabit during *huayno* events. Crucially, the state has perpetuated and amplified this identification, which has culminated in the marginalization of and a sense of 'existential anxiety' among Andean migrants based in Lima. *Huayno* spectacles, by contrast, become spaces where positive endorsement and acknowledgement of their migrant status may help neutralize such concerns. This is intensified by drinking, affect and the sentimentality invoked by song lyrics and expressive modes of vocal delivery. Excessive alcohol consumption emerges as a technology of the self that appears to be essential for the consolidation of subjectivation processes. Alcohol and its intricate social and moral connotations accompany a sensory overload and a surplus of emotional expression. This forcefully manifests, inter alia, the role of the body in bringing about an ethical self. What is of primary concern here, then, is an emphasis on the corporeality of *huayno* music spectacles.

In contrast, Evangelos Chrysagis traces the ethical trajectory of a former Glasgow-based music promoter based on the seemingly paradoxical views, reflective attitudes and practical judgements surrounding his adherence to a 'do-it-yourself' (DiY) ethos. In drawing attention to the improvisatory nature of music promotion and its attendant values, practices and conventions, his account construes extramusical activity as a critical site for the study of self-fashioning and offers an argument that resonates with and builds on certain developments in the anthropology of ethics and morality. By ethnographically operationalizing James Faubion's insights in his book *An Anthropology of Ethics* (2011), the author explores the promoter's effort to occupy and alter particular subject positions. In doing so, he considers the salience of exemplarity and judgement in the organization and execution of DiY music events and the ways in which promotional practices encourage the cultivation of specific dispositions. Although the narrative chronicles the ethical transformation of one individual, the ethnographic exposition of the promoter's entrepreneurial development through various forms of collaboration discloses the resolutely intersubjective nature of ethics. Spanning issues of financial moderation and excess, ethical conversion and informal pedagogy, the analysis foregrounds the fundamental role of music in shaping the personal, professional and ethical identities of promoters vis-à-vis material considerations and ideas about commercial sustainability. Thus, Chrysagis also opens up a space to examine the significance of ethics in relation to cultural policy and employment in the creative industries, by revisiting the tension between artistry and commercialism at a critical economic and political juncture for the U.K.

Part IV: Dancing in Time and across Space

Ruxandra Ana's lucid account of the Cuban rumba is a prime example of a music/dance complex and how it fosters and expresses ideas about politics and belonging. By tracing the emergence of rumba as a cultural commodity and an authenticating tool for local populations and tourists alike, the author provides a fascinating ethnography of *rumberos* in Havana and Matanzas. She asserts that rumba is at the forefront of the expansion of the tourist sector and the commodification of Cuban cultural heritage. However, *rumberos* do not reap the full benefits of such international attention, while many see this 'heritagizing' as a politically motivated process. This conviction is intimately related to the racialization of the dance and its perceived 'blackness'. Nowhere is this more apparent than in the actual spaces where rumba is danced. Becoming the nexus where tourists, rumba aficionados and locals meet, dance venues encapsulate antagonistic ideas about rumba, blackness and Cubanness. Venues are also the contexts in which bodily assets are transformed into economic capital and where the bodies of *rumberos* come to stand for 'roots' and the 'authentic'. As Ana succinctly observes, 'the rumba appears to function as an embodied souvenir that makes "Cubanness" available' to tourists. Within a globalized tourist industry, blackness seems to take on 'positive' connotations. But rumba is further linked to other domains of Afro-Cuban tradition, such as religion, which contributes to its ambivalent position, while explaining rumba's deliberate racialization on the part of the state.

In her exploration of the recent financial downturn in Greece, Mimina Pateraki examines Hellenic cinematic history and its wealth of music and dance resources. The author suggests that paying attention to these films will enable us to fully grasp how inhabitants of Korydallos, an Athens suburb, use cinematic dance as the means to articulate a critical response to 'the crisis'. The chapter focuses on two iconic scenes from the early 1970s films *Evdokía* and *Oratótis Midén* to demonstrate how cinematic dance endows current narratives of the recession with cultural meanings. The author contends that, through these narratives, Greeks manage to enact a transtemporal understanding of their national history by reworking embodied memories. The significance of cinematic dance, therefore, dwells in its capacity to animate an assemblage of historicities. Yet, on a more mundane level, local dance events also afford people the opportunity to get together, share a dance, engage in acts of solidarity and collectively work through the conundrums of 'the crisis'. So, while economic hardship is experienced as a form of stasis or 'stillness', dance puts things back into motion. As Alkis, one of Pateraki's informants, explains, it is the '*zeibékiko* of Evdokia' that 'can put in motion the whole world for me .... It's an "antidote" to the crisis'. The contemporary situation is seen as the 'point zero', which is similar to the predicament of the main character in *Oratótis Midén*. Having reached their nadir, the country and its people seek a way out.

Part V: Motion, Irony and the Making of Lifeworlds

Panas Karampampas demonstrates how Athenian goth performances on the dance floor and in everyday life can be apprehended through notions of 'nihilistic' and 'liberal' irony. His analysis draws on social media and audiovisual resources, while bringing together ethnographic works that have explored irony in relation to language and politics in Greece. An important ethnographic particularity is that in modern Greek the word 'irony' is used interchangeably with sarcasm, parody and mockery and, therefore, the chapter also addresses issues of incommensurability between existing theoretical frameworks and native categories. The author examines irony from two interrelated perspectives: first, the ways in which it is embodied in actual goth dance performances and, second, how goths employ irony when they reflect on their own and other people's dance practices. The reader also learns about methodological complexities stemming from the discrepancy between research participants' verbal statements and their somatic postures, which result in an array of contradictions. Ironically enough, Athenian goths do not always practise what they preach. Based on the terms of nihilistic irony, goth ideas are realized in action, whereas from the standpoint of liberal irony, goth ideology and Athenian goths' practices occasionally clash and diverge from each other. This brings us to the analysis of inclusion and exclusion in relation to stereotypes, three notions that are directly related to the use of liberal irony. Ultimately, Karampampas argues that, even when goth practices seem antithetical and self-contradictory, the whole spectrum represents the embodiment of liberal irony.

Borut Telban explores the dancing, singing and drumming of Papua New Guinea's Karawari-speaking people by describing an all-night ceremony in the Ambonwari village of the East Sepik Province that facilitates the enactment of beauty, morality and love. His delightful storytelling and ethnographic account of *yamin siria* (song-dance of the house) encompass a host of cultural ideas and cosmological beliefs, such as the interrelation between sound, movement, image and the natural environment, the association between body decoration and the spirit world and the affinity between song-poetry and cultural memory. The author also points towards the alliance between movement/stasis and the recreation of landscape through treading specific paths. The link between the flow of song/dance and the ceaseless formation of the Ambonwari lifeworld is further exposed by the ceremony's potential to initiate sexual liaisons. The explicit content of the song lyrics attests to that, while the all-night dances become a ritual reevaluation of gender roles. Telban's captivating account demonstrates a depth of knowledge that only long-term fieldwork is able to impart and traces the ethnographer's gradual transition from sympathetic outsider to cultural facilitator and producer. For example, the author remarks that, after 2001, he was the only person that had access to the complete songs of *yamin siria*. As a result, when imported music and dance genres seemed to have captured the imagination of Ambonwari youth, the anthropologist emerged as the mainstay of tradition, partaking in what Telban, following Sahlins (2013), calls the 'mutuality of being'.

By grappling with these issues, we intend to illustrate the benefits of dissolving sound and movement into everyday practice. This retains the primacy of musicality and expressive motion in the lives of our informants. Essentially an agglomeration of bodily practices, technologies of self-fashioning and forms of place-making, sound and movement open up social pathways and conjure up life trajectories that are neither predetermined nor teleological, but generative and in flux. As people adjust such pathways and trajectories and in turn become attuned to them, anthropologists should continually adapt to fleeting circumstances and embrace the imagining of alternative futures. We hold that musical sounds and dance moves have the potential to spark our imagination and transform it into creative action, thus providing novel ways of being, becoming, doing and relating.

Evangelos Chrysagis initially trained in History and Archaeology at the University of Ioannina, Greece, before embarking on postgraduate studies in Social Anthropology, earning an M.Sc. and a Ph.D. from the University of Edinburgh, where he was also a guest lecturer until 2015. His doctoral research explored the intersection of do-it-yourself (DiY) music-making and ethics in Glasgow. He has published on the themes of publicity and invisibility in DiY practice, and is currently completing an ethnographic monograph based on his Ph.D. thesis.

Panas Karampampas is a post-doctoral researcher at the Institut Interdisciplinaire d'Anthropologie du Contemporain (IIAC), École des Hautes Études en Sciences Sociales (EHESS). He currently works on Intangible Cultural Heritage policies and global governance. Previously he was a guest lecturer in the Department of Social Anthropology at the University of St Andrews, where he also completed his Ph.D. His doctoral research focused on the goth scene, digital anthropology, dance and cosmopolitanism. He has also conducted ethnographic research on Roma education as a scientific associate in the Centre for Intercultural Studies at the University of Athens.

Note

1. Unless otherwise stated, italics in quotations are used by the original author.

References

Appadurai, A. 1995. 'The Production of Locality', in R. Fandon (ed.), *Counterworks: Managing the Diversity of Knowledge*. London: Routledge, pp. 204–25.
Baxstrom, R. 2008. *Houses in Motion: The Experience of Place and the Problem of Belief in Urban Malaysia*. Stanford, CA: Stanford University Press.
Bennett, A., and R.A. Peterson (eds). 2004. *Music Scenes: Local, Translocal and Virtual*. Nashville, TN: Vanderbilt University Press.
Bigenho, M. 2008. 'Why I'm Not an Ethnomusicologist: A View from Anthropology', in H. Stobart (ed.), *The New (Ethno)musicologies*. Lanham, MD: Scarecrow Press, pp. 28–39.
Bizas, E. 2014. *Learning Senegalese Sabar: Dancers and Embodiment in New York and Dakar*. Oxford: Berghahn.
Blacking, J. (ed.). 1977. *The Anthropology of the Body*. London: Academic Press.
———. 1979a. 'Introduction', in J. Blacking and J.W. Kealiinohomoku (eds), *The Performing Arts: Music and Dance*. The Hague: Mouton, pp. xiii–xxii.

———. 1979b. 'The Study of Man as Music-Maker', in J. Blacking and J.W. Kealiinohomoku (eds), *The Performing Arts: Music and Dance*. The Hague: Mouton, pp. 3–15.
Born, G. 2011. 'Music and the Materialization of Identities', *Journal of Material Culture* 16: 376–88.
——— (ed.). 2013. *Music, Sound and Space: Transformations of Public and Private Experience*. Cambridge: Cambridge University Press.
Bramwell, R. 2015. *UK Hip-Hop, Grime and the City: The Aesthetics and Ethics of London's Rap Scenes*. New York: Routledge.
Buckland, T.J. (ed.). 1999. *Dance in the Field: Theory, Methods and Issues in Dance Ethnography*. Basingstoke: Palgrave Macmillan.
Bull, C.J.C. 1997. 'Sense, Meaning, and Perception in Three Dance Cultures', in J.C. Desmond (ed.), *Meaning in Motion: New Cultural Studies of Dance*. Durham, NC: Duke University Press, pp. 269–88.
Butterworth, J. 2014a. 'Andean Divas: Emotion, Ethics and Intimate Spectacle in Peruvian Huayno Music', Ph.D. dissertation. London: Royal Holloway, University of London.
———. 2014b. 'The Ethics of Success: Paradoxes of the Suffering Neoliberal Self in the Andean Peruvian Music Industry', *Culture, Theory and Critique* 55: 212–32.
Chrysagis, E. 2013. 'Becoming Ethical Subjects: An *Êthography* of Do-it-Yourself Music Practices in Glasgow', Ph.D. dissertation. Edinburgh: University of Edinburgh.
———. 2016. 'The Visible Evidence of DiY Ethics: Music, Publicity and Technologies of (In)Visibility in Glasgow', *Visual Culture in Britain* 17: 290–310.
Classen, C. 1993. *Worlds of Sense: Exploring the Senses in History and across Cultures*. New York: Routledge.
Cobussen, M., and N. Nielsen. 2012. *Music and Ethics*. Farnham: Ashgate.
Cohen, S. 1991. *Rock Culture in Liverpool: Popular Music in the Making*. Oxford: Clarendon Press.
———. 1995. 'Sounding Out the City: Music and the Sensuous Production of Place', *Transactions of the Institute of British Geographers* 20: 434–46.
Collingwood, R.G. 1938. *The Principles of Art*. Oxford: Clarendon Press.
Corsín-Jiménez, A. 2003. 'On Space as a Capacity', *Journal of the Royal Anthropological Institute* (N.S.) 9: 137–53.
Cowan, J.K. 1990. *Dance and the Body Politic in Northern Greece*. Princeton, NJ: Princeton University Press.
Cresswell, T. 2004. *Place: A Short Introduction*. Oxford: Blackwell.
Csordas, T.J. 1993. 'Somatic Modes of Attention', *Cultural Anthropology* 8: 135–56.
Dankworth, L.E., and A.R. David (eds). 2014. *Dance Ethnography and Global Perspectives: Identity, Embodiment and Culture*. Basingstoke: Palgrave Macmillan.
Davida, D. (ed.). 2011. *Fields in Motion: Ethnography in the Worlds of Dance*. Waterloo, ON: Wilfrid Laurier University Press.
DeNora, T. 1999. 'Music as a Technology of the Self', *Poetics* 27: 31–56.
———. 2000. *Music in Everyday Life*. Cambridge: Cambridge University Press.
———. 2013. *Music Asylums: Wellbeing through Music in Everyday Life*. Farnham: Ashgate.
Desmond, J.C. (ed.). 1997. *Meaning in Motion: New Cultural Studies of Dance*. Durham, NC: Duke University Press.

Dodds, S. 2001. *Dance on Screen: Genres and Media from Hollywood to Experimental Art*. Basingstoke: Palgrave Macmillan.
Dodds, S., and S.C. Cook. 2013. *Bodies of Sound: Studies across Popular Music and Dance*. Farnham: Ashgate.
Duranti, A., and K. Burrell. 2004. 'Jazz Improvisation: A Search for Hidden Harmonies and a Unique Self', *Ricerche di Psicologia* 27(3): 71–101.
Eisentraut, J. 2013. *The Accessibility of Music: Participation, Reception, and Contact*. Cambridge: Cambridge University Press.
Engelke, M. 2007. *A Problem of Presence: Beyond Scripture in an African Church*. Berkeley: University of California Press.
Erlmann, V. (ed.). 2004. *Hearing Cultures: Essays on Sound, Listening and Modernity*. Oxford: Berg.
Farnell, B.M. 1994. 'Ethno-Graphics and the Moving Body', *Man* (N.S.) 29: 929–74.
———. (ed.). 1995. *Human Action Signs in Cultural Context: The Visible and the Invisible in Movement and Dance*. Metuchen, NJ: Scarecrow Press.
———. 2012. *Dynamic Embodiment for Social Theory: 'I Move Therefore I Am'*. Abingdon: Routledge.
Farnell, B.M., and C. Varela. 2008. 'The Second Somatic Revolution', *Journal for the Theory of Social Behavior* 38: 215–40.
Farnell, B.M., and R.N. Wood. 2011. 'Performing Precision and the Limits of Observation', in T. Ingold (ed.), *Redrawing Anthropology: Materials, Movements, Lines*. Farnham: Ashgate, pp. 91–113.
Fassin, D. (ed.). 2012. *A Companion to Moral Anthropology*. Oxford: Wiley-Blackwell.
Faubion, J.D. 2011. *An Anthropology of Ethics*. Cambridge: Cambridge University Press.
Feld, S. 1996. 'Waterfalls of Song: An Acoustemology of Place Resounding in Bosavi, Papua New Guinea', in S. Feld and K.H. Basso (eds), *Senses of Place*. Santa Fe, NM: School of American Research Press, pp. 91–135.
Feld, S., and D. Brenneis. 2004. 'Doing Anthropology in Sound', *American Ethnologist* 31: 461–74.
Finnegan, R. 1989. *The Hidden Musicians: Music-Making in an English Town*. Cambridge: Cambridge University Press.
———. 2003. 'Music, Experience and the Anthropology of Emotion', in M. Clayton, T. Herbert and R. Middleton (eds), *The Cultural Study of Music: A Critical Introduction*. New York: Routledge, pp. 181–92.
Foster, S.L. 2011. *Choreographing Empathy: Kinaesthesia in Performance*. Abingdon: Routledge.
Frith, S. 1996. 'Music and Identity', in S. Hall and P. Du Gay (eds), *Questions of Cultural Identity*. London: Sage, pp. 108–27.
Geurts, K.L. 2002. *Culture and the Senses: Bodily Ways of Knowing in an African Community*. Berkeley: University of California Press.
Giurchescu, A. 2001. 'The Power of Dance and Its Social and Political Uses', *Yearbook for Traditional Music* 33: 109–21.
Goffman, E. 1990 [1959]. *The Presentation of Self in Everyday Life*. London: Penguin.
Grau, A. 1993. 'John Blacking and the Development of Dance Anthropology in the United Kingdom', *Dance Research Journal* 25(2): 21–31.

Helmreich, S. 2007. 'An Anthropologist Underwater: Immersive Soundscapes, Submarine Cyborgs, and Transductive Ethnography', *American Ethnologist* 34: 621–41.

Hirschkind, C. 2001. 'The Ethics of Listening: Cassette-Sermon Audition in Contemporary Cairo', *American Ethnologist* 28: 623–49.

———. 2006. *The Ethical Soundscape: Cassette Sermons and Islamic Counterpublics.* New York: Columbia University Press.

Holmes, D.R., and G.E. Marcus. 2008. 'Collaboration Today and the Re-imagination of the Classic Scene of Fieldwork Encounter', *Collaborative Anthropologies* 1: 81–101.

Kaeppler, A.L. 1978. 'Dance in Anthropological Perspective', *Annual Review of Anthropology* 7: 31–49.

———. 2000. 'Dance Ethnology and the Anthropology of Dance', *Dance Research Journal* 32(1): 116–25.

Keane, W. 2015. *Ethical Life: Its Natural and Social Histories.* Princeton, NJ: Princeton University Press.

Keil, C. 1966. *Urban Blues.* Chicago, IL: The University of Chicago Press.

Keil, C., and S. Feld. 1994. *Music Grooves: Essays and Dialogues.* Chicago, IL: The University of Chicago Press.

Kohn, T. 2008. 'Creatively Sculpting the Self through the Discipline of Martial Arts Training', in N. Dyck (ed.), *Exploring Regimes of Discipline: The Dynamics of Restraint.* Oxford: Berghahn, pp. 99–112.

———. 2010. 'The Role of Serendipity and Memory in Experiencing Fields', in P. Collins and A. Gallinat (eds), *The Ethnographic Self as Resource: Writing Memory and Experience into Ethnography.* Oxford: Berghahn, pp. 185–99.

Konrad, M. (ed.). 2012. *Collaborators Collaborating: Counterparts in Anthropological Knowledge and International Research Relations.* Oxford: Berghahn.

Koutsouba, M. 1999. '"Outsider" in an "Inside" World, or Dance Ethnography at Home', in T.J. Buckland (ed.), *Dance in the Field: Theory, Methods and Issues in Dance Ethnography.* Basingstoke: Palgrave Macmillan, pp. 186–95.

Kringelbach, H.N. 2013. *Dance Circles: Movement, Morality and Self-Fashioning in Urban Senegal.* Oxford: Berghahn.

Laidlaw, J. 2002. 'For an Anthropology of Ethics and Freedom', *Journal of the Royal Anthropological Institute* (N.S.) 8: 311–32.

———. 2014. *The Subject of Virtue: An Anthropology of Ethics and Freedom.* Cambridge: Cambridge University Press.

Lambek, M. (ed.). 2010. *Ordinary Ethics: Anthropology, Language, and Action.* New York: Fordham University Press.

Lassiter, L.E. 2005. *The Chicago Guide to Collaborative Ethnography.* Chicago, IL: The University of Chicago Press.

Lefebvre, H. 1991. *The Production of Space*, trans. D. Nicholson-Smith. Oxford: Blackwell.

Low, S.M., and D. Lawrence-Zúñiga. 2003. 'Locating Culture', in S.M. Low and D. Lawrence-Zúñiga (eds), *The Anthropology of Space and Place: Locating Culture.* Oxford: Blackwell, pp. 1–47.

MacIntyre, A. 1981. *After Virtue: A Study in Moral Theory.* Notre Dame, IN: University of Notre Dame Press.

Mahmood, S. 2005. *Politics of Piety: The Islamic Revival and the Feminist Subject*. Princeton, NJ: Princeton University Press.
Marcus, G.E. 1997. 'The Uses of Complicity in the Changing Mise-en-Scène of Anthropological Fieldwork', *Representations* 59: 85–108.
Massey, D. 2005. *For Space*. London: Sage.
Mazzarella, W. 2009. 'Affect: What Is it Good for?', in S. Dube (ed.), *Enchantments of Modernity: Empire, Nation, Globalization*. New Delhi: Routledge, pp. 291–309.
Narayan, K. 1993. 'How Native Is a "Native" Anthropologist?', *American Anthropologist* 95: 671–86.
Ness, S.A. 1992. *Body, Movement, and Culture: Kinesthetic and Visual Symbolism in a Philippine Community*. Philadelphia: University of Pennsylvania Press.
———. 1996. 'Dancing in the Field: Notes from Memory', in S.L. Foster (ed.), *Corporealities: Dancing Knowledge, Culture and Power*. Abingdon: Routledge, pp. 129–54.
Pandian, A. 2010. 'Interior Horizons: An Ethical Space of Selfhood in South India', *Journal of the Royal Anthropological Institute* (N.S.) 16: 64–83.
Parviainen, J. 2002. 'Bodily Knowledge: Epistemological Reflections on Dance', *Dance Research Journal* 34(1): 11–26.
Pateraki, M., and P. Karampampas. 2014. 'Methodological Insights in Dance Anthropology: Embodying Identities in Dance Celebrations in the Context of Metamorphosis of Sotiros in Sotira, South Albania', in V. Nitsiakos, I. Manos, G. Agelopoulos A. Angelidou and V. Dalkavoukis (eds), *Balkan Border Crossings: Third Annual of the Konitsa Summer School*. Berlin: LIT, pp. 149–74.
Pink, S. 2007. *Doing Visual Ethnography: Images, Media and Representation in Research*, 2nd edn. London: Sage.
Pipyrou, S. 2015. 'Governance, Theatricality, and Fantasma in Mafia Dance', in A. Flynn and J. Tinius (eds), *Anthropology, Theatre, and Development: The Transformative Potential of Performance*. Basingstoke: Palgrave Macmillan, pp. 147–66.
Potter, C. 2008. 'Sense of Motion, Senses of Self: Becoming a Dancer', *Ethnos* 73: 444–65.
Reed, S.A. 1998. 'The Politics and Poetics of Dance', *Annual Review of Anthropology* 27: 503–32.
Rice, T. 2010. 'Learning to Listen: Auscultation and the Transmission of Auditory Knowledge', *Journal of the Royal Anthropological Institute* (N.S.) 16(s1): S41–S61.
Robbins, J. 2013. 'Beyond the Suffering Subject: Toward an Anthropology of the Good', *Journal of the Royal Anthropological Institute* (N.S.) 19: 447–62.
Rouch, J. 2003. *Ciné-Ethnography*, ed. and trans. S. Feld. Minneapolis: University of Minnesota Press.
Royce, A.P. 1977. *The Anthropology of Dance*. Bloomington: Indiana University Press.
———. 2004. *Anthropology of the Performing Arts: Artistry, Virtuosity, and Interpretation in a Cross-Cultural Perspective*. Walnut Creek, CA: AltaMira Press.
Sahlins, M. 2013. *What Kinship Is–and Is Not*. Chicago, IL: The University of Chicago Press.
Samuels, D.W., et al. 2010. 'Soundscapes: Toward a Sounded Anthropology', *Annual Review of Anthropology* 39: 329–45.
Senay, B. 2015. 'Masterful Words: Musicianship and Ethics in Learning the *Ney*', *Journal of the Royal Anthropological Institute* (N.S.) 21: 524–41.

Sheets-Johnstone, M. 2011. 'The Imaginative Consciousness of Movement: Linear Quality, Kinaesthesia, Language and Life', in T. Ingold (ed.), *Redrawing Anthropology: Materials, Movements, Lines*. Farnham: Ashgate, pp. 115–28.

Skinner, J. 2010. 'Leading Questions and Body Memories: A Case of Phenomenology and Physical Ethnography in the Dance Interview', in P. Collins and A. Gallinat (eds), *The Ethnographic Self as Resource: Writing Memory and Experience into Ethnography*. Oxford: Berghahn, pp. 111–28.

Skinner, R.T. 2015. *Bamako Sounds: The Afropolitan Ethics of Malian Music*. Minneapolis: University of Minnesota Press.

Sklar, D. 2000. 'Reprise: On Dance Ethnography', *Dance Research Journal* 32(1): 70–77.

———. 2008. 'Remembering Kinesthesia: An Inquiry into Embodied Cultural Knowledge', in C. Noland and S.A. Ness (eds), *Migrations of Gesture*. Minneapolis: University of Minnesota Press, pp. 85–112.

Spencer, P. (ed.). 1985. *Society and the Dance: The Social Anthropology of Process and Performance*. Cambridge: Cambridge University Press.

Stokes, M. 1994a. 'Introduction: Ethnicity, Identity and Music', in M. Stokes (ed.), *Ethnicity, Identity and Music: The Musical Construction of Place*. Oxford: Berg, pp. 1–28.

———. (ed.). 1994b. *Ethnicity, Identity and Music: The Musical Construction of Place*. Oxford: Berg.

———. 1997. 'Voices and Places: History, Repetition and the Musical Imagination', *Journal of the Royal Anthropological Institute* (N.S.) 3: 673–91.

Telban, B. 1998. *Dancing through Time: A Sepik Cosmology*. Oxford: Clarendon Press.

Thomas, H. (ed.). 1997. *Dance in the City*. Basingstoke: Palgrave Macmillan.

———. 2003. *The Body, Dance and Cultural Theory*. Basingstoke: Palgrave Macmillan.

Tuan, Y.-F. 1977. *Space and Place: The Perspective of Experience*. London: Edward Arnold.

Turino, T. 2008. *Music as Social Life: The Politics of Participation*. Chicago, IL: The University of Chicago Press.

Turner, V.W. 1969. *The Ritual Process: Structure and Anti-Structure*. Chicago: Aldine Publishing.

Van Zile, J. 1999. 'Capturing the Dancing: Why and How?', in T.J. Buckland (ed.), *Dance in the Field: Theory, Methods and Issues in Dance Ethnography*. Basingstoke: Palgrave Macmillan, pp. 85–99.

Whiteley, S. 2004. 'Introduction', in S. Whiteley, A. Bennett and S. Hawkins (eds), *Music, Space and Place: Popular Music and Cultural Identity*. Aldershot: Ashgate, pp. 1–2.

Wilf, E. 2010. 'Swinging within the Iron Cage: Modernity, Creativity, and Embodied Practice in American Postsecondary Jazz Education', *American Ethnologist* 37: 563–82.

———. 2015. 'Modernity, Cultural Anesthesia, and Sensory Agency: Technologies of the Listening Self in a US Collegiate Jazz Music Program', *Ethnos* 80: 1–22.

Williams, D. 1991. *Ten Lectures on Theories of the Dance*. Metuchen, NJ: Scarecrow Press.

Wulff, H. 1998. *Ballet across Borders: Career and Culture in the World of Dancers*. Oxford: Berg.

———. 2007. *Dancing at the Crossroads: Memory and Mobility in Ireland*. Oxford: Berghahn.

Zigon, J. 2008. *Morality: An Anthropological Perspective*. Oxford: Berg.

PART I

Sound, Meaning and Self-Awareness

Chapter 1

Being in Sound

Reflections on Recording while Practising Aikido and Shakuhachi

Tamara Kohn and Richard Chenhall

> I *become* in the sensation and something happens through the sensation, one through the other, one in the other.
>
> —Deleuze, *Francis Bacon: The Logic of Sensation*

This chapter examines both a methodological conundrum and an auto-ethnographic analysis of how one's position within and beyond the production of sound and movement affects one's experience. We draw from our own sonic field research in Japan with aikido and shakuhachi practitioners, examining some of the methodological and theoretical implications of how bodily practice within both of these different sonic contexts affects sensory awareness. These are compared with a different modality of recorded sound that is captured electronically and reflected upon by people who were, or were not, involved in the production of the sound. Finally, we begin to provide a relational framework for understanding how bodily 'being in sound' contributes to a multisensory[1] and dynamic process of self-production.

The research that informs this chapter arises from a project that sought to examine sound production and reception in Japan. Through ethnographic research, we examined the positions (and in some cases the 'role') of sound in three domains: space and place; physical and artistic practice; health and therapy. This meant spending time sensorily traversing and, in some cases, engaging with others in streets, train stations, workplaces and places of leisure and healing. The everydayness of these locations was important as we planned to document and analyse sound as part of the experience of everyday life in Japan, including the uncertainties associated with the position of sonic practice in relation to people's senses of emotional and physical well-being. The project aimed to answer these questions:

1. How are people's daily lives structured by sound in urban Japan and, in turn, how is human agency manifested in sonic practice?
2. How have people's understandings of sounds and silences in their daily lives changed over time, especially given their recognition of sonic environments as important communicative sources of information?
3. How do sonic practices in Japan affect people's senses of emotional and physical well-being?

We contend that the meaning of sound is never to be found solely in production, transmission and reception. Rather, weaving insight from work in linguistic anthropology (Bauman and Briggs 1992; Gal 2003; Silverstein 2003) into work on the senses (Classen 1993; Howes 1991, 2003), we seek to explain how sound, both produced and received, is positioned within sociality. Meaning is the product of interaction in social context; we must not presume that the perceptions of sound are experienced the same way for all people, even those who share linguistic, cultural or spatial attributes. In fact, it is the differences that arise between descriptions of experience that can afford the most nuance and depth of understanding about the social fabrics that bind sonic producers, managers and listeners together.

One small part of this project has involved the development of a digital sound repository, called *Sonic Japan*, to store information on a range of urban sounds that people encounter and contribute to as they navigate various public and semi-public environments in their everyday life, moving in and through train stations, shopping centres, fish markets, restaurants, sports halls, parks and so forth.[2] The sounds recorded and stored there range from the bodily noises of slurping noodles to electronic noises, and from temple bells and tourist chatter to directional instructions or political messages projected from loudspeakers.

In this chapter, we reflect on two soundscapes that are produced in the context of bodily training in Japan – one is a *dōjō* (training place) where the martial art of aikido is practised and the other is a site for learning to play the shakuhachi, the Japanese bamboo flute. What joins these two examples together is that the sets of audio recordings that were made in these spaces were produced while we were ourselves practising – when we were physically engaged with others in the activities that produced the sounds. When we returned to Melbourne, weeks after recording the sounds, we posted clips we selected from the recordings on our new sound repository along with photos and short descriptions that provided a modicum of cultural, historical and situational information. As one might expect, when we created the repository we were struck by the differences between our corporeal memory of actively being in sound as opposed to passively listening to sound. The recordings, we felt, were ironically both richer and poorer for their disentanglement from the 'noise' of the other bodily senses, thoughts, feelings and emotions that actively making the sounds involved. We want, however, not just to observe these differences here, but to figure out a way to account for them, to begin to identify a vocabulary to interrogate their significances and to be able to include what we learn in our ethnographic sensory toolkit.

Anthropologists are now very interested in sonic studies (as this volume demonstrates) but we are still struggling to find ways to capture the nuances, both in terms of describing different qualities of sound and in terms of recognizing the very different levels of experience that our own bodies in practice and those of our informants encounter. Interesting ways of thinking through these experiential nuances have been developed in other disciplines such as music studies, art, geography, physiology and philosophy. The relational aspects of being in sound, for example, whether it is between a body and its instrument or between a body and other bodies and material surroundings, has been a productive space to explore in music, dance, art theory and human geography. Terms such as 'sounding' (Brown 2006), 'proprioception' (Montero 2006), 'haptic sensation' (Rebelo 2006) and 'kinaesonics' (Wilson-Bokowiec and Bokowiec 2006) have been adopted and adapted in various cases to help explain this relationship. Such terms have been embedded within creative projects including soundscapes, soundwalks and sound art/installations.

Finding a paucity of studies focusing on sound in anthropology, Samuels and colleagues have argued that anthropology's 'entwinement with histories of technology, aesthetics, and mediation has led it to a critique of representation in the visual field while largely neglecting issues of sound, recording and listening' (2010: 339). They go on to suggest that 'ethnographers could bring aural sensibilities to the worlds inhabited by the people with whom they work and consider those sounded worlds as more than performance genres to be extracted from their contexts' (ibid.).

But 'aural sensibility' can refer to many things. It includes what Schafer named the 'soundscape': a total acoustic environment that encompasses audible sounds as well as a sense of history and cultural context (1977). It also speaks to what Feld referred to as 'acoustemology' – attending to people's 'sonic way of knowing and being in the world' (see Feld and Brenneis 2004: 462). Additionally, the aurally sensitive ethnographer needs to develop what Clifford has called 'the ethnographic ear' (1986: 12). But where is the ethnographer's own experience of a sonic environment that they too become a part of, placed against the mission to attend to others' experiences?

We would suggest that there is a clear sense of purpose to more effectively share 'other' people's experiences in most sonic/sensory ethnography. Such perspectives offer a view that emphasizes the relational aspect of sonic practices. This takes into account a Bakhtinian view of the dialogical nature of the relationship between different communicative events, where 'meaning making' emerges from the messy interactions between sonic events and human experience (Bakhtin 1982). Feld engages with the dialogic in his approach to auditing and editing (1987) with his recordings of the sounds of voices and activities in the rainforest amongst the Bosavi (2000) and the Kaluli of Papua New Guinea (see Feld 1990; Feld and Brenneis 2004). Feld played back recorded sounds to participants in order to elicit their own understanding of how they listened and how they understood sounds in the forest. This was then elaborated upon through ethnographic texts to build a picture of their sonic environs and experience. In the very different Western urban context of New York City, Andrew Irving's sensory ethnographic work (2013) has involved gathering sound recordings of participants walking and talking as they traverse particular urban built environments (e.g., sound over bridges, which often seem to evoke associations and emotions). The work moves beyond the playing of everyday sounds of social and environmental interaction (as in Feld's work) into a space of participant verbal reflection in order to bring the other's meaningful experiences triggered through contact with meaningful environments closer to the outside observer/listener (and ethnographer). Sarah Pink celebrates the way in which ethnographers such as Irving harness movement as a significant source of understanding in sensory work (2015: 134). However, the bodily movement is of the other and the experience of being in the movement is primarily a recorded representation of the other's experience.

And yet, sounded worlds in the making are potentially perceived not just through the ears of the ethnographer and not just by considering, after the fact, what sounds signal or mean to individuals in different social, cultural and historical contexts. Aural sensibility in ethnography needs to go further to understand how sounded worlds are perceived through the body as a whole and in relation to other bodies and objects. It follows that the only way to approach the full bodiliness of sound is through awareness of what making sounds entails through one's own sonic practice and reflection upon that practice, alongside the aural traces of the total sonic environment in which such practice occurs. How this 'embodied sounding' is then communicated through discursive text, field recordings and so on is a further challenge in the communication of knowledge and experience of being in sound.

Sounded worlds in the making is something musicologists have tried to understand in terms of the way in which performance has the potential to dissolve the distinction between the subject and object. 'In *playing* music, the object really is within the control of the subject, because perception and action – held apart for listeners in concert culture – are in dynamic relation with one another' (Clarke 2005: 150–51).[3] What that dynamism does to the experience of the sound itself and the implications that this has for thinking about the multiple ways that people hear (and attribute meaning to) different things within one sounded environment can only be understood through an embodied and reflexive ear.

The empirical examples we introduce in the next sections based on our own participation within aikido and shakuhachi practice environments in Japan will allow us to think about how a 'sounded anthropology' (Samuels et al. 2010) can consider and compare awarenesses to sounds as they are produced as well as to the 'cleaner', recorded sounds extracted from the messy conditions of their making. We want to think about what practical methodological issues we need to be 'attuned' to here (no pun intended). We also want to theoretically interrogate the relational aspects of sonic production, to consider how 'being in' (the production of sound) also entails 'being with'[4] (other bodies and objects). The first example in the next section takes us to a place of disciplined and rigorous bodily training where vibrations and sounds of movement and interaction are distinctive (to the trained ear) but not necessarily consciously attended to.

Sounds from an Aikido Mat

Aikido is a Japanese martial art that is practised in a training hall or other space called a *dōjō*. A number of different recording clips taken in and around different *dōjō*s in Japan can be found and played at our online repository. The brief introduction to the history and form of practice that is offered later in this section makes some reference to one of these clips recorded in Tokyo, entitled 'Hombu Aikido Dojo with Doshu'.[5] When this recording was played to an Australian work colleague without any contextualizing hints or explanations, he listened carefully and said: 'popcorn noise'. He chose to use the word 'noise' rather than 'sound' – a description that often serves to separate the unknown from the known audible worlds (see Attali 1985). For any listener, however, who has experience with the martial art of aikido, the known, familiar *sound* of training in the recording may powerfully evoke emotions and memories and practical knowledge, and attending (as ethnographers) to that evoked and reflective experience shared by the other could, in itself, be interesting for a study of the sound's socio-cultural life. If we added to the disembodied recording a picture or two and a descriptive text, then anyone (within or outside of the aikido community) could get a closer understanding of the 'soundscape'. We would suggest, however, that this may still not be enough.

We want to consider how sonic ethnography both is and is not served by attempts to collect, share and represent sonic moments in any kind of recorded medium (and in this case we are critically referring to our own sonic repository). Before explaining any limitations, it is important to note that recordings of the sonic world are extremely useful for more than just producing an archive. We would not have invested so much time in the development of the sound repository if we did not believe this. Recordings (nowadays made digitally) may be of educational and historical benefit by salvaging contemporary sounds for a future that might sound quite different. They may be used as objects for cultural illustration; they may be compared to sounds 'captured' in other places or recorded at other times. They bring a textual description of a soundscape to sounded life. But they also, we believe, in providing an object we then label 'the sound of X', presume a representative completeness of sorts that we must, as ethnographers, be wary of. Not only do different *dōjō*s (made up of different teachers, styles, students etc.) sound quite different from one another,[6] but also different teachers within the same *dōjō* will evoke a different soundscape. But what this chapter is concerned with is how the soundscape experienced within the movement itself includes sensory elements that are often indistinguishable from the sound but obviously absent in the recordings consumed later. It is necessary to provide the reader with both a contextual narrative and then autoethnographic reflections on training – on being in sound – to explain this more fully.

Hombu *dōjō* is the world headquarters of the International Aikido Federation, located in a residential area in Shinjuku, Tokyo. Aikido was founded by Morihei Ueshiba (1883–1969), known as '*Ō Senseī*' (Great Teacher) to his students, and combined his knowledge of judo, sword and spear work and hard *jūjutsu* practice with principles of Shinto and Zen Buddhism. The name *aikido* can be translated as the way of harmony of spirit, from *ai* (harmony), *ki* (spirit) and *dō* (way or path). As a 'modern manifestation of the Japanese martial arts (*budō*)' (Ueshiba 1984: 14), aikido is a defensive practice where students learn to 'blend' with and then deflect or neutralize the energy of an attack. In this practice, emphasis is put on upon the correct 'feeling' of contact in the technique rather than on visual 'correctness' of the form (Kohn 2008: 101). This is achieved through a commitment to regular, even daily (for many), practice over many, many years – through a pattern of observation and mimesis of a teacher's training and the absorption through all the senses of form and contact through training with others. Elsewhere, Kohn has analysed the ways in which notions of 'discipline' in the creation and celebration of the self emerge from the study of such a 'disciplined leisure' craft (see 2007, 2008). Furthermore:

> [O]nce embodied, the tacitly 'known' physical and 'unknown' 'spiritual' and/or aesthetic elements in training can be understood as intrinsic parts of one state of being. This state of being in practice is a state of working towards what Zukav referred to as a state of enlightenment, or what Japanese martial artists call *mushin* or 'no mind', or towards what Bateson (following Huxley and Whitman) called a state of grace. (Idem 2011: 46–47)

Aikido practice is always paired with partners alternating their role as either *tori* (the one practising the aikido defensive techniques) or *uke* (the partner who receives the throw through rolling and/or breaking their fall). The predominant 'popcorn'-like sounds audible in the Hombu recordings are the sounds of *ukemi* – the sounds *uke* makes in contact with the mat for falling and rolling safely. To enter Hombu *dōjō*, remove one's shoes near the door, don practice clothes[7] in a changing room and then enter the matted space, kneel and bow at its edge and stretch quietly to get ready before the class begins, is to leave the rest of the world (of work in the city, commuting, home life) behind and to dedicate one's body and mind to the intensity of training.

As such, the *dōjō* is understood as a special space that feels different. One senior teacher at Hombu spoke about the special atmosphere – the special quality of 'air' – that a teacher strives to produce on the training mat with students. This air, he suggested, is invisible but found also in nature: the air you might find in a church or temple. The sound of training, then, is a product of movement and can be felt in the air of the *dōjō*. The senses work together through movement and are thus often indistinguishable on the mat – 'feeling' air, therefore, is understood to be part and parcel of the sounding of the training space.

In the Hombu recording, the chief instructor, Ueshiba Mitsuteru, the grandson of the founder (and known as the *Dōshū*), is in the midst of teaching his regular 6.30am class. He begins the class with rituals of bowing; next he leads students in a series of stretching exercises. Then students rush to the edges of the mat to watch him demonstrate a basic aikido technique with one of his *uchideshi* (live-in students) for a few throws. The students then pair off to practise what they have absorbed from the demonstration. Shortly after participating in this training session, Kohn reflected in writing on her sensory memories from that class:

> The partner who bowed to me on that morning was a young, fit *uchideshi*. His pace felt too fast for my ageing, stiff body at first; I could hear and feel my heart beating deep in my chest and my breath clutching for sustenance in order to get up and go again after each throw. I felt the energy of contact with my partner; I felt the power of his throw vibrate through my body. I then heard my own slapping of the mat only as part and parcel of the repetitive feel of the mat's sting on my palm and forearm. Frequently I heard sounds that helped me sense the potentially dangerous proximity of other bodies whirling and rolling around me in a very limited training space (due to the large number of practitioners that day). The sound became one entangled part of my *zanshin* (martial awareness), honed after more than twenty years of practising. This awareness is framed in martial discourse as 'ten-direction eyes', but it is just as much about hearing as it is about seeing. It relies on proprioception – the awareness of one's own body in space, as well as a felt awareness of other bodies in one's immediate space. It is relationally meaningful. Being in this sound as it is sounding is about feeling through the eyes, ears and fingers. Being in this sound as a practitioner is to attend to the sounds that are related to one's own and to others' bodies moving in space. The recording was made by our research assistant who sat with the audio-recorder just off the mat. To

listen later, from a safer, less dynamic space and to hear the recorded percussive, 'popcorn-like' sound of mat slapping seemed both totally familiar but also totally bereft of the feeling and aurality of being in the sound when training. And yet, despite the disembeddedness, an aikido teacher who listened to the recording with me also picked up subtle nuances in the sounds that my ear had ignored in training – the crispness and urgency of the *ukemi* sounds spoke to him of an accomplished level of training – a very different quality to a beginners' class or to the sound of *ukemi* in his *dōjō* in Australia. As for me, I was genuinely surprised to hear sounds of chatter and laughter from some of the old, senior men who train in one corner of the *Dōshū*'s class every morning. That wasn't meant to be there – no students are meant to talk while training in Hombu senior classes – one learns by seeing and feeling and through years of repetitive bodily practice. But the recorder didn't lie – the talking did take place, but it was not in the sounded space of my training – it didn't imprint itself on my aural consciousness – during that class.

What is clear from this excerpt of notes and reflections is that every 'hearing' is partial and shaped on the mat by circumstance, by necessity, by the body's total sensory awareness of itself in relation to others, as well as by expectation. It is also clear that thinking about different ways of engaging with sound is potentially fruitful in considering how to add sonic experience(s) to our ethnographic toolkit. The philosopher Jean-Luc Nancy, in his treatise on listening, draws on the distinction in the French language between 'listening' (*écouter*) and 'hearing' (*entendre*), suggesting that the latter term encompasses both hearing and 'understanding' (2007). He challenges philosophy to rethink the act of listening (to music) without necessitating a search for understanding. He asks: can senses merely resound without meaning? If the answer is yes, then perhaps the different actors in the above *dōjō* recording scenario can be considered with some reference to the different possibilities that *being with/near* or *being in* training-sound affords. To 'listen' with all one's being, according to Nancy, is to bypass the search for meaning and allow for bodily senses to resound (ibid.). Kohn's reflections from the aikido mat suggest that through the contact with a partner and the sensation of falling and rolling and feeling other bodies' proximity, she is listening in this resounding way. To listen fully in that moment is to absorb a throw and feel the concomitant sensual resonances of movement and contact with things and other people.

The attention to a recording after the event, however, is where people with differently educated ears struggle for meaning. Is it popcorn noise? 'I *hear* popcorn', says the outsider to the practice, while a teacher, perhaps, who has embodied many years of aikido training and teaching, *hears* something much closer to the mark, filtered through many memories of being in that sound. He knows instantly the sounds of *ukemi* and then listens for meaningful nuances that tell him something about the intensity and the style and the quality of that training. It is only the actor within the sound that is truly free from the search for meaning in those moments because of the complexity of the sensory realm: the relations of sight, touch/vibration and sound – the as-it-is-ness of their training.

It is relevant here to note that sounds in aikido practice are produced from the exertions of the body interacting in space and are unremarkable (that is, not usually worth talking about) until they are remarkable (until they stand out somehow – e.g., sound wrong, sound inattentive, sound chatty, sound unconnected). The sound is never perceived as a product or object of practice, but a consequence of it. The mat is slapped to break a fall; the breath is heavy to fuel the body. The sounds emerge from these activities and a well-trained teacher can include sound in her sensory understanding of how people are training, but it is not understood as a product or object in itself and most beginners will not make note of the sounded nature of training. Some other practices, however, reverse the order – the body must train itself to produce the right sort of sound. Sound is one purposeful product (even if it is never a finite product) – it is what people outside of the training remark on and what the beginner hopes to produce. The next section introduces the second of our sonic practice environments to offer a different empirical, reflexive example for this chapter.

Sounds from a Shakuhachi Lesson

The shakuhachi is a Japanese end-blown flute made from bamboo. The shakuhachi became popular in Japan during the seventeenth century when it was associated with a Buddhist sect called the Fuke-shū, although the shakuhachi has a much longer history in Japan stretching back to the twelfth or thirteenth century (see Lee 1992; Linder 2012). This sect replaced sutra chanting with *sui zen* (blowing zen on the shakuhachi) and the sect went on to attract samurai who became itinerant preachers known as the *komusō* (priests of emptiness). Wearing large baskets over their heads (*tengai*) to symbolize their detachment from the world, the aim of the *komusō* was to obtain enlightenment through a single tone, *ichi on jōbutsu* (Deeg 2007: 30). While the *komusō* have all but disappeared, what remains of their sonic practice is an ensemble of traditional pieces called *honkyoku* (original pieces).

Gaining the right pitch in shakuhachi is very difficult, given that this is determined by embouchure and the angle of the player's airstream for which there are no preset positions. Learning pitch is a matter of remembering the sound of the correct pitch, which is reinforced by the individual reproducing his or her own specific bodily positions to achieve the same pitch consistently. The way in which a player holds and adjusts their body in order to play the shakuhachi is vital to the production of sounds that are then judged in terms of their sonic quality by a teacher. Body skills in shakuhachi playing include awareness of breath and diaphragm control, embouchure and inner-mouth position, in addition to more technical features related to finger and head positions. This all requires frequent practice so that the body unconsciously remembers all of the different bodily adjustments that fit together to produce the 'right' sound. Drawing on Merleau-Ponty, various scholars have pointed out the embodied nature of music learning, with Alerby and Ferm stating that to 'acquire and incorporate the structures of music, we have to experience them with our body' (2005: 181). The embodiment of shakuhachi sound production is a key concept reinforced through the methods of teaching. However, among the traditional *komusō* players of the Fuke-shū during the Edo era (1603–1867, a period of relative internal peace, political stability and economic growth in Japan that saw the crystallization of workmanship associated with the traditional arts), it was not production of sound that was necessarily the focus: it was the awareness of the body during its production that could lead to enlightenment.

In the digital repository is a sound file of Richard Chenhall and his teacher playing the fundamental note on the shakuhachi, called RO in Japanese notation.[8] They are just playing one note repeatedly but in playing that one note he is trying to learn the teacher's tone by listening and imitating his teacher's bodily movements. There are but a few verbal explanations; demonstration is the main form of communication. In Japan, when learning the shakuhachi there is often very little verbal communication. A student arrives to a lesson and there are other students present, all of whom hear each other's lesson. Some kind of warm-up activity may be shared by the teacher and students. In this particular shakuhachi school, RO is played by both teacher and student and this might be followed by some comment by the teacher. The verbal comment may be a simple statement asking the student to play 'more', implying the teacher wants to hear a louder, fuller-sounding tone, or if the student is experiencing problems in sound production, the teacher may offer some technical advice. This is followed by the student playing the piece they are currently learning. The teacher and student then play the piece together. The teacher may make some comments but these comments are, again, often general ones about the overall 'feeling' of the piece. Specific technical difficulties may be addressed; however, the transmission of knowledge is through being attentive not only to the sound but also how that sound is produced and embodied. Linder (2012: 259) refers to this as 'audial instruction', rather than 'verbal instruction', in his study of shakuhachi tradition and transmission.

Attempts to imitate a teacher's sound and imagine the total bodily practice in playing the shakuhachi creates an experience of being both inside and outside of the production of sound. Shortly after the time of recording, Chenhall recalled in writing his thoughts and feelings:

> I was overly conscious of my teacher's very loud and proficient sound that overwhelmed my own; I could feel the vibration from his flute

resonating around the room. I can feel my own flute vibrating and incorporating the sound of my teacher's flute. In the recording, this presence is not captured in the same way that I felt it. We can hear two flutes; one is louder than the other but the vibrational resonance, as I experienced it, is lost in the recording. While making the recording, I become conscious of my own sound when I make a mistake and it jars against the sound my teacher makes. Other times, I am caught up in the movement and rhythm of the sound production. At times it feels like I am not connected to the sound production at all and in that moment I lose focus and make a mistake; I am brought back to the struggles in my own body about forming the sound. It's difficult to hear this in the recording, even for me when listening to this later. I hear some technical mistakes, but not the internal struggles I was experiencing. A passive listener would be more likely to focus on the tone and melody rather than the relational qualities of the two players.

As stated earlier, in Chenhall's experience of learning the traditional *honkyoku* repertoire, his teacher would often comment on the 'feeling' of the sounds produced. This feeling is connected to 'understanding'. However, understanding a piece does not necessarily mean that a student becomes competent in the technical aspects of playing a specific *honkyoku*. In learning the traditional *honkyoku* repertoire, Chenhall may learn an individual piece for up to two or three months and for longer pieces the time required to memorize and perform the piece to a teacher's satisfaction may be longer. At each lesson, Chenhall reflected on his progress and whether he would be allowed to move to a new piece. Similar to the fieldnote excerpt above, in the following extract Chenhall notes the experience of being both in and out of the sound he is producing, but here this is connected by his teacher to a sense of understanding the feeling of the piece:

> I am walking to my teacher's house and whilst walking I am rehearsing the piece I am to play to him in my mind. Each phrase courses through my body as I walk, my head moves as if I am playing an invisible shakuhachi. I can hear the sounds in my head as my body moves, unconsciously reflecting the internal voicing of the sounds. Have I memorized the piece correctly? Will my embouchure and embodiment required to produce the sounds come together correctly in the act of performance? Have I internalized the piece? At the lesson, I play the piece. I feel that the 'I' that is producing the sound is slightly outside myself, observing the body that is making the sounds. I am only made aware of myself when I make a mistake, a note is off pitch, a phrase is rushed, a sound is lost. My body stumbles, my consciousness refocuses on my body and its failure to produce the correct sound. In that shifting of awareness I lose

some connection to the sound that I held previously. Rather than the perception of being moved along by the sound I am now struggling to move it forward. After I have finished, my teacher encouragingly states: 'Very good, very good but ... but ... you have not quite understood the piece, I did not feel it. One more week, I think'.

The teacher here may well be referring to his student's ability to either express or give meaning to the performance of a specific piece. Expression has been variously defined; for example, Newcomb states that 'expressiveness results from the metaphorical resonances or analogies that a viewer-listener-reader finds between properties that an object possesses and properties of experience outside the object itself' (1980: 625). Expression is, then, a result of the intrinsic properties of music but also of the metaphorical resonances these properties have for the listener. With titles such as *Yamagoe* (crossing a mountain) and *Daha* (pounding waves), each *honkyoku* piece carries with it a specific story that has some expressive value. *Yamagoe*, a composition from the Kyushu region, literally refers to going over a mountain, but in Japanese this title is interpreted as overcoming difficult obstacles. This in turn has been related to the discovery of the self-limiting idea of life and death in Zen Buddhist philosophies, experienced through overcoming severe obstacles in life (International Shakuhachi Society 2016a). *Daha*, often translated as 'breaking of the waves', represents self-discipline and the will to break all ties to terrestrial life to attain enlightenment (idem 2016b). There is a large body of literature about the expressive aspects of music around the world (see for example Kivy 1980; Newcomb 1980). Kivy sees music as expressive of emotional life because it bears structural resemblances to emotional life. Others, such as Howard (1971), have objected to this 'isomorphic' theory of music and emotion, arguing that just because one thing is identified as similar to another does not mean that one is a sign of the other. Newcomb summarizes these various arguments in his article 'Sound and Feeling' and emphasizes that music has specific expressive resonances founded upon its musical properties, but these resonances are interpersonal and part of a 'shared enterprise that is culture, as a way of transmitting, changing and adding layers' (1980: 638).

Referring back to the above descriptions of 'listening' to the sounds of aikido, a trained shakuhachi player listens to the music in a different way to a novice, informed by the layers of understanding embodied through sustained, committed practice. Listening to a recording of sounds of practice with a well-trained ear affords nuanced interpretations. However, listening with one's training/playing body in the production of sounded movement and music reaches beyond interpretation towards a multisensorial as-it-is-ness, as illustrated through both examples we have offered in this chapter. Chenhall's recounting of the sensation of being 'outside' of the music demonstrates Nancy's (2007) mode of 'listening' with all one's being, rather than simply 'hearing' the technicalities required in the body to produce the sound. In putting to one side the search for meaning through hearing music, the act of listening creates the very 'feeling' or 'understanding' that the shakuhachi teacher refers to in his comments to his student. And the committed practitioner sees how such bodily training contributes to the development of one's personhood – one's growing sense of self and other in the cosmos more generally. For the shakuhachi player, at least in principle, this training is directed towards capturing the essence of the original *honkyoku* pieces by the Zen Buddhist monks, in order to achieve enlightenment through the one or eternal sound.

Reflections

So, what *is* the sound of shakuhachi? Is it the sound captured in a recording? Is it the vibrational aesthetic felt by the player, or the feelings evoked in the listener? Is it in our analytic reflections on all of these things? Similarly, we can ask: what *is* the sound of aikido training at Hombu *dōjō*? The popping sound of the mat slapping? The sensations of sound in a training body? The reflections on the various associations that the sounds may evoke in many who listen to the recording over the years? Or all of these? If part of our aim (as sonic ethnographers) is to share the embodied experience of being in sound, what is the best way to represent this? What are the relations between player and instrument, player and teacher, player and environment that inform various qualities of sound? How can we capture and share those multivocal qualities of sound that are holistically embedded in the sensuous, vibrating body in motion? How can we better consider how auditory knowledge is variously expressed by practitioners and by listeners with a range of practical knowledge and with different sensitivities?

In posing these questions at the last hurdle, we are not expecting to find (nor offer) simple answers. Gerschon (2013: 259) argues that 'representing sounds sonically' gives the producers of sound an important voice, allowing the listener to experience an affective quality of the sound and helping to retain information, such as tone and tenor, that would be lost when translated to text. However, what we have found is that we must not be fooled into thinking that our sounded recorded data is a total reality. Like texts, a recording is one possible representation, around which an interpretative act is framed. Jonathan Sterne argues that a sounded ethnography embraces 'sonic imaginations [that are] necessarily plural, recursive, reflexive, driven to represent, refigure and redescribe' (2012: 5, cited in Gerschon 2013: 259). We extend this to our own work to say that the multivocality of sounded data is an important addition to the repertoire of our sounded ethnographic methods. Our two examples highlight how involvement in the production of sound may be relationally and physically felt and listened to differently in situ than it is when extracted from a site and heard apart from the multiple sensations that produced it. Involvement in this production extends beyond experience and reportage as it embraces the practitioner and affects her sense of being. To be in sound is, as the quote by Deleuze reminded us at the start (Deleuze 2005 [1981]: 31), to become through the sounded practice.

The two examples of sonic practice in this chapter illustrate how learning to 'be and become in sound' is a key tool for ethnographers who are also practitioners – listening through the ears and pores is part of our habitus, as part of our training, as part of our sense of being in and feeling vibration and movement in the sounding space. It requires deeply holistic 'somatic modes of attention' (Csordas 1993: 138), as well as a fair amount of individual sensory 'inattention' to some details in the sonic environment. Because sounds are embodied, both in their production and in their perception, they allow for the creation of a shared, collaborative intimacy between humans and places. This intimacy can be forceful when the slap of a mat reverberates around the fallen *uke* or it can be gentle, seductive even, when the sounds of shakuhachi float through the air – when teacher and student's melodies intertwine with 'vibrational affect' (see Gerschon 2013). Being in sound affords a bodily awareness to an often-jumbled totality of sensations. If we can increasingly recognize these nuances in our own practices then we should at least have a better sense of what is required to interrogate other people's bodily and sonic experiences.

Acknowledgements

We would like to acknowledge the Australian Research Council for funding this research (Sonic Practice in Japan – DP130102035) and also to thank Carolyn Stevens (coresearcher and lead investigator for the project) and the volume editors, Evangelos Chrysagis and Panas Karampampas, for their helpful comments. In addition, Chenhall would like to thank Kaoru Kakizakai of the International Shakuhachi Kenshukan, and Kohn extends her grateful appreciation to Dōshū Moriteru Ueshiba, Dōjō-cho Ueshiba Mitsuteru and other instructors and administrators of the Aikikai Foundation and Hombu *dōjō*, and Yoko Okamoto Shihan of Aikido Kyoto, for their support of our project.

Tamara Kohn is Associate Professor of Anthropology in the School of Social and Political Sciences, University of Melbourne. Her current research interests include death studies, digital commemoration and the anthropology of the senses in communities of practice. Relevant recent publications include: 'Crafting Selves on Death Row', in D. Davies and C. Park (eds), *Emotion, Identity and Death: Mortality across Disciplines*, pp. 71–83 (Ashgate, 2012); 'Appropriating an Authentic Bodily Practice from Japan: On "Being There", "Having Been There" and "Virtually Being There"', in V. Strang and M. Busse (eds), *Ownership and Appropriation*, pp. 65–85 (Berg, 2011); and with C. Graham, M. Arnold and M.R. Gibbs, 'Gravesites and Websites: A Comparison of Memorialization', *Visual Studies* 30: 37–53 (2015).

Richard Chenhall is Associate Professor in Medical Anthropology in the Melbourne School of Population and Global Health, University of Melbourne. His recent works include articles related to the study of alcohol and self-help groups in Japan and books related to the anthropology of sleep, the social determinants of Indigenous health and Indigenous alcohol and drug treatment. Publications include: coedited with K. Glaskin, *Sleep around the World* (Palgrave Macmillan, 2013); coedited with B. Carson, T. Dunbar and R. Bailie, *Social Determinants of Indigenous Health* (Allen & Unwin, 2007); and *Benelon's Haven* (Melbourne University Press, 2007).

Notes

1. See also Chapter 10 in this volume on the 'multisensual' in Ambonwari emic expressions of song-dance experience.
2. http://sonicjapan.clab.org.au. Accessed 9 April 2016.
3. Note that all italics within quotes in this chapter appear in the original source.
4. See phenomenological discourse on different states of (social) being, especially Nancy (2000) on the fundamental state of 'being with'.
5. https://soundcloud.com/sonicjapan/hombu-aikido-dojo-with-doshu. Accessed 9 April 2016.
6. For example, the recordings made at Hombu *dōjō* in Tokyo and those made at Iwama *dōjō* in Ibaraki Prefecture contain very different sounds representing somewhat different styles, different instructors and different practice cultures around vocalization (or not). At Iwama, practitioners vocalize with a sound called a *kiai*, that comes from their centre/belly or *hara* upon contact (e.g., gripping or striking) or when throwing a partner. These usually begin with a vowel sound as in 'eeeeup!' or 'aiiuuup!', etc. At Hombu, in contrast, students attempt to train 'silently' even if they are still engaging their centre and extending their *ki* (life energy) in the movement.
7. These clothes include the white robe (*keiko gi*), a white or black belt depending upon rank, and, for *yudansha* (students with black belts), *hakama* (pleated and long skirt-like trousers in black or dark blue cloth).
8. https://soundcloud.com/sonicjapan/shakuhachi-lesson. Accessed 9 April 2016.

References

Alerby, E., and C. Ferm. 2005. 'Learning Music: Embodied Experience in the Life-World', *Philosophy of Music Education Review* 13: 177–85.

Attali, J. 1985. *Noise: The Political Economy of Music*, trans. B. Massumi. Minneapolis: University of Minnesota Press.

Bakhtin, M. 1982. *The Dialogical Imagination: Four Essays*, ed. M. Holquist, trans. C. Emerson and M. Holquist. Austin: University of Texas Press.

Bauman, R., and C. Briggs. 1992. 'Genre, Intertextuality, and Social Power', *Journal of Linguistic Anthropology* 2: 131–72.

Brown, N. 2006. 'The Flux between Sound and Sounding: Towards a Relational Understanding of Music as Embodied Action', *Contemporary Music Review* 25: 37–46.

Clarke, E.F. 2005. *Ways of Listening: An Ecological Approach to the Perception of Musical Meaning*. Oxford: Oxford University Press.

Classen, C. 1993. *Worlds of Sense: Exploring the Senses in History and across Cultures*. New York: Routledge.

Clifford, J. 1986. 'Introduction: Partial Truths', in J. Clifford and G.E. Marcus (eds), *Writing Culture: The Poetics and Politics of Ethnography*. Berkeley: University of California Press, pp. 1–26.

Csordas, T.J. 1993. 'Somatic Modes of Attention', *Cultural Anthropology* 8: 135–56.

Deeg, M. 2007. 'Komuso and Shakuhachi-Zen: From Historical Legitimation to the Spiritualisation of a Buddhist Denomination in the Edo Period', *Japanese Religions* 32: 7–38.

Deleuze, G. 2005 [1981]. *Francis Bacon: The Logic of Sensation*, trans. D.W. Smith. Minneapolis: University of Minnesota Press.

Feld, S. 1987. 'Dialogic Editing: Interpreting How Kaluli Read Sound and Sentiment', *Cultural Anthropology* 2: 190–210.

———. 1990. *Sound and Sentiment: Birds, Weeping, Poetics, and Song in Kaluli Expression*, 2nd edn. Philadelphia: University of Pennsylvania Press.

———. 2000. 'Sound Worlds', in P. Kruth and H. Stobart (eds), *Sound (The Darwin Lectures)*. Cambridge: Cambridge University Press, pp. 173–200.

Feld, S., and D. Brenneis. 2004. 'Doing Anthropology in Sound', *American Ethnologist* 31: 461–74.

Gal, S. 2003. 'Movements of Feminism: The Circulation of Discourses about Women', in B. Hobson (ed.), *Recognition Struggles and Social Movements: Contested Identities, Agency and Power*. Cambridge: Cambridge University Press, pp. 93–118.

Gerschon, W.S. 2013. 'Vibrational Affect: Sound Theory and Practice in Qualitative Research', *Cultural Studies <=> Critical Methodologies* 13: 257–62.

Howard, V.A. 1971. 'On Musical Expression', *British Journal of Aesthetics* 11: 268–80.

Howes, D. (ed.). 1991. *The Varieties of Sensory Experience: A Sourcebook in the Anthropology of the Senses*. Toronto, ON: University of Toronto Press.

———. 2003. *Sensual Relations: Engaging the Senses in Culture and Social Theory*. Ann Arbor: The University of Michigan Press.

International Shakuhachi Society. 2016a. 'Yamagoe'. Retrieved 15 April 2015 from http://www.komuso.com/pieces/pieces.pl?piece=2535.

———. 2016b. 'Daha'. Retrieved 15 April 2015 from http://www.komuso.com/pieces/pieces.pl?piece=1823.

Irving, A. 2013. 'Bridges: A New Sense of Scale', *The Senses & Society* 8: 290–313.

Kivy, P. 1980. *The Corded Shell: Reflections on Musical Expression*. Princeton, NJ: Princeton University Press.

Kohn, T. 2007. 'Bowing onto the Mat: Discourses of Change through Martial Arts Practice', in S. Coleman and T. Kohn (eds), *The Discipline of Leisure: Embodying Cultures of Recreation*. Oxford: Berghahn, pp. 171–86.

———. 2008. 'Creatively Sculpting the Self through the Discipline of Martial Arts Training', in N. Dyck (ed.), *Exploring Regimes of Discipline: The Dynamics of Restraint*. Oxford: Berghahn, pp. 99–112.

———. 2011. 'Gravity and Grace: A Study of Martial Movement and Discourse', in G. Hage and E. Kowal (eds), *Force, Movement, Intensity: The Newtonian Imagination in the Humanities and Social Sciences*. Melbourne: Melbourne University Press, pp. 40–52.

Lee, R.K. 1992. 'Yearning for the Bell: A Study of Transmission in the Shakuhachi Honkyoku Tradition', Ph.D. dissertation. Sydney: University of Sydney.

Linder, G.J. 2012. 'Deconstructing Tradition in Japanese Music: A Study of Shakuhachi, Historical Authenticity and Transmission of Tradition', Ph.D. dissertation. Stockholm: Stockholm University.

Montero, B. 2006. 'Proprioceiving Someone Else's Movement', *Philosophical Explorations* 9: 149–61.

Nancy, J.-L. 2000. *Being Singular Plural*, trans. R. Richardson and A. O'Byrne. Stanford, CA: Stanford University Press.

———. 2007. *Listening*, trans. C. Mandel. New York: Fordham University Press.

Newcomb, A. 1980. 'Sound and Feeling', *Critical Inquiry* 10: 614–43.

Pink, S. 2015. *Doing Sensory Ethnography*, 2nd edn. London: Sage.

Rebelo, P. 2006. 'Haptic Sensation and Instrumental Transgression', *Contemporary Music Review* 25: 27–35.

Samuels, D.W., et al. 2010. 'Soundscapes: Toward a Sounded Anthropology', *Annual Review of Anthropology* 39: 329–45.

Schafer, R.M. 1977. *The Tuning of the World*. New York: Random House.

Silverstein, M. 2003. 'Translation, Transduction, Transformation', in P.G. Rubel and A. Rosman (eds), *Translating Cultures: Perspectives on Translation and Anthropology*. Oxford: Berg, pp. 75–108.

Sterne, J. 2012. 'Sonic Imaginations', in J. Sterne (ed.), *The Sound Studies Reader*. Abingdon: Routledge, pp. 1–17.

Ueshiba, K. 1984. *The Spirit of Aikido*. Tokyo: Kodansha International.

Wilson-Bokowiec, J., and M.A. Bokowiec. 2006. 'Kinaesonics: The Intertwining Relationship of Body and Sound', *Contemporary Music Review* 25: 47–57.

Chapter 2

Performing and Narrating Selves in and through Classical Music
Being 'Japanese' and Being a Professional Musician in London

Yuki Imoto

Stories

Sumiko

Sumiko[1] was born in a small city in Hokkaido, the northern region of Japan. Her music education started at the age of three when her mother took her to the Yamaha music school for Eurhythmics classes. When she was four years old she asked her mother if she could take up the piano and she started having piano lessons with her neighbour, who happened to be a piano teacher. Her parents did not take her early music education seriously, and it was valued more for the 'cultivation of sentiments' than for its capacity to cultivate Sumiko's musicianship. When Sumiko was six her family moved to the larger city of Sapporo where she took up piano lessons with a reputable teacher. She started practising more intensively and began entering competitions, while her mother became more and more involved. It was not until the second year of secondary school, however, that she started thinking seriously about becoming a musician. Her parents were adamantly against this idea and Sumiko could not convince them to let her follow her 'calling'. She explained: 'It's definitely a tough job and difficult to sustain a living as a musician. My father (a professor of English literature) wanted me to pursue literature and my mother had her ideas too; it was natural that they had hopes for me, being an only child'.

When Sumiko was seventeen, her father took a sabbatical year and the family moved to Cambridge, U.K. Sumiko experienced life abroad for the first time. She reflected that she had never had much interest in Western culture, nor had she been aware of the link between classical music and Western culture, until her family moved to England. She asserted that, overall, her move did not affect her musical identity: 'Music always meant Western music and I played the piano to enjoy the bodily sensations that music produced in me. It was a much more primitive desire'.

Sumiko started taking piano lessons from an English music instructor, and this encounter was a crucial turning point that convinced her that she should become a pianist. The instructor encouraged her in a way no teacher in Japan had done and for the first time she felt that people appreciated and felt the music and the sensations that she was trying to communicate. During that year, she made her recital debut in Cambridge. On returning to Japan, she entered university to study English literature, although continuing to study the piano and occasionally being invited for recitals by her instructor in Cambridge. She eventually made up her mind that after her graduation she would go to England to study at the Royal Academy of Music. Although her parents did not believe she would be able to realize her dream, Sumiko managed to receive a scholarship and went on to pursue a postgraduate degree in London, where she has been residing for sixteen years.

Dai

Dai began violin lessons at four years old, though initially he did not take his studies seriously. It was when he entered the junior school of the Toho Gakuen Music School at the age of twelve that he realized he wanted to become a violinist. He recounted: 'At the Toho junior school I met people of my age studying music seriously. Playing with them in orchestras and ensembles made me think: "Wow, this is amazing!"' Dai entered the secondary school attached to Tokyo University of the Arts (*Geikou*) and went on to study towards an undergraduate degree (*Geidai*). From a young age, Dai held a great interest in Europe and its culture. He had lived in Paris for half a year when he was three, owing to his father's business, and, therefore, he felt an affinity towards Europe. He explained: 'Seeds had been sown early on'.

In his first week at *Geidai* his teacher told him: 'You must get out!' (*Deteikinasai*!). His teacher, having studied in France himself, encouraged Dai to leave Japan and go abroad to study music as soon as possible and to never come back. He told him: 'Just find your grave there and never come back! ... The Chinese, the Koreans ... We all have the same oriental face, but they're like the Jews; once they leave, they don't come back. The Japanese somehow become soft and want to come back and they do come back'. It was, however, only during his third year at *Geidai* that Dai first left to study abroad. He went to Los Angeles to study with a Russian teacher for three years. Following that, he moved to London and entered the Royal Academy of Music. He is now married to a British musician and has lived in England for fourteen years.

Music, Identity and the 'Japanese Self'

Sumiko and Dai are two musicians I met through mutual Japanese friends in 2005 when I was studying and conducting research in England. I was a Ph.D. student in anthropology, but one of the hidden reasons that I wanted to pursue my degree in England was because of my passion for playing the violin – something my Japanese parents forbade me from pursuing professionally. In fact, during my first years at graduate school, I probably spent more time practising and performing music in Oxford and London than I did studying anthropology. As my interest in anthropology crossed with my interest in music and with my perspective of looking at 'Japan' from the 'outside', questions that I had never before considered began to emerge. Why did I want to come to Europe to play classical music? What does it mean for me to play classical music? What does it mean for professional musicians to play classical music? My musician friends all had fascinating stories to tell – both through their music and through our conversations. How would an anthropologist analyse their stories, as well as mine?

Based on the research project that thereafter unfolded, this chapter explores how Japanese professional musicians who go to London to study and perform classical music narrate their experience and identity. More theoretically, the issue that eventually emerged from my interview-based fieldwork and upon which this chapter is focused, is how Japanese national identity, overlapping with ethnic and racial identity – a shared feeling of 'Japaneseness' explained and imagined in terms such as 'blood', 'history' or 'culture' (Yoshino 1992), is expressed and experienced in the 'West'.

As Frith articulates: 'Music, like identity, is both performance and story, describes the social in the individual and the individual in the social, the mind in the body and the body in the mind' (1996: 109). In framing my inquiry and analysis, I bring two further perspectives to this remark. The first is that of language – or more specifically the 'language about music' perspective (Feld and Fox 1994: 32). As Feld and Fox explain, people talk about music and this discourse about music intersects with music itself. Musical meaning and experience is difficult to translate into verbal-analytic discourse, but musicians are involved in verbally explaining their experience and understanding of music in various ways – whether with fellow performers, students, audiences, journalists or (occasionally) anthropologists. Both the experience of music and that of identity can only ultimately be told through language.

The second perspective is that of self. Here, I specifically refer to the anthropological depictions of 'the Japanese self', which Gordon Mathews describes (1996). Mathews refutes the dominant view in the anthropological literature of Japanese selfhood that contrasts the 'Western' self as 'individualistic' and the 'Japanese' self as 'sociocentric' and 'lacking essential cores of individuality' (ibid.: 720). He argues instead that all selves shape themselves over their life course and that this can be understood as a process of self-construction using an array of overlapping cultural conceptions. He presents a three-tiered model of the Japanese self: a deep level of the taken-for-granted, which includes one's native language, as well as the cultural habitus that one has acquired from childhood; the middle level, which is about dealing with Japanese social norms and roles; and the shallow level of the 'cultural supermarket', which is about how one can actively consume and perform identity from the range of cultural repositories available. It should be noted that this model is neither essentially 'Japanese', nor applicable to all Japanese; it is employed here to make sense of the variations in identity processes. One can imagine that cosmopolitan professional musicians will identify less with institutional social identities compared to Japanese expatriates and their wives dispatched abroad by the company (see Kurotani 2006). Musicians will, rather, perform by utilizing the cultural repositories of the 'deep level' of habitus, and narrate through bringing this to consciousness, and by utilizing 'language about music' and 'language about Japaneseness' from the 'shallow level' of the cultural supermarket.

In what follows, first the meaning of the 'West' – a highly problematic category against which modern 'Japanese' identity is defined – will be unpacked, mainly through the history of classical music and musicians in Japan. Next, the methodological background of the research will be provided. Interview data will then be presented to describe how Japanese musicians through 'language about music' narrate self-identity. As I demonstrate, the language of classical music becomes enmeshed with ideology (Woolard and Schieffelin 1994) – that is, the language of cultural distinctiveness and nationalism/race/ethnicity – reminding us of the legacy of Western classical music in Japan and its development as part of the nation's dual quest of modernization and westernization.

The Historical and Social Context of Classical Music in Japan

Music is a powerful symbol that can be used to create, express and enforce national identity. In the case of Japan, as in other modernized nations, music has played its part – starting with the introduction of military bands in the 1850s and 1860s. From the 1870s, the Meiji government systematically introduced Western music; a national anthem was created, *gagaku* imperial court music was reestablished, standardized songs were taught in schools and military music was utilized as a means of instilling nationalistic ideologies (Eppstein 1994). From the late nineteenth century onwards, the fervent importation of Western music from the U.S.A., Germany, France and England left an influence so prominent and persistent that its code has been completely naturalized in the soundscape of contemporary Japan (see also Chapter 1) and the sensibilities of the urban Japanese population.

What is particularly intriguing in the Japanese case is the emergence and development of Western classical music as a form of high art that, for the new intellectual middle class that participate in this discursive field (Bourdieu 1993), is at once a tradition of the Western Other and a means of self-identification and expression.

Today, Japan has one of the largest industries of classical music in the world, with forty-one music conservatories or university departments; a postwar legacy of piano-learning as a cultural practice of middle-class life, driven in large part by the success of Yamaha Corporation; and over one thousand amateur orchestras around the country. Those who become professional performing musicians are only a handful, however. The boundary between 'professional' and 'amateur', as discussed in other national contexts, is ambiguous and subjective (Baily 1988; Finnegan 1989; Cottrell 2004). However, it is significant that the majority of students in Japan's music conservatories are female and that many will become private music teachers or locally performing musicians supported by their husbands' income. Making a living solely out of music requires investment of money and constant long hours of dedicated practice from a young age (particularly for pianists and violinists), with generally low returns in terms of social and economic capital. For the handful who do pursue a professional career, studying – and if possible, launching one's career – in Europe or the United States has been a rite of passage ever since the late nineteenth century, when Koda Nobu first went to the U.S.A., then to Europe, to study and teach the violin (see Mehl 2012).

Collaborative Intimacies in Narrating Experience

Between September 2005 and April 2006, I conducted a series of semi-structured interviews in London and Tokyo, with classical musicians of Japanese nationality. From a total of twelve interviewees, five were violinists (of whom one was also a conductor), one a violist, another five pianists (of whom one was also a composer) and one a bassoonist.[2] All were born in Japan, were aged between twenty-nine and fifty-eight, had started their musical training in Japan, and then had gone on to study at music conservatories in Europe and/or the U.S.A. All, apart from two that had returned to live in Japan, were based as performers in London, though travelling frequently around the U.K. and to other parts of Europe. They also continued to retain contact with Japan through performances, as well as family ties, though to varying degrees.

They were all of a middle- to upper-class upbringing; that is, from families where the father was, for example, an academic, a medical doctor, a diplomat or a businessman of a large company, and where the mother was typically a housewife or a teacher. Many of my interviewees had academic or literary interests; for example, one informant had a Ph.D. in music, specializing in seventeenth-century English music; another was a qualified medical doctor and neurologist; one held an English literature degree and another a philosophy degree (both from prestigious universities in Japan); and another had been a Visiting Fellow of sociology at Oxford University.

The narratives introduced here do not provide a comprehensive picture of Japanese classical musicians abroad, while the backgrounds provide a comparative and alternative account from those of the musicians that appear in Yoshihara's (2007) study of Asian musicians in the U.S.A.

My informants' backgrounds – as well as the presentation of myself as a young, Japanese, female graduate student, though with relatable musical and transnational experiences – affect the nature of anthropological research (see also Chapter 4). Ethnographers are both reflexive and interactive selves, and are implicated in relations of power as well as intimacy. My interviewees narrated their stories in relation to the identities I carry and perform, as well as the level of collaborative intimacy that we forged. The fact that I reached my informants through introductions meant that the 'academic and literary interests' of my informants were consonant with my own interests and my status as a student at Oxford University. I was invited to the homes of the musicians, went to their concerts, was introduced to their other Japanese musician friends and rehearsed and performed with some of them.

The above issue of reflexivity and complicity is inseparable from my position as a 'native anthropologist' (see Narayan 1993). I am 'native' firstly in the sense of having grown up to feel at 'home' in both Japanese and British culture. As a 'returnee', having received education in the U.K. and in Japan, I myself, like my informants, have lived along national, cultural and linguistic borders. I am also 'native' in the sense that I have grown up immersed in classical music, having been playing the violin since the age of five. Because I have studied and performed music in both Japan and Europe, I 'hear' or, at least, 'feel' that I can understand the sorts of 'Japanese' qualities in musical performance that are perceived and discussed by the musicians. I also share the native language – Japanese – in which the interviews were conducted. During the interviews, therefore, I could empathize with the interviewees' views but had to always check on myself to keep a critical anthropological eye.

As in Yoshino's study (1992) on the consumption of sociological theories by the middle-class businessmen and educators he interviewed, many of my informants' narratives would also have been affected by their knowledge of literature, philosophy, psychology and sociology, as well as mass media. They are aware of terms such as 'identity' that the anthropologist works with and indeed I was frequently advised on books to read and topics to consider for my research. Just as I was obliged to continually problematize my interview methods and techniques and to consider whether, as a result, I was enforcing essentialized differences between the 'West' and Japan or other categories, my informants were well aware of the dangers or the potential traps of generalization.

It must thus be noted that all ethnographic writing is 'partial' (Clifford 1986) and that realities can only be represented through a subjective lens. As Clifford suggests, ethnographies are 'cultural fictions based on systematic and contestable exclusions, silencing incongruent voices' (ibid.: 6). I am complicit both in creating fiction with my interviewees, and in excluding certain versions of the story. That I am writing about musical experiences – a nonverbal, embodied realm, heightens the dilemmas of representation. The realities and experiences seem too complex and contextually fluid to be represented and analysed in the scope of this chapter. So what then *can* be represented and analysed? This chapter will focus on how 'national character' or distinctiveness/difference manifests itself in language about music. While some of what my interviewees state is contestable from an anthropological viewpoint because of the assumptions of essentialized culture/race/ethnicity that they posit, the first step is to suspend my judgements and to attempt to represent the perceptions and understandings of the interviewees through their explanations and narratives.

Cultural Distinctiveness of Musical Performance and *Nihonjinron*

The musicians' explanations of the perceived distinctiveness of Japanese characteristics of playing classical music, in relation to 'Western', 'European' or 'English' cultures, came in diverse forms. For some, difference in musical performance was explained as a difference of language. One pianist attributed the Japanese style of playing each note separately rather than in a flowing phrase to how the Japanese language clearly separated each syllable, while most European languages were more 'flowing' so that the sounds of one word often merged into the next. The notion of language and music as affecting one another is a prevalent discourse, resonating with a 'particularist' view of culture and notions of linguistic relativity (Sapir 1956; Woolard and Schieffelin 1994).

Others gave genetic/biological explanations; for example, reference was made to the theory that the Japanese and Westerners 'used their brains in different ways' (see Tsunoda 1985). One female violinist, Yumiko, noted that Japanese teachers and conductors encourage 'singing' a melody (see also Ingold 2007: 29–33); emphasis is placed on lyricism rather than the overall structure. She explained: 'Japanese traditional music is linear, and traditional Japanese folk songs are very emotional, nostalgic and lyrical – but classical music places more emphasis on structure and the logic of harmony'. The idea that, in Europe, musicians place more emphasis on structure and logic appeared in several of the interviews I conducted. It seemed that what is identified as the 'European style' of approaching classical music in an analytical and intellectual manner was particularly emphasized in order to differentiate European musicians' style of playing and interpretation from the 'Japanese way'.

A common view of the characteristics of Japanese audiences was that they were more 'passive' than European audiences. In Europe, interviewees claimed, one can feel the audience 'reacting and communicating with the music'. One male violinist explained:

The Japanese feel music in an experiential way. The Japanese are most concerned that they hear the music and this is the goal, like, 'yes we experienced the music and felt it'. In Europe music is more 'relativized' [*soutaika-sareteiru*] and the listener is more actively involved in interpretation. So, in Europe many people come to the performer after the concert with questions about the music they performed, or with comments and points of discussion. This almost never happens in Japan. When it does, comments are usually something like '*kandou shimashita*' [I was deeply moved] or '*namida ga demashita*' [it made me cry].

For some interviewees the main form of explanation was environment and custom (everyday embedded practices), such as the sense of rhythm being linked to a certain place (e.g., Stokes 1992; Cohen 1994); one argument being that, in Europe, there was always a sense of an 'upbeat', which was lacking in Japan. Reference was also made to a distinct 'European sound', which could not be achieved unless one experienced living in Europe. This was explained in terms of the humidity affecting the sound resonance and the environment in which one was able to practise. One female Japanese violinist in her fifties noted: 'In Europe, the sound can ring without force, especially as there is a lot of playing in churches and places with good acoustics. If you practise every day in a *tatami* [bamboo flooring] room, or in a cramped soundproof room, you're not going to be able to bring out the same sort of sound'.

Interviewees noted almost unanimously that there is a certain bodily or physical disposition (*kishitsu*) in the playing of Japanese musicians: each note is important and needs to be heard, playing is neat and clean, and emphasis is on accuracy. One pianist noted that even when pianists acquire a European style through studying abroad, 'a few years in the Japanese musical environment and performers are moulded back into this disposition'. A recurring theme was that the Japanese are very concerned with detail, and perfection is aimed for in terms of playing all the notes accurately and playing neatly and together in ensemble. A commonly arising expression was 'sensitivity' (*komayakasa, sensaisa*). While playing neatly and accurately does not necessarily entail positive meanings, sensitivity is used as a positive trait of Japaneseness, not only within music performance but also as a general personal characteristic.

'Sensitivity' and 'perfectionism' are further related to a particular work ethic. To attain perfection, my interviewees argued, Japanese musicians are willing to put in many hours of rehearsal and practice. One musician explained that this was because Japan had adopted the Germanic style of playing music; Germans also rehearsed in depth and in detail. This style of music practice, they said, suited the national character of both the Germans and the Japanese. By contrast, in England, ensembles and orchestras have very few rehearsals. The English were, therefore, more *iikagen* (remiss) but also *kiyou* (clever; skilful), in that with very little practice they could 'seem' to play well. Because of this scarcity of rehearsals (which one musician pointed out is not only the result of custom but also because of particular financial circumstances), musicians in England have good sight-reading and ensemble ability. One female violinist noted:

> Sometimes orchestral players look at the music for the first time at the dress rehearsal; this is unthinkable in Japan. It's difficult for a Japanese musician to work in an English orchestra or with English musicians and keep up because Japanese musicians aren't used to this 'crude' style of music practice. They have to spend many more hours than their colleagues preparing for the performance and 'polishing' their repertoire.

A bassoonist remarked with regret that, in English orchestras, musicians are very 'professional', which often leads to a remove from the 'emotionality' of music. For many, it has become an automatic and technical job. In Japan, he claimed, players 'care' more about each piece and the quality of the performance. Other musicians were of the view that, because there are fewer rehearsals, there is more spontaneity in the actual performance, and it allows something 'special' to be produced between the players and the audience; 'This sort of spontaneity does not occur among Japanese musicians', one violinist remarked.

In two cases, explanations of cultural difference were predominantly sociological. The claim was that it was the postwar Japanese society and its homogenizing education system, the loss of culture as a result of wartime bombings and the subsequent industrialization and the advent of consumerism that led to the present 'lack of individuality' among musicians. The 'common history' of the Japanese was discussed, with the underlying idea that 'we are not on the same grounds' – referring to the perceived lack of tradition and history, because Western music was 'only imported to Japan 250 years ago'. Common heritage was also raised with reference to 'our race/ethnicity' (*minzoku*), such as in the following comment: 'I believe that the race that has superior "[culinary] taste" is superior in all aspects of culture. The Arabs, in this sense, are wonderful. I think the Japanese have the best culinary taste in the world'.

In most cases, musicians did not feel that one way of listening to music was superior to the other; only that there were clear differences. In the case of one conductor, however, there was clearly a sense of Japanese superiority, as he talked of the Japanese audience as 'the best in the world':

> The Japanese audience and also the Japanese performing musician is 'introversive' rather than 'expansive' [he specifically referred to the words 'introversive' and 'expansive' in English even though the conversation was otherwise in Japanese]. I don't use this word in the negative sense – it is indeed very positive. I think it is a quality that some Japanese

people have – please note I'm saying *some* and not all. The Japanese are a race [*minzoku*] that reacts very sensitively to concentration. The Japanese have a sense of focus towards music in the same way they do for sports – very intense. Japanese musicians and audiences have a great capacity for concentration.

Contested Discourses of Individuality, Emotion, Discipline and Education

We have thus far seen that there are diverse forms of 'Japaneseness' that are used to explain cultural differences and distinctions in musical practice. These overlap with the larger discourse of *Nihonjinron* – theories of Japaneseness – that proliferated in Japan and have been consumed and read widely since the 1980s. The reinforced sense of national identity supports Fujita's (2009) observation about cultural migrants in London – whose senses of Japanese national identity often seemed to be strengthened in the process of border crossing and marginalization.

One violinist pointed to certain 'cultural values', such as the notion of talent, as being a factor in explaining the difference between Japanese and European music practice and education. Here, one cannot ignore the influence of the Suzuki Method – the method devised by Suzuki Shin'ichi and popularized throughout the postwar period – which emphasized that every child had musical talent, because music was like language and thus all children had the ability of acquiring the mother tongue (see Peak 1998; Yoshihara 2007).

The meaning of discipline could be interpreted as positive or negative by interviewees, but in either case there was a specific value of 'Japaneseness' associated with the concept and its practice. All musicians acknowledged the positive outcomes of a strictly disciplined approach in music education.[3] Some recounted their own experiences of how strict their mother and teachers had been. Looking back, they were grateful for the discipline they received, for without hard practice one could not achieve the technical skills that were crucial for a professional musical career. Central to the notion of discipline is the teacher–pupil relationship. One violinist commented that:

> When asked why the Japanese become good musicians, I answer that this can be linked to the traditional practices of Japanese arts – the *iemoto* system.[4] The teacher is respected and the student must accept and imitate what is transmitted to them. Japanese music students, therefore, are 'good students' [*yuutoosei*]. In the West, students are not as concerned with following the teacher's wishes.

While the above comment implies the strengths of a 'Japanese' approach to musical education, the more negative connotations include the Japanese lack of individuality and lack of opinion. These were explained by one violinist to be the result of the *iemoto*-system type of disciplined and submissive learning:

> In Japan, you are not expected to question, but to do as you are told. This is true in music education also. In England and in Europe, teachers explain the reasons for their opinion and interpretation of music in terms of structure and harmony or the historical and social context. The interpretation is left to the student. The worst thing about music education in Japan is that music is thought to be something that is taught.

Some interviewees viewed the Japanese musicians' propensity to imitate their teachers and masters as an unfortunate trend that hindered many from getting beyond a certain level of recognition in music conservatories abroad. Others, however, saw the diligence of Japanese musicians as the key to their success. The U.S.-trained pianist Kazumasa, for example, has reflected on how his playing, which is most often described as being *koseiteki* (having individuality), typically meets divided opinion. Even at the entrance examination for *Geidai*, the opinion was apparently divided between those who thought 'there is no more for him to learn at *Geidai*' and those who thought 'this isn't Beethoven'.

The link between education and the notion of individuality becomes apparent here. 'Individuality' has ambiguous meanings. One musician noted that individuality and expression alone cannot bring about good music; one needs to have the sufficient technique to express one's individuality. She felt that it was unfortunate that many students in England lacked this technique because of their less rigorous attitude towards technical training, which she explained as coming from a stronger belief in their intrinsic individual 'talent'. This ultimately hindered progress towards attaining adequate tools to express themselves musically. For some, lack of individuality was explicitly linked to 'Japanese culture'. But generally, while recognizing that there were indeed traits in Japanese social organization that tended towards group conformity, there was a feeling that the 'West' held a prejudiced view that only saw the superficial aspects of Japanese culture. It was noted that the stereotypical view of collectivism is linked to the stereotypical view that the Japanese 'do not express themselves'. One bassoonist commented:

> Yes, I did make the point that Japanese culture makes expression through classical music difficult and, therefore, Japanese musicians typically cannot express themselves naturally through classical music. However, there are other channels through which the Japanese express themselves; it is wrong to say that the Japanese have no self-expression. Their expression appears in more subtle and almost subconscious forms, and I don't think English people understand this.

The violinist, Dai, made a similar assertion, saying:

I think that, concerning emotion, the Japanese are a very passionate people. Japanese emotion is one that surges inwards. This is the same for the British too. They have to give effort to let their feeling come out. They have to 'perform' to bring out their inner emotions. Like in a 'kabuki' sort of way, because it takes effort to bring it out, the performance becomes formalized to certain set patterns. This type of expression is different from the type of expression in classical music, where feeling has to flow naturally. This difference is what raises the view that the music of Japanese musicians lacks expression.

This formalization process takes place in areas outside of music as well. Japanese businessmen are typically said to have no emotion and no humour. You know this isn't true. They are funny and emotional people. But they can't or won't express this in a natural way because, as they become adults, society imposes norms on them: manners and honorifics and so on. But when they were children, they could still freely express their emotions. That's why it's important to provide an education that preserves this freedom and that's what music can do. This is something that should be considered in Japanese education and it's the problem of classical music education in Japan.

The violinist Dai, with whom I held several hours of discussion both in person and over e-mail, revealed to me the emotional, 'spiritual' experiences of playing music, particularly in live concert performances as a soloist. He also spent considerable time discussing the issue of being a Japanese musician playing classical music in Europe:

> We don't have the historical background that Europeans take for granted, so when we try to play like the Europeans, it is difficult. There is a line that we just cannot cross.
>
> Of course, we have to acquire the basic background, because after all it's European music. If we don't, it will end up as some strange music. But in Japan, in music lessons, we are educated to catch up with the Europeans, the Americans, the Russians, in terms of performance level; to catch up and, if possible, to overtake. But this only works to a certain extent and we can't win with just this because we are not on equal grounds. We have to set the goals at the same level as the Europeans; otherwise it's impossible. So, to bring forth the feelings that they have had within them from many generations before, we have to bring out what the Japanese have had from the generations of our ancestors. Otherwise, we can't compete.
>
> In the end, we have to use the qualities that we have as Japanese, which have been with us from before we were born. And, in addition,

we have to acquire the European tradition. I think this is the way and it's what I personally try to keep in mind.

Appropriating Identities from the 'Cultural Supermarket' or Rediscovering the 'Deeper Self'?

Taylor Atkins, the author of *Blue Nippon: Authenticating Jazz in Japan* (2001), cites the following example of a 'Western' interpretation of 'Japanese' musical performance. A review in the Japan Times stated that: 'If jazz is an international language, every country has its own dialect. In Japan some people leave more space in the music. You could call it the Zen approach to music, sort of like less is more' (cited in ibid.: 31–32). To this, Atkins remarks that:

> Zen is a rigorous spiritual practice that is as alien and unnatural an approach to life to most Japanese as it is to most Americans. I had never met a jazz musician who had studied Zen, let alone self-consciously incorporated its aesthetic principles into performances. Furthermore, respect for space is nothing unique to any country or philosophy, as the musics of Thelonious Monk, Miles Davis, the Art Ensemble of Chicago, and Sun Ra attest. (Ibid.: 32)

While Zen may certainly be 'an alien and unnatural approach to life' for many in contemporary Japan, my empirical data opens up questions, for some individuals did consciously incorporate aesthetic principles of Zen in their performance and were influenced by its philosophy. This may be a result of the kinds of books that my interviewees were reading, as well as their reactions to the kinds of discourses of 'Japanese culture' they were exposed to outside of Japan. They may also have been responding to my own interest in the 'anthropology of Japan' and also to my seeming lack of familiarity and knowledge about 'Japanese culture' in spite of being 'Japanese'.

The violinist Dai recounted how he had found his playing being identified with 'Japaneseness' by audiences. People had commented on how his playing embodied an 'aura of calm' or how it related to Zen. On reflection, he could understand how such an interpretation could arise, as his playing style was not an aggressive one and he performed by 'creating a space that is congruent with nature'.

The pianist Matsuyama (male, in his fifties) noted: 'It is interesting that, within European music, aspects of Japanese music are being incorporated, such as the notion of *ma* [space; betweenness] or *mu* [nothingness]. These kinds of emotions, or rather the absence of emotion, are originally of the Orient and belong to our culture'. A younger pianist, Hirota, likewise mentioned that many Western musicians were incorporating concepts of Zen to enhance their performance so that a counter-importation was occurring.[5] He explained:

I have always been interested in Zen but not of the academic, difficult kind such as Nishida Kitaro's philosophy; more of the practical philosophy of Zen. I see music as one kind of *dō*道 [way] – as part of the spiritual discipline, which includes *shodō* [the way of calligraphy] and *sadō* [the way of tea]. It is a means of taking away idle thoughts and to reach a state of *muga* [nonself]. You could call it *ongaku* [music]-*dō* or *piano-dō*.

Would such narratives have emerged had they not left Japan and crossed borders? The incorporation of Zen into strategies of performance and/or in reaching a state of nonself in music could be regarded as responses to being an Oriental/Asian/Japanese Other in the field of classical music. Such narratives could, at the same time, be an indication of how Japanese musicians are bringing alternative conceptualizations and languages of musical performance into the Western classical music context.

Classical musical performance can be a highly ritualized but intense process that may bring upon performers the physical effects of nervousness, leading to uncontrollable shaking and/or memory lapse, as well as invoking heightened emotions. Zen is a slippery, ambiguous and oft-politicized concept, but one which cannot be separated from meditative 'practice', and more broadly the integration of body and mind in Eastern philosophical traditions (Yuasa 1987). It thus seems to have been consciously incorporated by some musicians in order to explore ways to think about and enhance one's performance – ultimately an act of physical and mental integration – regardless of their nationality, religion or ethnicity.

For Japanese musicians of Western classical music, however, the incorporation of Zen becomes symbolically multilayered. Zen emerges as an example of how cultural codes are chosen as self-identity from the 'cultural supermarket' at the shallow level of identity. But it is further entwined with the deep level (the unconscious) and also the middle level of social constraint – thus becoming a survival strategy.

It must be mentioned that many musicians would reject essentialized associations of classical music and 'culture' and ethnicity. This is discussed by Yoshihara (2007), who was rejected several times when making requests for interviews because the musicians were apprehensive that she would make a connection between ethnicity and music – which they found to be deplorable. When I asked a younger female musician, 34-year-old Hanae, about the use of *ma* in music, which was mentioned by Matsuyama above, she answered as follows:

> Concerning *ma*, I don't really think about it at a conscious level, but I probably think about it at the natural level. In ensemble performance, the flow of the music, the energy of myself and the other players and our breaths are all synthesized into one, and this is *ma* for me. In England, when we play in ensemble, we don't discuss things [like where to place

the *ma*] so much in detail. We talk about how to create the musical phrase, the flow, and I think the *ma* is something that naturally comes about in this process. I think of it as the energy in between a phrase and another phrase.

Ma is a concept derived from Buddhist aesthetics but also used in common parlance in Japanese. Hanae made no connection of the term to 'Japaneseness' or to Zen in her narrative. For Hanae, who has lived in England for thirteen years, it is about the way 'we' (including herself) make music in England, versus the way 'they' make music in Japan. When thinking about the opportunities that exist for her in London, with its active classical music scene, as well as what she considers to be a 'more mature and engaged audience' in Europe, she does not want to return to Japan permanently. In England, she can challenge herself and play repertoires that would be difficult to perform and may not be appreciated in Japan. Her musical home is England.

Concluding Remarks

The series of interviews, of which extracts have been presented in this chapter, revealed a common and continuing discourse of linking Japanese characteristics to issues of performance of classical music, as well as practices relating to music and musicians. However, the way this discourse was consumed or internalized seemed to vary according to the musician in question. It is, therefore, not constructive to question which of the assertions of Japanese qualities are 'real' practices and which are ideological claims. It can only be concluded that there are certain ways transnational musicians talk about Japanese characteristics of Western classical music, performance and reception, as well as everyday social experiences.

To give a tentative generalization, 'Japaneseness' can be: embraced and adhered to as an essential culture and self-identity; objectified and narrated from a detached viewpoint, at times rejected as irrelevant to identity; or consciously manipulated as an authenticating strategy for artistic interests. The way 'Japaneseness' is consumed is affected by the social values and collective memory inculcated through education, media and social interaction. Therefore, it is likely that the length of stay in Japan or abroad, as well as other factors such as class, age and gender, will lead to differences in the expression of national identity and this is a crucial problem that must be explored in further research.

I return here to the question of whether I am imposing a 'problem' that is not always recognized by the interviewees themselves and, second, whether my research is itself partly working to construct narratives of 'Japaneseness'. There is a constant contradiction as musicians move through different levels of narrative and self-identity. My interviewees commonly pointed out that while they regarded themselves as Japanese, this was not important, and that what *was* important was the 'individual'. They would then, however, delve into their own stories and reflect on their observations of musical performance using the language of 'Japaneseness': 'But when I am playing music, being Japanese has no significance. I surrender myself to the music – self and identity is meaningless in these moments', the pianist Yu emphasized.

The excerpt below from an interview with the London-based pianist Uchida Mitsuko published in *Kangaeru Hito*, a Japanese arts magazine, shows some of the frustrations that international musicians may face regarding how they are represented in the media, and also reveals commonly held ideals of universality of music and of borderless identities:

> If I return to Japan now, people would make a fuss over me. ... This is not something unique to Japan, to flatter an individual of one's own country. It is said that nationalism is a phenomenon that came about in the early nineteenth century, but it seems that from then onwards it has resided within most people. But I don't have interest in national sentiment. For me, the human being is the most important and music is important. (2005: 48)

Increasingly, Japanese media and musical institutions are placing musicians of mixed race and musicians of plural, hybrid cultural identities into the spotlight. Increasingly, musicians are crossing borders – not only geographically, but also in terms of genre and style – as Asian performers take centre stage in the most prestigious competitions and concert venues for classical music. While the prominent rhetoric among my interviewees was about Japaneseness as conquering and overcoming Westernness, it is likely that the identities of younger generations will be more hybrid and fluid. The uses of 'Japanese' concepts and characteristics, or Asian, Eastern and Zen Buddhist notions, will increasingly be about 'circulation' and 'fusion' (Baudrillard 1981; Willis and Murphy-Shigematsu 2007), rather than importation and reimportation. As the industry of classical music diversifies, individuals' appropriation of images, sounds, rituals and stories from the global cultural supermarket will increasingly be about reflexively creating and recreating the self (Giddens 1991) and the music that is embodied, in each moment of practice and performance.

Yuki Imoto is Assistant Professor at Keio University, Japan. Her research interests lie in the anthropology of education, language, music and Japan, and her works converge on the issue of cultural identity in globalizing contexts. Her publications include the volume *A Sociology of Japanese Youth: From Returnees to NEETs* (Routledge, 2011), coedited with Roger Goodman and Tuukka Toivonen; and the volume *Foreign Language Education in Japan: Exploring Qualitative Approaches* (Sense, 2015), coedited with Sachiko Horiguchi and Gregory Poole.

Notes

1. All names of interviewees are given as pseudonyms.
2. My focus is limited to instrumentalists. Different historical and social contexts apply for singers and composers, as Mari Yoshihara (2007) points out.
3. On education and learning in Japan see Singleton (1998), Rohlen and LeTendre (1999) and Cave (2009).
4. The *iemoto* system is the organization of schools of traditional Japanese arts, such as flower arrangement and tea ceremony. It is a hierarchical system that gives the master the complete, unquestioned authority. Its model can be seen in other domains of social organization, such as business organizations, the mafia and sports. Anthropologists, such as Hsu (1975), have used the *iemoto* system model to explain the success of Japan's industrialization.
5. Ohnuki-Tierney notes: 'The supreme irony in the Japanese imitation of the West, however, is that the latter is now increasingly imitating Japan' (1990: 204). She also points out that mutual borrowing or bidirectionality of imitation has a long history: 'The Japanese self has been constructed and reconstructed always as it affects and is affected by other cultures' (ibid.: 205). The 'passing around' of the images of Zen is a lucid example of the bidirectionality of the mechanisms of Orientalism. Zen was 'exported' to the West in the nineteenth century, through a form of self-orientalism on the part of Japanese Meiji intellectuals asserting *Nihonjinron*-type ideas. The image of Zen was thereafter consumed and transformed to meet the needs of the West. Today, the Japanese are consuming this Western-influenced version of Zen, so that the 'self' of this second round of self-orientalism is now objectified. For an interesting account of the manipulation of Zen in Japanese nationalism see Sharf (1993).

References

Atkins, E.T. 2001. *Blue Nippon: Authenticating Jazz in Japan*. Durham, NC: Duke University Press.
Baily, J. 1988. *Music of Afghanistan: Professional Musicians in the City of Herat*. Cambridge: Cambridge University Press.
Baudrillard, J. 1981. *Simulacra and Simulation*, trans. S.F. Glaser. Ann Arbor: The University of Michigan Press.
Bourdieu, P. 1993. *The Field of Cultural Production: Essays on Art and Literature*, ed. R. Johnson. Cambridge: Polity Press.
Cave, P. 2009. *Primary School in Japan: Self, Individuality and Learning in Elementary Education*. Abingdon: Routledge.
Clifford, J. 1986. 'Introduction: Partial Truths', in J. Clifford and G.E. Marcus (eds), *Writing Culture: The Poetics and Politics of Ethnography*. Berkeley: University of California Press, pp. 1–26.
Cohen, S. 1994. 'Identity, Place and the "Liverpool Sound"', in M. Stokes (ed.), *Ethnicity, Identity and Music: The Musical Construction of Place*. Oxford: Berg, pp. 117–34.
Cottrell, S. 2004. *Professional Music-Making in London: Ethnography and Experience*. Aldershot: Ashgate.
Eppstein, U. 1994. *The Beginnings of Western Music in Meiji Era Japan*. Lewiston, NY: The Edwin Mellen Press.
Feld, S., and A.A. Fox. 1994. 'Music and Language', *Annual Review of Anthropology* 23: 25–53.

Finnegan, R. 1989. *The Hidden Musicians: Music-Making in an English Town*. Cambridge: Cambridge University Press.
Frith, S. 1996. 'Music and Identity', in S. Hall and P. Du Gay (eds), *Questions of Cultural Identity*. London: Sage, pp. 108–27.
Fujita, Y. 2009. *Cultural Migrants from Japan: Youth, Media, and Migration in New York and London*. Lanham, MD: Lexington Books.
Giddens, A. 1991. *Self and Society in the Late Modern Age*. Cambridge: Polity.
Hsu, F.L.K. 1975. *Iemoto: The Heart of Japan*. New York: Halsted Press.
Ingold, T. 2007. *Lines: A Brief History*. Abingdon: Routledge.
'Interview with Uchida Mitsuko'. 2005. *Kangaeru Hito* Spring Issue: 34–55.
Kurotani, S. 2006. *Home Away from Home: Japanese Corporate Wives in the United States*. Durham, NC: Duke University Press.
Mathews, G. 1996. 'The Stuff of Dreams, Fading: Ikigai and the "Japanese Self"', *Ethnos* 24: 718–47.
Mehl, M. 2012. 'A Man's Job? The Kôda Sisters, Violin Playing, and Gender Stereotypes in the Introduction of Western Music in Japan', *Women's History Review* 21: 101–20.
Narayan, K. 1993. 'How Native Is a "Native" Anthropologist?', *American Anthropologist* 95: 671–86.
Ohnuki-Tierney, E. 1990. 'The Ambivalent Self of the Contemporary Japanese', *Cultural Anthropology* 5: 197–216.
Peak, L. 1998. 'The Suzuki Method of Music Instruction', in T. Rohlen and G. LeTendre (eds), *Teaching and Learning in Japan*. Cambridge: Cambridge University Press, pp. 345–68.
Rohlen, T., and G. LeTendre (eds). 1999. *Teaching and Learning in Japan*. Cambridge: Cambridge University Press.
Sapir, E. 1956. *Culture, Language, and Personality: Selected Essays*, ed. D.G. Mandelbaum. Berkeley: University of California Press.
Sharf, R.H. 1993. 'The Zen of Japanese Nationalism', *History of Religions* 33: 1–43.
Singleton, J. (ed.). 1998. *Learning in Likely Places: Varieties of Apprenticeship in Japan*. Cambridge: Cambridge University Press.
Stokes, M. 1992. *The Arabesk Debate: Music and Musicians in Modern Turkey*. Oxford: Clarendon Press.
Tsunoda, T. 1985. 'Remarks on Transitivity', *Journal of Linguistics* 21: 385–96.
Willis, D.B., and S. Murphy-Shigematsu (eds). 2007. *Transcultural Japan: At the Borderlands of Race, Gender and Identity*. Abingdon: Routledge.
Woolard, K.A., and B.B. Schieffelin. 1994. 'Language Ideology', *Annual Review of Anthropology* 23: 55–82.
Yano, C.R. 2002. *Tears of Longing: Nostalgia and the Nation in Japanese Popular Song*. Cambridge, MA: Harvard University Press.
Yoshihara. M. 2007. *Musicians from a Different Shore: Asians and Asian Americans in Classical Music*. Philadelphia, PA: Temple University Press.
Yoshino, K. 1992. *Cultural Nationalism in Contemporary Japan: A Sociological Enquiry*. Abingdon: Routledge.
Yuasa, Y. 1987. *The Body: Toward an Eastern Mind–Body Theory*, ed. T.P. Kasulis, trans. N. Shigenori and T.P. Kasulis. Albany: SUNY Press.

PART II

Pedagogies of Bodily Movement

Chapter 3

Kinaesthetic Intimacy in a Choreographic Practice

Brenda Farnell and Robert N. Wood

> I want people to see a *person* dancing, not someone in the role of 'dancer' – a person with all their spiritual, dispositional and dynamic presence.
>
> —Robert Wood

'What are people doing when they dance?' This was a question proposed by Drid Williams as a useful starting point for a social anthropologist of dance (1991: 15). This chapter proceeds from a variation of Williams's question by asking: what is a choreographer doing when s/he makes a dance?[1] This leads to a detailed excursion into the intricate world of Robert Wood, a New Zealand-American choreographer and contemporary dance artist based in New York City, in whose works intimacy between choreographer and dancers is a prerequisite to artistic exploration – rather than such collaboration leading to intimacy.[2]

Before proceeding, it is relevant to note that the intellectual partnership between one author's choreographic investigations and the other's cultural and linguistic anthropological interests entails additional intimacies that move well beyond the traditional anthropological model of scholar-and-informant. Robert Wood disrupted that model from the outset by making collaboration an implicit precondition for an ethnographic entrée into his world. What began and sustained the conversation (vocal and kinaesthetic) was the shared goal of furthering knowledge of who we are as human beings through investigating the artistic activity of people exploring space, time and energy, and what that means and/or produces. We also seek to exploit a space wherein artistic imagination and creative procedures – which envision movement as the enactment of a whole body intelligence – meet a social-scientific orientation towards body movement as dynamically embodied meaningful action that is culturally and historically situated.

How best to document this collaboration in writing has presented ongoing challenges, resulting in a working process that consists of cowriting and coanalysing – including coediting each other's voices. The result is a dialogue of sorts, grounded in long-term ethnographic field research on the one hand and artistic practice on the other, in a format that seeks to represent and respect the coauthors' different areas of expertise.[3]

Introduction and Outline

In popular usage, the word 'intimacy' implies emotional attachment, an affective connection, a bond formed through knowledge and experience of another person.[4] We suspect that most English speakers assume 'physical intimacy' to be characterized by romantic or passionate attachment or sexual activity. But contemporary dancers[5] share a physical intimacy that involves none of the above. Indeed, Robert Wood talks of dancing as 'a way to physical intimacy that is not about physical contact per se'. So what constitutes this alternative realm of physical intimacy among these dancers and choreographers? How best can we understand it, and of what significance is it to anthropological practice and broader understandings of who we are as human beings? We propose here an aesthetic – or, more accurately, a kine-aesthetic (kinaesthetic) – intimacy specific to the movement arts. Robert provides an enticing point of entry via the following statement:

> The social trust required for working physically, personally and intellectually on mature movement creates a lifetime emotional relationship or bonding. I remember the feel of all my [dance] partners – the shape of their bodies, their aroma; I can still see their faces in different emotional states. I can remember the feel of their hands, and also feel the remembrance of their hands – the sensation creates the image and the image subsequently amplifies the sensation. You don't feel because you see [visually] – you are also 'seeing' or attaining kinaesthetically.[6]

We find resonance here with Michael Herzfeld's concept of 'cultural intimacy' (1997)[7] and Elizabeth Povinelli's 'intimate grammars' (2006; Webster 2015), noting that human movements, too, are replete with 'feeling tones' (Sapir 1921: 39–41; 1929) created and expressed through kinaesthetic sensitivities that are psychologically salient, engage felt connections and bodily memories and build up over time through individual use. Through an articulation of Robert's artistic process and pedagogy that foregrounds his own oral narratives, we seek to illustrate how multisensory explorations initiate and permeate choreographic choices, thereby affording a highly developed kinaesthetic intimacy. We aim for a 'fine tuning' of anthropological experience (Friedrich 2006: 40) inclusive of an embodied poetics of motion.[8]

The chapter is organized into five sections: (i) provides select biographical information that briefly, but accurately, situates Robert Wood's approach historically, culturally and personally; (ii) examines specific choreographic procedures; (iii) contains an account of kinaesthesia and what we mean by 'kinaesthetic intimacy'; (iv) explores the centrality of personhood and disposition in Wood's work; and (v) describes how intimate group formations grounded in whole-body understandings create a 'common sociality' among the dancers – a 'cultural intimacy' defined in part by outsider perceptions (Herzfeld 1997). The concluding statement reflects on the significance of all this in relation to broader cultural concerns as well as theoretical issues in the social sciences.

The Choreographer

The concepts, procedures and principles that instruct the choreographer's craft are many and varied, but often unfamiliar to those outside of the professional dance arts community. We can begin to understand and appreciate the significance of Robert's artistic and choreographic vision if we consider his points of departure as a braiding of distinct strands: a New Zealand/Oceanic viscerality and physicality that embraces selected features of Japanese butoh and Zen Buddhism, brought into an environment of experimental choreographic structuring within North American modern, postmodern and contemporary dance.[9] Robert possesses extensive first-hand, embodied knowledge of how the craft of choreography was being developed during an important era in North American concert dance, having worked with a wide range of prominent New York contemporary dance-makers from 1983 to 1992 after arriving in the U.S.A. from his native New Zealand.

Robert developed a professional performing career as a soloist and featured artist in the New York dance companies of Merce Cunningham, Martha Clarke, David Gordon and Donald Byrd during the postmodern florescence of North American concert dance at this time. Cunningham (see below) invited Robert to join his company in 1987 and set his own role in the signature work *Rainforest* on Robert when he no longer wished to perform it himself, thereby bestowing a rich legacy.[10] Robert performed nationally and internationally as a featured member of this company from 1987 until 1992, when he chose to leave in order to develop further his own choreographic process.

He subsequently established his own movement arts organization, Robert Wood Dance – New York Inc. (hereafter RWD), which integrated his native New Zealand/Oceanic sensibilities and influences from the teaching of Tadashi Suzuki in Japan with his North American contemporary dance lineage to produce a distinct aesthetic signature.[11] Cosmopolitan in outlook, with a commitment to using dance as diplomacy in international contexts, RWD includes Asian and European as well as ethnically diverse American dance artists, and frequently works overseas.

Oceanic Formations – New Zealand

The aesthetics of New Zealand (*Aotearoa*)'s remarkable natural landscapes defy brief description: from the country's mountain air and astonishing clarity of light to the dark mysteries of its primeval, moss-draped forests; and from ever-changing ocean swells that lap pristine sandy beaches to the snow-capped backbone of *Te Waka-a-Māui* [the canoe of Māui] of Maori creation (see Illustration 3.1).[12] All this and more provided fertile environments for a quiet, imaginative young person to explore and fine-tune his physicality as an essential way of being-in-the-world. For example, the sensation of shifting one's weight, timing and balance, while accelerating a road bike along the curving coastal roads of the North Island – from Plimmerton through Pauatahanui to Paekakariki and back up the Pukerua Bay hill to Porirua – with their sweeping vistas and ever-changing light and shadow as the sun sets on shining water; then turning inland to shift and tilt with the camber of small, winding country roads between gently rolling hills with their small, scattered farmsteads on every turn. Or allowing the body to surrender to the swells and ever-changing tidal pull of the waves while surfing and swimming in the ocean. And all this in contrast to harnessing one's strength, weight and energy both with and against other bodies while playing the national sport of rugby football.

> The environment establishes who you are – physically, perceptually and spiritually. We luxuriated in our physicality – there's something robust about us … not a 'toughness' but a different understanding of timing – functioning with empathy towards the physical landscape (land, sea, sky, weather) … .
>
> As a young person I was very quiet but I sensed a great deal – that seemed to be how I worked. I was built to function that way, but it's not recognized [as a way of knowing]. A few teachers could see it, but not many. My memory was interesting: I could tell you what the teacher wore and how she moved and stood, but couldn't remember what the third line of the poem was! In a theatrical play, I addressed remembering the lines by making them up – my exterior senses didn't allow me to learn within that system.[13] … It was best for me to work through my imagination. I found a way to be good at something and focus on it – specialize. That came from exploring movement. I had a fascination with space and the body moving because I was shy and didn't think I had anything of value to speak about!
>
> Right from the beginning I was working my body from the visceral, not dressing it from the outside.

The physicality generated by a *Pākehā* (fair-skinned New Zealander) cultural upbringing was richly complemented by indigenous Maori understandings

Illustration 3.1 An onsite movement exploration for the camera, near Te Anau, on the South Island of New Zealand. The Piwakawaka *(*The Fantail*) section of Robert Wood's recent development of the work* Koru *(2014). Dance artist: Ling Fen Chien Wood.*

of relatedness between human and nonhuman worlds, filtered through regular exposure to Maori social, spiritual and ceremonial responsibilities via Robert's Maori and Pacific Islander friends in adolescence, as well as training in Maori language, stories, dances and songs in the local Marae.[14] Maori understandings of ancestral knowledge and relatedness remain deeply connected to the formation of the islands, their natural features and journeying across surrounding seas (see Mead 2003). This, together with the centrality of ceremonial dancing and action chants to sensorial understandings of Pacific Islander and Maori cultural knowledge and its aesthetic sensibilities, were deeply influential and formative of Robert's art well in advance of his New York career.

> When I arrived in New York I was confident enough to believe that I knew what I was doing. I came from a culture that does things early [in life], and so I found that, compared to a young American dancer, I had a lot more experience – of live performance, film and TV. I brought a physicality from New Zealand that I used to make some early works. *Portal-to-Portal* (1985)[15] was [a solo] dance on film designed to show that physicality; to make the point that a New Zealand mindset is not like yours.
>
> It was an experiment to take a pretty good piece of pop music and drop it randomly on top of a series of theatrical vignettes. Using transitions of human mood and action that fold into each other with gestures, it shows

a physical young man of a certain age and the anguish and anxiety of leaving a paradise and ending up in a small box in New York City – an image of me in my small apartment in the wee hours. I intended to perform it myself, to show this New Zealand information and who I was.

I built it on another young man so I could see the structure, activity, time and locations ... but when I realized how useful it became to him as a process that gave him confidence, I wanted him to perform. I was being influenced by film, and as with Fellini's use of real people, I wanted to see *a real person moving* rather than the image of a dancer. But it was not about technical expertise – *he* is in there, being human. It's not the performativity of it – but what it shows of *us* because truly experienced by the person making it. And it's not just making material about ourselves, but exploring an area of information about which we are trying to find out more. It was about bringing my [Oceanic] environment into this new environment – the mood of it, the way of it. *Stems from the Garden* (1982) was also made soon after my arrival in NYC [with memories of New Zealand]. It references a child's vision of a natural world that is alive – a kind of animistic vision.

Oceanic Formations – Butoh

I found that closest to the physicality I brought from New Zealand was [Japanese] butoh,[16] which utilizes cultural structures and patterns and an intense physicality that seemed to apply accurately to my New Zealand understandings – it also addresses nature in an in-depth way. I had studied with Tadashi Suzuki while in Japan for the Arts Festival in Osaka (1986) with David Gordon's Pick Up Company. I used butoh as a portal; a way to explain to Americans something of what I was bringing from Oceania. Butoh had been written about in English and so had been structured and interpreted by Westerners (e.g., Holborn and Hoffman 1987; Sanders 1988). I was coming to sense why Americans were interested in butoh and why they read it the way they did. Many Americans seemed fascinated with their perceptions of the elegance, ceremony and graciousness of Japanese culture, yet may not have associated this with the historical depth, reach or sacrificial pain, violence and darkness of Japanese culture that this new art form reveals (see Sanders 1988; Skuld 2014).

North American Formations – Postmodern Dance

A third strand in Robert's artistic development, North American modern and postmodern dance, involves several significant figures, but here we focus on the particular influence of his extensive experience with the musician John Cage and the dance artist Merce Cunningham during the 1980s in New York City, the birthplace of North American modern dance in the early twentieth century and self-proclaimed 'capital' of the modern/postmodern dance world.[17] Cunningham had developed an inspired and astonishing creative 'abstraction' of human movement and gesture. He sought to free concert dance from the dramatic storylines and symbolic representations of the human psyche, so prominent in North American modern dance and ballet at the time (Cunningham 1968, 1985, 1992; Copland 2004). It would be a mistake, however, to think that such abstraction meant that Cunningham was reducing human beings to the status of machines or merely physical objects. On the contrary, instead of accepting any loss of human agency and its freedom, Cunningham employed new compositional strategies such as 'chance procedure' (the roll of a dice or the I Ching), perhaps as a way to find a place for human freedom in the generation of new movement. It was also a strategy for removing the influence of his personal movement preferences or habits from his choreographic selections. His works are undoubtedly a product of the ironic, urban, postmodern New York environment that also produced renowned visual artists such as Andy Warhol, Jasper Johns, Robert Rauschenberg and others (see Copland 2004).

In retrospect, however, what seem to have been absent from Cunningham's modern and postmodern dance are whole realms of additional human experience – cultural, historical and personal dimensions. It is the cultural dimension and its expressiveness in the movements of skilled dance artists that Robert is recovering. What is meant by 'cultural' here is a framework of meaning and identity, within which people understand each other and come to know themselves, so as to live purposefully. Dancers, like all of us, reveal various aspects of cultural groundings in the way they move, both inside and outside of the dance studio. As Marcel Mauss (1935) pointed out a long time ago, the way we walk, sit, stand, gesture when talking, dig, swim and hold a child all have an 'accent', as it were, that indexes our cultural origins. While most of us remain unaware of the social origins of such *technique du corps* until we meet a contrasting case, the heightened kinaesthesia of a trained dancer and choreographer make this embodied information a potential resource for choreographic exploration. Robert expressed this heightened sensibility as follows:

> I can feel a New Zealander across the street.
>
> I have felt my land from someone's voice on the telephone, or from a photograph or picture of New Zealand that I might not even be familiar with.
>
> Ancient molecules and energies are still with us, in the dust, in the earth – they are still here to be recovered. An expansive environment that opens the body allows information from this library to come in.

Just as Cunningham, in forging a postmodern turn with John Cage, rejected the primitivism, naturalism, psychologism and narrativity of earlier modern dance (see Cunningham 1968, 1985; Copland 2004), Robert is finding ways to embody essential human qualities without returning to dramatic storylines or explicit symbolic expressionism. However, he departs from Cunningham's frequently depersonalized and a-sensual handling of bodies in space wherein partners are seemingly manipulated objects.[18] Instead, he seeks to recover an emotionally rich and humanized sense of physicality and state of being, which proposes to access the actual and imagined dimensions of space and time as perceptual and experiential human resources. This is grounded in an 'open-procedure' approach to the choreographic process that can best be described as a humanist and sometimes theatrical expansion of Cunningham's and Cage's legacy.

Choreographic Procedures and Process

> We are not aiming to make beautiful dances from this methodology.
> —Robert Wood

Operating within a broad set of general principles, Robert explores specific questions or parameters in the making of work and chooses methods of working generated by these, referring to his choreography as 'movement works' or 'movement explorations' rather than 'dances'. A movement exploration is an investigation into knowledge that can be accessed or discovered through the moving body. Testing ideas here is a research practice driven from moving itself – ideas come *from* here, not the reverse (that is, 'ideas' are not imposed onto the moving). To use Gilbert Ryle's (1984 [1949]) useful distinction, it is not thought *about* something but thoughtful engagement within the practice of moving that is central to movement investigations.

While explorations do cross over into considerations of the choreographic craft or method, this is not the focal point of the construction. Indeed, crafting, as it is usually understood, is used sparingly and yet, in some cases, remains productive. It is closely associated with variations on a procedural theme that has its own structure.

> From the early experience of using 'chance procedure' in sound and dance, we learned to establish information by adhering to a procedure that was selected or that showed itself.
>
> In fact, structurally speaking, in this section [of *siLenCe*] there are twenty-seven shapes with seventeen transitions; there are nine sub-transitions and another thirteen shapes. One can maintain a personal detachment – addressing the mathematical or geometrical aspects of the piece. One can also access other aspects of nature using the intelligent qualities that arise through casual [open] procedure. It doesn't just involve recall, it creates self-perpetuating new knowledge – embracing what was, what is and what could be. It is key to these states of high

functioning to be self-perpetuating. A calm waiting for the factors that reply to these energies brings us to appreciate planes of understanding and perceptual realms-within-realms.

Robert's process of making movement works also entails a rejection of the somewhat normative 'choreographer as master' system, in which 'I tell you how to move from what I know about my body'. But neither is this improvisation or democratic group collaboration. Instead, the dance-maker works from each dancer's self and personhood as these show themselves, both in the studio and outside, making selections from chance occurrences according to the principles of 'open' or 'casual' procedure. It is 'how I know your body, imagine your process', a deeply personal and interpersonal visceral-visual searching, producing story that creates imagery; a seeking that continues live in performance:

> It's the dancer's choice whether to explore or serve the choreography – all are equally empowered. It's not about always doing it, it's about the fact that they *could* choose to do it, like in the *siLenCe* 'Samurai'.[19] Do I play with cause and effect today? What is my state of being today? Do I go for something or stay in this zone of kinaesthetic exploration? Kinaesthetic being is the key to the whole thing – the brain feels this visceral imagery.
>
> The exploration is driven by the director, yet the dancer as explorer also has autonomy as well as the responsibility to seek. Reasoning for the directing/selecting comes from an effective continuation of decades of the exploration.
>
> Procedure adjusts to social context; and adjusts and adapts to the cultural proclivities of practitioners. In contrast to most choreography – which is 'set' – it changes. The organization and selections require knowledge of previous dance procedures, as well as a way to move what occurs into a functioning piece of investigation and information.
>
> The casual [open] procedure employed is not just happenstance; the action is moved to a whole other frequency – a kinaesthetic calibration is going on that is addressing the higher functioning that is shown in and through the work – [the higher functioning] shows itself.

This reveals deeply our shared humanity, accessible through a pleasurable process of discovery both on and off stage that confirms its validity:

> The goal is not to make the ultimate piece or era of choreography, but to take the high-functioning knowledge of the discipline [of dance] and mature dancers at their peak to establish a means of seeking human

information/knowledge ... a way of establishing belief and a permission to explore from a new intellectual/artistic space.

Developing kinaesthetic intimacies is a prerequisite to this mode of artistic exploration and collaboration. It requires personal dispositions of the artists that include transparency, vulnerability and reciprocity, qualities that make for exquisite kinaesthetic dialogue, as essential features of the 'shared trust' necessary to support this approach to choreography as both art and research.

Kinaesthetic Intimacy

This account foregrounds kinaesthesia as a primary sensory resource for constructing embodied knowledge. Missing from the traditional Western taxonomies of the five senses,[20] it is this ab(sense), as it were, that provides whole-body and body-part information to any human mover about her/his individual spatial orientation and location vis à vis other persons and the immediate environment.

Kinaesthetic awareness also provides proprioceptive feedback as to the dynamic qualities of one's actions. This allows skilled dancers to calibrate such elements as the speed of their movements, precise timing, fluctuations in muscle tension, energy flow and the size of actions – the degree of extension (stretch) of limbs and so forth. This can be supplemented by a simultaneously inward corporeal awareness of other bodily sensations such as blood flow, balance and even digestive processes, awareness of which varies from dancer to dancer.

The dancers in RWD also describe the importance of sensing a vibrational energy that emanates from them into the intersubjective space between and around them. A locational sensitivity comes into play that allows one to feel the presence of the other dancers and their human state of being. As one dancer wrote:

> One more thing is the *state of being*. I can sense the energy vibrating through the space when we're doing a group piece. He didn't give specific cues but most of the time we have to feel each other's movements and feel as part of the group. I enjoy this because a lot of the time when dancers are learning from choreographers they spend a lot of energy learning the movement, but often forget about the intention of our own moving body. In this piece I can feel the *present* when I'm dancing and not obsess about getting the timing and correct steps and movements, I really feel the energy in the space. (Ling Fen Chien Wood, performer, *siLenCe* 2006, personal communication)[21]

A shared awareness of the rhythm and sounds of each other's breathing also provides important cues for coordinating action in a performing space, along with sounds such as the feet landing and pushing off from the surface of the dance floor (see also Chapter 1). The uses of both regular vision and peripheral vision supplement kinaesthetic awareness. Regular vision involves using the eyes to locate points in the external performance space as well as other moving bodies; peripheral vision involves a sort of 'not looking' sideways per se but locating both sides of the 180-degree visual sphere available to us.

All these finely tuned skills and modes of sensory awareness develop during years of repetitive, daily technical training in the studio; training that builds not only the muscle strength and joint flexibility required, but also the necessary corporeal, personal and interpersonal levels of awareness. Robert highlights the difference as follows:

> A highly trained professional dancer has a very strong muscle mass. This easily creates the misconception that it is athletic ability that makes a dancer so well-tuned, but a dancer also requires a heightened sensorial library. This allows one to go to the next level rather than thinking of using muscles. You almost de-embody yourself to find a sensory essence; your idea/perception of the movement is the most important thing, not muscle power. Your energy sources come from places other than your fitness and power – one has an awareness of each other's worlds and we are moving in many spaces simultaneously.
>
> People say, 'Oh, you must have trained to get that', as if your mind, your muscles, your repetition must have created that. I am more interested in a seeking sensationally, which changes muscular usage, so we achieve a floating buoyancy in space – a kind of letting go to *be*.

Several layers of additional knowledge require our ethnographic attention to understand the processes that enable this attainment; knowledge that is familiar primarily to the creative artist and practitioners as 'inside' experts, and which enriches its meaningful potential for performers and observer/participants alike. An illustrative example of such 'letting go to be' can be seen in *Reverence* (see Illustration 3.2).[22]

> They are bringing their own humanity, their own physicality, emanating an energy, a vibration. The body may be the heightened receptor in this bodily state of heightened sensual awareness/consciousness. [Paula] dreams a different dream than me – I gave her the movement (one time only) but she makes it her own. It's a visceral pleasure – this is how she is feeling it. It's a less-than-conscious state of being – a new mode, hyper-kinaesthetic perhaps – not heavy, not dark, but gentle.
>
> Kelly is going directly to a place of experiencing; it's enjoyable and pleasure moves us towards things. Paula has a consciousness of performing; she sees herself in what she is doing. It's still a visceral activity but

Illustration 3.2 Kelly Slough enters a visceral foray in Reverence, *section six from Robert Wood's evening-length work* Ascension, *New York (1996). Photographic progression is by Chris Ramirez, costume design by Anne Dixon and lighting design by Lee Squires.*

at different levels. We are still seeing her human attributes more pronounced. She is bringing energy from herself, of her spirit, rather than muscular. We are aiming to bring out the heightened or special information uniquely accessible to Paula. The outcome might be quite different each time because the dancer's path is influenced by the choices they make according to their disposition each time they go through the procedure – again removing the choreographer as controller while retaining a focus for the searching or experimenting in ways that are not cerebral or linguistic. This moves quickly into vast and quite sophisticated knowledge and insight about whole body and environment.

Acknowledging the sophistication of danced movement as 'whole-body intelligence' at work in an environment that is always adapting and changing, Robert reflects that:

> As moving intelligence, the whole body in motion is immensely stimulating. Choreographing this way provides access to multiple planes of knowing ... the senses are heightened, the mind is getting additional oxygen ... This creates an enhanced ability to focus and explore several things at once while simultaneously letting go of the usual patterns of thinking, and travelling over the ideas ... being insightful.

Below, further selections from Robert's narratives illuminate what constitutes kinaesthetic intimacy in this choreographic practice.

Sensory/Sensational/Sensual/Sensibility
Robert's technical vocabulary includes several variations of the term 'sensual':

> There is purely sensational movement that comes from the experience of moving, not to be subsumed under other things .... One deploys a sensual imagination, then you need to edit – it's impossible to address everything that happens in a sensual idea, you aim to select. The knowledge or information has its own sensorial state. You ride the sensation of it and that gives you the pictures (as visceral imagery) or the state of being in an imagined or perceived bodily environment – a humanly generated environment, not simply a physical space.
>
> The right things show themselves – there is an accuracy of occurrence that validates this as an information-seeking procedure. A previously undetermined piece of information is intimated to you through a sensation. A 'picture' may emerge that is not necessarily visual.
>
> It's a study of time – of creating 'in the moment' when new patterns or structures are suggested. We work with a tight focus but one that is

available for broadening in its outcomes. It's about *human* structures – dancers find a warm-up plan to access their higher, whole-body functioning. For example, [dancer] M looks at material cerebrally first but also has a sensibility to her own feelings of how to structure the input to get there [to a plane of higher functioning]. She can get there automatically now. [Dancer] B got it immediately – she was experiencing visceral things that gave her enormous pleasure to realize. Her state of body [after her recent pregnancy] made it perfect timing for her to let go [of her classical ballet training]. You need to have the right environment that allows you to do that. We are not repeating, but constantly seeking new material, or new takes on what was travelled and known before.

These multiple variations of the word 'sense' (e.g., 'sensorial state', 'sensation', 'sensational movement', 'sensual imagination', 'sensual idea') remind us that kinaesthesia and touch, as well as the visual and aural, are primary creative resources in this world of movement exploration. A multisensory array of possibilities for the exploration of both feeling (sensation) and feelings (emotion and affect) becomes available to the artistic imagination. Such heightened sensuality is not to be conflated or confused with sexuality, however. Such conflation is a plausible root cause of the popular understanding of physical intimacy as necessarily sexual, not surprising perhaps, because this error was also Freud's in attributing sexuality rather than sensuality to infants and children. For the dancer, it requires sufficient trust in the working environment and artistic director to allow the personal to become transparent – an openness to vulnerability within intimate social space.

On Viscerality

[My artistic works] stem from hyper-visceral explorations that require a dancer to locate an internal visceral focus on the movements and develop a sensational rather than a visual sense of shape – it's not about 'steps' between the 'shapes'.

I seek through viscerality, and then sense a possibility, and my imagination and discipline provide me with an image of a path … and while moving – in my focus, in my concentration – information from a lateral sphere becomes plausible or possibly shows itself.

Rather than focusing with [just] the brain's functionality, we are inclusive of movement and human visceral fields – all of the states. This is a sensory field, which addresses things in one of the realms – when we tune in we find more realms.

When you access your 'structures', or your 'library of information', you go in viscerally – it's a bit like auto-writing and imagining from words.

'Visceral' here becomes a central trope that adds depth and inwardness, invoking deep-seated, deeply rooted or literally 'gut' feelings.[23] Although it is most often conceptualized in Western thought as being the opposite of 'cerebral', having to do with the response of 'the body' in contrast to 'the intellect', or 'feeling' separate from 'thinking', this is turned on its head in Robert's deliberately anti-Cartesian notion of kinaesthetic intelligence and whole-bodied information. He instead describes feelingful information flowing or 'emanating' between inside and outside:

> [We are] continually stepping to known platforms, then moving outwards, as registered realms provoke an oppositional coming inward ... seeking emanation in multiple directions while supporting ourselves perceptually at the centre.
>
> Movement exploration does not have to be a literal 'reaching out' – it can be found by moving inwards or not moving at all.
>
> In exploring time and space – we are not trained to be one person but to be an antenna – what happens from your inside out as you explore the exterior realms? How did you get there and what are they? As your imagination and discipline mature, in parallel with high-functioning thinking ... you choose the route to go inside with your imagination. Rather than being out and more visual in focus, you find an interior imagery that uses your visual capacities less, much like the martial arts, because other powers and paths become available.

Robert's narratives are full of such affectively salient terms as 'hyper-visceral', 'emanation' and 'live accessing' – words that could readily be misconstrued as 'mystical' by outsiders. In fact, they are carefully selected words that keep possible interpretations wide open while also constituting a technical vocabulary that requires careful translation. Such terminology refers to different facets of a non-vocal realm of human sensory resources, simultaneously conceptual, that become readily available to highly skilled movement artists. They are components of what is meant by 'moving intelligence'. They are also references to unobservable entities that require the kind of theoretical imagination that is in principle no different from theoretical physics.[24] Only when outsiders begin to understand the exploratory expansions of mundane space and time that inform his creative work do phrases such as 'moving in many spaces simultaneously' or 'seeking emanation in multiple directions while supporting ourselves perceptually at the centre' become comprehensible.

This knowledge structure undermines the familiar Cartesian dualisms that define 'the senses' as a source of emotion and feelings located in the materiality of the body, separate from 'the intellect' as the site of cognition and knowing located in a nonmaterial mind. Such a dualistic ontology positions the very notions of embodied knowledge and kinaesthetic intelligence as fundamentally oxymoronic.

Concepts of Time-Space

To find the sophisticated our thinking has to come from simple questions. Our own knowledge, history and experience of how to perceive this provide all the complexity of the result. We are not just using our ability to move; we access the notion that we are exploring space and time itself and the human potential of that.

This choreographic process allows past, present and future time to become available in ways beyond the chronological:

[The dancer] is experiencing it at a slower pace because of the pleasure it creates inside her body – her experience of time is not the viewer's time. There is a time-within-time due to this sensual primary selection (see Illustration 3.3).

The intelligence that brings [the movement exploration] where it goes at one point in time comes from the last time it was visited. It may be accessing or addressing this same information or it may not. The spirit of the work's exploration may move things forward to another place – it's built to move forward – it allows the dancer, sensing internally, to recalibrate or calibrate to the present time while also working from memory of the earlier search. It is these understandings that are at the centre of this moving process for the dancer – an ability to go somewhere – that's what we mean by bodily knowledge.

A manipulation or 'bending' of time takes place via this appeal to a higher level of awareness:

This functioning is interesting because the senses enhance the intellectual rigour of it and provide other dimensions of information. If you are organizing the parameters of your movement – whether using visceral intellect, conscious recall or future anticipation, or using insight and being involved – you are moving towards these possible realms and/or they move towards you.

In service of the exploration, Robert also aims to bypass the idea that the dancers are 'learning' something from without, and replace it with the notion that they are *finding* information that is useful to them – a realization of his theoretical premise that:

The agency and authorship of the dancer should be of primary concern if the dance is to fulfil its promise as a way of knowing and being.

Illustration 3.3 'I no longer "perform" – I'm walking through time'. Mariel Lowe after her performance of Wood's evening length work Coreografia 2, *Santa Fe, 2012. The dance artist Mariel Lowe's internal reconnaissance may entice the participating onlooker to move to a place where they think she is going or perhaps believe her to be. Photo copyright Robert Wood Dance – New York Inc.*

The focus on progressive discovery in the moment is central to this premise – it requires instantaneous realizations (sudden insights) within the flow of action, something that is extremely difficult to describe in words and can be easily disrupted outside of a conducive environment.

It is in some aspects of Robert's attention to dimensions of time (manifested in at least three dimensions of space) that the influence of butoh and Zen philosophy emerges; in emphasizing slow movement, active stillness and 'being in the moment' so that things 'show themselves'. In addition, acceleration and deceleration (in both working process and movement content), 'bending' and 'expanding' time all become dynamic resources for making movement works.

Personhood and Disposition

When talking about the way in which they work with dancers when composing, it is not uncommon to hear leading North American choreographers of contemporary dance and ballet to state that they function within a 'dictatorship' (e.g., Balanchine 1984; Paul Taylor in Diamond 1998; Morris 2004) – benign, perhaps, but nevertheless a dictatorship in which their ideas predominate. In their established positions, these choreographers have attained the right to control the content and process of making their work. Under such choreographic regimes, the dancer becomes a means to an end – by all accounts a beautiful, skilled, dynamic body, whose personal and human qualities may or may not be central to the resulting artwork, but a consenting body-object nevertheless, subject to the manipulations of the choreographer's needs and desires.

At the risk of overgeneralizing here, one might say that at the other end of the spectrum, it is also not uncommon to find contemporary choreographers whose modus operandi is more democratic (for example, David Gordon's Pick Up Performance Company). They aim to collaborate with dancers in the making of work, creating community, sharing ideas and building work together. However, in these cases too, the focus of attention is likely to be the movement ideas and themes they have chosen to be danced about, and the dancer remains the dynamic means to those ends.

In both these cases, the dancer as a person – with a unique disposition as well as a personal and cultural history – is not the primary focus of attention or source of movement material and knowledge. In contrast to this, Robert's work seeks to reveal to the viewer attributes of the dancer's personal and cultural being, as this is constructed through and revealed in their movement.[25] People are, for Robert, fundamentally moving beings, not the theatrically conditioned dancers of a Balanchine, moving to the choreographer's desires in musical space and time, nor the complex, dynamic, organic entities of Cunningham, where chance defines the movement vocabulary in abstract fields of space, time and sound.

This work involves creating environments that allow the mover/dancer to discover for her/himself, encouraging and anticipating a state of being, which draws deeply upon their unique personal, cultural and ancestral dispositions and experiences. At the same time, and without contradiction, movement explorations also seek to know and reveal deeply who we are as human beings, beyond the particular differences of social, cultural and historical conditions – a cosmopolitan ideology of humankind that resonates with Nigel Rapport's universal 'anyone' (Rapport 2010, 2012). 'Ancestral' here refers to inherited knowledge and ongoing sensory awareness of land and sea as the stories that situate one 'in place(s)' and in time. This stems from the practice of 'accessing' deep time (historical, archaeological and geologic time in Western terms) via imagination, memory and body movement in relation to the structuring of the present. Indigenous peoples in many parts of the world, including Oceania, hold similar concepts of 'ancestral' as connected to places of origin (cf. Feld and Basso 1996), as well as moral obligations connected to 'living tradition' (MacIntyre 1981: 190–209).

The section *Reverence* in *Ascension* (Wood 1996), again illustrates this beautifully. No uniformity of body type or technical movement vocabulary is at work here. Instead the dance artists reveal, and draw us into, a deeply sensuous, corporeal viscerality – a transparency and vulnerability that can be simultaneously intensely inwardly focused and connected through softly surrendering gestures reaching to infinite space.

The *New York Times* dance critic Jennifer Dunning (1998) described this as follows:

> *Reverence* is a ceremony of slowly changing patterns ... giving [the women] the look of graceful columns. *Reverence* is a gradual journey towards exaltation undertaken by strong, mature performers who gave each move and gesture a quiet glow.

Robert describes the dancer's experience inside the dance as follows:

> Tuned into each other and sharing an agreed, visceral sympatico that does not require words generates an efficient use of time and energy, an environment that is built selectively outside of the outside world.

The 2006 evening-length movement exploration *siLenCe*[26] also illustrates how Robert uses choreography to address the dancers' understandings of self and their personal dispositions in ways that relate to who they are, how they are working and what they want to achieve. Developed with a group of classically trained Italian dancers, it seeks to reveal the personal qualities of the individual dancers and enhance their sense of authorship over their movement, thereby moving away from the tradition familiar to them of learning and then executing 'the steps'.

> Here is a simple movement exploration that addresses multiple possibilities for the dancer. It is kept relatively simple choreographically – it's not about the visual movement, but what occurs *from* its doing. For the young dancer it offers an experiential position for searching without observing him- or herself and disrupting focus by being self-conscious.

The exploration also seeks to expand the dancers' understandings of time as described above. The simple cannon structure presents the idea that rather than being exact in musical timing, the dancer can permit her/himself to address a more independent human timing or phrasing that simultaneously addresses their histories, yet is in the moment and nevertheless responsive to the group:

> It's not that each phrase must be 'three beats apart' but rather that as each dancer begins to move she [this section involves seven women] takes her own time to explore further the visceral, sensational quality of the action and permits a vibrational response – a searching of her own being in place.
>
> [This is a] wonderful procedure for these classically trained dancers because they have been brought up on 'counts' rather than their own sense

of timing ... within explorations that are actively seeking what kind of knowledge might be available to their dispositions, their being and their relationships to everything, both next to them and infinitely distanced.

The footage freezes one particular performance – body-movement-wise they are 'out', musically they are 'out' – but this is the point: someone went into a dream or explored something ... and came to their understanding of how they wish to address themselves.

The documentation on film did not serve what actually happened live – the most interesting occurrences and casual interactions or relationships occurred in the initial phases of it – this type of work is addressing change and it's most successful when disorganization occurs. The greatest experience for many of these dancers is when it 'doesn't work' on stage – they search into other places and something interesting happens – another arrangement occurs or shows itself, is invited or arrives.

This procedure also diplomatically addresses body type:

> It also liberates them [classical ballet dancers] from the idea that 'perfect placing' relates to the height and weight and body type of the dancer. Perfect placing in this context is whatever occurs in the moment, in relationship to each time it is explored. It's a big leap from perfectionism to a casual human precision.

These different facets can have a profound effect on the dancer's self-conception, as prior personal knowledge and unfolding discoveries about self are recognized as being of artistic value to the choreographer, not only in the making of specific works but by contributing significantly to the progress of the art form, as well as the dancer's personal growth and artistic maturity. Not all dancers are able to respond in productive ways. In some cases prior training can condition expectations about 'performing' and 'choreography' that make the transparency and vulnerability required to work in this way somewhat threatening to preconceived notions of self as 'dancer' or 'stage performer'. In addition, the risk and sacrifice entailed in committing to an artistic way of life are not for everyone (see below on 'internal goods').

Common Sociality

A process of intimate group formation happens both inside and outside of the studio. The social trust mentioned above requires

> an agreement on the part of the dancer – a respect for the discipline, a respect for the choreographer. This doesn't mean being impersonal, but being personal with each other resides in [my] guiding them, providing

them with elevated or mature information that makes kinaesthetic intelligent sense. There is a way to intimacy that is not about physical contact per se. I rarely go in 'cold' with someone, but when I do there has to be some kind of mutual recognition that each is happy to reveal [who they are].

This procedure of intimate group familiarization exponentially adds a dispositional dimension to a human exploration of knowledge and information – the intimacy as each one learns or knows or senses more of their partners and also of themselves (see Illustration 3.4). We identify our [own] personal attributes more and more as they are reflected from our intimate working partners.

In my partnering with D we did not need to say very much at all – a brief gesture would suffice – almost a telepathy.

Such activity can seem telepathic because the two-way flow of multisensory information shared between embodied self and other(s) in motion becomes extremely familiar through practice, is anticipated and requires few, if any, vocal or external cues.

If a group of intimate movement/environment explorers 'tunes in', so to speak, the human equations that appear are far more socially interesting, humanly intricate and valuable.... Working intimately within a group, as a group, also heightens our intimacy and understanding among ourselves. This again points to the self-awareness that is developed through a danced career or life. This has tended to happen with mature dancers because one needs experience [to be able to work in this way].

There is a larger social understanding as well; once identified and shared it becomes a reality [among the dancers]. The dancers know I am looking at a larger picture, beyond the discipline. All this information is accessible and available to the dancers: we have placed ourselves in a position to use our creative imagination and intuition.

This discourse resonates with Herzfeld's 'cultural intimacy' in the sense of illustrating in words the kinds of whole-body understandings that create a 'common sociality' among the RWD dancers. This is, in part, constructed from an awareness of contradictory but often negative external views of themselves that reflect back from an advanced capitalist society such as the U.S.A. In contrast to athletes, who become high-earning, valuable commodities within hugely profitable business ventures, finding a sustainable level of economic support for movement artists in the U.S.A. is enormously challenging and unpredictable. Alternatively trivialized as 'entertainment' or pushed upstairs as 'fine art', there is always a potential risk of negative evaluation from outsiders because

Illustration 3.4 Robert Wood and Margie Gillis in Devotion, *section four from Wood's evening-length work* Ascension. *Photograph by Chris Ramirez, costume design by Anne Dixon, lighting design by Lee Squires. New York 1996.*

contemporary concert dancers and choreographers are not only working outside of capitalist financial norms and the related ideology of competition, which defines sports, but also with a range of contra-normative knowledge constructs and values regarding what it means to be human, that come from within and are specific to the group.

Alasdair MacIntyre's concept of 'internal goods' (in the sense of values or virtues) is helpful here (1981: 175–81). MacIntyre first defines a 'practice' as

> any coherent and complex form of socially established cooperative human activity through which *goods internal to that activity* are realized in the course of trying to achieve those standards of excellence which are appropriate to and partially definitive of that form of activity, with the result that human powers to achieve excellence, and human conceptions of the ends and goods involved are systematically extended. (Ibid.: 175; italics added)

He identifies two kinds of 'goods' to be gained in a practice thus defined: 'external goods', such as prestige, status and money, are contingent and not to be confused with goods internal to the practice, which can only be obtained by participation.[27] Goods internal to dance arts as practice in MacIntyre's sense would include the excellence of the products – the performance and each movement composition. Such excellence, MacIntyre argues, has to be understood historically. A second kind of internal good is to be found

> in participation in the attempts to sustain progress and respond creatively to moments. ... For what the artist discovers within the pursuit of excellence in [dancing/choreographing] and what is true of the practice of the fine arts in general is the good of *a certain kind of life*. ... It is in the [dance-maker's] living out of a greater or lesser part of his or her life as a [dancer/choreographer] that is the second kind of good internal to the [dance arts]. (Ibid.: 177; italics added)

It is this dedication to the dance arts as providing a 'certain kind of life', often in spite of the absence of external goods, that sustains the cultural intimacy of the kind Robert and RWD artists practise.

Forged within a nonvocal social poetics by embodied persons moving energy in space-time, such common intimacy is largely exclusive of spoken discourses. One does not hear RWD dancers talking about what they know, although they frequently demonstrate their understandings kinaesthetically, in playful exchanges during moments of relaxation as well as in their work. This makes ethnographic representation of dancers' voices somewhat challenging and is one of the reasons for their absence in this text.[28]

However, the common sociality that develops also emerges from a shared recognition that in social contexts outside of the studio and theatre they can expect, on occasion, to be negatively stereotyped by potential patrons, arts administrators, academics and upper-class members of the general public with whom they come into contact at various social events as inarticulate or lacking intelligence and education because they do not talk about what they know. In spite of being aware of such negative external evaluations, they frequently choose to uphold their contra-normative position. This furthers their identity as 'dancer' in common sociality with other dancers, within both RWD and the broader subculture of dance artists in New York and elsewhere, in contrast to those who would treat them as Other. For example, Robert recalls occasions when journalists and other writers would visit Merce Cunningham's New York studio:

> When interviewers came to learn about MC's work, they interviewed dancers, who are somewhat programmed to respond with simple answers. What one should do [as a journalist/writer] is build a sensational relationship and enquiring method or procedure, which parallels the one in which *they* work. Dancers do talk but not in ways that you expect them to. So these writers' frames were too limiting. ...
>
> When I work with dancers, in their training or in an investigation, we communicate directly along visceral procedural lines – the act of going there is one that is best achieved somewhat wordlessly.

In other words, when dance-maker and dancer are working in the studio implementing a choreographic procedure, the broad multisensory semiosis described above communicates better than words.

Within Western modes of thought, such embodied knowledge, if acknowledged at all as anything other than physical skill, is considered separate from 'language' and 'mind'. This means that dance artists must consistently embrace contra-normative values about what *counts* as 'real' (ontology) and how one is going to *know* the real (epistemology). The specialized discourse cited above refers to largely unspoken realms of shared understanding, which provide these dancers as insiders with their assurance of a common intimacy within a social space. This is insider knowledge – translated into words with difficulty and for the anthropologist's benefit, from the kinaesthetic and other sensory modalities understood by the dancers.

There may be some benefit for the dancer in learning to translate this process into words; at the very least as a means to counter negative stereotypes by establishing themselves in the eyes of admirers, as well as detractors, as 'knowers' and not merely 'doers'. While recognizing that 'talking *from* the body' is a dance artist's vernacular, so to speak, intellectual resources to think reflexively about what they do – 'talk *about* the body' – provide another option (Farnell and Varela 2008: 218).[29]

In Conclusion

The authors see dancers/movers as embodied persons with dispositions that literally incorporate personal, historical, cultural and ancestral knowledge and experience. This represents a post-postmodern recovery of the person, of significance to broader cultural concerns as well as theoretical issues in the social sciences. It resonates, for example, with current research in biology (in evolutionary theory, cognitive science and neuroscience) in seeking to identify the correct relationship between 'person' and 'organism': that is, to recover the person from being reduced to some aspect of one's organism such as the brain or the Freudian unconscious, or some other cognitive variation (Varela 2003). The increasing popularity of robotics (both real and imagined) and dissemination of findings from brain research, neuroscience and genetics, widely understood as providing 'really real' explanations of who we are as human beings, present a reductionist concept of personhood. This is fertilized by an education system in the U.S.A. that is increasingly dominated by STEM[30] subjects with the goal of producing citizen subjects capable of serving neoliberal political economies, to the exclusion of artistic ways of knowing and being. Robert's artistic vision dislodges that agenda, reminding us of alternative exploratory pathways to understanding who we are as human beings. In addition, his insistence on the value of communicating through live performance challenges the seduction of increasingly ubiquitous mediated communication technologies. Robert should have the last word:

> This knowledge stems not from the written word but from human experience – as we amplify the access – the light, the aroma, the tone of that day, that rehearsal, the social exchanges while travelling. It also involves a detachment from other things, including complicated media. The goal is to work towards an elevated hyper-visceral place of addressing tasks, questions, processes and procedures – this is dance!

Acknowledgements

Thanks are due to our editors for insightful comments and patience; to Charles Varela for his careful reading and ongoing support; to Patricia Morgan for her lifetime collaboration with Robert; and to the extraordinary knowledge and artistry of Paula Swiatkowski, Kelly Slough, Margie Gillis, Mariel Lowe, Ben Mielke and Ling Fen Chien Wood.

Brenda Farnell is a Professor of Anthropology at the University of Illinois at Urbana-Champaign. Her book *Do You See What I Mean?* (University of Texas Press, 1995), challenges the dominant Western view of language as essentially verbal and shows to the contrary that words and gestures participate equally in the creation of meaning. Her most recent book, *Dynamic Embodiment for Social Theory: 'I Move Therefore I Am'* (Routledge, 2012) uses the philosophical resources of Critical Realism to argue against the conventional division between the semiotic and the somatic.

Robert N. Wood is a New Zealand-American artistic director and choreographer of Robert Wood Dance – New York Inc. He has produced over forty choreographic works, receiving awards and grants from organizations in the U.S.A., France, Canada, Palestine, Italy, the Czech Republic, mainland China and Hong Kong. Pursuing insights from the perspective of a native New Zealander, as an independent observer of cultural expression, he has been working towards the inclusion of New Zealand information in the larger global flow of intellectual understandings.

Notes

1. Although evidence suggests that all peoples possess forms of dancing, many do not choose to recognize individual dance-makers, nor do they consider their dances and dancing a creative art. Indeed, the term 'dance' itself has proved problematic for anthropologists of human movement (see Gore 1994: 59 and references therein). In other contexts, a dance-maker may be recognized by name, referred to as a 'choreographer', and considered a professional creative artist whose products are performed for paying audiences. Readers will readily distinguish between the Western genres of ballet and modern dance and many social forms of dancing in this regard, often categorized as 'folk dance' or 'traditional dances', 'ballroom' or 'swing', etc. Social dance forms rarely recognize individual dance-makers and do not, for the most part, require the kinds of professional training and advanced skills necessary to becoming a professional artist. Competition and commercialization can radically alter this, of course, as is the case with ballroom dancing (see Marion 2010).
2. Although certain aspects of Robert's artistic philosophy are shared by some of his contemporaries, he is clearly unique in many respects. However, the significance of the present account lies not simply there, but in its detailed exegesis of how embodied knowledge works within one choreographer's processes and procedures, articulated through an anthropological perspective.
3. Brenda Farnell was first invited to conduct ethnographic research with Robert Wood Dance in 2005, and has travelled with the company to residencies in Prague, Florence and Hong Kong, as well as New York and Santa Fe. In addition to hours of conversation with the choreographer, the field research has included attending and documenting workshops,

guest lectures, studio work, rehearsals and performances, as well as informal interviews with dancers, staff, theatre technicians, audience members and international hosts. She also learned much about the inner workings of a nonprofit movement arts company by contributing to the work of fundraising and administration.
4. The online Oxford Dictionary (https://en.oxforddictionaries.com/definition/intimate. Accessed 18 September 2016) defines the verb 'intimate' as to '[s]tate or make known' (as in 'the lawyer intimated that the trial would be postponed'). As an adjective it refers to detailed insider knowledge (e.g., 'she has an intimate knowledge of the archives'). In its noun form, a person who provides such inside information is an 'intimate'. Which of these applies at any one moment depends on where the social actors are in relation to each other within a field of action.
5. In keeping with artists in the U.S.A. and Europe, we refer to Robert's choreographic work as 'contemporary dance'. The term distinguishes current practices from earlier genres, from which they have both evolved and/or departed. See Note 9.
6. Indented quotations throughout the chapter are selected from notes and recordings taken by Brenda Farnell between 2005 and 2015, during Robert Wood's structured sharing of spoken information and new thoughts arrived at through the body – that is, through visceral accessing sessions, utilizing the immediacy of insights that emerge prior to, during and after rehearsal or elsewhere, in ways consistent with his working procedures. This is thus a specific style of discourse about the body in motion, neither interview nor conversation.
7. See also Stoler (2002) on colonial intimacies.
8. Theoretical developments in the social sciences and humanities over the past fifty years reveal an interesting trajectory regarding the concept of embodiment (see Farnell and Varela 2008; Farnell 2011, 2012). Having (re)discovered 'the body' during the first somatic turn of the 1970s and 1980s, research interests then moved towards 'the senses' and more recently towards 'emotion' and 'affect' – hence arriving at the current focus on 'intimacy'.
9. At the beginning of the twentieth century, experimental forms of American and European dance as an art form emerged that departed radically from classical ballet, in line with a modernist point of view that suffused many art forms at the time, such as the visual arts and architecture. Although generating numerous choreographic styles and content, they became known collectively as 'modern dance'. In the 1960s, 'postmodern dance' emerged as a second revolution, rejecting many of the premises of the modernist movement. 'Contemporary dance' labels more recent genres of concert dance arts in the U.S.A. and Europe. See Reynolds and McCormick (2003). It also serves to identify a fine arts approach, practised by formally trained dancers, as well as distinguishing these practices from many hybrid genres of concert dance performance that do not necessarily seek to continue or contribute to this choreographic tradition.
10. *Rainforest* premiered in 1968 with a highly acclaimed score by David Tudor, Mylar pillow decor by Andy Warhol and costume design by Jasper Johns. The Cunningham dancer Robert Swinston shared this inheritance. This was the first time one of Merce Cunningham's roles was bestowed upon another dancer.
11. A wide variety of short, medium- and evening-length works have since been made for his own company and as commissioned works. See www.robertwooddance.org. Accessed 8 April 2016.

12. Video clip 1: The *Piwakawaka* (*The Fantail*) section of the work *Koru* (2014). http://robertwooddance.org/media-2/. Accessed 8 April 2016.
13. Robert continued: 'Memorizing movement is different – is not mathematical – it's seeing the whole thing from different perspectives and then addressing speed and time. That's the first step to addressing a sequence or section of movement. Seeing from above or from different directions and getting a sense of its time – then in a more sophisticated response, because it suits me, I connect the directions and sense and shape of what the sequence is. If I am concerned about it not being perfect it shuts down my learning procedure'.
14. A Marae is a communal, sacred place with buildings and open spaces that serve religious and social purposes in Maori society. The Marae is a vital part of everyday life. See Mead (2003). Also influential was the performing community that developed out of a Polynesian song, chant and dance group at Tawa-Porirua led by Ani Bosch, in addition to friendships with Chris Wall and Eddie Grace.
15. Video clip 2: *Portal to Portal*, Sean Kelly (*Delicate Mind* night video), Midnight Blue Studios, NYC (1985). http://robertwooddance.org/media-2/. Accessed 8 April 2016.
16. Butoh is a form of dance theatre that emerged in post–World War II Japan through collaborations between the founding artists Tatsumi Hijikata and Kazuo Ohno. According to the actor/dancer Akaji Maro: 'Butoh draws its strength from Japanese Culture. It began as a spirit of revolt, to break the rules and upset forms. It is the suspension of decision-making. We let the body speak for itself. To reveal itself. To reject the superficiality of everyday life' (cited in Skuld 2014; see also Holborn and Hoffman 1987; Sanders 1988). According to the butoh scholar Mark Holborn, butoh deliberately breaches social conventions and explores taboo subjects, and is often grotesque, violent, sexuality explicit and full of images of anguish. It draws from Japanese archaic traditions, reimagined in a contemporary context. Butoh was not just something practised in the studio but a form of life (Holborn, cited in Skuld 2014). Since the 1980s, selected aspects of butoh, translated into Western cultural frameworks, have become a creative resource for North American and European contemporary dance-makers. The Japanese photographer Eiko Hosoe and the director and performance theorist Tadashi Suzuki also influenced Robert's work.
17. See Kourlas (2005) for a critic's review that makes the case for a decline in this status.
18. Exceptions are Cunningham's 'memory pieces' (Vaughan 1997: 232) such as *Fabrications* (1987), *Shards* (1987) and *Quartet* (1982). See Vaughan (1997) for further discussion.
19. Video clip 3: *The Blind Swordsman*, opening section *siLenCe* (2004). http://robertwooddance.org/media-2/. Accessed 8 April 2016.
20. See Farnell and Varela (2008); Sheets-Johnstone (2011). The traditional 'five senses' consist of vision, hearing, touch, smell and taste. A concept of kinaesthesia is also prominent in alternative approaches to medicine, as well as bodywork (somatic) techniques of many kinds related to dancing and sports. For a brief summary of the physiological structure and functions of the human kinaesthetic system see Farnell (2016).
21. Video clip 4: *Women's Trio*, a section from *siLenCe* (2004). http://robertwooddance.org/media-2/. Accessed 8 April 2016.
22. Video clip 5: *Reverence*, Kelly Slough and Paula Swiatkowski in section six from Robert Wood's evening-length work *Ascension*, New York (1996). http://robertwooddance.org/media-2/. Accessed 8 April 2016.

23. See the Latin *viscera* (any internal organ of the body).
24. Such unobservables are plausible candidates for Rom Harré's 'third realm' of causally active entities, processes and events, which are not available to observation. Realm one is the ordinary world of experience. Realm two is the world of indirect experience: observations of the activity of things such as viruses and bacteria that require instrumentation to extend human perception. Realm three is the world beyond possible experience: only the manipulation of the effects of the activity of things are available to scientists in this realm, e.g., black holes, neutrinos, mental structures, social structures. See Varela (1995: 375–76).
25. See also the Canadian choreographer Jean-Pierre Perreault in the documentary film *Danser Perreault*, directed by Tim Southam (2005).
26. Video clip 6: The *Little Street* section from *siLenCe* (2004). http://robertwooddance.org/media-2/. Accessed 8 April 2016.
27. The kinds of external goods available to a contemporary dance-maker and dancers might be fame, social status and some power and influence in the dance and arts worlds generally. The external good of personal wealth would be extremely rare, although sustaining financial support is attainable for a few.
28. The integrated spoken and gestural discourse of dancers as they talk about their work is, however, a topic to be covered in a future book project by the authors of this chapter.
29. The option to develop spoken and written discourses in which to express embodied understandings has, of course, been taken up by dance artists who are also university graduates and doctoral researchers.
30. STEM is an acronym for science, technology, engineering and mathematics, which are considered the 'core' subjects in the U.S. educational curriculum.

References

Balanchine, G. 1984. *Balanchine Parts 1 & 11. American Masters*. Documentary TV programme, shown on PBS, 14 January 2003. Producer: Judy Kinberg. Originally broadcast in 1984.

Copland, R. 2004. *Merce Cunningham: The Modernizing of Modern Dance*. New York: Routledge.

Cunningham, M. 1968. *Changes: Notes on Choreography*, ed. F. Starr. New York: Something Else Press.

———. 1985. *The Dancer and the Dance: Merce Cunningham in Conversation with Jacqueline Lesschaeve*. New York: Marion Boyars.

———. 1992. 'Time, Space, and Dance', in R. Kostelanetz (ed.), *Merce Cunningham: Dancing in Space and Time*. Pennington, NJ: A Cappella Books, pp. 37–39.

Diamond, M. 1998. *Dancemaker*. Documentary film, broadcast on PBS 2007.

Dunning, J. 1998. 'Review of Robert Wood's *Coreografia* Program, Joyce SoHo', In Performance; Dance, *The New York Times*, 26 October. Retrieved 8 April 2016 from http://www.nytimes.com/1998/10/26/arts/in-performance-dance-541044.html.

Farnell, B.M. 2011. 'Theorizing the Body in Visual Culture', in M. Banks and J. Ruby (eds), *Made to Be Seen: Perspectives on the History of Visual Anthropology*. Chicago, IL: The University of Chicago Press, pp. 136–58.

———. 2012. *Dynamic Embodiment for Social Theory: 'I Move Therefore I Am'*. Abingdon: Routledge.

———. 2016. 'The Kinesthetic System', in H.L. Miller, Jr. (ed.), *The SAGE Encyclopedia of Theory in Psychology*. Thousand Oaks, CA: Sage, pp. 483–85.

Farnell, B.M., and C.R. Varela. 2008. 'The Second Somatic Revolution', *Journal for the Theory of Social Behavior* 38: 215–40.

Farnell, B.M., and R.N. Wood. 2008. 'Choreography as Live Theoretical Practice', in A.C. Albright, D. Davida and S.D. Cordova (comps), *Re-Thinking Practice and Theory: International Symposium on Dance Research. Thirtieth Annual Conference of the Society of Dance History Scholars, Paris, 21–24 June 2007 (Conference Proceedings)*. Riverside, CA: Society of Dance History Scholars, pp. 407–16.

———. 2011. 'Performing Precision and the Limits of Observation', in T. Ingold (ed.), *Redrawing Anthropology: Materials, Movements, Lines*. Farnham: Ashgate, pp. 91–114.

Feld, S., and K. Basso (eds). 1996. *Senses of Place*. Santa Fe, NM: School of American Research Press.

Friedrich, P. 2006. 'Maximizing Ethnopoetics: Fine-Tuning Anthropological Experience', in C. Jourdain and K. Tuite (eds), *Language, Culture and Society: Key Topics in Linguistic Anthropology*. Cambridge: Cambridge University Press, pp. 207–28.

Gore, G. 1994. 'Traditional Dance in West Africa', in J. Adshead-Lansdale and J. Layson (eds), *Dance History: An Introduction*, 2nd edn. London: Routledge, pp. 59–80.

Herzfeld, M. 1997. *Cultural Intimacy: Social Poetics in the Nation-State*. New York: Routledge.

Holborn, M., and E. Hoffman. 1987. *Butoh: Dance of the Dark Soul*. New York: A Sadev Book – Aperture.

Kourlas, G. 2005. 'How New York Lost its Modern Dance Reign', Critics' Notebook, *The New York Times*, 6 September. Retrieved 8 April 2016 from http://www.nytimes.com/2005/09/06/arts/dance/how-new-york-lost-its-modern-dance-reign.html?_r=0.

MacIntyre, A. 1981. *After Virtue: A Study in Moral Theory*. Notre Dame, IN: University of Notre Dame Press.

Marion, J. 2010. 'Circulation as Destination: Considerations from the Translocal Culture of Competitive Ballroom Dance', *Journal for the Anthropological Study of Human Movement* 17(2): n.p.

Mauss, M. 1979 [1935]. 'Techniques of the Body', in *Sociology and Psychology: Essays by Marcel Mauss*, trans. B. Brewster. London: Routledge and Kegan Paul, pp. 95–135.

Mead, H.M. 2003. *Tikanga Māori: Living by Māori Values*. Wellington: Huia Publishers.

Morris, M. 2004. Post-Performance Discussion. Krannert Center for the Performing Arts, University of Illinois at Urbana-Champaign, April.

Povinelli, E. 2006. 'Intimate Grammars: Anthropological and Psychoanalytic Accounts of Language, Gender, and Desire', in C. Jourdain and K. Tuite (eds), *Language, Culture and Society: Key Topics in Linguistic Anthropology*. Cambridge: Cambridge University Press, pp. 190–206.

Rapport, N. 2010. 'Apprehending *Anyone*: The Non-indexical, Post-cultural, and Cosmopolitan Human Actor', *Journal of the Royal Anthropological Institute* (N.S.) 16: 84–101.

———. 2012. *Anyone: The Cosmopolitan Subject of Anthropology*. Oxford: Berghahn.

Reynolds, N., and M. McCormick. 2003. *No Fixed Points: Dance in the Twentieth Century*. New Haven, CT: Yale University Press.

Ryle, G. 1984 [1949]. *The Concept of Mind*. Chicago, IL: The University of Chicago Press.
Sanders, V. 1988. 'Dancing and the Dark Soul of Japan: An Aesthetic Analysis of "Butō"', *Asian Theatre Journal* 5: 148–63.
Sapir, E. 1921. *Language: An Introduction to the Study of Speech*. New York: Harcourt, Brace & Company.
———. 1929. 'A Study in Phonetic Symbolism', *Journal of Experimental Psychology* 12: 225–39.
Sheets-Johnstone, M. 2011. 'The Imaginative Consciousness of Movement: Linear Quality, Kinesthesia, Language and Life', in T. Ingold (ed.), *Redrawing Anthropology: Materials, Movements, Lines*. Farnham: Ashgate, pp. 115–28.
Skuld. 2014. *Dance of Darkness: Documentary on Butoh Dance*. https://www.youtube.com/watch?v=xVZi8zuJExo. Accessed 8 April 2016.
Southam, T. 2005. *Danser Perreault*. Documentary Film. Montréal, QC: Les Films de l'Isle.
Stoler, A.L. 2002. *Carnal Knowledge and Imperial Power: Race and the Intimate in Colonial Rule*. Berkeley: University of California Press.
Varela, C.R. 1995. 'Ethogenic Theory and Psychoanalysis: The Unconscious as a Social Construct and a Failed Explanatory Concept', *Journal for the Theory of Social Behaviour* 25: 363–85.
———. 2003. 'Biological Structure and Embodied Human Agency: The Problem of Instinctivism', *Journal for the Theory of Social Behaviour* 33: 95–122.
Vaughan, D. 1997. *Merce Cunningham: Fifty Years*, ed. M. Harris. New York: Aperture.
Webster, A.K. 2015. *Intimate Grammars: An Ethnography of Navaho Poetry*. Tucson: University of Arizona Press.
Williams, D. 1991. *Ten Lectures on Theories of the Dance*. Metuchen, NJ: Scarecrow Press.
Wood, R. 1982. *Stems from the Garden*. New York City.
———. 1985. *Portal-To-Portal*. Solo choreographed for film. New York City.
———. 1996. *Ascension: Where Angels Travel*. Evening-length work. Performed at several venues in U.S.A. and Canada.
———. 2006. *siLenCe*. Evening-length work commissioned by the Florence Dance Company. Performed by Florence Dance Company and members of RWD, Teatro Goldini, Florence, Italy.
———. 2012. *Coreografia 2*. Evening-length work. Lensic Theatre, Santa Fe, New Mexico.
———. 2015. *Choreographic Intimacies*. Website Vimeos 1–6. Robert Wood Dance. http://robertwooddance.org/media-2/. Accessed 8 April 2016.

Chapter 4

The Presentation of Self in Participatory Dance Settings
Data Collecting with Erving Goffman

Bethany Whiteside

Introduction

Slim females with their hair in a bun walk up a set of nondescript stairs. One dancer supports the weight of her partner on her hip, lifting her and lowering her down in a graceful arc. Line dancers settle into performing 'Flobie Slide' and 'Wagon Wheel Rock' in unison. A young woman, dressed for a Cuban night, hears the beat of salsa music as she makes her way through a Glasgow nightclub. Highland dancers break in a new pair of ghillies before adjusting and fastening the laces. Children shout and laugh as they 'set to' during a 'Dashing White Sergeant'. Unremarkable at first glance, nevertheless these examples reflect the everyday dance scenes that I found myself part of during fieldwork in Glasgow. The challenge I faced was assimilating myself within these scenes, to gain data that was useful and trustworthy. I needed to understand not only the accepted etiquette of the social worlds that I was entering, but how my actions and behaviours were actually shaping the very settings I was researching. The desire to be reflexive throughout the data collection process that involved six case studies – a professional ballet class, an inclusive creative dance class, a line dancing class, a Highland dancing class, a salsa club and dance in primary education – led me to situate myself as researcher within Erving Goffman's 1990 ([1959]) dramaturgical framework, the model subsequently used to frame and analyse the data gathered. This chapter explores the behaviours and the 'presentation of self' that I made as part of a larger aim, to understand the multiple experiences or 'realities' in each setting; defined as 'a matter of scripts and performances created and sustained by human interaction' (Clark and Mangham 2004: 41).

Goffman has been described as a scholar who departed 'radically from the mainstream sociological tradition' and one whose work is 'a protean sociology of the common man in mass society' (Williams 1986: 349). Goffman's main contribution to social theory, his model of dramaturgy, is most clearly stated in the seminal text *The Presentation of Self in Everyday Life* (1990 [1959]), which uses the metaphor of the stage to explain the portrayal and management of face-to-face social interaction. This groundbreaking work 'not only announced his arrival as an important, if unorthodox social commentator[; it] also ushered in a new approach to sociology: a sociology of everyday life' (Birrell and Donnelly 2004: 49). Goffman aimed to 'promote acceptance of this face-to-face domain as an analytically viable one ... a domain whose preferred method of study is microanalysis' (1983: 2).

As drawn together by Whiteside and Kelly (2016), Goffman's dramaturgical model has been applied within a range of settings, including corporate management, erotic performance, leisure, outdoor education, the operating theatre and sport.[1] As Young argues, the greater part of Western society constitutes a dramaturgical one, where 'the technologies of social science, mass communication, theatre, and the arts are used to manage attitudes, behaviours, and feelings of the population' (1990: 71). Yet Goffman's theoretical framework has had a limited impact on dance scholarship. Despite the centrality of aesthetic practice in everyday society, ethnographic dance studies that adopt specific social-theoretic frameworks firmly focus on the concepts and models of Pierre Bourdieu and Michel Foucault (concerning the latter, in relation to notions of docile bodies, surveillance and power), with the majority centred on vocational and professional ballet and contemporary dance practices (see Whiteside 2013; Whiteside and Kelly 2016).[2] This most recent body of work builds on sociological dance studies that first began in the early 1980s (Brinson 1983a, 1983b; Thomas 1986) and subsequent studies that consider social structures and interactions in dance settings and the link between dance and society (Prickett 1990; Sussman 1990; Thomas 1995, 1997, 2003; Wulff 1998).

Dance anthropology as a distinct area of study has existed since the 1960s (see Reed 1998) and in contrast to sociological developments, dance has a long history within anthropology, owing to the previously longstanding notion that 'dance is a primary expression of the "non-rational" world of primitive people' (Thomas 1986: 10). Here is a story of a sub-discipline that began decades earlier, with the embracing of dance by the earliest proponents of anthropology (i.e., Franz Boas, Edward Evan Evans-Pritchard, Bronislaw Malinowski and Alfred Radcliffe-Brown) and subsequent developments in both academic anthropology and dance departments in the U.K., mainland Europe and the U.S.A. in particular, which saw research approaches cemented. Seminal anthropology of dance scholars and more recent proponents such as the scholars in this anthology have a determined focus: to interrogate and record dance as a power both shaping and being shaped by cultural value-systems, as viewed by those doing the dancing, predominantly through ethnographic means (see, for example, Kealiinohomoku 1970; Hanna 1979; Buckland 1999; Grau 2005; Wulff 1998, 2007). Of particular relevance to the present study is Wulff's (2007) notion of 'yo-yo fieldwork', whereby the mobile researcher participates in a number of different local settings linked to a central piece of research, necessitating an individualized approach within each. My own interdisciplinary approach saw 'yo-yo fieldwork' take place in a micro sense; data was collected across six case studies encompassing six different dance activities and practices, each taking place within a distinct social setting, all within the city of Glasgow.

Sociology of dance within a dance studies context may be described as the 'nascent' sibling of dance anthropology (Buckland 1999: 6). The latter has flourished within dance studies, taking a founding and pivotal role in the 'theoretical turn' that occurred in the 1980s (Manning 2006: 2), while the former is still cementing its place and status. Yet, as this chapter demonstrates, Goffmanian methodology can be valuable for anthropological investigation due to the shared focus of the sub-disciplines on the cultural and social worlds of dance and the long-standing tradition of social theory within anthropology.

In what follows, the applicability of Goffman's framework to dance scholarship is interrogated and illustrated primarily through situating the author as an ethnographic researcher within the dramaturgical model: the duo of central themes throughout the analysis presented is collaboration and reflexivity. First, the potential of Goffman's dramaturgical model to dance research is presented and the key concepts explored with ethnographic examples; and second, the methodological virtues of Goffman's framework are highlighted ethnographically through framing and interpreting data-collection experiences within the model. Goffman's framework allowed critique of the interactional microelements in worlds that were not easily accessible through providing the means for me as the researcher to reflexively interpret and shape the 'performances' that I gave.

Potential for Goffmanian Dance Scholarship

Expanding upon existing discussion in Whiteside (2013) and Whiteside and Kelly (2016), four overarching factors contribute to the argument that Goffman's dramaturgical framework is eminently suitable for adoption in dance research, and specifically to explore the social mechanisms operating within participatory dance settings. Firstly, Goffman focuses on social establishments, defined as 'any place surrounded by fixed barriers to perception in which a particular kind of activity regularly takes place' (1990 [1959]: 231). This notion mirrors the operation of dance activities and practices that take place behind closed doors, including all six case studies in this research. Many dance settings could be described as closed 'systemic programs of instruction' (Foster 1997: 238), and in particular the studio, the 'front stage' space, exists explicitly for the purpose of dance.

Secondly, Goffman notes the role of 'pre-established pattern[s] of action' within a 'performance' (1990 [1959]: 27) and this key characteristic reflects those activities where the format that unfolds is dictated by the dance practice under investigation. For example, within the current study, the ballet class unfolded in the universal format of barre, centre practice, adage and allegro; the inclusive creative dance class often began and ended with an exercise carried out in a circle. The line dancing classes began with easier dances before moving on to intermediate and advanced ones, and a mixture of both new and familiar dances were performed; following basic exercises at the barre and stretching in the centre, the Highland dancing class also worked through individual dances before moving on to harder performances.

Thirdly, 'performances' are also viewed as 'theatrical ... contextual ... non-verbal, [and] presumably unintentional' (ibid.: 16), a statement that could be used to describe the purpose and nature of dance as 'a transient ever-shifting art' (Smith-Autard 2013: 153). Moreover, Goffman's proposal that the dominant models of what he terms 'sincere' performances (whereby an individual believes in their performance) and 'false' performances (whereby an individual knows that they are 'pretending') are simultaneously in existence, can translate to a dance setting. There, '[m]acro choreographed performance[s] (the dancing) merge with micro individual performances' (Whiteside 2013: 53), providing a setting rich for ethnographic exploration.

Lastly, Goffman pre-empts criticism that the focus on immediate incidents and scenarios results in neglect of the greater cultural, historical and social context (as argued by Gouldner 1971; Blumer 1972; Dawe 1973), through warning against the attraction of generalizing conclusions that are unsustainable. The solution advised is to focus on smaller units 'or classes of establishments' (Goffman 1990 [1959]: 238).

Within the literature, 'participatory' dance has connotations of a social or community-building function and the focus tends to be on aerobic and creative dance and the link between dance activity and health (e.g., Shigematsu et al. 2002; Lobo 2006; Hui et al. 2009), or to provide pedagogical advice (e.g., Amans 2008; Williamson 2009). Within the present study, the line-dancing class case study could most obviously be fitted to this tradition, yet the stance taken does not limit the concept of 'participatory dance' by equating it with 'social dance'. Rather, the term 'participatory' encompasses all dance settings where both social and dance interaction takes place between groups of individuals and the one shapes the nature of the other.

Erving Goffman's Model of Dramaturgy

Goffman was 'arguably the most influential American sociologist of the twentieth century' (Fine and Manning 2000: 457). As such, his approach and tradition have attracted considerable critique from his contemporaries (e.g., Gouldner 1971;

Blumer 1972) and continue to invite commentary and examination (e.g., Scheff 2006; Smith 2006; Jacobsen 2010). Attention is centred largely on Goffman's uneasy stance between structuralism and symbolic interactionism and his attempts to 'bridge situations and structures' (Williams 1986: 351): the result of a pioneering interest in the seemingly insignificant interactional encounters of everyday life as one strives to control the impression that they give to another. The dramaturgical model is centred on social performance, defined as a period of social interaction that occurs in front of and shapes the impressions of a single observer or group of observers. Goffman explains that two possibilities regarding an individual's performance exist: an individual may be taken in by their own act or cynicism will prevail. However, the 'object of a performer is to sustain a particular definition of [a] situation' (Goffman 1990 [1959]: 90). Projection of the 'reality' aimed for is fostered through 'impression management' – that is, the means by which the individual aims to influence the perceptions of others and the process guiding all face-to-face interaction (Whiteside and Kelly 2016). This 'reality' will be ostensibly, at least, often believed and supported by both the performer and their audience. The nature of its 'portrayal' is dependent on the assumptions and expectations characterizing the social situation and individual roles inhabited within them.

As highlighted by Whiteside and Kelly, 'roles are performed in conjunction with three interconnected elements: the physical environment ("setting"); the appearance and manner of the performer ("personal front"); and the collective, situational expectation ("front")' (2016: 16). Settings are located within specific 'regions', defined by Goffman as any space with physical boundaries, preserving the interaction taking place within. 'Front stage' constitutes the primary performance space, inhabited by both performers and audience members (for example, a studio), and 'back stage' is a space reserved for performers only (for example, a changing room). The concepts of 'front' and 'personal front' are of more relevance here.

'Personal Front'

Understanding of the social interaction being played out in a performance setting is gained through sign vehicles: the manner and appearance of an individual, labelled as 'personal front', that convinces both performer and audience of the performance being given. Their manner (for example, etiquette specific to a particular dance activity and practice, such as the wearing of one's hair in a bun for ballet) is more susceptible to change than their appearance (for example, adhering to the 'ideal', slim and flexible female ballet body). Before entering the dance and social setting of each case study, I consciously thought about and planned the outfit(s) that I would wear, how I would dress my hair and if I would wear make-up or not.

Personal front can fracture in a variety of ways: maintaining a certain impression can be emotionally and physically exhausting. In rather more poetical terms:

'a single note off key can disrupt the tone of an entire performance' (Goffman 1990 [1959]: 60). For Goffman, 'unmeant gestures' and 'incidents' challenge the desired reality, necessitating the adoption of particular techniques – for example, 'tact' – to mitigate the situation at hand. Contradictions between emotions felt, and performances given, most obviously arise when an individual's personal front and the macro team and situational 'front' that the individual as a performer is simultaneously part of become conflicted. The next section demonstrates where and how a tension between the threefold roles of researcher, dancer and observer that I adopted shaped the performances that I gave to my audience: my informants.

'Front'

Goffman defines the concept of 'front' as 'that part of the individual's [or group's] performance which regularly functions in a general and fixed fashion to define the situation for those who observe the performance' (1990 [1959]: 32). As Whiteside and Kelly explain: 'Collective expectations ("fronts") become institutionalized to the extent that performers and onlookers ("audience") are familiar with patterns and obligations' (2016: 16). Goffman uses the phrase 'vocabulary of fronts' to describe the knowledge (in terms of behaviour and etiquette) that performers draw upon to present themselves in the 'correct' way. Hence, within the different case studies, I adopted different attitudes. For example, I knew to not engage in conversation (or only minimal conversation) in the ballet and Highland classes, but to act in a highly engaged ('happy') way in the salsa club. Knowing how one 'should' behave, and responding accordingly, was necessary in order for me to gain a place in the relevant 'team'.

Goffman defines a team as 'a set of individuals whose intimate cooperation is required if a given projected definition of the situation is to be maintained' (1990 [1959]: 108). For example, within the line dancing class, the banter directed by the teacher to select individuals was a means of cementing their place in the team; communicating that their long-term, committed attendance had been noted and was appreciated. 'Dramaturgical loyalty' is more likely to occur between team members who are closely related in age, class, ethnicity and gender. All of the case studies were defined by a certain demographic: the majority of ballet dancers were white and aged between twenty and thirty-five; the majority of the participants of the inclusive creative dance class, including clients (the term used by the organization to refer to their dancers with disabilities), support workers, teachers and volunteers, were white and aged over thirty. The participants of the line dancing class were almost all white, female, aged over fifty and from Glasgow; with only a handful of exceptions, the salsa club dancers originated from outside of Scotland; the teacher and Highland dancers (with the exception of one participant) all originated from Scotland and there was a profusion of 'Mc' and 'Mac' surnames within the class; within the primary school, naturally the majority of research participants, the pupils, were all under the age of twelve.

Being part of a team gives an individual a sense of security as the individual can rely on their colleagues to support them if he or she fractures the reality that all are supposedly striving to support. Within the inclusive creative dance class, when we were all called upon to make a shape, one support worker panicked and simply stood with his hands behind his back. The teacher played on his 'cool and nonchalant' action as we all repeated this action, infusing it with a sense of sophistication. The notion of vocabulary of fronts conveys the fact that individuals joining the team may function effectively almost immediately. However, a second scenario for new team members is possible: they may unknowingly be ignorant of the particular setting that they are attending. Those team members who are unable to recognize or perform correct behaviour may unwittingly adopt a 'discrepant role' (see Goffman 1990 [1959]). As explored subsequently, collaborating with teams of performers through attempting to communicate my knowledge, skill and understanding of the dance practice in question, while avoiding communicating my ignorance where felt, was central to the data collection process, with mixed success.

Within a team performance, one person often takes the role of directing and controlling that performance and he or she is termed the 'director' (ibid: 101). That person across the majority of the case study settings, (i.e., within the ballet, inclusive creative dance, line dancing, Highland dancing and primary school case studies), was the teacher or authority figure, who often adopted a disciplinary approach to varying degrees. The exception to this pattern was the salsa club, which followed a fluid and nondirected format. Thus, the ways in which students, pupils or participants within each class treated their teacher differed from how they engaged with one another. Significantly, the ways in which I interacted with my informants were shaped by whether I was interacting with a teacher or student/participant. Following years of experience in classical ballet and Irish step dance classes, I naturally fell back into the role of student or participant and was far more at ease with those I could consider my peers.

Participant Observation within the Case Studies

Table 4.1 illustrates the varying combinations of participant observation (using Gold's 1958 typology) drawn upon and tailored to each case study setting, reflecting both the researcher's dance ability and the social nature of the setting. A brief explanation of the mode(s) of participant observation within each setting complements the succeeding section, where a Goffmanian critique of the data collection process is provided.

Participant observation has been defined as observation carried out by a researcher who is 'playing an established participant role' in the setting being studied (Atkinson and Hammersley 1998: 111). Yet Goffman actually

Table 4.1 Participant observer roles adopted

Case Study	Observer Role
Professional ballet class	Observer as participant (Overt)
Inclusive creative dance class	Participant as observer Observer as participant (Overt)
Line dancing class	Participant as observer (Overt)
Salsa club	Complete participant (Covert)
Highland dancing class	Participant as observer (Overt)
Dance in primary education	Participant as observer Observer as participant (Overt)

'preferred the term observant participant to participant observer and participant as observer, implying that, irrespective of levels of personal participation, all social interaction could be observed' (Whiteside and Kelly 2016: 25). Participant observation in a dance setting allows the researcher to have greater interaction with other participants that, in turn, can create an atmosphere of trust and respect, and participating through dancing is crucial to kinaesthetically experience the practice under investigation (Green and Stinson 1999). Expanding upon this latter point, I sought to not only seek a measure of embodiment from the dancing, but also to understand the implicit 'action signs (bodily movement as kinaesthetic-spatial acts)' (Farnell and Wood 2011: 91). Rather like Jackson (1989) in his study of Kuranko social life, 'I discovered the value and necessity of paying equal and serious attention during fieldwork to learning visual-kinesthetic acts in addition to acts achieved with words (vocal gestures)' (Farnell 1999: 344).

I felt that the action of dancing within the case studies was particularly relevant where I had limited or no practical experience in the practice under investigation, i.e., contact improvisation (featuring in the inclusive creative dance class), salsa dancing, line dancing and Highland dancing. In addition, dancing with the participants provided me with the opportunity to not only witness face-to-face interaction between performers that shaped the realities in existence, but actually become part of this interaction myself, which allowed another level of analysis to take place. As Sklar (2001) wrestled with reconciling the authorial self with the role of observer to understand and interpret embedded and embodied knowledge, meanings and experiences, so too did I need to reflexively understand how my participation as a dancer-observer-researcher shaped the very 'realities' that I was researching.

I have current and previous experience as a dance participant, having undertaken years of vocational training, primarily in ballet, as a child and young adult and as a current and enthusiastic amateur of ballet and Irish dance. I was able, willing and happy to dance. In addition, my technical competence and sense of belonging (Sands 2002: 36) offset some of the disorientation experienced when participating in new dance practices; etiquette and knowledge were transferable to a certain degree across case studies. This personal history was integral to the collaborations that formed between me and groups of performers across the case studies as I was welcomed into various teams. However, irrespective of my personal relationship with the dance activities and practices that I danced, investigated and observed, I prepared for the case studies through undertaking a series of literature reviews and visiting and talking with various staff and members at the settings involved.

The professional ballet class was the only case study where the observer as participant role was solely adopted (i.e., I did not dance) owing to a range of reasons. Firstly, I did not have the necessary dance ability. Secondly, this was a professional working environment and so I respectfully felt that it was not a place to 'try and keep up'. Lastly, I already had a good working knowledge of the ballet class format and practice from previous vocational training and I knew how I felt when I was dancing ballet. However, adoption of this role meant that my interaction with, and presentation to, the ballet dancers was largely limited to the front stage space of the studio and constrained further by my sitting and watching, rather than standing and dancing. However, I danced within the inclusive creative, line dancing and Highland dancing classes, the salsa club and the dance sessions that took place at the primary school. Within all of these settings (with the exception of the salsa club) my presence and the nature of the project were known. Within the salsa club, I conducted observations covertly as a complete participant. The main justification for this was a logistical one; it simply was not possible to explain the study and issue the relevant paperwork to all the people operating (dancing and watching) in the space, constantly moving around in a haze of loud music and bright lights. Within the other case studies, where my ethnographic research role was overt, informed consent was gained from the organizations, institutions, venues and individuals involved in the research, and anonymity across all of the case studies ensured. As a dance participant, I also had access to key settings outwith the front stage space, including the green room and lunch space of the inclusive creative dance class, the bar and seating areas of the line dancing class and salsa club, the changing rooms of the private dance school where the Highland class took place and the staff room of the primary school. Wainwright (2004: 79) talks of feeling like an 'honorary member of their ballet company' in his ethnography of The Royal Ballet, and dancing within the key performance space, while having access to the back stage spaces, was an important contributor to my gaining 'honorary membership'.

By turning to local communities, rather than to the far-flung places that are the traditional destination of the anthropologist, I embraced a relatively new type of dance ethnography: 'art world dance ethnography' or 'artistic dance ethnography' (Davida 2011: 10, 7), merging 'hybrid methods' with 'traditional anthropological practices' (ibid.: 13). The interdisciplinary approach adopted drew on the tradition of dance ethnography and, in particular, the resource of the researcher's own body in accessing knowledge of the social phenomena under investigation.

The Presentation of Self in Participatory Dance Settings

The Ethnographic Researcher as 'Observer'

The micro behaviours and beliefs exhibited and shared across the participatory dance activities and practices were accessed, interrogated and often supported by myself as I danced and observed in all but one of the case studies. Having previously experienced, or experiencing within the case studies, the types of movement being performed allowed me to note how my enjoyment (or otherwise) of dancing affected my part in the various social interactions that unfolded. The collaborative nature of my behaviour respected the 'realities' that were in existence; as shall be explored, across the research settings I sought to reconcile my personal front with the macro front in existence and, in turn, the participants involved collaborated with me in my research. Here, Goffman's framework is drawn on to acknowledge and demonstrate the interactional role that the ethnographer can play in the data collection process, through interrogating examples of conduct and etiquette that I engaged in and the responses observed. Goffman's role of 'observer' constitutes neither audience nor performer, but the social theorist suggests that an observer may be familiar with the performance that he or she is witnessing, impacting on his or her experience and understanding:

> Instead of having to maintain a different pattern of expectation and responsive treatment for each slightly different performer and performance, [the observer] can place the situation in a broad category around which it is easy for him [*sic*] to mobilize his past experience and stereotypical thinking. Observers then need only be familiar with a small and hence manageable vocabulary of fronts, and know how to respond to them, in order to orient themselves in a wide variety of situations. (1990 [1959]: 36)

There were certain widely accepted actions and behaviours that I understood had to be performed for me to 'fit in' across the majority of dance settings; they included the tying back of long hair, removal of jewellery, wearing of appropriate clothing and footwear, engaging in a minimum of talking in the front stage space and obeying the teacher or figure of authority.

Goffman's vocabulary of fronts mentioned earlier and cited above, as a research resource, is complimentary to Schütz's (1967) phenomenological concept of an existing 'stock of knowledge': a familiar understanding of attitudes, experiences, stories and values. These concepts proved particularly important in the professional ballet class, where I only gave a social, rather than a dance performance, in the sense that my informants could only 'judge' me based on my social interaction (what I said and how I said it, my dress, my facial expressions and my body language) as my knee-high boots remained firmly on and my ballet shoes off.

Linked to the latter theme, a vocabulary of fronts could literally be translated into the vocabulary of ballet. Dancers in the front stage space wanted to know if I understood what was being said, in relation to the instructions being given and followed. Understanding of ballet vocabulary, an 'inside secret' (see Goffman 1990 [1959]), gave the dancers the means to check that the stranger in the studio was in some way a member of their 'team', that I shared and could demonstrate shared knowledge. Within the studio more than one dancer asked me if I 'knew what was going on', demonstrating the importance of being able to answer in the affirmative in order to gain a sense of membership. I entered this setting following fifteen years of amateur and vocational training in classical ballet; despite not being at the required professional standard to participate with my arabesques and pirouettes, my knowledge of ballet technique and social etiquette allowed me to gain 'partial membership' and thus an element of rapport and trust was established with the professional dancers. During the first class that I attended, I actually found myself sitting with my feet turned out and accentuated my posture, sitting upright rather than slouching. Prior to individual dancers seeking to sound out my understanding of their world, I felt the need to communicate that I had received ballet training previously through subtle, yet obvious, measures. After I was able to explain that I was, indeed, familiar with ballet pedagogy, I emotionally and physically relaxed in the setting, reverting to a stance with less of a ramrod back.

Within the primary school case study, I actually started off dancing with the pupils in all of the sessions operating within my period of data collection, including the Scottish ceilidh instruction with P4 pupils (aged between seven and nine), the whole-school Zumba sessions, creative movement with P1 pupils (aged between four and six) and the street dance sessions led by an external specialist for P5 pupils (aged between eight and ten). Within the former class, the raucous nature of the dancing was apparent and it did not seem to matter if I, as an adult researcher, was 'setting to' a child pupil during the dances. Within the whole-school Zumba sessions, the front stage space was very much shared between the adult teachers and child pupils as crucially everyone present in this space was dancing. During the P1 classes, I appeared to be viewed as something of a novelty figure and my presence was welcomed by the youngest pupils in the school. However, after fully participating through dancing in the first two P5 street dance sessions, it became apparent that, as the sole adult dancing with them, the preference of the pupils, really, was for me not to be doing so. This was realized through observing shared looks and gestures; the pupils were engaging in 'team collusion' (see Goffman 1990 [1959]) to subtly communicate their wish to enjoy being the sole dance performers and owners of a dance reality during a specialist activity that had been set up specifically for this class for a fixed period only. Given the centrality of inequality between adult researcher and child informant, it is interesting to note that it was actually particular groups of school pupils that denied me research access, or rather, dictated the terms of my participation.

This collective sentiment was particularly obvious during the first half of the street dance sessions led by the external dance specialist, which featured a series of movement-based games. One such exercise was called 'The Silent Picture Game'. The pupils were divided into two groups; a number such as '6' or a symbol or emoticon such as 'smiley face' was called out and the children had a limited amount of time to make this 'shape' on the floor; following a bout of several rounds the winning group of the game was announced. This competition format inspired play and saw the pupils working together in their own teams. This was one scenario where my willingness to collaborate was unwelcome; as a fairly unknown adult trying to join in, my position was superfluous. Thus, I wisely made the move from performer to observer, moving from dancing to sitting and watching. This action, together with my ready admittance to the iconic back stage arena of the school staff room and my aged appearance that obviously marked me out as an adult, meant that I naturally fell into the team of teachers as opposed to the one comprised of pupils. Indeed, throughout my time at the primary school, despite consistently explaining my role as a student researcher, both teachers and pupils viewed me as a dance teacher and responded accordingly. Before one of the Zumba sessions, the teacher leading the session was quick to tell me: 'It's not real dance you know, it's just me getting up and leading it from the front'. The pupils viewed me as a performer who was a dance teacher, in part due to my leading a discussion on dance, but also from seeing me dance in their classes and perhaps noting the way that I moved. One pupil asked me: 'Could you teach the school dancing and every day you teach a different class and every week you could teach us something different?' Significantly, the reality within (the interactional strategies that allowed both teachers and pupils to 'save face') was shaped by an external expectation that dance was taught. Within Scotland, dance is part of the Curriculum for Excellence under 'Expressive Arts'; the learning and teaching of dance is mandatory.

A second case study that also reflected a transition made from performer to one of observer occurred within the salsa club. However, in contrast to the primary school case study where my role moved from expected 'dancer' to unexpected 'spectator', brought about by differences in age and status, within the salsa club the issue was a discrepancy in dance ability. Concerning this latter setting, the reality sought was one that maintained and promoted a high level of technical performance and understanding. Noting my beginner level, some of my (male) partners chose to dance with me in the back stage space of the balcony and to the side of the bar, rather than leading me onto the front stage space of the dance floor. Their decision was not explained or expanded upon, but the strategy not only served to make me feel more comfortable through providing me with a 'safer' space to increase my knowledge and skill, but also ensured that my salsa ability could not threaten the desired 'authentic' and embodied reality being promoted largely through the dance performances taking place. Hence, I danced on the periphery and, given that the attendees, who were there to dance, wanted to have a more advanced dance experience than the one I could provide, observing rather than performing became my primary occupation during this case study. Nonetheless, engaging in both basic dance behaviour and etiquette, coupled with a competence and willingness to dance, proved crucial for moving from the role of observer to one of team player as the observation sessions progressed in each setting. Within the salsa club, although it was obvious that I was new to salsa, it also appeared to be obvious that I had engaged in previous training of some kind. I was told: 'Your frame is very good'. I was asked: 'Have you done this before?' Such assimilation was key to having the opportunity to observe and note routine team behaviours rather than those performances instigated and impacted upon by the presence of a researcher solely as observer. The very nature of salsa dancing shaped my behaviour: the way that I smiled and talked with my partner was shaped both by my being guided, spun and whirled about and through watching the dancing of other couples. The syncopation of the hip movements, the merging of physical and auditory rhythm, and the lights, colour and close physical contact with another human being served to shape the nature of social behaviours in the research process.

The Ethnographic Researcher as (Dancing) 'Performer'

As a dancing researcher, my dance performances facilitated, to varying degrees of success, my immersion in each setting. Goffman writes: 'we commonly find that the definition of the situation projected by a particular participant is an integral part of a projection that is fostered and sustained by the intimate cooperation of more than one participant' (1990 [1959]: 83). In other words, the nature of the 'intimate cooperation' existing in the varying dance settings had to be understood and performed by myself for team membership status to be obtained; this was integral to the collaborative nature of the research, which saw a level of trust established and enjoyed as opinions, stories, plasters and (dance) shoes were shared across settings.

The Highland dancing class constituted the most natural setting for me, from both a dance and social perspective, despite my lack of experience and knowledge of the dance form. This was owing to the rigid format of the class and the private dance school setting, both of which I had experienced before. During the first class, I actually entered the studio late, having been held up with explaining and obtaining informed consent in the reception area, and knew to go quickly and quietly to the barre and join in the plié exercise taking place. I also listened to the teacher and kept my talking to a minimum. I was drawing on an existing vocabulary of fronts. However, I argue that the concept of a vocabulary of fronts can also be applied to muscle memory and dance performances given. Previous experience in ballet and Irish dance meant that I was able to resemble a Highland dancer through my dancing; my body could perform the hallmarks of good posture, turnout and pointed feet. Indeed, one of the participants remarked: 'You're good at it for a beginner. You're able to pick it up. I think because of the other dancing you're able to pick it up so quickly and point your toes'. My body would not have been able to perform the shapes that it did without having been through a similar regime and, crucially, I would not have supported a traditional disciplinary dance training if I had not (whether consciously or unconsciously) supported one elsewhere previously.

As became apparent, the dominant dance reality in existence, which aimed to preserve and promote the physical, traditional and regulated nature of Highland dancing practice, was a source of tension in the class between the teacher and older participants (aged between eighteen and thirty), who supported this reality, and the younger participants (aged between seven and fourteen), who rebelled against it (all participants were female). The dance performance that I gave belied a certain previous social and cultural background and naturally allied me to the teacher and older participants. Doing the dancing and feeling the exact and powerful nature of the movement sensation also gave me a greater understanding of how and why the teacher and older participants felt so protective of the practice. The steps and dances performed, which also characterize and constitute the practice, made one feel brave and powerful. The rigid posture necessary, the straight legs, upright arms, splayed fingers resembling 'antlers' and the extreme turnout all served to give one a feeling of invincibility when dances and sequences were 'hit'.

Through conversations had (for example, discussion about various syllabuses, boards and associations) and gestures noted (stretching together, sharing plasters) I was subtly welcomed as a member of one 'sub-team' within the class. One incident in particular provided me with the means to gain sub-team membership. The teacher had been increasingly frustrated with the poor effort and commitment shown by the younger members of the class and at the penultimate session furiously shouted her opinions: 'This just isn't good enough. Am I going to have to go ballistic like I did just before the exams? *That was absolutely appalling.* Horrendous'. As somebody who was not the intended recipient of this tirade, I could have moved myself to the side of the room, or engaged a facial expression that was respectful, rather than downright guilty, but, mirroring the behaviours of the older participants in the setting, I followed suit. In other words, I collaborated with them. This response would have been understandable, as reaction is often instantaneous and unconscious, but I continued this performance of 'looking and feeling bad' into the back stage space of the changing rooms. Discussion focusing on how the older participants, myself included, needed to work harder to help and motivate the younger ones ensued. This was a performance that I acted consciously. I engaged in behaviour that was encouraged in a private, vocational dance school teaching a highly codified form of dance.

Previous to engaging in this research I had worked in the disability arts sector for a number of years and felt comfortable in an integrated environment. However, attaining a level of comfortableness with the main dance practice employed in the inclusive creative dance class, contact improvisation (CI), proved to be a challenge. As mentioned previously, the majority of my previous and current training was in ballet and Irish dancing and in settings where steps and dances were set by the teacher, rather than explored by the participants themselves. The bravery, creativity, flow, risk and trust that I felt was inherently necessary to engage in CI were challenged by my own lack of experience and fear of performing it. As with the salsa club, within the inclusive creative dance class the kinaesthetic sensation created and experienced was to some extent reliant on another human being. Contact improvisation has been described as a dance practice in which the 'impetus for motion stems entirely from the moment of improvisational immediacy. Although dancers learn methods of safe physical response to these impulses, contact's essence is all about riding the waves of unexpected partner movement' (Davies 2008: 44). This 'shared flow of energy' was a theme of both the salsa club and inclusive creative dance class case studies; however, the highly social nature of the salsa club, the pulsing music and the colourful and whirring bodies meant that, in contrast to the inclusive creative dance class, a smile was almost permanently on my face when salsa dancing. The more serious business of negotiating shared movement without a conventionally conceived 'leader', and through being in a studio rather than a club setting, shaped the way that I interacted with and interpreted the CI class. Yet it transpired over the course of the observation sessions that my nervousness was both noted and shared by other members of the class, most notably by the support workers and volunteers who also danced. One of the volunteers observed my apprehension and reassured me that the clients 'know what they're doing. They will help you'. The embarrassment experienced through engaging in and trying to perform CI 'correctly' (without fully understanding what that meant) gave us a shared experience to bond over. In contrast to the Highland dancing class, it was actually a lack of familiarity with the movement that led to my assimilation within the inclusive creative dance class. The full data collection process revealed the two-way relationship between dance performances given and the inclusive nature of the class, resulting in both positivity and tension, brought about in part by the different roles involved: clients, teachers, support workers, volunteers and students (including one Ph.D. student). Actually embodying one of those roles and having a shared empathetic connection with the support workers and volunteers gave me an insight as to the complex social make-up in existence.

Previously, when discussing the case study situated within a primary school, the collusion observed between the children, evidenced through their facial expressions and body language, was noted. During the inclusive creative dance class, it was my turn to collude with others who expressed discomfort, and in return I was confided in: 'I love movement, I always have done but you know, within a sports context. I mean dancer? Me? Nah. No … You're judged by how good you are and particularly when I started, I'm not a dancer, so I was afraid that I was going to stand up and look a complete idiot'. During one of the classes, which took the form of a rehearsal for an upcoming show, Siobhan (the stage manager) led a kind of pep talk. People were told that they needed to multitask: 'Enjoy it, learn it, do it'. 'Not much then', muttered one support worker who looked right at me with a smile. 'Defensive strategies' (Goffman 1990 [1959]: 24) adopted by the volunteers and support workers to manage the impression that they gave included a mixture of apologizing, self-deprecation and the full embracement of exercises and choreography within sessions, actions that I noted and replicated when I felt embarrassment creep up on me during a particular CI exercise or task.

As someone who was fully participating though dancing within the majority of settings, the possibility existed that I would commit actions and behaviours that were unwelcome. The most obvious example of such incidents occurred during the line dancing class. A performer may commit discrepant actions and faux pas, purposefully or unintentionally, even when they grasp the nature of the scenario and have an existing understanding of the intimate cooperation that is sought in the promotion of a sponsored reality. From the first observation session it was apparent that a sense of protective pride was felt by both the teacher and regular participants over line dancing practice; they were aware that dominant public perception viewed line dancing as 'uncool' and easy to do, and stressed to me, as well as to each other, the technical and progressive nature of the activity during classes. The common sentiment presented was: 'It's not what people think it is'. However, what could be termed my ballet 'habitus' (Bourdieu 1977) seeped through and shaped how the line dancing teacher and participants viewed me and, in turn, the impression that they sought to give of themselves.

On one occasion, I was waiting outside of the front door when two of the participants arrived. One of them suggested that we ring the bell that I was standing under and, being not much over five foot tall, the only way I could reach it was to jump or go on my pointes. When we got in, the teacher asked how we had gained access and on hearing that 'she went up on her tippy toes', felt the need to tell me: 'You know I used to be a ballet teacher'. This theme that I was associated with ballet continued throughout the case study: I had to constantly remind myself that it would be best if I did not point my feet to such a degree or use my head to spot when we turned in a dance. However, on more than one occasion, the following was shouted into the microphone: 'You're doing your ballet, Beth', causing everyone to turn round and look.

The connotations with ballet, viewed by the participants as being a 'superior' dance form, were obvious. As a result, I had to draw on particular strategies, including downplaying my technical dance ability, to show that I was respectful, serious and enthusiastic about learning line dancing and that I gained enjoyment from the practice. Familiarity was an important theme: participants performed in rows; they most often had 'their' place within the line, denoting their level of experience. I also found something comforting in dancing on my own (in the sense of having no physical contact), while feeling part of a coordinated and visual whole. I took pleasure in turning, performing grapevines and moving in a set sequence when, once a dance had been mastered, I could continue to perform on a sort of autopilot, allowing some disengagement between mind and body and giving the former some time out. The regularized nature of line dancing promoted a safety-in-numbers approach: being a 'cog in the wheel' permitted escapism of a different, less urgent and overt kind. There was very much a sense of dancing literally as a team, which transferred to socially interacting as a team. However, I was still known as 'ballet Beth' when I left and was presented with a goodbye card with a ballerina on the front at my last class. The concept of stereotypes had a role to play in this scenario; existence of a vocabulary of fronts in the line dancing class resulted in situational behaviour that reacted to the idea of (an) 'other' dance practice (Kelly 2007a). Actions observed suggest that it was the presence of a new observer in the line dancing class, one who was overtly present as both a researcher and a dance participant, which acted as a catalyst for an underlying reality to be explicitly promoted: line dancing as a technical, and thus valid, practice.

The kinaesthetic sensation experienced within the ballet and Highland dancing classes reflected the uniformity of the line dancing class (for example, each dancer has 'their' place at the barre; barre work is performed as a class). There is also something reassuring in settling into the first few minutes of a dance activity: a change in the mindset and in the body occurs. In the words of Goffman, these exercises constitute 'moments [where] one can detect a wonderful putting on and taking off of character' (1990 [1959]: 123); a process that is not limited to engaging in the more codified dance practices. Although this alteration is both felt internally and displayed externally, kinaesthesia plays a primary role in causing this transformation to occur. My social behaviour altered and to a significant extent was shaped by the physical movement that I was performing and feeling or, in the case of the professional ballet class, watching and feeling.

Conclusion

Attaining honorary team-member status through performing the 'researcher as (dancing) performer/observer' roles and having access to both front stage and back stage regions gave me the means to better seek out underlying individual patterns of behaviour and social interaction. Kinaesthesia was a shaping force that operated on multiple levels throughout the data collection process, both as an internal motivator and by demonstrating and inspiring dramaturgical cooperation and loyalty. Goffman's framework provided a means for me to understand both the contribution that I, as an ethnographic researcher, was making to the realities under investigation and how I was accessing information about these worlds through collaborating with my informants: my performances were tailored. This approach, of situating the researcher within the dramaturgical model, has been underexplored in the Goffmanian literature and the sociological dance studies cited previously and, more significantly, it may prove beneficial to the reflexive dance ethnographer. Within the field, crucially, I participated as fully as was possible (most obviously, with regard to dance ability) and appropriate (understanding and respecting the inevitable boundaries that would remain: for example, respecting the child-centred space of school pupils).

Impression management engaged in within the generally 'closed' dance settings reflected and revealed the social expectations and structural mechanisms surrounding the participatory dance activities and practices operating there; expectations and mechanisms that I had to understand and respect. Goffman's framework uncovers and interrogates patterns and incidents of social interaction to explain that 'what appear on the surface to be personally formed behaviours ... are actually rooted in pre-existing and well-established definitions of situations' (Whiteside and Kelly 2016: 16). '[S]ocial units ... become committed every time the individual performs his [*sic*] routine' (Goffman 1990 [1959]: 235), and the vocabulary of fronts I consistently engaged in helped to communicate and cement my commitment. A central example from this research concerns not only the nature of the relationships witnessed between the various figures of authority or directors of realities and the various participants or dancers that they taught across the case studies, but also the relationship between myself as an ethnographic researcher and the various teachers that I encountered. In each case, I mirrored the respectful and subservient behaviour of the learners and with each passing observation session cemented my commitment and so validated my place within each setting. Smith explains:

> Goffman showed how many of our seemingly insignificant and idiosyncratic concerns (our expletives when we drop a glass, our discomfort

when a stranger holds a glance at us too long) are consequences of the normative ordering of interactional conduct. Goffman ... is never more clearly present than when he is drawing our attention to the social sources of a feeling or item of conduct we had thought uniquely ours. (2006: 32)

The findings of the study – that is, the nature of the realities within the professional ballet class, inclusive creative dance class, line dancing class, Highland dancing class, salsa club and dance in primary education – are explored in detail elsewhere (e.g., Whiteside 2015). Yet the exciting and rich data that was gained, analysed, interpreted and presented resulted directly from the performances that I gave throughout the data collection process, shaped by how I thought I was expected to and how I did behave, dress, talk and dance.

Acknowledgements

This chapter draws on the author's Ph.D. study, 'The Hidden Dancers: A Goffmanian Analysis of Participatory Dance Activity and Practice in Glasgow'. The doctoral project, based at the Royal Conservatoire of Scotland and the University of St Andrews, is funded by the Economic and Social Research Council, 'Capacity Building Cluster' grant # RES 187-24-0014, with industry sponsor Creative Scotland. Ethical clearance was provided by the Royal Conservatoire of Scotland (RCS) following a successful ethics application to the RCS Research Degrees Committee.

Bethany Whiteside is undertaking an ESRC CASE Studentship in the sociology of dance at the Royal Conservatoire of Scotland and the University of St Andrews, sponsored by Creative Scotland. She has published in a range of peer-reviewed publications, presented at national and international conferences, is a guest lecturer at the University of Edinburgh and was a founding coeditor of the *Scottish Journal of Performance*. In 2014, she was a Visiting Research Scholar at the dance department of Temple University, Philadelphia, funded by the ESRC as an Overseas Institutional Visit.

Notes

1. See, for example, Enck and Preston (1988); Gardner and Martinko (1988); Grove and Fisk (1992); Dillard et al. (2000); Tanner and Timmons (2000); White and Hanson (2002); Birrell and Donnelly (2004); Riley and Manias (2005); Johansson (2007); Beames and Pike (2008); Wosick-Correa and Joseph (2008); Kelly (2007a, 2007b, 2013a, 2013b).
2. See, for example, Green (2001, 2003); Turner and Wainwright (2003); Wainwright (2004); Wainwright, Williams and Turner (2005, 2006, 2007); Heiland et al. (2008); Dryburgh and Fortin (2010); Alexias and Dimitropoulou (2011); Pickard (2012, 2013).

References

Alexias, G., and E. Dimitropoulou. 2011. 'The Body as a Tool: Professional Classical Ballet Dancers' Embodiment', *Research in Dance Education* 12: 87–104.
Amans, D. 2008. *An Introduction to Community Dance Practice*. Basingstoke: Palgrave Macmillan.
Atkinson, P., and M. Hammersley. 1998. 'Ethnography and Participant Observation', in N.K. Denzin and Y.S. Lincoln (eds), *Strategies of Qualitative Inquiry*. Thousand Oaks, CA: Sage, pp. 35–56.
Beames, S., and E. Pike. 2008. 'Goffman Goes Rock Climbing: Using Creative Fiction to Explore the Presentation of Self in Outdoor Education', *Australian Journal of Outdoor Education* 12(2): 3–11.
Birrell, S., and P. Donnelly. 2004. 'Reclaiming Goffman: Erving Goffman's Influence on the Sociology of Sport', in R. Giulianotti (ed.), *Sport and Modern Social Theorists*. Basingstoke: Palgrave Macmillan, pp. 49–64.
Blumer, H.G. 1972. 'Action vs Interaction: Review of "Relations in Public" by Erving Goffman 1971', *Society* 9(6): 50–53.
Bourdieu, P. 1977. *Outline of a Theory of Practice*, trans. R. Nice. Cambridge: Cambridge University Press.
Brinson, P. 1983a. 'Scholastic Tasks of a Sociology of Dance: Part 1', *Dance Research* 1(1): 100–7.
———. 1983b. 'Scholastic Tasks of a Sociology of Dance: Part 2', *Dance Research* 1(2): 59–68.
Buckland, T.J. (ed.). 1999. *Dance in the Field: Theory, Methods and Issues in Dance Ethnography*. Basingstoke: Palgrave Macmillan.
Clark, T.I., and I. Mangham. 2004. 'From Dramaturgy to Theatre as Technology: The Case of Corporate Theatre', *Journal of Management Studies* 41: 36–59.
Davida, D. (ed.). 2011. *Fields in Motion: Ethnography in the Worlds of Dance*. Waterloo, ON: Wilfrid Laurier University.
Davies, T. 2008. 'Mobility: AXIS Dancers Push the Boundaries of Access', *Text and Performance Quarterly* 28: 43–63.
Dawe, A. 1973. 'The Underworld of Erving Goffman', *British Journal of Sociology* 24: 246–55.
Dillard, D., et al. 2000. 'Impression Management and the Use of Procedures as the Ritz Carlton: Moral Standards and Dramaturgical Discipline', *Communication Studies* 51: 404–14.
Dryburgh, A., and S. Fortin. 2010. 'Weighing in on Surveillance: Perception of the Impact of Surveillance on Female Ballet Dancers' Health', *Research in Dance Education* 11: 95–108.
Enck, C., and J.D. Preston. 1988. 'Counterfeit Intimacy: A Dramaturgical Analysis of an Erotic Performance', *Deviant Behaviour* 9: 369–81.
Farnell, B.M. 1999. 'Moving Bodies, Acting Selves', *Annual Review of Anthropology* 28: 341–73.
Farnell, B.M., and R.N. Wood. 2011. 'Performing Precision and the Limits of Observation', in T. Ingold (ed.), *Redrawing Anthropology: Materials, Movements, Lines*. Farnham: Ashgate, pp. 91–113.
Fine, G.A., and P. Manning. 2000. 'Erving Goffman', in G. Ritzer (ed.), *The Blackwell Companion to Major Contemporary Social Theorists*. Oxford: Blackwell, pp. 457–85.

Foster, S.L. 1997. 'Dancing Bodies', in J.C. Desmond (ed.), *Meaning in Motion: New Cultural Studies of Dance*. Durham, NC: Duke University Press, pp. 235–57.
Gardner, W., and M. Martinko. 1988. 'Impression Management in Organisations', *Journal of Management* 14: 321–38.
Goffman, E. 1990 [1959]. *The Presentation of Self in Everyday Life*. London: Penguin.
———. 1983. 'The Interaction Order: American Sociological Association, 1982 Presidential Address', *American Sociological Review* 48: 1–17.
Gold, R. 1958. 'Roles in Sociological Field Observation', *Social Forces* 36: 217–23.
Gouldner, A.W. 1971. *The Coming Crisis of Western Sociology*. London: Heinemann.
Grau, A. 2005. 'When the Landscape Becomes Flesh: An Investigation into Body Boundaries with Special Reference to Tiwi Dance and Western Classical Ballet', *Body & Society* 11(4): 141–63.
Green, J. 2001. 'Socially Constructed Bodies in American Dance Classrooms', *Research in Dance Education* 2: 155–73.
———. 2003. 'Foucault and the Training of Docile Bodies in Dance Education', *Arts and Learning Research Journal* 19: 99–125.
Green, J., and S.W. Stinson. 1999. 'Postpositivist Research in Dance', in S.H. Fraleigh and P. Hanstein (eds), *Researching Dance: Evolving Modes of Inquiry*. Pittsburgh, PA: University of Pittsburgh Press, pp. 91–123.
Grove, S.J., and R.P. Fisk. 1992. 'Service Experience as Theatre', *Advances in Consumer Research* 19: 455–61.
Hanna, J.L. 1979. *To Dance Is Human*. Chicago, IL: The University of Chicago Press.
Heiland, T., et al. 2008. 'Body Image of Dancers in Los Angeles: The Cult of Slenderness and Media Influence among Dance Students', *Research in Dance Education* 9: 257–75.
Hui, E., et al. 2009. 'Effects of Dance on Physical and Psychological Well-Being in Older Persons', *Archives of Gerontology and Geriatrics* 49: 45–50.
Jackson, M. 1989. *Paths Toward a Clearing: Radical Empiricism and Ethnographic Inquiry*. Bloomington: Indiana University Press.
Jacobsen, M.H. (ed.). 2010. *The Contemporary Goffman*. New York: Routledge.
Johansson, C. 2007. 'Goffman's Sociology: An Inspiring Resource for Developing Public Relations Theory', *Public Relations Review* 33: 275–80.
Kealiinohomoku, J. 1970. 'An Anthropologist Looks at Ballet as a Form of Ethnic Dance', *Impulse 1969–1970*: 24–33.
Kelly, J. 2007a. 'The Flowers of Scotland: A Sociological Examination of the Relationship between Association Football, Rugby Union and National Identity in Post-Devolution Scotland', Ph.D. dissertation. Loughborough: Loughborough University.
———. 2007b. 'Hibernian Football Club: The Forgotten Irish?', *Sport in Society* 10: 514–36.
———. 2013a. 'Popular Culture, Sport and the "Hero"-fication of British Militarism', *Sociology* 47: 722–38.
———. 2013b. 'Football Fans in Pre-Referendum Scotland: Folk Devils, Space and Place', *East Asian Sport Thoughts* 3: 207–29.
Lobo, Y.B. 2006. 'The Effects of a Creative Dance and Movement Program on the Social Competence of Head Start Preschoolers', *Social Development* 15: 501–19.
Manning, S. 2006. 'Letter from the President', *Society of Dance History Scholars Newsletter* 26: 1–2.

Pickard, A. 2012. 'Schooling the Dancer: The Evolution of an Identity as a Ballet Dancer', *Research in Dance Education* 13: 25–46.

———. 2013. 'Ballet Body Belief: Perceptions of an Ideal Ballet Body from Young Ballet Dancers', *Research in Dance Education* 14: 3–19.

Prickett, S. 1990. 'Dance and the Workers' Struggle', *Dance Research* 8(1): 47–61.

Reed, S. 1998. 'The Politics and Poetics of Dance', *Annual Review of Anthropology* 27: 503–32.

Riley, R., and E. Manias. 2005. 'Rethinking Theatre in Modern Operating Rooms', *Nursing Inquiry* 12: 2–9.

Sands, R.R. 2002. *Sport Ethnography*. Champaign, IL: Human Kinetics.

Scheff, T.J. 2006. *Goffman Unbound!: A New Paradigm for Social Science*. Boulder, CO: Paradigm Publishers.

Schütz, A. 1967. *Phenomenology of the Social World*. Evanston, IL: Northwestern University Press.

Shigematsu, R., et al. 2002. 'Dance-Based Aerobic Exercises May Improve Indices of Falling Risk in Older Women', *Age and Ageing* 31: 261–66.

Sklar, D. 2001. *Dancing with the Virgin: Body and Faith in the Fiesta of Tortugas, New Mexico*. Berkeley: University of California Press.

Smith, G. 2006. *Erving Goffman*. Abingdon: Routledge.

Smith-Autard, J. 2003. 'The Essential Relationship between Pedagogy and Technology in Enhancing the Teaching of Dance Form', *Research in Dance Education* 4: 151–69.

Sussman, L. 1990. 'Recruitment Patterns: Their Impact on Ballet and Modern Dance', *Dance Research Journal* 22(1): 21–28.

Tanner, J., and S. Timmons. 2000. 'Backstage in the Theatre', *Journal of Advanced Nursing* 32: 975–80.

Thomas, H. 1986. 'Movement, Modernism and Contemporary Culture: Issues for a Critical Sociology of Dance', Ph.D. dissertation. London: Goldsmiths, University of London.

———. 1995. *Dance, Modernity and Culture: Explorations in the Sociology of Dance*. London: Routledge.

———. (ed.). 1997. *Dance in the City*. Basingstoke: Palgrave Macmillan.

———. 2003. *The Body, Dance and Cultural Theory*. Basingstoke: Palgrave Macmillan.

Turner, S., and S.P. Wainwright. 2003. 'Corps de Ballet: The Case of the Injured Ballet Dancer', *Sociology of Health & Illness* 25: 269–88.

Wainwright, S.P. 2004. 'A Bourdieusian Ethnography of the Balletic Body', Ph.D. dissertation. London: King's College London, University of London.

Wainwright, S.P., Williams, C., and B.S. Turner. 2005. 'Fractured Identities: Injury and the Balletic Body', *Health* 9: 49–66.

———. 2006. 'Varieties of Habitus and the Embodiment of Ballet', *Qualitative Research* 6: 535–58.

———. 2007. 'Globalization, Habitus and the Balletic Body', *Cultural Studies <=> Critical Methodologies* 7: 308–25.

White, R., and D. Hanson. 2002. 'Corporate Self, Corporate Reputation and Corporate Annual Reports: Re-enrolling Goffman', *Scandinavian Journal of Management* 18: 285–301.

Whiteside, B. 2013. 'High Kicks, Heel Stomps and High Cuts: Performing the Data Collection', in B.T. Clegg, J. Scully and J. Bryson (eds), *ESRC Research Capacity*

Building Clusters. National Summit Conference 2013, Birmingham, 25–26 June 2013 (Conference Proceedings). Birmingham: Aston University, pp. 50–57.

———. 2015. 'Salsa and the City: A Case Study on a Glaswegian "Community"', in C.F. Stock and P. Germain-Thomas (eds), *Contemporising the Past: Envisaging the Future. World Dance Alliance Global Summit 2014, Angers, 6–11 July 2014 (Conference Proceedings)*. Canberra: Ausdance. Retrieved 21 December 2015 from http://ausdance.org.au/articles/details/salsa-and-the-city-a-case-study-on-a-glaswegian-community.

Whiteside, B., and J. Kelly. 2016. 'Dancing with Goffman: The Presentation of Self in the Classical Ballet Class', *Research in Dance Education* 17: 14–27.

Williams, S.J. 1986. 'Appraising Goffman', *The British Journal of Sociology* 37: 348–69.

Williamson, A. 2009. 'Formative Support and Connection: Somatic Movement Dance Education in Community and Client Practice', *Journal of Dance & Somatic Practices* 1: 29–45.

Wosick-Correa, K., and L. Joseph. 2008. 'Sexy Ladies Sexing Ladies: Women as Consumers in Strip Clubs', *Journal of Sex Research* 45: 201–16.

Wulff, H. 1998. *Ballet across Borders*. Oxford: Berg.

———. 2007. *Dancing at the Crossroads: Mobility and Memory in Ireland*. Oxford: Berghahn.

Young, T.R. 1990. *The Drama of Social Life: Essays in Post-Modern Social Psychology*. New Brunswick, NJ: Transaction Publishers.

PART III

Music Practices and Ethical Selfhood

Chapter 5

The *Animador* as Ethical Mediator
Stage Talk and Subject Formation at Peruvian *Huayno* Music Spectacles

James Butterworth

It is a couple of hours into the show and the crowd has grown to a few thousand people. Jaime Ponce, the *animador* (literally, 'animator'), has been compering since the start but it will be several more hours before he clocks off around dawn. With the help of a handful of lesser-known *huayno* performers and a roaring trade in Cristal beer he has successfully built up an atmosphere of energy, intimacy and anticipation ahead of the arrival of the headline divas and idols. On stage, a harp player tunes up while the other musicians tease the crowd with various riffs and song fragments. Jaime moves towards the front of the stage, adjusts his charcoal pinstripe jacket and brings the microphone up to his mouth. In a heightened voice, he calls out: '*Dondé está la gente más allregreeeee!?*' (Where are the liveliest people!?).[1] His enquiry is a burst of syllables delivered in machine-gun style, the last of which cascades like the voice of a character falling down a deep hole. As members of the audience respond affirmatively, Jaime has already begun the next question: 'And the single ladies!? Where are the single ladies!?' Gesturing towards a group of screaming and waving young women, he says: 'Hey, look! They say they don't want to get married!'

Down in the crowd people drink, dance and chat, shouting to be heard over the extreme volume of the public address system. The musicians have now started vamping in a style that is a mix of *huayno* and *cumbia*, which causes Jaime to shift registers into a series of syncopated shouts: 'Palms in the air! Arms in the air! Palms in the air! Arms in the air!' He pauses. 'Ladies, do a turn! Ladies, do a turn!' Some of the women, who are already dancing, begin doing a slow 360-degree rotation with exaggerated hip movements. 'Sensual! Sensual!', Jaime chants. 'And the men!? Jump, guys, jump! Jump, guys, jump!' Shifting back into a conversational register, Jaime jokes: 'The guys who aren't jumping must weigh too much, their bellies are too big!' His comment catches the attention of pockets of the audience, causing a range of smiles, sniggers, smirks and finger pointing.

'That's it!', Jaime exclaims. 'Now, raise your glasses, the people from the south: Arequipa, Tacna!' He pauses. 'The people from the centre: Huancayo, La Oroya, Huancavelica! Cheers!' This naming of Andean towns and regions – as much two thousand kilometres apart – continues throughout the night and indicates the pan-Andean make-up of the public being addressed. While the concert is in Puente Piedra, a district in the northern outskirts of the coastal capital Lima, the vast majority of the migrant audience locate their ethnic origins elsewhere, in Peru's Andean highlands. Peering at a note passed up from the crowd, Jaime exclaims: 'Greetings to Reynaldo and Edwin Quispe Huaman from Abancay [a southern-Andean city]', before adding one of his personal clichés, 'where they drink by the truckload!'

The ethnographic focus of this chapter is *huayno* music spectacles in Peru. *Huayno* is the most widespread Andean music genre but its aesthetics, meanings and uses vary enormously across places, time periods and social classes.[2] The *huayno* referred to here is a contemporary mass-cultural variant, developed primarily in urban areas and especially in the national capital, Lima. The most famous singers tend to be women and instrumental accompaniment is usually provided by all-male ensembles, combining Andean harp, electric bass, drum machine, timbales and keyboard. Concerts usually take place at weekends and are attended by the Andean working classes, many of whom have migrated from the Andes to Lima's peripheral urban neighbourhoods.[3] Audiences range from a few hundred to tens of thousands depending on the financial investments of event organizers (see also Chapter 6 for a discussion of music promoters). While there are comparable events showcasing *cumbia* and *salsa* music, this chapter concentrates on *huayno* shows, which are much more heavily marked as Andean. This Andeanness is manifested through a combination of rhythms, melodies, instruments, harmonic progressions, dance steps, costumes, stage talk, accents and drinking practices.[4] With the exception of Alfaro (2005) and Butterworth (2014c) these popular folkloric events have received scant ethnographic attention. The observations and analyses in the present chapter derive from fifteen months of fieldwork conducted between 2010 and 2012, which involved multisited fieldwork in the commercial folkloric music industry in both Lima and the central Peruvian Andes. During this time, the author attended dozens of events, which, though varying in scale, were essentially similar to those discussed here.

In this chapter, *huayno* music spectacles are considered as ethical events that act as privileged sites for ethical subject formation. I am interested in the ways people choose, try on and are interpellated by generic identifications – such as migrant, Peruvian, lover, sufferer and drinker – as a means of developing stories about themselves and making sense of their own experiences. In particular, this study focuses on the role of the *animador* – in this case, Jaime Ponce (mentioned above) – as an important mediator in this ethical field, considering how he frames the event and the audience's experience of it, as well as the ways in which his own performance pushes and pulls audience members towards and away from particular ethical subject positions. While Jaime Ponce is widely viewed within the scene as one of *huayno*'s leading *animadores* (due to his wit, engaging delivery and association with top artists like Dina Paucar), the fundamentals of his performance are shared by many other lesser-known *animadores*.

Roughly equating to a compere, emcee or master of ceremonies, the *animador* takes a particularly active role during *huayno* shows and is responsible for holding much of the performance together.[5] The word *animador* comes from the verb *animar*, which can be variously translated as 'to encourage', 'to animate' or 'to enliven'. Through his or her verbal and gestural interactions with the audience and the other performers the *animador* must sustain the energy and intensity of the show, keep the attention of the crowd and frame how spectators experience what is seen and heard on stage. The patter of the *animador* features recurring themes, jokes and stock phrases, as well as spontaneous interjections in response to the crowd and other performers.

The figure of the *animador* appears to have little historical precedent in Andean music, seemingly developing out of the *chicha* music scene of the 1970s and 1980s. Up to and during this time, *huayno* music in Lima, in contrast to *chicha*, was performed in small venues where artists often played to an audience that sat and observed the show in a relatively passive manner (see Turino 1988). From the 1940s, roughly up until the 1970s, there was a limitation of audiences' senses beyond listening and watching. People did not drink, eat or dance. And while there was usually somebody responsible for introducing the artists to the audience and thanking them afterwards, such comperes were rarely involved during the performance of the song itself. During the 1980s, however, most of these music venues ceased to exist and in the early 1990s live *huayno* performances began to take a similar form to *chicha* events of the 1980s. Small concerts in tents became large, open-air spectacles. The audience's previously rather passive experience of sitting and watching the show became a more interpersonal, interactive and multisensory experience where people danced, socialized and drank, arguably more akin to music-making at *fiestas* in the (rural) Andes.[6] In this environment, I suggest, processes of ethical self-fashioning become increasingly visible, explicit and foundational to the experience of the music event. This is not to suggest that ethical subject formation ceases beyond the space-time nexus of *huayno* concerts but, rather, that such events foreground and intensify the ethical dimensions of performance and spectatorship.

There follows some theoretical framing in which the approach taken here to ethics and ethical subject formation is outlined, building on ideas laid out by Michel Foucault and Henrietta Moore, among others. The focus then shifts to the cultural particularities of *huayno* music spectacles. While elsewhere I have explored the ethical self-fashioning of *huayno*'s star singers (Butterworth 2014b), this chapter is primarily concerned with self-making in relation to the *animador* and *huayno* spectators. The way in which the 'selection' of and 'recruitment' to subject positions (Faubion 2011) at *huayno* spectacles is realized, through practices such as drinking beer and dancing, as well as the value-laden pull of ethnic (national, regional and migrant), sentimental and gendered modes of identification, is examined. Moreover, the pivotal role of the *animador* as an ethical mediator in this context is highlighted. Through this analysis, I aim to emphasize the importance of embodiment and intersubjectivity in processes of ethical subject formation.

Ethics: Some Theoretical Foundations

Ethics has long been a component of philosophy and theology, but over the last decade or so ethics has emerged as an increasingly common topic in anthropological inquiry (e.g., Lambek 2010; Faubion 2011; Laidlaw 2014). While much of this anthropological research has argued for an ongoing dialogue with moral philosophy, there has been a move away from thinking about ethics in abstract, hypothetical and absolute terms. Correspondingly, there has been a move towards a more grounded, empirical and contingent view of ethics as a practical and everyday mode of comportment. In other words, 'ethical' does not signify that which is right or good. Rather, it indicates a contested field in which people wrestle with the value of their thoughts, feelings, actions and judgements in particular and everyday contexts.

Much research in the anthropology of ethics is also concerned with subject formation (e.g., Hirschkind 2006), which is of particular interest here. I am concerned with how the thoughts, feelings and behaviours involved in self-making are shaped in relation to the influence of others and of discourse. Subject positions are value laden, often indicating paths towards notions of virtue and vice. While they may nudge people towards how they *ought* to think, feel and act in relation to the perceived thoughts, feelings and actions of others, subject positions are also malleable and in flux (Faubion 2011: 4). Subject formation may involve disciplinary social pressures and interpellation, but also self-stylization and intersubjectivity.[7] People are coaxed towards 'right feeling' (Stokes 2010), variously triggering co-option, resistance, ambivalence, pleasure and agency. The kind of ethics I am interested in here, therefore, has less to do with questions of right or wrong and more to do with what Foucault calls 'technologies of the self' (1997).

Foucault was successful in grounding the question of ethics in practice, in the mundane work that individuals perform on themselves in relation to socially determined categories of experience. In much of his earlier work, Foucault was concerned with analysing how the disciplinary power of discourse and institutions in society helped to create a subject, which, in turn, it conditioned.

However, in later writings Foucault shifted his emphasis towards conceptions of a more agentive subject that had a more active and intentional engagement with its own constitution. This was certainly a new direction for Foucault but one that still perpetuated his concern with the relationship between the individual and society, subjectivity and discourse. Foucault writes:

> I would say that if I am now interested in how the subject constitutes itself in an active fashion through practices of the self, these practices are nevertheless not something invented by the individual himself [*sic*]. They are models that he finds in his culture and are proposed, suggested, imposed upon him by his culture, his society, and his cultural group. (1997: 291)

For Foucault, as it is for me, the practice of self-constitution is a foundational element of ethics. From this point of view, ethics has to do with what Foucault terms the 'care of the self', a relationship the self has to itself. The 'care of the self', however, does not operate independently of moral norms but it has significant control over how it establishes its relation to them. This intentional process of relation is what Foucault refers to as 'subjectivation'. One of the reasons I find a Foucauldian view of ethics appealing is because it proposes that ethics is something more dynamic and unpredictable than simple rule following or the strict conformance to moral codes.[8] Lisa Downing summarizes this point nicely:

> There is a profound difference, Foucault thinks, between a system in which one understands the moral codes of one's culture and yet is free to adapt them creatively to one's own conduct, and a system in which an externally imposed series of moral rules governs the individual's conduct through that individual's fear of retribution. In the latter system, renunciation, rather than cultivation, of the self is the result. (2008: 101)

Foucauldian ethics, then, are bound up with 'technologies of the self', which 'permit individuals to effect by their own means, or with the help of others, a certain number of operations on their own bodies and souls, thoughts, conduct, and way of being, so as to transform themselves in order to attain a certain state of happiness, purity, wisdom, perfection, or immortality' (Foucault 1997: 225). However, while ethics may involve seeking to attain these kinds of virtues or ideals, the case of *huayno* music reminds us that 'the care of the self' just as often encompasses ambivalent and even cynical relationships with such normative virtues and ideals (see also Butterworth 2014a).

Foucault's writings have had a powerful influence on many anthropologists of ethics and his ideas have been reworked, adapted and extended by a number of scholars (Faubion 2011; Moore 2011; Laidlaw 2014). Henrietta Moore, for example, has compellingly extended Foucault's ideas via a concept she terms 'the ethical imagination': 'the way in which technologies of the self, forms of subjectification [subjectivation] and imagined relations with others lead to novel ways of approaching social transformation' (2011: 15). Moore's concept of the 'ethical imagination' complements Foucault's view of ethics in two crucial ways. First, Moore has a much greater emphasis on the role of self–other relations and intersubjectivity in ethical practice. Although Foucault concedes that the care of the self may imply a certain relationship with others (1997: 287), Moore grants this aspect much more weight – as do I (see also Chapter 6). In a mass-mediated and globalizing world, she argues, our perceived relations with those near and far become central to our ethical practice. She writes:

> [T]he ethical imagination has scalar dimensions ... that link us both to those with whom we are most proximate and intimate, as well as those who are very distant. Within the domain of the ethical, the fantasmatic nature of intersubjectivity plays a key role in maintaining forms of identity and belonging through establishing new possibilities for connection that are animated and propelled by hopes, desires and satisfactions. (2011: 22–23)

Thinking about the 'fantasmatic nature of intersubjectivity' that occurs between *huayno* stars and fans and across *huayno* publics is especially useful in linking up mass-mediated 'imaginaries' and the 'intimacies' of physical copresence, to use Byron Dueck's helpful distinction (2013b).

Second, Moore is concerned with developing Foucault's concept of 'problematization': the process through which 'human beings "problematize" what they are, what they do, and the world in which they live' (Foucault 1985: 10). For Foucault, problematization is fundamentally a 'work of thought' (idem 1997: 119), a process of (self-)distancing through which one establishes one's conduct 'as an object, and reflects on it as a problem' (ibid.: 117). However, for Moore, problematization should be understood as 'more than a work of thought or reflection' (2011: 21). In addition, she argues, it 'involves affect, emotion, the placement of the body, fantasy, and relations with objects, technologies and the material world' (ibid.).

Hovering in the background of Moore's writing is the 'affective turn' in the humanities and social sciences, which has foregrounded the relational nature of feelings, sensations and emotions and the importance of pre- or extracognitive bodily experience (Gregg and Seigworth 2010). Definitions and uses of affect vary enormously across disciplines and authors. For some, affect is primarily delineated by its capacity to operate outside of representation and semiotics (e.g., Thrift 2008). Others associate affect with sensations that fall between the cracks of relatively stable and culturally specific taxonomies of emotion.

According to Eric Shouse, '[f]eelings are *personal* and *biographical*, emotions are *social*, and affects are *prepersonal*' (2005: para. 2; italics in the original). Some stress the contagious nature of affect; that is, the ways in which feelings are transmitted both between people and between objects and people (e.g., Brennan 2004). Others, still, see affect as a means of deconstructing the notion of the autonomous, coherent and bounded human subject (e.g., Massumi 2002). However, as Moore writes, while '[a]rguing for the decentring of the rational, humanist subject and the reinstatement of somatic engagement with the world are important moves' (2011: 203), they are also historically and culturally contingent and 'perhaps it is too early yet to abandon a notion of the human subject' (ibid.: 204). For the purposes of this chapter, I do not provide my own definition of affect. Rather, I invoke affect as a means of highlighting the importance of feelings, the body and intersubjectivity in the ethical practices of *huayno* performers and spectators. However, while I do not construct any rigid boundaries between 'emotion' and 'affect', I use 'emotion' principally to refer to categories of feeling that are experienced and reflected upon at a discursive and relatively conscious level.

In the remainder of this chapter, various aspects of ethical subject formation at *huayno* music spectacles will be discussed. The study focuses in depth on the ethical framing performed by the *animador*, which involves encouraging audience members to adopt particular bodily behaviours – through drinking, dancing and other gestures – and inhabit particular subject positions, governed by intimate discourses of nation and migration. The effect of song lyrics, singers' voices and the expressive gestures of performers and spectators, which commonly rest on tropes of suffering and sorrow, are also considered. The discussion highlights that ethics does not necessarily involve affirmations of moral good; rather, the following illustrates how *huayno* spectacles engender often-ambivalent ethical stances, including in relation to public displays of emotional excess, suffering and alcoholic intoxication. Alongside such apparent ambivalent melancholy, however, one also finds jolly tunes, jokes and energetic and playful social dancing. In considering these various dimensions, I aim to demonstrate the cognitive, embodied and affective aspects of self-constitution. Moreover, I argue, such processes of ethical subject formation provide a bridge between performers and audiences that allow for intersubjective acts of evaluation, empathy and judgement, which, in turn, feed back into the process of self-fashioning among performers and spectators. In other words, the care of the self is intricately bound up with the care of others.

Stage Talk

It is New Year's Eve, 2011, and Lima's roads are characteristically gridlocked as people head to celebrations across the capital. Several thousands of them are headed to El Huarocondo, a well-known popular and folkloric music venue in

San Juan de Lurigancho, an Andean-migrant neighbourhood to the northeast of Lima. Like many large-scale music venues in Peru, El Huarocondo is an open-air venue with a huge scaffold stage, which looks out onto a large, empty yard surrounded by high brick walls and big iron gates. The crowd grows gradually throughout the night. After buying their tickets at the door, spectators stand around talking, drinking and dancing, with their eyes and ears orientated towards the stage. There are a mixture of couples and larger groups and, although spectators bump into the odd other person they know, the vast majority are unknown to each other; here, live music and sound enable both the intimacy of copresence and the anonymity of stranger sociality.

The *animador* for tonight's show at El Huarocondo is Jaime Ponce (mentioned above), one of *huayno*'s leading *animadores* and a familiar voice if not face for the majority of attendees. Over the course of a year in 2011–12, I accompanied Jaime to around a dozen recording sessions and live performances and twice conducted formal interviews with him. Raised in the central Andean city of Huancayo, Jaime grew up listening to Rod Stewart, The Bee Gees and ABBA, as well as Andean folklore and Latin popular music, fancying himself as a bit of a 'rocker'. Jaime recounted the excitement of holding a microphone for the first time at the age of twelve, after beginning to work as an errand boy at a local radio station known as '1550'. After several years, he got the chance to present his own radio show at around the time of the *chicha* music boom in the late 1970s and early 1980s. It was in the *chicha* scene that Jaime learned the ropes of being what he termed a 'social communicator', a role encompassing all kinds of verbal public performance, mass mediated or otherwise. But it is as an *animador* in the commercial folklore-music scene that Jaime has become most well-known. 'The *animador* is basic', Jaime explained to me. 'An artist without an *animador* does not have much to deploy on stage' (*no tiene mucho despliegue en el escenario*).

While tonight is a particular celebration to welcome in 2012, Jaime's set of responsibilities remains the same as ever: he welcomes artists to the stage and salutes them on their departure; he interjects with commentary on the lyrics of songs, sometimes earnestly, other times humorously; he employs a series of rhythmic calls, such as 'hands in the air!', 'move your waist!', 'jump!', 'get down!', 'enjoy, enjoy, enjoy!', which emphasize certain rhythms, add an extra layer to the musical performance and often correspond to particular bodily movements; he shouts out questions encouraging romantic, sexual and gendered modes of identification, including 'Where are the single ladies?', 'Where are the single men?' and 'Where are all the men who are under the thumb?' (*los hombres pisados*); he reads out messages and gives shout-outs to members of the audience and their home towns and regions in the Andes; and he perpetually makes references to drinking beer and getting drunk, saying 'cheers!' with the audience, asking 'Who's drunk yet?' and encouraging spectators to drink up.

Drinking as a Technology of the Self

The spectators at El Huarocondo go back and forth to kiosks selling beer that are dotted around the edge of the yard, bringing bottles and, sometimes, entire crates back to their circle of friends. Like at other Andean events, drinking here is an especially communal activity (Harvey 1994), involving a particular drinking ethic and etiquette. Revellers pass a single glass and a single bottle of beer around within small groups and take it in turns to pour and drink from the glass in fairly speedy succession. Excessive dawdling with the bottle will soon make you the butt of a collective joke, but refusal to drink altogether can be socially awkward, potentially signalling a lack of respect, mean-spiritedness or a disavowal of reciprocal relations.

Moral expectations surrounding drinking are also continually reinforced by performers on stage, especially the *animador*. Using one of his tried and tested formulae, for example, Jaime exclaims to the New-Year's-Eve spectators: 'Where are all those with [beer] bottles in their hands!? Where are all the boozers!?' (*la gente chelera*). In the act of raising their bottles and waving their arms in affirmation, spectators are hailed as drinkers, as participants in a collective intoxication. Jaime then characteristically addresses those who did not respond to his initial question: 'If you don't have a bottle in your hand, what are you doing here!?' His self-conscious laughter and explanation that he is 'only joking' do little to undermine the general moral expectations.

While the ethics and etiquette of drinking beer have deep social and cultural significance in the Andes, it is difficult to ignore the importance of beer to the financial profitability of *huayno* concerts. For example, when I asked Jaime what the response was when *huayno* concerts began to feature *animadores*, he replied:

> It was a boom! It was a great success [*golazo*], because I remember that even Samuel Dolores [the boss of the production company PRODISAR] told his *animadores* from that moment onwards that they had to animate like me, because ... I made people drink more beer. [I said to the crowd,] 'Hey, where are all the beer sales to the people from Huaraz [a northern city in Peru]?' You have to toast those details, you know. And it seems like a lie, but that impels you to go and get more beer ... just like now, you know, shouting 'raise your hands, raise your bottle, raise your glasses', which they do, you know. So we are indirect sellers of beer. We have a lot of influence so that the people dance and drink.

I do not think Jaime overstates the influence of *animadores* here. His comments indicate how he choreographs the beer drinking of audience members, often through reference to regional Andean identity markers (e.g., 'people from Huaraz'). Such place naming occurs throughout the show: 'Where are all the

Cuzco people?' 'Wave your hands if you're from Sicuani?' 'Anyone in from Apurímac?' 'Greetings to the guys from Huancayo, where they know how to drink!' Such questions and calls bring attention to the fact that, while the concert is taking place in Lima and most attendees are residents of the coastal capital, the majority are first- or second-generation Andean migrants that rarely identify as *limeño* (from/of Lima).

I asked Jaime about this habit of naming places and again he brought it back to beer drinking: 'For example, a guy from a town in Abancay, let's say Uripa, and nobody has ever mentioned his town and you say "Greetings for all the people from Uripa" – jeez, that guy wakes up and right there they drink the bar dry because they get excited'. Jaime's comments here can be contextualized within a long history of existential anxiety surrounding how to identify oneself as an Andean migrant living in Lima, especially given the historical 'othering' and marginalization of Andeans and the continuing hegemony of Lima and mestizo culture in representing the Peruvian nation. By being hailed so specifically as an *uripeño*, the spectator is greeted with a sense of recognition and visibility rarely available in the mainstream public sphere (see also Taylor 1994). This situation mirrors wide-reaching socio-political shifts in Latin America and beyond where consumption, rather than traditional democratic participation, has become the overriding basis for modes of citizenship and belonging (see Canclini 2001). Whether or not 'drinking the bar dry' amounts to an individual choice or moral pressure, it acts as a means of reinforcing the process of subjectivation as an *uripeño* and, more generally, an Andean migrant. By complying with the *animador*'s calls to drink up, wave bottles in the air and drown their sorrows', audience members adopt positions as drinking and drunken subjects, contributing to the maintenance of social ideals such as sharing and reciprocity as well as embodying affirmations of migrant identity. However, running parallel to readings of drinking as an act of social reciprocity is a more individualistic and introspective view of drinking related to *huayno*'s sentimental narratives of sensorial and emotional excess.

This latter reading is primarily in evidence in the lyrics of *huayno* songs. For example, 'Tomaré para no Llorar' (I Will Drink so as Not to Cry) by Dina Paucar and 'Dos Más' (Two More) by Sonia Morales both invoke the trope of drinking to escape or forget the pain of *desamor*, or love gone sour. Contemporary *huayno* lyrics tend to emphasize alcohol consumption as an individualistic activity based on self-interest and the overcoming of personal torments. As one *huayno* fan put it: 'In our country we have that old trick of drowning our sorrows with alcohol'. This escapist notion of drinking contrasts with the more social uses of alcohol discussed above, as well as the kinds of sacred uses of alcohol commonly associated with a range of cultural, agricultural and religious practices in the (rural) Andes (Harvey 1994; Jennings and Bowser 2009). In such practices, drunkenness is often a positive and achieved state of being. As Penny Harvey writes in relation to her research in Ocongate, intoxication ensures 'social reproduction through the integration of human beings both among themselves and with supernatural powers' (1994: 228). Harvey explains that drunkenness has, since colonial times, been frowned upon as a form of 'excess', from an elite and mestizo perspective (ibid.: 213). From an indigenous viewpoint, however, drunkenness has often been motivated by the desire for transcendence and sacrificial offerings to the land and the supernatural spirits. Thus, Harvey argues, the 'adverse judgments about Andean drinking practices ... failed to appreciate the total meaninglessness of drinking in moderation' (ibid.: 216). This situation provides an interesting contrast to Foucault's discussion of moderation as an 'ethical substance' (Foucault 1997). Here, by comparison, excess is itself an ethical substance, albeit one that may be experienced with deep ambivalence in the context of the racialized othering of Andean culture in hegemonic national imaginaries.

In the case of contemporary *huayno* pop one is unlikely to encounter discourses about the sacred uses of alcohol. In the lyrics, stage-talk and drinking practices at *huayno* shows one finds ambivalent responses to alcohol consumption, which are enmeshed in ethnic identity politics and tropes of emotional and sensorial excess. This ambivalence simultaneously generates both pride and embarrassment. Perhaps, getting drunk might be seen as providing a kind of emotional license, which creates an ethical context for the heart to get the better of the head. In discussing the prevalence of romantic pain in *huayno*, Jaime invoked an 'intimate' and 'ambivalent' (Herzfeld 1997; Stokes 2010; Dueck 2013a) view of national identity linked to alcohol and love, as well as market forces:

> It's because that's what sells; I mean, so that you drink beer it has to be like that. A Peruvian, through inheritance and through race, is romantic and from romanticism it becomes sentimental frustration: every Peruvian has his or her thing, usually a past where someone betrayed them, including he who speaks to you now. So when you drink a couple of beers you remind yourself of that and listening to those songs makes you drink more beer.

However, it is also important to recognize that such ambivalences surrounding emotional and sensorial excess are sustained by ethnic and class hierarchies in which working-class Andean migrants are more likely to be stereotyped as affectively unhinged and indulgent.[9] Furthermore, Andean migrant identity might be conceived as a fundamental subject position around which various other social categorizations and identifications (e.g., nation, class and gender) revolve.

In sum, drinking practices at *huayno* concerts can be interpreted in a variety of ways: as a manifestation of Andean social ideals of sharing and reciprocity; as the source of sensory and emotional pleasure and excess; as a marker of ethnic and migrant identities; and as the product of profit-making motivations. The polyvalence of drinking makes it a fascinating site of ethical subject formation, featuring a continual back and forth between individual and socially constructed categories of experience and identity.

Sentimental Subjects

In a lull between the departure of one artist and the arrival of the second, Jaime moves centre stage, taking responsibility for keeping the crowd's attention. He energetically calls: 'I want all the audience to embrace each other with joy, with euphoria, with excitement, with intimacy, with love, with feeling, because our homeland is cool [*chévere*]! Right!?'[10] Jaime's request puts national identity and public intimacy squarely in the frame together. Not only are the spectators hailed as members of a national community but also they are encouraged to identify as such in an incredibly intimate fashion: citizenship and public emotionality go hand in hand (Berlant 2008; Stokes 2010). Indeed, what is highlighted here is how spectators are encouraged to put emotion at the centre of their ethical self-fashioning as well as their ethical evaluation of singers.

'Where are the sufferers?', Jaime shouts. 'Where are those that have been betrayed?' Once again, Jaime creates a context for interpellation and self-fashioning. Spectators are hailed as sufferers, or at least provided with the opportunity to try on the subject position of sufferer for size. Suffering is a pervasive discourse in *huayno* songs as well as narratives about *huayno* performers and listeners. In the context of an overwhelmingly Catholic country like Peru, suffering has often been conceived as an inevitable experience and even a potentially virtuous act (see Butterworth 2014b).

However, while the *animador* (alongside the other performers) plays a powerful role in framing audiences' experiences and identifications, the audience is far from passive. Singers, in particular, are at the mercy of public evaluations, which frequently make use of ethical criteria as a means of assessing the relative value of artists. The extent to which artists are perceived to have worked hard to get where they are, felt deep emotions, endured suffering and remained humble ('ethical substances' to be worked on) is central to audiences' evaluations of performers.[11] The fact that ethics is so fundamental to such evaluations is not to deny the importance of aesthetics: rather, the ethical and the aesthetic are inextricably entwined. In addition to the circulation of their life stories, the ability of performers to meet the ethical criteria mentioned above is contingent upon the sound of their voices, their manipulation of language, their dress and their gestures. Vocal breaks, quivers and sighs, for example, all serve to demonstrate emotional vulnerability and feelingfulness. This is further emphasized by singing with a hand on one's chest or outstretched as if appealing to a higher power. Alternatively, a clenched fist may convey a sense of stoicism in the face of adversity. *Huayno* divas' dresses, too, communicate an ethical message: while many female celebrities in Peru often dress in an overtly sexualized manner (such as vedettes), female *huayno* singers' outfits are rather moderate by comparison, enabling them to maintain an ethical emphasis on sentiment as opposed to sexuality.[12]

The ethical work of performers is not only about caring for their own selves but also about demonstrating understanding of the ethical and emotional lives of others. This is distinct from Foucault's indication that the care of the self implies a certain relationship with others, as, for Foucault, this is a hierarchical, instrumental and pedagogical relationship in which 'listening to the lessons of a master' (1997: 287) becomes central to the care of the self. A more relevant reference point in the case of *huayno* performance is Adam Smith's writings on sentimentalism and sympathy (1982 [1759]), which extol the virtues of imagining what it might feel like to be in someone else's shoes. It is arguably this empathic impulse that makes sentimental public culture – such as *huayno* – so key to the way people feel emotionally connected to fellow members of social groups, publics and nations. Indeed, when I asked *huayno* fans why they liked the genre they consistently drew attention to the fact that singers give voice to and demonstrate understanding of the everyday trials and tribulations of ordinary people – a euphemistic label for a working-class, Andean-migrant public.[13] For example, when I suggested to my friend Fanny Corrales Quispe, a female *huayno* fan in her late twenties, that as far as *huayno* was concerned love always seemed to be 'something bad', she responded: 'Of course, because it makes you relive it, I mean, it's the life that you live; there *is* a lot of betrayal, a lot of suffering'. There was a sense of recognition, therapy and catharsis at work. As one Andean migrant from Ancash suggested (perhaps invoking a generic story about being a migrant rather than her own subjective experience):

> You come to the capital and it's not how you thought it would be. It's unpleasant, at times you earn very little, at times there's not even any work for you. All these things can make you sad, they contribute, and [you think] 'a matter of the heart, yes that's where they sing it to me, I'll take myself there and find refuge, with a couple of beers'.

At *huayno* concerts, the pleasures, pains and ambivalences of people's ethical and emotional lives are worked through as psychodrama. Audience members, and principally women, sing and gesture along with the 'autobiographies of collective experience' (Berlant 2008: vii) performed by *huayno* stars, sharing in an aestheticization of narratives of painful love, complicated family lives and homesickness – in other words, 'matters of the heart'. *Huayno* spectacles afford opportunities for subject positions to be tried on, whether sincerely or ambivalently, through intimate exchanges, physical copresence and shared embodiment. Furthermore, at events such as these this care of the self necessitates care of others.

Conclusion

This chapter has analysed *huayno* spectacles as ethical events and charted corresponding processes of ethical subject formation. It has emphasized the role of the *animador*, who, through his or her verbal and gestural performance, repeatedly constructs a series of moral expectations and ethical contexts in which spectators are coaxed into and afforded the opportunity to adopt particular subject positions. In conjunction with other elements of *huayno* performance, the *animador* encourages a series of behaviours and identifications surrounding alcoholic intoxication. Drinking beer at *huayno* shows is a polyvalent act, variously enabling the embodiment of social ideals of reciprocity and individualistic notions of escape and remembrance. Moreover, it has been argued here that drinking often functions as an embodied affirmation of Andean migrant identity, a subject position that people often inhabit with a sense of ambivalence due to long histories of ethnic discrimination. As spectators respond somatically to questions such as 'Who's drinking?' and 'Where are the sufferers?', notions of sensorial and emotional excess combine, creating crossovers between drinking/drunken and sentimental subjects. Public displays of emotion are a central component of ethical practices at *huayno* events. Through the *animador*'s patter, audience members are frequently hailed as emotional subjects that have loved and been betrayed. Spectators, too, typically evaluate performers on their ability to demonstrate lived experiences of such intense emotion through their vocal and bodily performance and, in turn, to empathize with the emotional and ethical lives of ordinary people. In sum, *huayno* spectacles act as privileged sites for embodied, affective and intersubjective ethical practices.

Acknowledgements

The fieldwork upon which this study is based was facilitated by an Arts and Humanities Research Council Doctoral Award. I would like to thank the many performers, audience members and friends in Peru that educated me in the ways of *huayno*. I am very grateful to the *animador* Jaime Ponce, who generously shared his time and wisdom with me and made this particular study possible. Finally, I would like to thank the editors for their patience and invaluable feedback.

James Butterworth received his undergraduate degree in Music from the University of Cambridge and Master's and Ph.D. in Ethnomusicology from Royal Holloway, University of London. His research centres on the anthropology and sociology of music, focusing specifically on Peruvian and Latin American music as well as hip-hop in Britain. In 2013 he was the recipient of the Society for Ethnomusicology's LACSEM prize for his paper entitled 'Divas and Entrepreneurs: Blurring the Boundaries between Art and Business in Peruvian

Commercial Huayno Music'. In 2015–16 he was a Research Associate on the AHRC-funded 'Performing Hip Hop Englishness' Project at the University of Cambridge, and in 2016 began as a British Academy Postdoctoral Fellow in Music at the University of Oxford.

Notes

1. All interlocutors' words in this chapter have been translated from Spanish to English by the author.
2. The type of *huayno* discussed here is referred to by Tucker (2013a, 2013b) as '*huayno norteño*' (northern *huayno*) and by Ferrier (2010) as '*huayno con arpa*' (harp *huayno*). Lloréns (1983), Turino (1988), Romero (2002) and Alfaro (2005) discuss various manifestations of *huayno* in Lima. Tucker (2013b) examines *huayno* from Ayacucho and its reputation for sophistication, refinement and artistry. For discussion of *huayno* in Ancash see Otter (1985), in the Mantaro Valley see Romero (2001) and in Conima see Turino (1993).
3. Mass rural–urban migration throughout the twentieth century has been fundamental in Peru's political, economic, social and cultural development. Peru changed from being 73.1 per cent rural in 1940 to 53 per cent urban in 1972 (Cotler 1978: 290). Fuelled by desires for better employment, education and living standards, as well as people escaping the violence of Peru's civil war in the 1980s, the population of the capital, Lima, has increased year on year until the present day where the number of inhabitants now exceeds eight million (almost one-third of Peru's entire population).
4. While sharing characteristics with *cumbia* in other Latin American countries, Peruvian *cumbia* has a distinct stylistic and social history, marked by interactions with music and musicians from the Amazon and the Andes (Romero 2002; Tucker 2013c).
5. It should be noted that most *animadores* tend to be men, though certainly not all. Women do also act as *animadores* but typically they enjoy some celebrity status beyond the context of *huayno*, often as models, presenters or media personalities.
6. For discussion of music-making at Andean *fiestas* see Turino (1993), Romero (2001) and Stobart (2006).
7. The use of the term 'interpellation' in this chapter refers to Althusser's notion that individuals are hailed as subjects that are always already the product of ideology or social structure (1971).
8. Distinctions between 'morality' and 'ethics' are often far from clear in anthropological literature. In this chapter 'moral' is used to refer to relatively stable, well-defined and socially agreed upon understandings about what one should and should not do and which one is typically compelled to follow. The term 'ethics', on the other hand, is used to refer to a practical, everyday and embodied mode of conduct, encompassing thoughts, feelings, actions and judgements.
9. See also Weismantel (1991) on the image of the 'drunken Indian' in the Ecuadorian popular imagination.
10. The word '*chévere*' is an extremely common colloquialism in Peru, which is less common in other Spanish-speaking countries and thus helps to emphasize the notion of a Peruvian 'homeland' linguistically.

11. Kringelbach (2013: 98–120) makes similar observations about the importance of moral ideas in public evaluations of celebrity dance performers and performances in Senegal.
12. I do not seek to aestheticize the ethical here, much like Faubion (2001), who refutes the criticism that Foucault was an aestheticist, having famously said: 'But couldn't everyone's life become a work of art?' (Foucault 1997: 261).
13. Similar discourses have been identified in U.S. country music (Fox 1992: 56) and in Greek *rebétiko* (Zaimakis 2009: 21).

References

Alfaro, S. 2005. 'The Cultural Industries and Ethnic Identities of Huayno' [Las Industrias Culturales e Identidades Étnicas del Huayno], in C.M. Pinilla (ed.), *Arguedas and Peru Today [Arguedas y El Peru de Hoy]*. Lima: SUR Casa de Estudios del Socialismo, pp. 57–76.

Althusser, L. 1971. *Lenin and Philosophy and Other Essays*, trans. B. Brewster. London: New Left Books.

Berlant, L. 2008. *The Female Complaint: The Unfinished Business of Sentimentality in American Culture*. Durham, NC: Duke University Press.

Brennan, T. 2004. *The Transmission of Affect*. Ithaca, NY: Cornell University Press.

Butterworth, J. 2014a. 'Andean Divas: Emotion, Ethics and Intimate Spectacle in Peruvian Huayno Music', Ph.D. dissertation. London: Royal Holloway, University of London.

———. 2014b. 'The Ethics of Success: Paradoxes of the Suffering Neoliberal Self in the Andean Peruvian Music Industry', *Culture, Theory and Critique* 55: 212–32.

———. 2014c. 'Rethinking Spectacle and Indigenous Consumption: Commercial Huayno Music in Peru', in H. Gilbert and C. Gleghorn (eds), *Recasting Commodity and Spectacle in the Indigenous Americas*. London: Institute of Latin American Studies, pp. 131–49.

Canclini, N.G. 2001. *Consumers and Citizens: Globalization and Multicultural Conflicts*, trans. G. Yúdice. Minneapolis: University of Minnesota Press.

Cotler, J. 1978. *Classes, State and Nation in Peru [Clases, Estado y Nación en El Perú]*. Lima: Instituto de Estudios Peruanos.

Downing, L. 2008. *The Cambridge Introduction to Michel Foucault*. Cambridge: Cambridge University Press.

Dueck, B. 2013a. 'Civil Twilight: Country Music, Alcohol and the Spaces of Manitoban Aboriginal Sociability', in G. Born (ed.), *Music, Sound and Space: Transformations of Public and Private Experience*. Cambridge: Cambridge University Press, pp. 239–56.

———. 2013b. *Musical Intimacies and Indigenous Imaginaries: Aboriginal Music and Dance in Public Performance*. New York: Oxford University Press.

Faubion, J.D. 2001. 'Toward an Anthropology of Ethics: Foucault and the Pedagogies of Autopoiesis', *Representations* 74: 83–104.

———. 2011. *An Anthropology of Ethics*. Cambridge: Cambridge University Press.

Ferrier, C. 2010. *Harp Huayno: Global Styles in the New Andean Popular Music [El Huayno con Arpa: Estilos Globales en la Nueva Música Popular Andina]*. Lima: PUCP.

Foucault, M. 1985. *The Use of Pleasure: Volume 2 of the History of Sexuality*, trans. R. Hurley. New York: Vintage Books.

———. 1997. *Ethics: Subjectivity and Truth*, ed. P. Rabinow, trans. R. Hurley and others. London: Penguin.
Fox, A.A. 1992. 'The Jukebox of History: Narratives of Loss and Desire in the Discourse of Country Music', *Popular Music* 11: 53–72.
Gregg, M., and G.J.J. Seigworth (eds). 2010. *The Affect Theory Reader*. Durham, NC: Duke University Press.
Harvey, P. 1994. 'Gender, Community and Confrontation: Power Relations in Drunkenness in Ocongate, Southern Peru', in M. McDonald (ed.), *Gender, Drink and Drugs*. Oxford: Berg, pp. 209–33.
Herzfeld, M. 1997. *Cultural Intimacy: Social Poetics in the Nation-State*. New York: Routledge.
Hirschkind, C. 2006. *The Ethical Soundscape: Cassette Sermons and Islamic Counterpublics*. New York: Columbia University Press.
Jennings, J., and B.J. Bowser (eds). 2009. *Drink, Power, and Society in the Andes*. Gainesville: University Press of Florida.
Kringelbach, H.N. 2013. *Dance Circles: Movement, Morality and Self-Fashioning in Urban Senegal*. Oxford: Berghahn.
Laidlaw, J. 2014. *The Subject of Virtue: An Anthropology of Ethics and Freedom*. Cambridge: Cambridge University Press.
Lambek, M. (ed.). 2010. *Ordinary Ethics: Anthropology, Language, and Action*. New York: Fordham University Press.
Lloréns, J.A. 1983. *Popular Music in Lima: Criollos and Andeans [Música Popular en Lima: Criollos y Andinos]*. Lima: Instituto de Estudios Peruanos.
Massumi, B. 2002. *Parables for the Virtual: Movement, Affect, Sensation*. Durham, NC: Duke University Press.
Moore, H. 2011. *Still Life: Hopes, Desires and Satisfactions*. Cambridge: Polity.
Otter, E.D. 1985. *Music and Dance of Indians and Mestizos in an Andean Valley of Peru*. Delft: Eburon.
Romero, R.R. 2001. *Debating the Past: Music, Memory, and Identity in the Andes*. New York: Oxford University Press.
———. 2002. 'Popular Music and the Global City: Huayno, Chicha, and Techno-cumbia in Lima, Peru', in W.A. Clark (ed.), *From Tejano to Tango: Essays on Latin American Popular Music*. New York: Routledge, pp. 217–39.
Shouse, E. 2005. 'Feeling, Emotion, Affect', *M/C Journal* 8(6). Retrieved 5 July 2015 from http://journal.media-culture.org.au/0512/03-shouse.php.
Smith, A. 1982 [1759]. *The Theory of Moral Sentiments*. Indianapolis: Liberty Fund.
Stobart, H. 2006. *Music and the Poetics of Production in the Bolivian Andes*. Aldershot: Ashgate.
Stokes, M. 2010. *The Republic of Love: Cultural Intimacy in Turkish Popular Music*. Chicago, IL: The University of Chicago Press.
Taylor, C. 1994. 'The Politics of Recognition', in A. Gutmann (ed.), *Multiculturalism: Examining the Politics of Recognition*. Princeton, NJ: Princeton University Press, pp. 25–73.
Thrift, N. 2008. *Non-Representational Theory: Space, Politics, Affect*. Abingdon: Routledge.
Tucker, J. 2013a. 'Producing the Andean Voice: Popular Music, Folkloric Performance, and the Possessive Investment in Indigeneity', *Latin American Music Review* 34: 31–70.

———. 2013b. *Gentleman Troubadours and Andean Pop Stars: Huayno Music, Media Work, and Ethnic Imaginaries in Urban Peru*. Chicago, IL: The University of Chicago Press.

———. 2013c. 'From the World of the Poor to the Beaches of Eisha: Chicha, Cumbia, and the Search for a Popular Subject in Peru', in H.F. L'Hoeste and P. Vila (eds), *Cumbia! Scenes of a Migrant Latin American Music Genre*. Durham, NC: Duke University Press, pp. 138–67.

Turino, T. 1988. 'The Music of Andean Migrants in Lima, Peru: Demographics, Social Power, and Style', *Latin American Music Review* 9: 127–50.

———. 1993. *Moving Away from Silence: Music of the Peruvian Altiplano and the Experience of Urban Migration*. Chicago, IL: The University of Chicago Press.

Weismantel, M.J. 1991. 'Maize Beer and Andean Social Transformations: Drunken Indians, Bread Babies, and Chosen Women', *Modern Language Notes* 106: 861–79.

Zaimakis, Y. 2009. '"Bawdy Songs and Virtuous Politics": Ambivalence and Controversy in the Discourse of the Greek Left on *Rebetiko*', *History and Anthropology* 20: 15–36.

Chapter 6

A Sense of Togetherness
Music Promotion and Ethics in Glasgow

Evangelos Chrysagis

The Music Promoter as an Ethical Subject

This chapter discusses the practices of Cry Parrot, a Glasgow-based music promoter under the creative control of one person, Stuart.[1] The account revolves around Stuart's promotional techniques, entrepreneurial strategies and the consideration of the practical judgements that informed and shaped his conduct over the course of my fieldwork (2010–11). On a basic level, concert promoters deal with the organizational and practical aspects of music performances (see Laing 2003). These may include, among other tasks, booking bands, hiring venues, providing food and accommodation for performers, arranging payment and coordinating the distribution of promotional material, such as posters and flyers. Evidently, the role of promoters is both intrinsically complex and highly flexible, demanding adaptability and careful judgement.

Concert promoters are now perceived as 'the new ruling class within the music industries' (Cloonan 2012: 155). Yet, as Elina Hytönen-Ng claims with reference to small-scale, local music promotion, 'the promoter cannot be viewed as a commercially oriented operator' (2015: 68). In an article about the significance of promoters in live music, Matt Brennan and Emma Webster ask: 'Are promoters corporate entities? Gig organizers? Rights holders?' (2011: 3). Their answer is that promoters can take all of these roles, but I further argue that the aforementioned characteristics can be nested within a promoter's subject position and that the study of promotional practices requires an emphasis on ethics. Thus, while 'promoters have been well aware that the environment in which they have to work is material as well as cultural and political as well as economic' (Behr et al. 2016: 6), here I seek to underscore the fact that promotional activities are also shaped by ethical considerations. In addition, my ethnographic analysis simultaneously traces the ways in which promotional practices contribute to the culmination of a particular ethos.

This chapter, therefore, will focus on the figure of the music promoter as an ethical subject. In an effort to account for the ethical modalities of Stuart's modus operandi, inspiration is drawn from James D. Faubion's *An Anthropology of Ethics* (2011). Faubion takes as his starting point Foucault's writings on ethics as a form of self-fashioning and embraces the parameters of ethical subjectivation, substance and telos (see Foucault 1985: 26–28), while acknowledging the importance of ethical work or *askēsis*, epitomized by technologies of the self (idem 1997: 223–51). Nevertheless, Foucault's fourfold apparatus was not completed and exhibits limitations that invite adjustments (see also Chapter 5). Faubion embarks on a painstaking reformulation of this schema, providing important revisions. For example, Foucault's approach fails to register 'ethical complexity', which conveys the possibility of actors – not necessarily 'individuals' – striving towards multiple ethical goals and indicates the ways in which different subject positions relate to one another.[2] Similarly, although Foucault's mode of subjectivation refers to how people engage with moral codes or rules, it does not acknowledge that these deontological possibilities may also include exemplars, ideals or 'role models' that compel subjects to undertake ethical work beyond duty (see Humphrey 1997). An important consequence of this is that Foucault does not adequately elucidate the intrinsic role of the 'other', especially in the form of the ethical pedagogue: someone who sets an example and not in the narrow sense of an instructor. A final lacuna detected by Faubion concerns the decisive role of judgement in shaping the subject's ethical telos, a capacity that is not formally addressed in Foucault's work. Faubion formally restores the cardinal importance of judgement by adding to Foucault's four parameters the mode of ethical judgement.

The mediation of ethical subjectivation by the mode of judgement suggests that actors may often demonstrate behaviour that is simultaneously ethical and 'immoral' (Stafford 2010: 188). Yet one of the indispensable features of the framework proposed by Faubion is the grounding of ethics within the intersubjective, without falling into moral obligation and the Durkheimian 'social' (see Laidlaw 2002, 2014: 16–23).[3]

The remainder of the chapter will describe ethnographically Stuart's engagement in live music promotion, his concrete practices associated with the process of hosting bands and the specific ideas and values that shaped Cry Parrot's promotional ethos. In other words, this chapter provides an account of Stuart's ethical subjectivation as a music promoter. Following the discussion of his initial involvement in music promotion is a detailed consideration of Stuart's promotional activities and his gradual conversion from a 'do-it-yourself' (DiY) register to what he called 'independent' promotion. Exercising judgement was crucial to this process. Then, Stuart's ethical complexity is discussed before his telos – which concerns the accomplishment and establishment of a particular ethos – is explored. The final section examines the object of Stuart's *askēsis*, the dimension of his practice targeted for ethical exercise and review: his ethical substance. What precedes the consideration of the parameters of Stuart's ethics is an ethnographic account of two music events that empirically exemplify his alleged conversion.

From Rags to Riches

Mitchell's was a small pub in Glasgow. Stuart explained to me that it was free to hire, but because a sound system was not installed appropriate equipment had to be carried to the venue in order to set it up for a gig. The venue was spread over two floors and the gig would take place downstairs, in a small basement area. As I entered the basement, there were musical instruments and other pieces of equipment placed on the ground, including two drum kits, guitar amplifiers and a vintage wooden case containing effects pedals, as well as a table on which Stuart had placed his laptop and a plastic cup full of change. Occupying half of the basement's space, musical equipment also served as the only visual boundary between the 'stage' and the area designated for the audience.

Stuart had cooked for the two bands in the line-up, consisting of Quack Quack and Sexy Entourage, while members of Leeds-based Quack Quack would sleep in one of his friends' flat tonight. Stuart attempted to connect the sound mixer and the main speakers to his laptop in his effort to play some background music before the event kicked off, but he eventually decided to use his laptop speakers because changing the set-up was seemingly complex and time-consuming. It was just after 9pm, the event's scheduled start time, but there were no more than fifteen people in the venue, including band members. People placed the cover charge for the night (£3) in the plastic cup and I did the same. Stuart welcomed everyone in a friendly manner and the atmosphere felt quite intimate and relaxing. However, Stuart looked a little disappointed at the low turnout, which according to him was due to other gigs taking place on the same night. By the time Sexy Entourage, a local band, were ready to begin their set more than thirty people were in the audience and the basement was packed. 'Every time it's like this, you don't know what will happen in the end', Stuart told me. After the bands' brief sets, I left Mitchell's with a feeling that I had been to a friendly musical gathering rather than what could be termed a 'gig'.

Stuart kept on hosting such small and intimate gigs but over time both the musical scope and the presentation of his events evolved and diversified considerably. Almost a year after that evening at Mitchell's, John Maus, a North American musician, was touring the U.K. and Stuart had booked him for a Glasgow event at Mono, which he expected to sell out. I had reserved my ticket online weeks in advance. When I arrived at Mono people were standing outside and I noticed a board stand with a poster advertising the event. Inside the venue there was a table with John Maus merchandise. There was also a vinyl record for sale by the London-based band Plug, who would also perform tonight. The show would be opened by a solo performance by Remember Remember, a local act.

Tom from *Crasier Frane* (a local fanzine) was sitting behind the table along with Alan, who occasionally helped Stuart with the gigs. I showed them my booking reference number and received a red 'CP' stamp on my wrist. Stuart, who was standing nearby, expressed his excitement about the gig and stated that he had made a substantial effort to promote it. This was understandable considering that John Maus was one of his favourite acts. I asked him what time Remember Remember would go on stage and after consulting his watch Stuart replied that the gig would start 'in seven minutes'. Mono had almost reached capacity and the only unoccupied area was in front of the wooden platform that served as the stage. The bar, opposite the stage, was also busy with people queuing for drinks. Remember Remember's set lasted half an hour, with the audience enjoying the performance; I spotted two photographers among the audience. After Plug's set and John Maus's dramatized performance the lights and background music came back on to signal that the gig was over. Tonight there were no technical issues or delays and Stuart seemed happy and relaxed. As I was leaving Mono, Stuart was standing near the exit saying goodbye to each one of us. He was holding a pile of flyers that advertised music events organized by Bryony from Tracer Trails, who was on the opposite side of the door also giving away flyers. I asked Stuart whether I could take the poster from the board stand and he agreed.

Junior Nuts and Seeds

A Motherwell native, Stuart resided there with the rest of his family and he would commute to Glasgow by train. In his early twenties, he was a good-natured and instantly likeable person. When I started my research in January 2010, Stuart was still studying for a degree in Film and Television Studies at the University of Glasgow. Shortly after his graduation in June 2010, the government announced its plans to abolish the U.K. Film Council, a decision that left Stuart wondering about the usefulness of his degree and his employability: 'I have a better CV in event management', he told me characteristically, hinting at his accumulated practical experience.

During his university years Stuart had a job at a supermarket. More recently, he had started DJ'ing in Glasgow bars and music venues. Stuart was not a musician. Following his graduation he continued his DJ'ing activities, and at the end of that summer he took up a six-month internship at the Centre for Contemporary Arts (CCA). In October, he became the music programmer for Nice 'n' Sleazy, a live music venue, and a few months later, after his internship had finished, he took over the schedule for the venue's club nights as well. While the CCA internship required him to work in the Centre from 10am to 6pm on weekdays, the job at Nice 'n' Sleazy was quite flexible and allowed Stuart to work remotely from the comfort of his home.

His educational and socioeconomic background aside, the form of Stuart's involvement in music promotion reflected a process of attempting to live up to specific values and ideals, encapsulated by promoters that had preceded Cry Parrot. Stuart had two such examples locally: one was Nuts and Seeds, a now-defunct DiY music promoter (see also Chrysagis 2016). Stuart praised their practice, which involved a substantial amount of care towards the bands they catered for. He followed their steps closely and as they decided to cease all activities Stuart became known as 'junior Nuts and Seeds'. Their demise left a gap in the city's stream of DiY gigs, a situation that Stuart, among others, strived to remedy. Moreover, Stuart was inspired by the local club promoters and music collective LuckyMe, whose events exhibited various characteristics that he sought to implement, such as memorabilia, a party atmosphere and what he perceived as a 'forward-looking and expansive' outlook. Furthermore, Stuart believed that the main reason for the recent resurgence and persistence of DiY activity in Glasgow was a common dissatisfaction with various promotion companies and their practices. This dissatisfaction largely stemmed from the notorious 'pay-to-play' policy.[4] Therefore, Stuart's ethical conditioning was fuelled by positive exemplars on the one hand and by examples to be consciously avoided on the other.

The idea of promoting gigs dates back to when Stuart was in secondary school, and it was Blake, Stuart's school friend, who had named Cry Parrot. It was only in university, and specifically in 2007, that they managed to put their ideas into practice, but Stuart ended up running Cry Parrot on his own two years after launching it. Shortly after Blake's voluntary departure Stuart recruited Graham, and this is how Cry Parrot was set up when I began my fieldwork. The first time I met Stuart he presented it to me as a joint effort between Graham and himself. Catherine, Stuart's girlfriend, would design posters and flyers, as well as contributing to the realization of music events. In October 2010, Graham left in order to take up a job with a well-known local promoter, from which time he was not allowed to take part in Cry Parrot activities due to a perceived conflict of interest. Just a few months earlier, Aidan had stepped in and he went on to become Stuart's right-hand man. He remained in this position for almost a year, but he eventually had to leave due to his other commitments, such as running the University of Glasgow's Subcity Radio. In the meantime, Stuart and Catherine had broken up. By the time my research was coming to an end, Cry Parrot had become an individual affair: 'It's me on my own, really', Stuart declared to me in June 2011.

Even when other individuals were involved in the organization of events, they seemed to play a peripheral role. This was evidenced by the ways in which

Stuart assessed, albeit hesitantly, their influence on him, saying that his former affiliates had not affected his ideas about music promotion. However, Stuart acknowledged their dedication, passion and acute awareness of all things musical. That Stuart was the main creative force behind Cry Parrot could also be illustrated by his supervisory role. His associates did have a degree of creative control, but the operation as a whole was overseen and commanded by him. In essence, then, Cry Parrot had been Stuart's project all along and he would assign specific tasks to certain people depending upon the circumstances at hand. In short, Cry Parrot had a hierarchical nature. Apart from the aforementioned frequent collaborators, Stuart also engaged other people in the project, such as Alan, who was on the door at the John Maus event, or when, for example, he had to make arrangements to accommodate touring bands for the night. For this, Stuart relied on his friends, usually from local bands. Visitors would sleep on 'couches, floors or mattresses', and to return the favour Stuart would enlist his friends' bands for future events.

The main reason why Stuart lived in Motherwell was his financial situation, which changed for the better once his unpaid internship at the CCA ended and his work for Nice 'n' Sleazy became a full-time job. As a result, when I finished my fieldwork Stuart was already in the process of moving to Glasgow. As he put it: 'My network is here and all my friends are here and quite happy as well'. As such, the city as a particular place with specific social and cultural dynamics can be perceived as an auxiliary moral agent (see also Basso 1996). Objects, too, impinge upon one's ethical self-fashioning, but they are gradually transformed into ethical 'tools' that assist rather than constrain the becoming of the subject. Various materials at once determined and facilitated Stuart's subjectivation. The money kept from successful gigs, for instance, was not seen as profit but would be invested in future gigs or the production of memorabilia, such as stickers and badges – exactly as LuckyMe had done previously. Yet some money from the proceeds was also put into paying off the debt that Stuart had accumulated due to his engagement in music promotion (see below).

The experience of organizing several small-scale gigs had solidified Stuart's practice, while the number of Cry Parrot shows remained relatively stable during my fieldwork. Whereas initially Stuart had to confront various issues due to his lack of experience, he was now more confident about his efficiency as a music promoter. For Stuart, certain aspects always had to be taken into account when organizing music events, including bookings, fees and combining appropriate bands in the line-up. Other considerations included communications, the production and distribution of promotional material, providing food and accommodation for the bands, setting up performance spaces and, last but not least, arranging payment. In the following section, the concrete practices associated with the promotion of Cry Parrot gigs are examined.

From DiY to Independent

Music listening preceded the formation of Cry Parrot and provided the thrust for Stuart's continuous involvement in music promotion. For example, the vast majority of Cry Parrot gigs featured bands and musicians whose music Stuart appreciated greatly. Stuart's interest in music could also be said to constitute a final but critical dimension of his ethical subjectivation. According to Hennion (2007), musical taste suggests primarily an *activity* that involves participation and reflection. Taste and distaste are, therefore, both pedagogical and reflective technologies of self-formation (Faubion 2011: 137–38). The ongoing cultivation of musical taste was a necessary technology for the delineation of Cry Parrot's subject position.

The main criterion with which different individuals were taken on board as Stuart's collaborators was their genuine enthusiasm for the musical diversity underpinning Cry Parrot's ethos. Both Graham and Aidan were recruited on the basis of attending Stuart's gigs and expressing their interest. Even when Graham moved to commercial music promotion he continued to attend most Cry Parrot shows. Stuart was respectful towards Graham's decision, but he pointed out that his new job would to some extent dictate the breadth of his music listening. As Martin Cloonan puts it: 'the more professional the promoter, the more they are subject to *other people's* tastes' (cited in Webster 2011: 38; italics in the original).

Cry Parrot did not occupy an office or any other establishment and organizational matters were arranged mainly through email. Stuart's critical objective was to stay up-to-date with his inbox. Initially, he would approach bands or booking agents, but as his gigs became increasingly popular and Stuart had managed to build a wide range of contacts in the music industry in and outside of Glasgow, booking agents would also contact him with gig offers. His personal preferences aside, Stuart would also browse the line-ups of music festivals to identify bands that would fit within Cry Parrot's musical scope. He hosted a wide range of musicians from the U.K., as well as abroad, with the latter mainly consisting of touring bands. This had the advantage of not incurring additional costs for travel and allowed Stuart to keep door and ticket prices to a minimum.

Local bands normally included young acts from Glasgow that would open the show for the headlining touring bands. Carefully choosing the line-up for these events constituted an important exercise because it combined and balanced an array of factors, such as Stuart's musical proclivities, logistics and audience expectations. This process required a certain amount of organizational skill but its ethical aspects were predicated upon self-examination. This, according to Stuart, stemmed from the idea that promoters allegedly had 'big egos', expressed in their decisions about which shows to promote and which not. However, Stuart remained open-minded regarding the musical dimension of Cry Parrot and his job at Nice 'n' Sleazy was a contributing factor.

Money was a thorny issue for Stuart. As a result, his attitude towards finances was perhaps the most important ethical exercise. When Stuart launched Cry Parrot, his jobs at the supermarket and as a DJ sustained his practice. Later on, he would organize fundraising gigs – what he called 'unofficial funding' – and towards the end of my fieldwork he could still keep Cry Parrot afloat thanks to his full-time wage from Nice 'n' Sleazy. For the most part, financial matters with touring bands were settled in advance, with Stuart being able to offer £50–80 as a guarantee. However, he could not afford any guarantees for local bands. When I enquired about the bands' response to this, Stuart replied that most of them recognized that it was impossible to receive guarantees considering the small-scale character of these events, but he also said that some acts were more 'career driven'. If audience turnout was satisfactory, all bands, including support acts, would receive additional funds.

Booking a venue for a music event was largely dictated by financial considerations and venue availability. Cheap or free venues were in high demand and Cry Parrot would regularly host gigs in places such as The 13th Note, the CCA and Mitchell's during the first half of my fieldwork. In venues that did not employ sound engineers Stuart would pay his friends to work on the sound. Although in most cases bands would receive more than what was initially agreed, there were instances when gigs had produced a deficit. Door charges were kept low, with most gigs around £4–5, but occasionally rising to £7–8 for 'bigger' bands. Stuart believed that by keeping the fees as low as possible more people would have the opportunity to attend the gigs. Ultimately, this would be beneficial for the bands, because initially he would give all the proceeds to them minus the costs, which would allow him to fund future ventures.

A particular approach towards money and financial decisions was thus shaped by necessity but also Stuart's will to support the bands and make Cry Parrot gigs accessible to audiences. Publicity for these events would consist of the circulation of posters and flyers, as well as online advertising via social media and Cry Parrot's website (see Chrysagis 2016). Despite his lack of financial resources, Stuart would try and accommodate bands for the night wherever possible. Another of Stuart's main principles was to prepare food for musicians in the line-up, which was a common practice among local DiY promoters. The absence of luxury and comfort for the touring bands did not prevent them from responding positively about their host and Stuart sought to ensure that bands had a nice time in Glasgow by taking them on short excursions around the city and spending time with them.[5] Stuart would cater for bands' other requirements too, which normally involved the sourcing of appropriate musical equipment. It was not unusual for Stuart to bring a drum kit to the venue or negotiate instrument borrowing between bands in the line-up. Moreover, creating an intimate atmosphere for bands and audiences alike meant decorating event spaces. This was not always the case, though, and when it did happen the decor was usually not very elaborate: small touches such as lit candles seemed to be sufficient to transform a generic pub basement into a welcoming and cosy venue.

Over time, Stuart raised the prices of Cry Parrot gigs, which were now ticketed as well. Halfway through my fieldwork Stuart announced that he would issue tickets for all Cry Parrot gigs. People would still have the option to pay on the door, but Stuart had realized that many audience members felt more comfortable when buying their tickets in advance. The plastic cup with change at Mitchell's, which was subsequently mentioned several times in my fieldnotes, ultimately gave way to tickets that were sold by Monorail, the record shop hosted within Mono, and WeGotTickets, an online ticket outlet operating a paperless ticket system. The former charged a booking fee of 50p–£1 per ticket depending on the ticket price and the latter 10 per cent of the ticket's face value. Listening and talking to the audience, therefore, as well as paying attention to their feedback, urged Stuart to implement further changes, as any good entrepreneur would do, by adjusting his promotional tactics.

For example, talking about posters, he once told me: 'I've realized over time that some posters in the past were printed on bad paper and that it's important to do things to a higher standard'. The gradual transformation of Stuart's practice was also evident in the bands that he booked for the gigs. The booking process remained more or less similar, but the names that appeared on the bill were of much wider appeal. The sites that hosted Cry Parrot music events were now mostly conventional venues, such as Mono, Stereo and Nice 'n' Sleazy. Ironically, the first time I met Stuart he had mentioned that these venues were expensive to hire. A year later, he was able to book Nice 'n' Sleazy for free, while some of his gigs would take place at Stereo. By employing well-known venues Stuart could also minimize the risk of technical issues and avoid the need to carry and install a public address system for the night. Bigger bands meant additional expenses, however, because these bands required hotel accommodation.

The money factor had influenced other parts of the organizational process. Whereas before, local bands would be informed that payment depended on the turnout, Stuart would now provide guarantees to most bands. This was correlated with an increased turnout and the anticipation of success of events featuring specific bands. Yet one direct result of such a policy was that Stuart put himself at risk of losing more money: his accumulated debt was largely the outcome of paying guarantees for gigs that had failed to attract a substantial crowd. By contrast, while certain DiY promoters would pay the cover charge for the gigs they hosted – something that Stuart initially did too – they would never guarantee any money.

The shift in Stuart's approach to promotion was influenced by his practical knowledge, by his interaction with bands, audiences and other actors involved in music-making and, finally, by reflecting upon his own practices. This form of conscious reflection became the juncture at which Stuart, in assigning himself to the DiY subject position, had to consider the available possibilities or alternatives. This process is what Foucault calls 'problematization' or 'thought' (1997: 117). However, thought is not only one's reflection upon a problem, but 'what establishes the relation with oneself and with others and constitutes the human being as ethical subject' (ibid.: 200).

Interlude: A Scene of Crisis

Stuart's promotional practices did not constitute a straightforward adoption of a script. Rather, his approach punctuated a conversion from a DiY register to an 'independent' modus operandi. Gradually, Stuart veered away from the DiY blueprint as this had been inherited from Nuts and Seeds. This passage can be traced, perhaps unsurprisingly, in Stuart's changing perspective on and use of financial resources:

> A big turning point for me was in January [2011], when I put on Moon Unit [a local band] and it was in Nice 'n' Sleazy's. There were two supports, both of which were local. One hundred and seventy people paid in at £5 and I paid Moon Unit £250 and gave their supports £130 each. I took £150 from that gig because, well, they're getting paid loads of money .... I'm taking £150 and that's maybe forwarded to something, you know? Normally I would just give it, like, before, I would just give it all away. I think I was just quite intensely strict on the ethics.

This event and no doubt many others to a lesser extent gave rise to Stuart's questioning of what valorized such 'strict' ethics that encouraged DiY promoters to hand over all the proceeds to the performers.

This incident resembles what Faubion, following Weber's analysis on charismatic authority (1946), calls a 'scene of crisis' (2011: 81–90). While Weber's 'primal scene' refers to the extra-ordinary, a crisis 'is often of small scale, and at that scale is not at all foreign to what we usually think of as everyday life' (idem 2013: 300). Employing the allegoric essence of the Weberian scene allows it to be adapted to Stuart's subjectivation in order that the latter may be described in comparable but ethnographic terms: the foregoing event was a moment of 'crisis' that made Stuart realize that his habitual ways of promoting music events were problematic. Sensing that elements of his routinized practice, consonant with DiY ethics, would fail to live up to the necessities of long-term engagement in music promotion, he started questioning his approach. The ethical possibilities opened up from such a problematization were by definition non-normative and open-ended. Very quickly, though, this anethical moment gave way to emerging patterns, elements of which were already present in the transformation of Stuart's thought into action. These routines were consistent with the established logics and operating principles of another register: that of the independent promoter.

The Stigma and the Dilemma

In light of the above, the following questions emerge: What other factors influenced Stuart's decision to embrace independent promotion? What kinds of judgements were pertinent to his conversion? As has been described, thinking and interacting with audience members and others encompassed and sharpened Stuart's decision-making. Crucially, both processes were mediated by judgement. The philosopher Hannah Arendt argues that thinking is an activity that animates a process of self-constitution (2003: 105), but she distinguishes between thinking as objective and ethically neutral and judgement as situated and communicative (Lambek 2010a: 26). And, while conversation seemed to be instrumental to the formation and establishment of Stuart's ethical criteria in relation to music promotion, the attachment of criteria to the terms of a discourse does not clarify whether they precede or follow from agreement in judgement, while recourse to criteria usually implies disagreement (idem 2010b: 43). What is more, in Stuart's case such discursive interaction was occurring upon shifting grounds and ill-defined criteria.

Unavoidably, the terms 'DiY' and 'independent' were the two axes along which such discourse took place. The definition of 'DiY' was a consistently favourite discussion topic between Stuart and myself. He seemed extremely interested in clarifying what was involved in the term, as well as confused and frustrated by its volatile meaning, owing to the plural ways in which it was interpreted and put into practice. This was a common predicament within the local DiY network (see Chrysagis 2013). For Stuart, who was previously a 'DiY promoter' and lately had become 'an independent promoter with DiY ethics', thus distinguishing between DiY as a label and DiY as practice, providing clear definitions was not an easy task. Stuart framed 'independent' as follows:

> It's as ambiguous as DiY .... I guess [it refers to] people or individuals or acts less focused on a commercial aspect of the music and strongly focused on being creative? Creativity and a sense of going out and trying to do it yourself, rather relying on other people? Reading it back about how to define Cry Parrot now, it is an independent promoter with DiY ethics. It's something very fluid, I guess.

About DiY ethics he believed that: 'Again, it's just like independency [*sic*], it's a strong focus on the arts, a strong focus on inclusivity, a strong focus on a scene and people being together; these are the ethics, I think, in my mind'. Notice how the two definitions not only share a similar level of ambiguity, but, in fact, they could be used interchangeably.

Stuart considered the *term* DiY problematic: 'DiY, I think, is something that was forged out of punk, but DiY also suffers from the stigma of laziness. If someone says he's a DiY promoter, then certain people can go "Well, that's a lazy promoter", you know, "That's someone not doing it right"'. Thus, the negative connotations of such a label were undesirable, the implication being that a number of bands would potentially refrain from booking their Glasgow gigs through Stuart. However, 'DiY' conveyed positive messages as well, according to Stuart: 'DiY is something that's formed upon ethics that are troublesome … but ultimately a positive thing. I think "independent" is perhaps the word … . For me it keeps a sense that I'm open minded and I'm trying to do my own thing in my own way. *I just want to be ethical.* I think I just struggle with defining'.

In essence, then, while the 'DiY' label would trigger negative responses, Stuart perceived DiY ethics as positive. Mary Douglas's observation that labelling involves an increasing bias that leaves our assumptions unchallenged (2002 [1966]: 46) is useful here. Following Douglas, we could say that, because the established assumption identifies 'DiY' with 'laziness', the idea of a competent and attentive DiY promoter should be rejected as a 'discordant cue'. Otherwise, 'the structure of assumptions has to be modified' (ibid.: 45). The process of labelling is never ethically neutral; more so because it is not a matter of specific negative attributes conferring such labels. Rather, what leads to stigmatization is the incongruous relationship between our preconceptions and the qualities of a person, group or entity in a particular context (Goffman 1990 [1963]: 13). As Stuart put it, the problem for outsiders was not 'laziness' per se, but the notion of DiY not fitting within the stereotype of an efficient concert promoter. Of course, stigmatization does not guarantee the subjection of the stigmatized (Faubion 2011: 62), because it does not address the 'reverse' discourse (see Foucault 1978: 100–2), namely how the image of an accomplished music promoter could be accommodated within DiY. It seems, to me, that Stuart's engagement in the discourse about DiY and independent promotion revolved around exactly this counter-possibility.

Being caught between these two registers had elicited a form of 'moral torment' (Robbins 2004). Stuart constantly questioned his choices pertaining to the organization of shows and he was reluctant to implement or introduce new elements from fear that his practice would fall outside of the limits of DiY. For example, he had repeatedly wondered about whether using a film projector in Cry Parrot gigs would be consonant with the DiY ethos, which generally promoted an aesthetic of simplicity. And, of course, taking money from the proceeds was taboo. However, contrary to Robbins's informants, who found themselves in the midst of two conflicting and mutually exclusive ethical realms, for Stuart, in principle at least, there was no dilemma in the sense of being called to embrace one and renounce the other. The multifaceted nature of DiY would render any such dilemma ambiguous at best. It was rather a matter of scrutinizing the possibility of expanding an existing register in order to encompass a wider set of ideas and practices, which he perceived as necessary for the viability of the register itself. Converting from DiY to independent, therefore, was a semiotic shift that designated Stuart's effort to embed characteristics from independent promotion within an existing DiY framework. From this perspective, his mode of subjectivation did not contribute to the reproduction of the homeostatic characteristics of DiY promotion, but mainly to its alteration and diversification.

Stuart's ethical trajectory thus echoes David Hesmondhalgh's conviction that '[i]n an era of pragmatic acceptance of collaboration with major capital, there is a need to (re)develop a case against the majors [major record labels] which does not rely on a simplistic romanticism' (1999: 53). A similar shift in the realm of music promotion necessitated Stuart's continuous problematization interspersed with periods when the tendency to follow specific examples was stronger. 'The question arises', writes Arendt, 'whether there is really nothing to hold onto when we are called upon to decide that this is right and this is wrong', and the answer is that we 'cannot hold on to [*sic*] anything general, but to some particular that has become an example' (2003: 143). Insofar as actors have recourse to examples, ethical judgements rarely depend upon either universal 'common sense' or subjective intuition. Yet, as Stuart's creative appropriation of available ethical examples demonstrates, 'the example as exemplar may create stability by alluding to a larger whole that people (are made to) subscribe to, [but] it may ... also contain within it a potential instability, a possibility for becoming something else' (Højer and Bandak 2015: 8). Ethically speaking, this points towards the fluctuating degrees of self-determination that subjects have at their disposal and the alternating and mutually reinforcing nature of ethics and morality.

A Flurry of Activity

Stuart exhibited 'ethical complexity'. In striving to occupy a subject position pertinent to his musical interests and promotional practices, Stuart simultaneously became the occupant of another subject position, namely the one conditioned by his work in Nice 'n' Sleazy. One side effect was his relative lack of time and energy to treat the bands as he used to. Organizing an average of eight gigs per month, plus the regular club nights, plus the Cry Parrot shows, was both hard work and emotionally draining due to the interpersonal communication involved in the job. However, this tension was gradually neutralized and the two subject positions began to overlap considerably. While Cry Parrot progressively mutated to an independent promoter, it was Stuart's experience in DiY promotion that had allowed him to work for Nice 'n' Sleazy. In turn, the ethical scope of his initial position would be affected by Stuart's work experience in Nice 'n' Sleazy and the CCA. The ethics of Cry Parrot takes on further complexity if we account for Stuart's associates. Although relations with his affiliates were asymmetrical in the sense that Stuart was ultimately in command of the operations, at times Cry Parrot consisted of a subject position with multiple occupants.

This intrasubjective complexity was intensified by the accommodation of other subjects external to Cry Parrot, through Stuart's numerous collaborations with other promoters, venues and organizations. For instance, Stuart had formed a 'partnership' with the SWG3 Studio Warehouse, where he hosted monthly after-parties for the SWG3 gallery's exhibitions. Cross-promotion and collaboration with other institutions and organizations were not uncommon and Stuart saw his involvement in such mutual efforts as strengthening these events, by enabling him to bring different musical strands and diverse audiences together, nurture established connections and initiate new ones. Cross-promotion and other joint initiatives had the additional benefit of permitting Stuart to undertake projects of larger scale, such as the three-day festival he and Bryony from Tracer Trails were planning for September 2011.

Over time, Cry Parrot became a competitor within the local live-music industry, which Graham's company had recognized by banning him from continuing his promotional alliance with Stuart. Cry Parrot's ethical environment further included younger actors under Stuart's pedagogical supervision. One example was *Crasier Frane* and another was Red Room, a young promoter who had sought advice from Stuart for setting up a one-day festival. In his belief that the organizational aspects of live music promotion were essentially straightforward, Stuart's aim was to enhance the confidence of these young promoters in putting on their own events. To this end, he had also published an informative piece on noncorporate funding in the fanzine *Don't Make a Scene* (2014), a collection of essays, interviews and illustrations that was geared towards providing advice to aspiring DiY promoters. Stuart had the foresight to understand that Cry Parrot's long-term viability was correlated with the general well-being of the DiY music network in Glasgow (and beyond). Therefore, providing advice was directed towards ensuring continuous creative stimulation in music practice. By assisting other promoters and attracting new crowds to his events, Stuart facilitated local music's growing potential and established links between different actors, thus supporting their prolific activities and preventing them from fading out.

A Sense of Togetherness

Stuart's collaborative spirit had given rise to an idea of novelty and movement. In practical terms this involved hosting Cry Parrot music events in different venues so as to avoid becoming formulaic. Stuart entertained that:

> It would piss me off if Cry Parrot just felt stagnant. If you're continually putting on smaller bands you are generally getting the same people in every time and there's no push forward. I think what I'm basically trying to do is extend ... I'm not really aiming towards a certain thing as such; it's purely to try and solidify, perfect what this is all about.

Stuart's objective was to create a feeling of a 'gathering' or a 'party'. He believed that gigs should be based on mutual trust between promoters, musicians and audiences, whereas the music event as a whole should aim to foster 'a sense of togetherness'. I still remember his expression of disapproval and surprise when somebody stole my bottle of wine at a thirteen-band all-nighter at the Audio Lounge studio in Maryhill, where Stuart was DJ'ing. He said: '*Who* would do such a thing?'. This specific event had attracted around three hundred people. Stuart was not being naive but articulating his strong belief, stemming from his experience, that people attending similar events were conscious of the 'sense of togetherness' advocated by the local DiY network. Perhaps a similar feeling of intimacy was the reason for my inattentive behaviour in the first place.

Even if Stuart accomplished his telos, even if Cry Parrot became the exemplification of collaboration and intimacy, it would not be the end of the line:

> I guess people can rely on it [Cry Parrot]; they continue turning up and the network has expanded ... . That's what I want; I want to keep it exciting all the same, though. I think that's the big thing: I just want to keep it fresh. If you keep it dynamic, if it's something that's moving like a dynamic entity, to me, that brings more people on board.

Stuart's view resists complete routinization, that is, the process of transforming ethical value into habitual practice. While it unavoidably reduces ethical complexity, instituting a routine is not the telos of ethics but its temporary retraction (Faubion 2011: 114–15). Faubion argues that, once actors securely occupy their positions, ethics becomes dispositional (ibid.: 37). Yet this does not necessarily imply that the end of subjectivation – the occupancy of a subject position as the actor's ethical telos – amounts to a form of unreflective reproduction. For example, Stuart was not confined by the DiY subject position and he implemented various changes as a result of his *askēseis*. On the other hand, as Stuart's trajectory further demonstrates, ethical innovation is best conceived of through its relation to prescribed courses of action and as a form of adjustment of what is already in place, rather than operating completely outside of such regimens, giving rise to something novel.

Generosity

When Foucault speaks of 'ethical substance', he does not necessarily mean one's body: 'when a philosopher was in love with a boy', he writes, '[t]he problem was: Does he touch the boy or not? That's the ethical substance' (1997: 264). In reformulating Foucault's question, I would suggest that the problem for Stuart, his ethical substance, can be phrased as follows: Does he keep the proceeds or not? Does he give it all away or not? Of course, one obvious difference is that his problem, as opposed to the philosopher's predicament, admits of various degrees. But Stuart's ethical substance, what can be best referred to as 'generosity', has all the characteristics of malleability and neutrality that make it an appropriate candidate for the target of *askēsis* in bringing about his ethical telos (cf. Lambek 2010a: 20; Faubion 2011: 55). Generosity demanded ethical work. Hence the hallmark of Stuart's mode of subjectivation: how to *limit* his generosity that was detrimental to his long-term engagement in music promotion.[6] It was one or another use of money that pervaded Stuart's subjectivation: financial management as an ethically valorized practice and not merely as an impersonal, calculated and functional strategy (see also Ortiz 2013).

While generosity (or its absence) is usually manifested as a personal disposition, it belongs to the normative dimensions of systems, in this case to the DiY mode of conduct. Its regulation is not handed down as a set of rules, however, but such moderation is predicated upon a *'savoir-faire'* on the part of the subject (Foucault 1985: 62), a practice mediated through particular attitudes, themselves acquired through specific exercises. Stuart never conceded that he perceived or kept the proceeds from his promotional transactions as personal income or profit. It was evident, though, that the differences between his early and later practices were inextricably linked to a changing use of money. I would argue that the reason for such a shift was twofold: it related, first, to Stuart's experience of working in the local art and music industries, and second, to the financial deficit that certain Cry Parrot gigs had incurred. These reasons were interrelated, as both provided a glimpse into the economy of live music promotion.

Stuart's unpaid internship at the CCA was a case in point. Although it did not have a specific focus, towards the end of his tenure he was asked to produce the Centre's music programme. Stuart eventually refused on the basis of this task being 'a proper, full-time, paid job', which he would be keen to undertake had he been properly employed by the organization. Receiving a wage from Nice 'n' Sleazy had enhanced his conviction that the effort and time invested in music programming and promotion had to be financially rewarded. A common feature of both the CCA and Nice 'n' Sleazy was that they provided Stuart with an opportunity to deal with the more commercial aspects of the art and music worlds. This experience was not overtly positive: the CCA internship afforded him some insight into arts funding, which amid a global financial crisis Stuart believed that was 'crumbling apart', feeling that pursuing a career in the creative industries by following a publicly funded route was a risky affair. On the other hand, he became convinced that organizations in need of external funding tended to lose their focus on creative matters due to their explicit orientation towards attracting necessary resources for their projects.

Stuart's changing approach towards finances was also partly owing to the losses he had made over the years. He claimed that music promotion was not a profitable venture and he would cite as examples local commercial promoters who had decided to quit. Regarding the idea of keeping money from gigs to cover his earlier losses, Stuart mentioned that: 'I don't think it's a bad thing making money back that you've lost in a gig'. As mentioned above, Stuart did this with the most successful gigs and fundraising events, while he would forward some of the proceeds to future projects, memorabilia and equipment – to different kinds of 'investments', as he called them. Working through the conundrums and risks of particular uses of money necessitated considerable effort and diverse *askēseis*, because seemingly trivial changes in business practice immediately signalled a shift of ethical positioning. Nevertheless, the rhetorical question Stuart once posed to me revealed his intentions about the future of Cry Parrot: 'Why not take a wage if it consistently becomes something that is so busy all the time and acts are being paid really well?'

Conclusion: ~~Cry~~ Bye Parrot

The last time I saw Stuart was at the 'Bye Parrot' event in Stereo in December 2014 (Illustration 6.1). Stuart had recently managed to get a job in London as the Senior Producer at Cafe OTO, an internationally famous avant-garde music venue. Although Cry Parrot would go on an indefinite break, Stuart would still retain his musical affiliations in Glasgow through his role as a cocurator of Counterflows music festival. After having curated three instalments of Music Language festival (initially with Bryony from Tracer Trails), which incurred financial losses in 2013, Stuart was convinced that festival organization could not be sustained without external financial support, ideally from noncorporate sources, which Counterflows eventually managed to attract. Despite his repeated efforts, Stuart had only lately succeeded in securing some public funding for Cry Parrot music events, but this was not enough to sustain operations.

These recent developments partly reflect the relative lack of appropriate music infrastructure in Glasgow, as opposed to other cities such as London (see Williamson, Cloonan and Frith 2003). They also confirm Stuart's early intuition that promoters could not rely exclusively on public funds, especially due to the uncertain and volatile economic climate. In essence, as Keith Negus notes and as Stuart knew, music promotion 'can be a risky business' (1992: 130). This chapter has traced ethnographically Stuart's ethical trajectory and his emergence as a small-scale entrepreneur with a sense of vocation that cut across different types of music promotion (see Frith et al. 2013: 15–16). Although the notion of the concert promoter as entrepreneur is becoming 'increasingly misleading' (Brennan and Webster 2011: 3) or, at least, insufficient (cf. Scott 2012; Forbes 2016), the

Illustration 6.1 'Bye Parrot' poster. Design by David Shrigley, used with permission.

story of Cry Parrot indicates the extent to which ethics can inform the work of cultural entrepreneurs (see also Banks 2006: 457) and epitomizes a series of issues pertinent to cultural policy and employment in music and the arts within a particular period in Scotland. Despite the fact that Scotland is no longer a 'stateless nation' (McCrone 1992), whether devolution has facilitated and can contribute, especially since the Scottish independence referendum in 2014, towards the development of a music industry sensitive to local concerns, remains to be seen (see also Symon and Cloonan 2002).

For Glasgow, bringing musical culture to the foreground would primarily involve not public intervention but support for the vibrant informal networks of musicians already based in the city. As Simon Frith writes, 'local, small-scale do-it-yourself promotion remains as necessary to the live music ecology as Live Nation' (Frith et al. 2010: 3). The live music sector, especially at the grassroots, should be approached with particular sensitivity because it is the vast number of undocumented practices that nourish creativity and sustain cultural production locally, in addition to more established actors and institutions (see Lowndes 2010). Ethnographic studies can help highlight such interconnections and demonstrate the practical issues and challenges faced by concert promoters, while foregrounding their hopes and aspirations.

Stuart once told me that Cry Parrot was ultimately his 'musical identity'. Owing to its ethical indeterminacy and pluralism, identity cannot be reduced to what is usually referred to as 'status' or 'role', nor to some combination of these (see Faubion 2011: 101–4). As my ethnographic discussion clearly shows, Stuart *was* Cry Parrot, but Cry Parrot encompassed Stuart's collaborators, too. It follows that identity – musical, personal, professional – is better conceived of as being intimately related to one's subject position. Stuart inherited and disseminated a pluralistic ethics, and his form of subjectivation underscores the fact that an anthropology of ethics cannot be squarely centred upon 'the individual'; rather, it studies complex subjects who strive to occupy or who pass through positions (ibid.: 119). Crucially, there are temporal constraints in the study of ethics, because anthropologists will most likely not be able to trace ethical trajectories in their entirety. However, as Ulf Hannerz remarked some time ago: 'The construction of whole lives may seem to be biography rather than ethnography' (1980: 255). I remain sensitive to these methodological limitations and I have been able to address them only partially by employing the past tense throughout. This is consonant with the shifting attitudes that characterized the music practices of my informants during the time of my fieldwork, but I hope that some of the issues raised here will have a more lasting resonance.

Acknowledgements

I would like to thank Stuart for the spirit of collaboration and generosity he demonstrated throughout my field research. I wish him all the best for the future.

For extensive and insightful comments on earlier versions of this material, I am grateful to Richard Baxstrom, James Laidlaw, Nick Prior and Alexander F. Robertson. Discussions at the University of Edinburgh and especially suggestions by Siobhan Magee also helped clarify my argument. Any remaining deficiencies are, of course, my own. A shortened version of this chapter was presented at the 'Working in Music: The Musicians' Union, Musical Labour and Employment' conference in Glasgow in January 2016.

Evangelos Chrysagis initially trained in History and Archaeology at the University of Ioannina, Greece, before embarking on postgraduate studies in Social Anthropology, earning an M.Sc. and a Ph.D. from the University of Edinburgh, where he was also a guest lecturer until 2015. His doctoral research explored the intersection of do-it-yourself (DiY) music-making and ethics in Glasgow. He has published on the themes of publicity and invisibility in DiY practice, and is currently completing an ethnographic monograph based on his Ph.D. thesis.

Notes

1. Personal names have been changed in order to preserve anonymity and confidentiality.
2. Faubion writes that '[t]he subject position – or subject, more briefly put – is always socially, culturally and historically specific' (2011: 36). For a thorough exposition of the notion of 'subject position', as employed and developed by Faubion, see Robbins (2012).
3. For a concise overview of various distinctions between ethics and morality see Laidlaw (2014: 110–19).
4. Certain promoters allegedly exploited mainly young and unknown bands that would be asked to sell an allocated number of tickets in order to receive payment for their performance. The pay-to-play model was not limited to this practice and could also involve a band directly paying a fee to the promoter in order to secure a slot (see Webster 2011: 83–85).
5. The ethics of the host are quite ambiguous, even paradoxical, as Derrida has shown (Derrida and Dufourmantelle 2000; see also Candea and Da Col 2012). Stuart's hospitality could thus be seen as part of his effort to preserve complete control over Cry Parrot's organizational matters.
6. According to Lambek (2010a: 20), it is 'the balance between prodigality and meanness' that characterizes generosity. On 'excess' as ethical substance see Chapter 5.

References

Arendt, H. 2003. *Responsibility and Judgment*, ed. J. Kohn. New York: Schocken Books.
Banks, M. 2006. 'Moral Economy and Cultural Work', *Sociology* 40: 455–72.
Basso, K.H. 1996. *Wisdom Sits in Places: Landscape and Language among the Western Apache*. Albuquerque: University of New Mexico Press.
Behr, A., et al. 2016. 'Live Concert Performance: An Ecological Approach', *Rock Music Studies* 3: 5–23.

Brennan, M., and E. Webster. 2011. 'Why Concert Promoters Matter', *Scottish Music Review* 2: 1–25.
Candea, M., and G. da Col (eds). 2012. 'Special Issue: The Return to Hospitality: Strangers, Guests, and Ambiguous Encounters', *Journal of the Royal Anthropological Institute* (N.S.) 18(s1): Siii–Siv, S1–S217.
Chrysagis, E. 2013. 'Becoming Ethical Subjects: An *Êthography* of Do-it-Yourself Music Practices in Glasgow', Ph.D. dissertation. Edinburgh: University of Edinburgh.
———. 2016. 'The Visible Evidence of DiY Ethics: Music, Publicity and Technologies of (In)Visibility in Glasgow', *Visual Culture in Britain* 17: 290–310.
Cloonan, M. 2012. 'Selling the Experience: The World-Views of British Concert Promoters', *Creative Industries Journal* 5: 151–70.
Derrida, J., and A. Dufourmantelle. 2000. *Of Hospitality: Anne Dufourmantelle Invites Jacques Derrida to Respond*, trans. R. Bowlby. Stanford, CA: Stanford University Press.
Don't Make a Scene: A Field Guide to Putting on DIY Gigs, 2nd edn. 2014. Comps R. St. John and B. Owl. Self-published.
Douglas, M. 2002 [1966]. *Purity and Danger: An Analysis of Concepts of Pollution and Taboo*. Abingdon: Routledge.
Faubion, J.D. 2011. *An Anthropology of Ethics*. Cambridge: Cambridge University Press.
———. 2013. 'The Subject that Is Not One: On the Ethics of Mysticism', *Anthropological Theory* 13: 287–307.
Forbes, K. 2016. 'Live Music', in A. Dumbreck and G. McPherson (eds), *Music Entrepreneurship*. London: Bloomsbury, pp. 113–40.
Foucault, M. 1978. *The History of Sexuality, Volume I: An Introduction*, trans. R. Hurley. New York: Pantheon Books.
———. 1985. *The Use of Pleasure: Volume 2 of the History of Sexuality*, trans. R. Hurley. New York: Pantheon Books.
———. 1997. *Ethics: Subjectivity and Truth*, ed. P. Rabinow, trans. R. Hurley and others. London: Penguin.
Frith, S., et al. 2010. 'Analysing Live Music in the UK: Findings One Year into a Three-Year Research Project', *IASPM@Journal* 1(1): 1–30.
———. 2013. *The History of Live Music in Britain. Volume I: 1950–1967*. Farnham: Ashgate.
Goffman, E. 1990 [1963]. *Stigma: Notes on the Management of Spoiled Identity*. London: Penguin.
Hannerz, U. 1980. *Exploring the City: Inquiries toward an Urban Anthropology*. New York: Columbia University Press.
Hennion, A. 2007. 'Those Things that Hold Us Together: Taste and Sociology', *Cultural Sociology* 1: 97–114.
Hesmondhalgh, D. 1999. 'Indie: The Institutional Politics and Aesthetics of a Popular Music Genre', *Cultural Studies* 13: 34–61.
Højer, L., and A. Bandak. 2015. 'Introduction: The Power of Example', *Journal of the Royal Anthropological Institute* (N.S.) 21(S1): 1–17.
Humphrey, C. 1997. 'Exemplars and Rules: Aspects of the Discourse of Moralities in Mongolia', in S. Howell (ed.), *The Ethnography of Moralities*. London: Routledge, pp. 25–48.

Hytönen-Ng, E.T. 2015. '"A Musician Who Puts on a Gig": Local Promoter's Multiple Roles and Hierarchies at a Small British Jazz Club', *IASPM@Journal* 5(2): 58–72.

Laidlaw, J. 2002. 'For an Anthropology of Ethics and Freedom', *Journal of the Royal Anthropological Institute* (N.S.) 8: 311–32.

———. 2014. *The Subject of Virtue: An Anthropology of Ethics and Freedom*. Cambridge: Cambridge University Press.

Laing, D. 2003. 'Promoter', in J. Shepherd, D. Horn, D. Laing, P. Oliver and P. Wicke (eds), *Continuum Encyclopedia of Popular Music of the World, Volume 1: Media, Industry and Society*. London: Continuum, pp. 561–62.

Lambek, M. 2010a. 'Introduction', in M. Lambek (ed.), *Ordinary Ethics: Anthropology, Language, and Action*. New York: Fordham University Press, pp. 1–36.

———. 2010b. 'Toward an Ethics of the Act', in M. Lambek (ed.), *Ordinary Ethics: Anthropology, Language, and Action*. New York: Fordham University Press, pp. 39–63.

Lowndes, S. 2010. *Social Sculpture: The Rise of the Glasgow Art Scene*. Edinburgh: Luath Press.

McCrone, D. 1992. *Understanding Scotland: The Sociology of a Stateless Nation*. London: Routledge.

Negus, K. 1992. *Producing Pop: Culture and Conflict in the Popular Music Industry*. London: Edward Arnold.

Ortiz, H. 2013. 'Financial Value: Economic, Moral, Political, Global', *HAU* 3(1): 64–79.

Robbins, J. 2004. *Becoming Sinners: Christianity and Moral Torment in a Papua New Guinea Society*. Berkeley: University of California Press.

———. 2012. 'On Becoming Ethical Subjects: Freedom, Constraint, and the Anthropology of Morality', *Anthropology of this Century* 5. Retrieved 30 March 2016 from http://aotcpress.com/articles/ethical-subjects-freedom-constraint-anthropology-morality/.

Scott, M. 2012. 'Cultural Entrepreneurs, Cultural Entrepreneurship: Music Producers Mobilising and Converting Bourdieu's Alternative Capitals', *Poetics* 40: 237–55.

Stafford, C. 2010. 'The Punishment of Ethical Behaviour', in M. Lambek (ed.), *Ordinary Ethics: Anthropology, Language, and Action*. New York: Fordham University Press, pp. 187–206.

Symon, P., and M. Cloonan. 2002. 'Playing away: Popular Music, Policy and Devolution in Scotland', *Scottish Affairs* 40 (First Series): 99–122.

Weber, M. 1946. 'The Sociology of Charismatic Authority', in H.H. Gerth and C.W. Mills (eds), *From Max Weber: Essays in Sociology*, trans. H.H. Gerth and C.W. Mills. Oxford: Oxford University Press, pp. 245–52.

Webster, E. 2011. 'Promoting Live Music in the UK: A Behind the Scenes Ethnography', Ph.D. dissertation. Glasgow: University of Glasgow.

Williamson, J., Cloonan, M., and S. Frith. 2003. *Mapping the Music Industry in Scotland: A Report*. Glasgow: Scottish Enterprise.

PART IV

Bodies Dancing in Time and across Space

PART IV

Bodies Dancing in Time and across Space

Chapter 7

Rumba

Heritage, Tourism and the 'Authentic' Afro-Cuban Experience

Ruxandra Ana

In February 2014, while doing research in Havana,[1] I participated in the Cuban Experience Project, a workshop that brought together professional competitive ballroom dancers, judges and teachers from more than twenty countries and professional Cuban dancers from the National Folkloric Ensemble (Conjunto Folklórico Nacional). The aim of the project, as described by the organizers, was to provide participants with the best possible information about Cuban dances, practical knowledge and an appropriate learning environment, thus offering them the opportunity to discover the sources of competitive Latin-American dancing and to gain insight into the contexts of these dances.[2] The organizer of the workshop explained to me the reasons that stood behind her decision to initiate the project:

> My first time in this country was twenty years ago and since the first time I felt that the country had a very rich musical and movement tradition, and of course in our competitive dancing we have two dances, cha-cha-cha and rumba bolero, and their movement and musical background come from this country, so I was interested in researching the real, authentic background. And I believe that going and drinking from the source is the best way to get the energy. That's why people who come here open so beautifully and feel so happy, because they perceive something within themselves, which connects with their own essence, the essence of Mother Nature. Of course, authentic dance keeps much closer to ... nature than our Western world.[3]

Illustration 7.1 Participants in the Cuban Experience Project during the workshop at Conjunto Folklórico Nacional in Havana, Cuba, February 2014. Photo by the author.

The workshop consisted of dance classes (Illustration 7.1), lectures, concerts and demonstrations, as well as a final performance at Mella Theatre in Havana, which involved all participants, who presented in front of the Cuban public different dance styles, in their Cuban and competitive forms. The opening and closing events of the project, in Havana and Matanzas, focused on Afro-Cuban dance and rumba demonstrations, with which most of the participants were unfamiliar. While most ballroom dancers have at least some basic knowledge of one or more styles of salsa dancing, the Cuban version of the rumba remains widely unknown, because international-style rumba, performed in dancesport competitions around the world, differs fundamentally in its technical aspects and interpretation.[4] Therefore, knowledge of the 'authentic Cuban rumba' proved to be one of the keys to deeper and better understanding of the music and dance traditions of the island, thus bringing participants closer to achieving the goals of the workshop. In our conversations during the breaks, many of them mentioned being fascinated with and inspired by the 'raw energy', 'passion', 'vitality', 'connection' and 'spontaneity' that, according to them, characterized the way Cubans danced. These were all considered very desirable attributes that most of the participants appeared to be willing to adapt to their own competitive dancing, in this way improving their performance. Similar adjectives were used to describe the demonstrations and concerts that were also included in the programme.

The last day of the workshop was dedicated to attending an 'authentic rumba performance in Matanzas, with Afro Cuba de Matanzas', as the programme of the workshop described it. While not on the most popular tourist track on the island, Matanzas, the capital of the province with the same name, is known in Cuba as the birthplace of Afro-Cuban traditions, music and dance, and in recent years it has increasingly been presented as such to foreign visitors as well. For example, travel guide discourse has incorporated the element of Afro-Cuban heritage in describing a city that is otherwise recommended only for a short stopover, without many attractions for travellers. Even though Matanzas attracts far fewer tourists than Havana or the neighbouring Varadero, it remains a popular destination among dance and music aficionados, who come from all over the world to take classes with some of the best professional musicians and dancers on the island.

Only a few hours before the scheduled concert of Afro Cuba, it turned out that none of the band members knew they were supposed to perform for the workshop participants. However, the concert carried on as scheduled, only with a different band on stage. I arrived at the venue together with Ana, one of my close acquaintances and a key interviewee. As the former lead singer and dancer of Los Muñequitos de Matanzas (one of Cuba's most renowned and appreciated rumba groups), she was instantly recognized by the representative of the Ministry of Culture, who was present at all the events throughout the workshop. When we asked about the change in the schedule and about the replacement of Afro Cuba de Matanzas with a different band, we were told that Afro Cuba were currently touring in Europe, therefore a last-minute change had been in order. The carefully presented argument was difficult to back up when the director of Afro Cuba called from his home in Matanzas, concerned that tourists from Europe had been promised a concert with Afro Cuba and had instead been offered a different band, without being informed of the change. At that point, the main concern was not whether Afro Cuba were touring in Europe or not, but whether I was Cuban and, subsequently, whether it was appropriate or not to be having this conversation in my presence. The state officials who were involved in organizing the event on behalf of the Cuban side declared an investigation was to be completed upon returning to Havana, in order to establish the reasons behind the change in schedule. However, the concert carried on without informing the public, largely made up of workshop participants and a few locals who happened to be passing by, that the band on stage was, in fact, not Afro Cuba.

For the workshop participants this had little or no meaning, as they attended an 'authentic rumba performance' in the city of Matanzas, as scheduled. Some of them waved it off as being too 'touristic' – most of the participants showed constant preoccupation with their status, deeming 'touristic experiences' as something undesirable, fake, designed for the masses they did not identify themselves with, as opposed to the 'authentic learning experience' they were seeking during the workshop. Yet most participants, regardless of the change in the programme, appreciated the afternoon in Matanzas as it added a new layer to the learning experience and to a week already filled with dance, music and performances.

Shifting Perspectives: Divergent Rumba Narratives

This ethnographic example, which is not an isolated one as I had noticed during my previous field research trips to Cuba, has deeper implications that I believe to be symptomatic of the current situation of the rumba, its practice and its perception on the island and outside of it. This chapter looks at the integration of the rumba into the global tourist circuit, addressing the relations established between various social actors in maintaining and developing the rumba in Cuba's western provinces. Regarded as a hybrid practice influenced by Spanish and Central/West African traditions, brought together into a form that was brand new and described entirely as Cuban (Carbonero and Lamerán 1979; Daniel 1995; Moore 1997), the rumba emerged as a genre that accompanied parties and festivities in poor, black and racially mixed communities in western Cuba. Cubans who migrated from the countryside to the cities of Havana and Matanzas after the abolition of slavery in 1886 brought along their music and dance traditions, which were kept under strict supervision from the government. After the revolution of 1959, in an attempt by the socialist government to erase racial inequalities, the rumba and other Afro-Cuban practices were institutionalized and gained increased support from the state (Daniel 1995). The concept of a raceless society, which stood behind revolutionary ideology, brought along a series of reforms that were aimed at eliminating structural racism (Gawrycki and Bloch 2010; Lisocka-Jaegermann 2011) but did not, by any means, solve any of the problems of the deeply rooted racism that is still part of everyday life on the island. Although the rumba benefited greatly from the official support, some scholars (e.g., Daniel 1995) suggest that such measures were taken not only to serve the egalitarian agenda of the government, but also to keep the rumba and its practitioners under strict supervision, to avoid undesirable behaviours or possibilities of a revolt, remote as they may have been.

In what follows, the tensions and ambiguities that characterize the dance are explored by addressing the narratives constructed around racialized bodies, as well as the emergence of diverse perspectives on authenticity and tradition. The rumba appears to have gained broader acceptance and increased visibility in recent years, including among foreign visitors. Yet, to many of its practitioners, as well as to some members of the rumba communities in Havana and Matanzas, this only seems to be a generic acceptance, which in many instances does not incorporate concrete manifestations. Singular instances and examples such as the one above reveal that practice is not always congruent with the discourse around the dance. The material I gathered in the field and discussions with many of my interviewees suggest that there exists a certain ambivalence that characterizes current attitudes around the rumba. When discussing the episode described above with members of Afro Cuba and Los Muñequitos, it became clear, once again, that performers themselves perceived the entire situation regarding the concert and the schedule change as being racially motivated and having deeper economic implications that arise from the current status of the rumba and its practitioners.

This analysis, therefore, looks at how official and unofficial practices and strategies for the promotion of heritage are related to definitions of identity. In doing so, it examines how Afro-Cuban heritage is situated in relation to other types of heritage and how Afro-Cuban practices become integrated into mainstream forms of tourism, in which the rumba comes to function as an epitome of 'authentic' Cuban dance. For a particular type of tourist, who seeks immersion in the culture of the country visited, beyond the possibilities offered by mass tourism and in order to legitimize the ultimate 'authentic' experience, the rumba encompasses several aspects related to the Cuban strategies for making the idea of 'Cubanness' accessible to non-Cubans. Two of the direct consequences that derive from the articulation of Afro-Cuban heritage in relation to cultural tourism are related to the tensions created around the dance in defining one's identity as *rumbero* and the coexistence of various perspectives on what is considered to be 'authentic' dance. These tensions will be addressed here in light of the broader phenomenon of the transnational movements of Cuban dance, which have made the rumba accessible and increasingly popular in the context of dance schools and dance events in Europe.

This research has been informed by music and dance scholars, analysing aspects related to race, gender and class and the political implications behind the institutionalization of the rumba (Daniel 1995), the role of music in the formation of national identity (Moore 1997, 2006) and the social and economic conditions of the rumba's development (Knauer 2005). My findings converge with those of the ethnomusicologist Rebecca Bodenheimer (2010), who explored the racialization of regional identities and their performance through rumba innovations, and also reveal a complex system of narratives around racialized bodies in light of both Cuban and non-Cuban perspectives. Building on the arguments put forward by these authors, this examination of the racial aspects of the rumba also shows the ambivalence that surrounds them in various contexts, especially in regard to the instances when blackness appears to be valorized positively in an increasingly competitive cultural market. This, in turn, reshapes to a great extent how authenticity is defined and understood in relation to the practice of the rumba, in the context of expectations and anticipations that characterize the dynamics of tourist encounters (Skinner and Theodossopoulos 2011).

In the following section, the racialized discourse that functions in Cuba and its connection to the rumba and its practitioners are examined; the chapter then turns to an analysis of how the dance is created as a commodity on the tourist market, in an economy characterized by growing inequalities and social stratification. The venues where the rumba is performed and the racialization of the dance in light of tourist encounters are discussed, and it is suggested below that the rumba comes to function as an epitome of Afro-Cuban culture in the spaces commonly associated with blackness. The final sections of this chapter look at the diverse discourses that emerge in relation to 'authentic' dance practices and the way they are employed by locals and by non-Cubans who learn the rumba on the island and outside of it.

'Four, Six, Ten Negroes with a Drum Is Something that Worries a Lot of People'

During my first research trip, I encountered the strongly racially marked discourse about the rumba before actually participating in any rumba event. The moment I mentioned my research interests to my hosts in Habana Vieja, Miriam, the landlady, showed great concern and did not hide her disapproval: 'My beautiful white girl does not want to be white any more, she wants to be black', was her first comment on hearing my question about rumba venues in Havana.[5] Over the years, I discussed my research and my reasons for being in Cuba with her and her husband and, while they did show appreciation for my academic interests, they were very sceptical about my topic of choice and tried to warn me about how dangerous it was to get too involved with Afro-Cuban people. This issue related not only to the racial aspect, but also to a difference in class and social status: as a tourist, I was expected to avoid interacting with the lower classes and, according to my hosts, I could do equally valuable work by investigating other dances, more 'appropriate' for a white, educated, middle-class young woman.[6]

Later on, as they got to know me better and witness the developments in my fieldwork and my progressive immersion in the world of the rumba, they showed appreciation for some of the people with whom I had come to establish closer relationships (the musicians and dancers of well-known rumba groups, such as Los Muñequitos de Matanzas, Clave y Guaguancó and Afro Cuba de Matanzas). Yet they remained doubtful about my attending dance events in places they considered dangerous, kept warning me about the necessity of guarding my personal belongings and on more than one occasion advised me not to go to a specific event alone, but to seek the company of my Cuban friends who were not involved in the rumba scene. In Miriam's opinion, I was spending too much time with people who were not like 'us', as 'they' had different values from 'ours' – the core of this difference being, in her opinion, the system of beliefs, as people who practise Santería[7] and perform rituals that involve animal sacrifice are not to be trusted. Thus, she suspected that I might become an easy prey for those seeking new converts, especially among tourists willing to open their wallets in order to become initiated into the religion.

During my last week in Havana in 2011, I expressed my intention to go and see a rumba group in San Miguel del Padrón (a municipality in the outskirts of Havana, notorious for the coexistence of musicians, dancers and Afro-Cuban religious practitioners) and Miriam's concern went as far as to actually have a family friend who is a taxi driver take me there and wait for a few hours while I conducted the interviews and observed the rehearsal. It was unconceivable, she said, for me to go by myself and spend time alone in that part of Havana, as she and her husband were responsible for me, as owners of the *casa particular* (private house) I lived in. They were also very concerned because I had become a close acquaintance, and thus they did not want me to become exposed to any dangers.

The Cuban ethnomusicologist Olavo Alén expressed a similar point of view during one of our interviews:

> Sometimes they [*rumberos*] are good, but sometimes, because they like to show off, they end up getting into big fights, they end up killing people. But this is what I call the rumba attitude of Cuban people. Pure *rumberos* are very difficult to find, mostly they are tied to Afro-Cuban people.[8]

On several occasions it was pointed out to me, especially during conversations with Cubans who were not involved in the rumba scene, that while the rumba can still be seen in performances, it is not part of Cubans' daily reality, or at least not to the extent that it used to be. One of my interviewees, Carlos, who sometimes gives dance lessons to tourists at the *casa particular* his family runs, made the following comment during a night out dancing:

> If you want to see a rumba, you have to go to a performance, but when we go to parties we dance mostly salsa or reggaeton. Rumba is just for shows and sometimes after religious ceremonies. Most young people don't even know how to dance it. It used to be very popular a while back, but now it [has] completely disappeared from our daily life.

Other interviewees pointed out the 'advantages' of salsa over rumba, thus attempting to explain its greater popularity along gender lines. Yusleidy, a dancer whom I met through my dance teacher, explained:

> At parties we dance mostly salsa; the rumba is mainly a dance of the people with pagan beliefs, strongly connected with our folkloric music. Salsa is very feminine; it allows you to show your body and allows the man to watch it. Yes, you have to do what the man wants you to do, but you can show your attributes. The rumba does not give you this possibility. Seduction is not that obvious; you do not respond to the man in the same way.

Almost all rumba-related contexts of my research indicated the complicated relationship between race, class, gender, religion and definitions of identity. The above examples are symptomatic of a more general attitude of a larger segment of the population, generating deeper stratifications not only because of individual prejudice, but also due to institutional tensions and double standards that have characterized the dance throughout its evolution. Recent studies (Prieto and Ruiz 2010; Clealand 2013) indicate that racial discrimination in Cuba is still, in fact, the result of structural racism and not just an incident of individual prejudice, arguing that racial discrimination generates a contradiction between the realities of everyday life and the rhetoric of racial democracy in Cuba. This was pointed out to me during an interview with the Cuban writer Tato Quiñones, a scholar of Afro-Cuban religion and culture: 'This is the dialectic, the dynamic of the rumba. Four, six, ten Negroes with a drum is something that worries a lot of people. The rumba has been and stays marginal. Starting a rumba in a street corner makes you the official candidate for a meeting with the police'. The opinion that rumba has remained a marginal practice throughout the years was not uncommon among rumba practitioners too, yet many of them pointed out that new opportunities had been created in the past few years, coming along with the changes in policies regarding tourism.

Selective Heritage and the Touristic Global Marketplace

The tourist sector has had a dynamic expansion especially after the collapse of the Soviet Union, which determined a series of radical changes in Cuba, including significant growth in transnational tourism. Over the past two decades, this sector became a rather influential substitute for what sugar used to be – a monocrop that serviced the accumulation of foreign capital. Most of my interviewees pointed out that Afro-Cuban traditions and art are considered exotic and attractive for tourists and, therefore, constitute key components that, in their essentialized form, can and do generate revenue when presented in front of an international audience. However, these opportunities, set against the rapidly changing, market-oriented economy, do not always translate into direct benefits for the practitioners themselves. Discursive and institutional valorization of the rumba does not always mean that there exists economic or practical support for its performance (see Bodenheimer 2010).

This aspect has been pointed out to me on several occasions since the beginning of my fieldwork, but became particularly obvious in 2012, when UNESCO declared the genre to be part of the cultural heritage of the Cuban nation (see UNESCO Regional Office for Culture in Latin America and the Caribean 2012). This marked an important step towards having the rumba included in the List of Intangible Cultural Heritage, but among practitioners of the rumba the opinions about this decision varied. Especially among the older *rumberos*, there were claims that such symbolic recognition would, in fact, not change anything.

Others saw it as a great opportunity, a chance for publicity, for making the rumba more visible and hence more appealing to tourists, while emphasizing the need to legitimize the genre by having it included in the broader discourse around heritage. One of my informants, Rodrigo, who comes from a family with very rich music and dance traditions and is currently the lead singer of a young and very popular rumba band, told me that, in his opinion, having the rumba declared part of the national heritage was a big step towards repairing the harm that had been done over centuries to the people of African descent. Such an interpretation, indicating the link between the new opportunities surrounding the rumba and a sense of compensation for the previous marginalization of the genre, was offered by Luis, who was a constant presence at all rumba events in Havana, performing on a weekly basis with various groups: 'Now the rumba is [officially recognized as part of the nation's] heritage, you can do a rumba in the street and you won't have problems with the police. But we have problems with discrimination, you understand that? There can be problems if they see an ugly Negro with a tourist'.

While for the younger generations the official recognition of the rumba as part of national heritage signalled an optimistic tone and was viewed as a boost and encouragement to those directly involved in its making, for the older generations it appeared to be a political manoeuvre without real consequences or benefits for the practice of the dance. Leaders and members of older rumba bands in the country appeared to be more sceptical about the decision, pointing out that real implications, which would contribute to a change in the status of the dance, were lacking. This was the case of Ana, a former member of Los Muñequitos de Matanzas, now retired, for whom 'nothing changed and nothing will change', even with the recognition given to the dance; or Minini, Afro Cuba's founder and director, who phrased it as follows: 'We're like puppets. They come looking for us when they need us, when they want to demonstrate [the rumba], when they want to show our traditions and our roots. But they are never here when we need them'.

The bottom line in many discussions and interviews was that state officials and institutions only showed interest for rumba performances when they were organized for specific purposes, such as demonstrations for groups of tourists, television shows or documentaries. However, there appears to be a fundamental lack of institutional support as far as the daily activities, rehearsals and performances of the rumba musicians and dancers are concerned. Most of the time, the interpretation given by my informants was directly linked to issues of race, class and social status. Although the recognition of Afro-Cuban traditions created new financial opportunities for rumba practitioners, promotion was still insufficient and their earning power remained limited in an economy dominated by rising inequalities and social stratification that arose as direct effects of market socialism (see Morris 2008). In short, it was not very often that *rumberos* could make a living solely from their art.

Living under the pressure of the dual-currency economy, most of them had to rely on interactions with tourists in order to have access to foreign capital. Contact with tourists usually occurred via performances (although money earned from gigs at various venues could sometimes be very little and payments made very late) or private dance lessons. Prices for lessons usually varied between ten and twenty CUC, but could sometimes go as high up as forty CUC (the average state salary in Cuba is around 25–30 CUC per month, the equivalent of 19–23 GBP). In recent years, many young dancers who had trained in institutions of higher education, especially in Havana, started working with dance schools aimed exclusively at foreigners, teaching rumba and Afro-Cuban folkloric dances. It was not uncommon for them to also teach outside of the class, usually private lessons in their homes or in the *casas particulares* that the tourists were renting. In most cases, they were formally trained as dancers, specializing in one area (e.g., contemporary, ballet or folkloric), and it is to such dancers that dance schools tended to turn, in this way professionalizing the dance-school scene and the rapidly emerging business around them. This often excluded practitioners without formal training, as well as those who came from families of self-taught *rumberos* or acknowledged performers, who did not have the same opportunities to interact with tourists.

Tourist Encounters and the Racialization of Dance

Venues where the rumba is performed also create the opportunity for other sources of profit, sometimes only partly related to the dance itself (Daniel 1995; Knauer 2005; Bodenheimer 2010), as it is especially in these cultural spaces most commonly associated with blackness and through interactions with tourists that skin colour can be capitalized upon. Currently, probably the most popular venue among foreign visitors is Callejon de Hamel (Illustration 7.2), a project initiated in the 1990s by the Cuban artist Salvador Gonzales. The initial purpose of the venue, as declared by its founder, was to offer Afro-Cuban dancers and musicians a space where they could present their art to the Cuban public, primarily targeting local audiences. However, the narrow street, with its psychedelic murals and regular rumba performances, shortly became one of the most popular tourist spots in the neighbourhood of Centro Habana and, to my knowledge, still remains the only free-of-charge rumba venue in the capital.

The other rumba venues, with entrance fees ranging from five to ten CUC, can hardly compete with Callejon de Hamel when it comes to attracting locals. Their presence at the weekly performances, combined with the fact that it is one of the few instances when Cubans can be actually seen dancing 'in the streets', maintains the aura of 'authenticity', as the narrow, colourful street is almost always filled with locals ready to offer advice and assistance to the foreigners attracted by the enthusiastic descriptions found in almost every travel guide, such as this from Lonely Planet: 'Aside from its funky street murals and psychedelic art

Illustration 7.2 Rumba dancers and members of the public at Callejon de Hamel, in the neighbourhood of Centro Habana, Havana, Cuba. Photo by Karolina Chmiel, used with permission.

shops, the main reason to come to Habana's high temple of Afro-Cuban culture is for the frenetic rumba music that kicks off every Sunday at around noon. For aficionados, this is about as raw and hypnotic as it gets' (Sainsbury 2007: 139).

Based on evidence provided by this particular venue, it has been argued that the rumba can be interpreted as a counter-example to the privilege of whitened tourist spaces, providing a setting 'in which tourists are tolerated on the margins, while Cuban society's most marginalized occupy the centre of action' (Roland 2013: 114). My findings converge with this conclusion in regard to the central place held in rumba venues and performances by a marginalized segment of the population. However, they also indicate that rather than being tolerated, tourists were actively sought, while their presence was appreciated as a positive aspect, not only for their potential financial contribution, but also as the means to increase visibility of the genre and the performers. As Rafael, a young, self-taught *rumbero*, explained one Sunday morning before dancing at Callejon, he liked that place most 'not because it's the best dancing, but [because] many tourists come here and they always take pictures and videos and put them on Facebook and YouTube and then when other tourists come they will recognize me'. Blackness becomes positively valued and the presence of (usually white) tourists was something many of the rumba performers sought and appreciated as a desirable aspect that was central to their work, which was mainly motivated by economic hardship and the struggle for foreign currency. Rumba venues usually attracted many self-professed dance teachers who usually employed the racial argument before the professional one ('I'm black, of course I can teach you how to dance the rumba, it is natural') and so in some instances being black became equivalent with being able to dance and teach. This, in turn, complicated even more the already blurred tourist imaginary, whereby Cubans are 'born with the dance in their blood', or 'learn dancing before learning how to walk', only to grow up 'dancing in the streets' and being permanently joyful despite economic hardship.

While dance lessons were usually the first byproducts to be offered to tourists, at other times discussion about dance was followed by questions about religion, as it was assumed that if one was present at such an event, one either had some knowledge of Afro-Cuban religion or was at least interested to gain some, which in turn could open the path towards the commoditization of religion (Holbraad 2004). Also, it was not uncommon for these venues to offer the appropriate setting for those seeking friendships or romantic involvement with tourists, although this was not something specific of rumba venues exclusively, as recent studies of tourism in Cuba have demonstrated (Simoni 2012).

For some of the *rumberos*, as well as for some Cuban researchers of the rumba community, the increased visibility of the practice in tourist spaces is not necessarily valued positively, as was the case for the ethnographer Tato Quiñones:

> The rumba was a folkloric fact [*hecho folklórico*] that appeared in a spontaneous manner, done by the people in the street. They would gather in a *solar* [tenement building], on street corners or in someone's house, and there were clear aesthetic and ethical rules for the rumba. And in the past years it started gaining other spaces, where you can go and see a performance, which in turn gave birth to groups of *rumberos* who are semi-professional and their purpose is no longer just pleasure, but how to make this professional. And as soon as the tourists arrive[d], a specific fauna arrived – tobacco sellers, prostitutes, pickpockets, because tourists attract these people. So the people in the neighborhood started feeling as if they were part of a show – a show that the tourists were supposed to enjoy.

The double-edged sword in regard to race was not an uncommon occurrence during my fieldwork and I noticed that in many situations blackness was considered a prerequisite for good performance of the rumba. One of my dance teachers in Havana told me one day before class that, while watching some of the videos of ballroom dancing I had given him, his neighbour, 'one of these black women in the neighbourhood', made a comment about the dancers and characterized them as 'stiff' and 'without emotion' and affirmed her preference for the rumba the way it is danced in Cuba. My teacher's observation was that her disapproval came from a lack of understanding of such 'refined European dancing'. However, when we started working on the rumba later that day, he reassured me I would get appropriate training: 'Don't be fooled by the fact that I am white. We all have black blood in our veins'. The naturalization of ideas about racialized bodies (Desmond 1998; Bosse 2007) sometimes goes as far as replacing technical explanations about how the dances should be performed. In a rumba workshop I took in Poland with Isabel, a Cuban instructor, participants were told that dancing was supposed to be on a bent knee, not a straight one, because: 'These dances are not soft. These are dances of the black people. Tired'. Jürgen, a German dance educator and trainer who works with competitive couples across Europe, teaching and giving lectures, and who has conducted extensive research on the origins of Latin American dances, expressed a similar point of view: 'All good dancing comes from black people. They were slaves, they did not have the time to figure out how these things work, and somehow they had a perfect 'lead'. What they do is not structured but there is a high quality to what they do'.[9]

The racial aspect becomes incorporated in a broader discourse about cultural otherness and claims of authenticity stand out as the most desirable assets of intercultural encounters in the era of global tourism. In many instances, mediated by travel-guide and media discourses, blackness is semantically reduced and essentialized as a central feature of Afro-Cubanness. As will be seen in the following section, this in turn becomes the equivalent of 'the roots' or 'the source' of many dance styles specific of Cuba.

Dancing back to the Roots: The Quest for Authenticity

Anthropologists of tourism (MacCannell 1973; Cohen 1988; Urry 1995; Alneng 2002; Bruner 2005) have extensively discussed questions related to authenticity and how it shapes the tourist experience and the modes of perception and visualization, being not only a purpose in itself, a gate of access to the depths of the cultures visited, but also a tool for legitimizing and validating the tourist experience. The constant negotiations between expectations and anticipation (see Skinner and Theodossopoulos 2011) involve and empower different actors whose aspirations meet in a perpetual redefining of the tourist experience. The misleading nature of authenticity has been analysed in depth by Theodossopoulos (2013), who suggests looking into the simultaneity and multiplicity of authenticities in discussing the authentic/inauthentic binary opposition. Recent studies also indicate that, while acknowledging the socially constructed nature of heritage and the lack of innocence in this process (Brett 1996; Klekot 2014), a merely deconstructive approach to authenticity is very likely to ignore the popular demand for authenticity and the meaning of external recognition for the distinctive character of a given culture.

In this respect, Brumann suggests 'heritage agnosticism' as a path in the study of heritage, which 'is a good vantage point to take such popular demands seriously and to contribute to assessing factual claims about historical roots and continuities, not all of which are fabricated to the same degree' (2014: 81). Researchers of cultural heritage have pointed out the intersections between commodification and tradition (Pietrobruno 2009), as well as the functioning of intangible cultural heritage as a strategy that makes culture available and consumable in a global market (Tauschek 2011), showing how a strong focus is placed on the colourful and exotic examples that represent nationally valued events or performances that coincide with Western perceptions (Smith 2006). In the majority of cases, these perceptions operate with the assumption that there is only one 'real' cultural identity (Bruner 2005), which can be discovered and experienced, thus favouring a strongly exoticized version of the authentic.

For the participants in the Cuban Experience Project mentioned at the beginning of this chapter, as well as for many of the non-Cuban dance aficionados I met during my research, dance forms and bodily practices appeared to be valued for their 'pure', 'unchanged' and 'original' characteristics. This was explained in many instances by a closer connection to nature, which was perceived as allowing one to have a better connection to one's 'true self', and through participation in a community whose image was constructed in opposition to the one the dancing tourists usually came from. Imagination plays a key role in this construction and authenticity becomes 'a way to imagine and idealize the real, the traditional and the organic in opposition to the less satisfying qualities of everyday life' (Deloria 1998: 101). In other words, the process of 'tourismification' (Salazar 2011: 581) is grounded in romanticized and nostalgic visions, similar to Fabian's (1983) 'denial of coevalness'.

In the Cuban case, the quest for the authentic had been doubled and supported by one of the most common assumptions that were still functional among tourists: that Cuba remained unchanged, 'frozen' in time and isolated from the rest of the world for more than half a century, after the changes in the political system in 1959. The shattering of this fantasy in light of recent events had resulted in a media boom, which brought Cuba back to public attention, generating thousands of commentaries, predictions and possible scenarios regarding the future of the island and its development after Raul Castro and Barack Obama announced in December 2014 the renewing of diplomatic ties between the two countries, suspended in 1961. All of a sudden, potential tourists from all over the world appeared to be facing their last chance to see 'Cuba before it changes', 'before the Americans get there', 'before capitalism'.[10] A sense of urgency mixed with nostalgia for a world that escapes definition but needs to be experienced were recurring elements in most of the articles that covered the news. The approach, however, was not new in itself, but rather part of a complex apparatus that was developed over time and involved official promotional campaigns, tour operators and an entire industry in a perpetual quest for unspoiled experiences and local colour.

Set against this background and accumulation of expectations, certain aspects of Cuban heritage have been functioning, over the years, as key symbols of cultural tourism, constantly redefined and negotiated, and placed into hierarchies as a result of approaches to culture in light of neoliberal practices and ideas (Scher 2011). Cultural practices and symbols that ensured recognition as well as revenue gained meaning both locally and internationally, and Cuba became increasingly appealing for foreign consumption (Babb 2011). The nostalgia for the land 'frozen' in time mixed with prerevolutionary extravagance and revolutionary culture appeared to be the main focus of most travel guides, organized tours and local businesses aimed at foreign visitors, employing a discourse that naturalizes the exotic and a rhetoric of lightheartedness, sensuality and passion. In fact, this vision of a country where time stood still was behind the notion that Cuban dance had such a particular character – Cuban Experience Project participants described the dancing of Cubans as 'free', 'intuitive', 'authentic', 'sensual' and 'sincere', descriptions that were regularly intensified by oppositions and contrasts with European dances, both in their competitive and social forms.

In this way, dancing not only provides the venue for the articulation of neocolonial imaginaries, but also creates idealized versions of the practice and its practitioners, oriented towards the 'recovery of an essence' (Bendix 1997: 8). Anticipation fuels the tourist experience prior to arrival at the destination and shapes to a great extent the choices made: 'Such anticipation is constructed and sustained through a variety of nontourist practices, such as film, newspapers, TV, magazines, records and videos which construct the gaze. Such practices provide the signs in terms of which the holiday experiences are understood, so that what is then seen is interpreted in terms of these pre-given categories' (Urry 1995: 132).

Both the official campaign of the Cuban Ministry of Tourism, 'Auténtica Cuba', and the dominant discourse of the tourist industry were built around a set of symbols most commonly associated with the island, promising unforgettable experiences on sunny beaches where tourists could relax while sipping mojitos and daiquiris and enjoying real Cuban cigars, or discover the country's cultural richness by touring in an old American car and attending music and dance performances. This system of representation relied heavily on images of 'authentic' dance and music that shaped to a considerable degree touristic modes of visualization and experience. In fact, these cultural products were more and more often part of the programmes offered by most tour operators that sold trips to Cuba and it was very likely that many tourists would attend at least one salsa night while in Cuba. However, there were different regimes of presenting and selling dance to foreign visitors, and preferences for particular genres were quite visible across the island.

While the majority of tourist guides acknowledged the presence of music and dance as unquestionable components of Cuban daily life, emphasizing the richness and diversity of genres, the rumba was presented as 'Cuba's hypnotic dance music', 'raw, expressive and exciting to watch' (Sainsbury 2007: 37), 'sensual' (Thomas Cook 2005), 'dynamic and seductive' (Rzeczpospolita 2008) and a most powerful expression of the nation: 'Cuba is an island of dancers. For the inhabitants of this country, rhythmic movements are not so much a type of entertainment, but rather a way to express emotion. Out of all Cuban dances, the most popular one is the rumba' (ibid.: 134).

Exciting as this perspective might appear to rumba aficionados, the dance still remains less visible and less present than salsa (the generic term used to describe Cuban *casino*, especially in interactions with tourists), although recent years have seen an increase in the number of venues where the rumba is performed, the inclusion of rumba groups in venues that up until recently were dedicated to salsa/timba (Yoruba Andabo at Casa de la Música) and better promotion of the already well-established rumba performances, like the ones at Callejon de Hamel or Conjunto Folklórico Nacional. Furthermore, a distinct visual identity of the rumba, emphasizing vibrant colours, drums and symbols of Afro-Cuban culture, which tourists can access outside of the spaces where the dance is usually performed, has become easier to notice through the inclusion of rumba pictures in the media (placing the rumba on several lists of 'must see/must do' things in Cuba), leaflets promoting events, guided tours or postcards. In this way, the dance becomes similar to other souvenirs that function as 'selective templates' (Benson 2004), parts of a reality that has been fragmented in order to become comprehensible.

Embodied Cuban Souvenirs

For foreign visitors, the rumba becomes the epitome of Afro-Cuban cultural manifestations and a less 'commercialized' genre than salsa, which remains a lot more visible, at least in the western part of the island, and a lot more popular among tourists.[11] With the increasing popularity of salsa congresses and festivals in Europe and the globalization and increased commercialization of the dance and music (Skinner 2007), situated between cultural heritage and leisure commodity (Pietrobruno 2009), many dance aficionados outside of Cuba have become familiar with these dances through classes, workshops and constant participation in dance events, which usually include a Cuban section. Rumba workshops are still less numerous than *casino* or 'Cuban-style' workshops, but the rumba is increasingly present in these latter classes as an addition that can enrich one's style of dancing *casino*, making its overall appearance more 'authentic'. In this way, the rumba appears to function as an embodied souvenir that makes 'Cubanness' available and, in a way, portable, through the body that experienced it. The ultimate declared purpose for many of the tourists attending rumba classes is to dance 'as Cubans do', which is sometimes met with mixed feelings by some of the Cuban instructors teaching outside of the island, as was the case of Javier, one of the dance instructors I interviewed in Poland:

Mixing rumba steps in [with] *casino* actually started from the music. But *casino* was already a mixture of *son* [a Cuban genre of music and dance which gained worldwide popularity in the 1920s–1930s] and rumba.... Anyway, it starts in the music, I think it started with Los Van Van and then it started happening in the dance because people understood what they were singing and some of them were religious ... you know how it is. But now they teach it as a rule in dance schools, that it's cool to mix rumba or Afro in *casino*, and people just do it. You can't do whatever you feel like only because you think that's what you saw Cubans doing. Because your dance will be empty.

A similar opinion was expressed by another Cuban instructor in Poland, Francisco, who also mentioned the importance of musicality and understanding basic rhythmic patterns and the need to focus on 'enjoying the dance, rather than showing off... knowledge of all Cuban styles'. At the same time, Francisco pointed out that presentations of the dance, shows and performances, which are a consistent part of every congress or workshop, are a very good means of disseminating information about the dance and raising awareness, as long as they keep the original meaning (not necessarily the technique).

These aspects were also pointed out by my interviewees in Havana and Matanzas, indicating that, for the local community, authenticity was understood rather as a process that could accommodate change and evolution, as long as such changes did not affect the essence of the dance or the musical structure. Thus, from the community's point of view, dance was understood rather as a process, blending the original context of the dance (its 'first existence') with its public display ('second existence'), integrating them rather than excluding each other.[12] The presence of tourists and their interest in public displays and performances of dance did not necessarily diminish authenticity, at least not from the locals' perspective (see also Comaroff and Comaroff 2009). In fact, many of my interviewees suggested that a stronger presence of the dance in venues that attracted foreign visitors was beneficial, not only because of the financial opportunities created, but also because it reinforced the importance of the dance for the community and drew attention to less promoted aspects of Cuban culture. It was also pointed out to me, repeatedly, that the will to understand the dance and to gain knowledge about it was essential in order to avoid responding to an increasing expectation and demand for exoticism, raw sexuality, flashy colours and aggressive movements. One of my interviewees in Havana, Rafael, a dancer of the younger generation, was particularly critical of this tendency, which, in his opinion, had become stronger in recent years and had led to changes in the structure of the dance: 'Sometimes you don't even know if what you are seeing is rumba or not; it's easier not to train hard and just do whatever you feel like and deceive tourists. They won't even know they were deceived'.

Within the rumba communities in both Havana and Matanzas, a strong accent was placed on historicity and continuity, which were strongly related to knowledge, understanding and remembering. Skill acquisition from a young age was extremely important, and metaphors were used to describe how knowledge becomes embodied: 'You either have the rumba or you don't. It's there, in you'; or, 'you need to carry the *clave* [fundamental rhythmic pattern in Cuban music] in your heart'; or, 'once you practise long enough, you will have the *clave* in your blood'. This was the type of message transmitted to the younger generations but also to non-Cubans willing to become familiar with the rumba, thus distinguishing it from other dance practices, which only require a good command of specific sets of steps, lead-and-follow skills and a developed sense of rhythm.

Training in the sounds and bodily movements associated with the rumba almost always came along with a clearly stated need to understand both Afro-Cuban traditions and history in order to be able to perform the dance, thus connecting it to its origins and evolution in time. Also, as already mentioned, the dance appeared to function as a path towards other layers of traditional culture, as very often discussions about the rumba, even in the most touristic settings and contexts, led the way towards discussions on religion and Afro-Cuban heritage, which came to play an important role in the construction of identity, creating new experiences and defining a sense of belonging.

'How Come This Girl Can Dance but She Cannot Play nor Sing a Rumba?'

This ambivalence of the rumba, which appeared to occupy the place between a secular and religious practice, was also key to another episode, this time in Matanzas, in the house of one of my interviewees, who came from a family with rich music and dance traditions and devoted Santería practitioners. I had spent the morning playing cards and dominos with her eight-year-old nephew, who then decided to teach me how to dance. He had seen me before, on several occasions, during my dance lessons with his grandmother, which would sometimes turn into dance lessons with several members of the family, each of them eager to teach me something new, correct my mistakes or show me how to improve the overall quality of my dance. Learning from such a young instructor was something I had not experienced before and I happily accepted his invitation. He took me by the hand and we walked into the living room, where he showed me a statue of San Lazaro. 'He takes care of sick people and heals those who pray to him. Now put your hand here', he said, and showed me where to touch the statue. He then took my camera and took a picture of me next to San Lazaro, so that I would remember him. Next, we moved on to a shrine with votive offerings and representations of Changó, the Orisha of masculinity, drums and thunder. The boy explained the importance of this particular Orisha and took a picture so that I would remember him, too. He did the same with all the other altars in the house, in what I came to view as a private tour of a house so filled with religion it could have very well been a museum of Afro-Cuban beliefs and traditions.

Once the tour was over and I had been provided with all the important information about the Orishas, their powers, characteristic colours and foods, he told me: 'Now you know about religion, you are ready to learn how to dance'. I asked him whether dancing without knowing things about religion was possible and he told me that it was, but all good dancers should know these things, therefore so should I. Then, in order to show me the basic rumba steps, he brought a drum that he placed in front of me and asked me to play a rumba. I told him I didn't know how to play the drums, which judging by the look on his face must have been very puzzling. He came up with a solution quickly and told me we could still learn the dance without the drums, as long as I sang a rumba he could dance to, then he would sing and I would dance. Slightly embarrassed by now, I had to admit to not being able to sing. Luckily, just when I thought my newfound teacher would give up on me and his mission, he switched on the DVD player and the room filled with the rumba of Los Muñequitos de Matanzas. We had barely managed to go through three or four basic steps, when he stopped me and told me I was doing it wrong, because I was doing the exact same moves as he was, when in fact I was supposed to dance 'more like a woman', placing accent on hip movement, which he then demonstrated. Our lesson was interrupted when his grandmother came home and my teacher was eager to know one thing: 'How come this girl can dance but she cannot play nor sing a rumba?'

His surprise at noticing my incomplete knowledge was not a surprise to me, as I had become familiar, over the years, with groups of children who had started learning the dances and the music at a very young age, in informal settings, training on a weekly basis and as much as on a daily basis before performances (Illustration 7.3). In many instances, the groups were organized as community projects that brought together children from the neighbourhood in order to provide them with knowledge they did not receive at school. As explained by Ana, who was teaching such a group of around thirty children, it was very important to teach children in such organized settings, because they had become less and less exposed to 'traditional' forms of dancing:

> What I see now is the loss of tradition and of the roots of our culture. That is why I work with children; we have to make sure we pass on our knowledge. People have started mixing techniques and this will slowly lead to losing the essence of the dance. Of course, we all have problems and needs and life is difficult, but we have to remember the difference between selling the rumba and keeping it alive.

Ana's observation points towards an increased need for a type of training, which, although not formal, still follows a well-defined set of rules, aimed at

Illustration 7.3 Rumba rehearsal in Santiago de Las Vegas, Havana. Photo by the author.

not just passing on technique and providing contexts for performance, but first of all teaching the content and meaning of the dance. Although the rumba is defined by its practitioners as a secular practice with almost no exception, it is strongly connected to performances of Afro-Cuban folkloric dances (dances of the Orishas) and it is slowly strengthening its position as a cultural niche product with increased popularity and growing visibility.

For tourists already familiar with other forms of Cuban dancing, especially through the dissemination of Cuban-style salsa in dance schools and dance congresses around the world, the rumba becomes the epitome of Afro-Cuban heritage and holds the promise of authentic dance experiences. However, although the dance has become more popular in the past few decades, having a stronger position in the cultural market and diverse grassroots strategies for promotion, the practitioners are still confronted with economic difficulties. This is a result not only of the more general imbalances that characterize the Cuban economy, but also of racial discrimination. Tourist venues become central spaces for the infusion of foreign capital and lead to increased competition among performers in terms of offering their services to foreigners, while at the same time providing one of the few instances when blackness gains positive connotations. In this context, therefore, tourist encounters contribute to the diversity of narratives around racialized bodies and reshape the defining elements of a cultural product, the rumba, within the broader frame of market socialism.

Acknowledgements

Many thanks to the editors of this volume, Evangelos Chrysagis and Panas Karampampas, for their helpful critique and suggestions, and to Grete Viddal and Valerio Simoni for their valuable comments and observations. I am very grateful to all my Cuban friends and interviewees, for letting me have insight into their fascinating world. Their contribution to this research is incommensurable.

Ruxandra Ana is a Ph.D. candidate in Ethnology and Cultural Anthropology at the University of Warsaw, specializing in dance anthropology and the anthropology of tourism in Latin America and the Caribbean. Her main research interests include Afro-Cuban dances, social and competitive ballroom dance, race and gender in performance, ethnicity and cultural heritage and touristic development in postcolonial contexts.

Notes

1. This chapter is based on approximately five months of fieldwork in the western provinces of Cuba, in the course of three trips in 2011, 2012 and 2014. Much of the background information and observations that helped structure the material came from my own participation in Cuban dance classes, workshops and events, mainly in Poland, but also in other European countries. Multisited ethnography (Marcus 1995) supplied the data for analysing the creation and dissemination of narratives of Cubanness. My informants were mainly Cuban practitioners of the rumba, most of them identifying themselves as being of Afro-Cuban descent. Some of them were professional musicians and dancers; others were performers without formal training. Some of the foreign tourists were dancers themselves, others were dance educators or instructors, and the majority of people I met at dance venues had some connection with the salsa scene in their countries of origin, taking classes and participating constantly in salsa events. None of my Cuban informants worked directly in the tourist sector, which means they only had access to foreign currency through contact with tourists and their main income sources were gigs and performances in different venues, or private classes offered to tourists. None of them could be classified as wealthy, in Cuban terms. Unless otherwise stated, all interviews have been originally conducted in Spanish and were translated by the author. Some of the interviewees have been anonymized according to their wishes.
2. International-style Latin-American dancing consists of five couples' dances: samba, cha-cha-cha, rumba, paso doble and jive.
3. This interview was conducted in English.
4. For an extensive analysis of the difference between Afro-Cuban rumba and ballroom rumba see McMains (2010).
5. My position as a foreigner meant that I was able to develop particular types of networks and collaborations with my research participants. Yet, as I appeared to have a fair amount of knowledge of Cuban culture and traditions, spoke Spanish and danced, I managed

to build closer relationships with some of them. My being white meant that I was never excluded from tourist venues (see also Roland 2013). However, it also turned out to be a very important aspect in my research and in my dance practice. For example, I was told on several occasions while working on the rumba during dance classes that I should 'not worry' about being white and that I would eventually learn to dance.
6. While 'class' is not a term used in Cuba to describe difference (as noted by Lundgren 2011), there is a class discourse embedded in the racial one, as there is a strongly marked difference functioning in Cuban society between 'high' and 'low' culture. I noticed that, in many instances, Afro-Cuban religion and music appeared as the most common denominators for 'low' culture; however, it must be pointed out that some of my Cuban interviewees were highly esteemed members of society, as they had gained recognition through their art (see also Saunders 2009).
7. Santería is a syncretic religion based on Yoruba beliefs and traditions, influenced by and syncretized with Roman Catholicism.
8. This interview was conducted in English.
9. This interview was conducted in English.
10. On the relationship between nostalgia, imagination and everyday life in present-day Cuba see Behar (2015).
11. Many of my Cuban interviewees suggested that the popularity of *casino* among foreigners was mainly due to the fact that it was easier to learn, allowing even those with no previous experience in dancing to achieve a level of proficiency that, in a rather short amount of time, would make them feel comfortable at most venues and dancing events. Another reason repeatedly cited was that for learning *casino* there was no need to understand the history of the dance or of the people who created it, something that was a prerequisite for the rumba. On the other hand, my non-Cuban interviewees indicated that the rumba was a lot more challenging because of the increased difficulty of the rhythmic patterns and the movements, especially those of the hips and torso.
12. For an extensive discussion on 'first' and 'second' existence of dance see Nahachewsky (2001).

References

Alneng, V. 2002. '"What the Fuck Is a Vietnam?": Touristic Phantasms and the Popcolonization of (the) Vietnam (War)', *Critique of Anthropology* 22: 461–89.
Babb, F.E. 2011. 'Che, Chevys and Hemingway's Daiquiris: Cuban Tourism in a Time of Globalisation', *Bulletin of Latin American Research* 30: 50–63.
Behar, R. 2015. 'The Fantasy of a Cuba Where Time Stood Still', *Huffington Post*, 15 January. Retrieved 11 July 2015 from http://www.huffingtonpost.com/ruth-behar/the-fantasy-of-a-cuba-whe_b_6479872.html.
Bendix, R. 1997. *In Search of Authenticity: The Formation of Folklore Studies*. Madison: University of Wisconsin Press.
Benson, S. 2004. 'Reproduction, Fragmentation and Collection: Rome and the Origin of Souvenirs', in D.M. Lasansky and B. McLaren (eds), *Architecture and Tourism: Perception, Performance and Place*. Oxford: Berg, pp. 15–36.
Bodenheimer, R.M. 2010. 'Localizing Hybridity: The Politics of Place in Contemporary Cuban Rumba Performance', Ph.D. dissertation. Berkeley: University of California.

Bosse, J. 2007. 'Whiteness and the Performance of Race in American Ballroom Dance', *Journal of American Folklore* 120: 19–47.
Brett, D. 1996. *The Construction of Heritage*. Cork: Cork University Press.
Brumann, C. 2014. 'Heritage Agnosticism: A Third Path for the Study of Cultural Heritage', *Social Anthropology* 22: 173–89.
Bruner, E.M. 2005. *Culture on Tour: Ethnographies of Travel*. Chicago, IL: The University of Chicago Press.
Carbonero, G.C., and S. Lamerán. 1979. *Cuban Folklore I II III IV* [*Folklore Cubano I II III IV*]. Havana: Editorial Pueblo y Educación, Ministerio de Cultura.
Clealand, D.P. 2013. 'When Ideology Clashes with Reality: Racial Discrimination and Black Identity in Contemporary Cuba', *Ethnic and Racial Studies* 36: 1619–36.
Cohen, E. 1988. 'Authenticity and Commoditization in Tourism', *Annals of Tourism Research* 15: 371–86.
Comaroff, J.L., and J. Comaroff. 2009. *Ethnicity, Inc.* Chicago, IL: The University of Chicago Press.
Daniel, Y. 1995. *Rumba: Dance and Social Change in Contemporary Cuba*. Bloomington: Indiana University Press.
Deloria, P.J. 1998. *Playing Indian*. New Haven, CT: Yale University Press.
Desmond, J. 1998. 'Embodying Difference: Issues in Dance and Cultural Studies', in A. Carter (ed.), *The Routledge Dance Studies Reader*. London: Routledge, pp. 154–62.
Fabian, J. 1983. *Time and the Other: How Anthropology Makes Its Object*. New York: Columbia University Press.
Gawrycki, M., and N. Bloch. 2010. *Cuba* [*Kuba*]. Warsaw: Trio.
Holbraad, M. 2004. 'Religious "Speculation": The Rise of Ifá Cults and Consumption in Post-Soviet Cuba', *Journal of Latin American Studies* 36: 643–63.
Klekot, E. 2014. 'Self-Folklorization: Contemporary Folk Art through the Perspective of Postcolonial Criticism' [Samofolkloryzacja: współczesna sztuka ludowa z perspektywy krytyki postkolonialnej], *Contemporary Culture* [*Kultura współczesna*] 1(81): 86–99.
Knauer, L.M. 2005. 'Translocal and Multicultural Counterpublics: Rumba and la Regla de Ocha in New York and Havana', Ph.D. dissertation. New York: New York University.
Lisocka-Jaegermann, B. 2011. 'Black Americas' [Czarne Ameryki], in M. Gawrycki (ed.), *Facts of Latin American Culture* [*Dzieje kultury latynoamerykańskiej*]. Warsaw: Wydawnictwo Naukowe PWN, pp. 163–73.
Lundgren, S. 2011. *Heterosexual Havana: Ideals and Hierarchies of Gender and Sexuality in Contemporary Cuba*, Ph.D. dissertation. Uppsala: Uppsala University.
MacCannell, D. 1973. 'Staged Authenticity: Arrangements of Social Spaces in Tourist Settings', *American Journal of Sociology* 79: 589–603.
Marcus, G.E. 1995. 'Ethnography in/of the World System: The Emergence of Multi-sited Ethnography', *Annual Review of Anthropology* 24: 95–117.
McMains, J. 2010. 'Rumba Encounters: Transculturation of Cuban Rumba in American and European Ballrooms', in S. Sloat (ed.), *Making Caribbean Dance: Continuity and Creativity in Island Cultures*. Gainesville: University Press of Florida, pp. 37–48.
Moore, R.D. 1997. *Nationalizing Blackness: Afrocubanismo and Artistic Revolution in Havana, 1920–1940*. Pittsburgh, PA: University of Pittsburgh Press.

———. 2006. *Music and Revolution: Cultural Change in Socialist Cuba*. Berkeley: University of California Press.

Morris, E. 2008. 'Cuba's New Relationship with Foreign Capital: Economic Policy-Making since 1990', *Journal of Latin American Studies* 40: 769–92.

Nahachewsky, A. 2001. 'Once Again: On the Concept of "Second Existence Folk Dance"', *Yearbook for Traditional Music* 33: 17–28.

Pietrobruno, S. 2009. 'Cultural Research and Intangible Heritage', *Culture Unbound* 1: 227–47.

Prieto, R.E., and P.R. Ruiz. 2010. 'Race and Inequality in Cuba Today', *Socialism and Democracy* 24(1): 161–77.

Roland, L.K. 2013. 'T/Racing Belonging Through Cuban Tourism', *Cultural Anthropology* 28: 396–419.

Rzeczpospolita. 2008. *Cuba [Kuba]*. Warsaw: Rzeczpospolita/New Media Concept.

Sainsbury, B. 2007. *Havana City Guide*, 2nd edn. London: Lonely Planet.

Salazar, N.B. 2011. 'The Power of Imagination in Transnational Mobilities', *Identities* 18: 576–98.

Saunders, T.L. 2009. 'Grupo OREMI: Black Lesbians and the Struggle for Social Space in Havana', *Souls* 11: 167–85.

Scher, P.W. 2011. 'Heritage Tourism in the Caribbean: The Politics of Culture after Neoliberalism', *Bulletin of Latin American Research* 30: 7–20.

Simoni, V. 2012. 'Dancing Tourists: Tourism, Party and Seduction in Cuba', in D. Picard and M. Robinson (eds), *Emotion in Motion: Tourism, Affect and Transformation*. Farnham: Ashgate, pp. 267–81.

Skinner, J. 2007. 'The Salsa Class: A Complexity of Globalization, Cosmopolitans and Emotions', *Identities* 14: 485–506.

Skinner, J., and D. Theodossopoulos. 2011. *Great Expectations: Imagination and Anticipation in Tourism*. Oxford: Berghahn.

Smith, L. 2006. *Uses of Heritage*. Abingdon: Routledge.

Tauschek, M. 2011. 'Reflections on the Metacultural Nature of Intangible Cultural Heritage', *Journal of Ethnology and Folkloristics* 5(2): 49–64.

Theodossopoulos, D. 2013. 'Laying Claim to Authenticity: Five Anthropological Dilemmas', *Anthropological Quarterly* 86: 337–60.

Thomas Cook. 2005. *Cuba [Kuba]*. Warsaw: Hachette.

UNESCO Regional Office for Culture in Latin America and the Caribbean. 2012. 'The Rumba is Declared Cultural Patrimony of the Cuban Nation', 23 February. Retrieved 19 September 2016 from http://www.lacult.unesco.org/noticias/showitem.php?uid_ext=orcalcadmin_1&getipr=&lg=2&pais=0&id=3269.

Urry, J. 1995. *Consuming Places*. London: Routledge.

Chapter 8

Cinematic Dance as a Local Critical Commentary on the 'Economic Crisis'
Exploring Dance in Korydallos, Attica, Greece

Mimina Pateraki

This chapter examines the social engagement of dance[1] in Greece during a critical historical period known as the 'economic crisis'.[2] The intention is to explore the ways people critique the contemporary sociopolitical situation, the financial crisis and their own personal choices through the engagement of certain cinematic dance scenes in their oral narratives and everyday practices. In particular, the focus is on Greek films in which dance plays a prominent role, and the ways in which people comment on these dance scenes and articulate their critique are addressed. More specifically, two particular dance scenes that were filmed during the military Junta period in Greece (1967–73) are elaborated on. These scenes derive from two different films: *Oratótis Midén* (Zero Visibility), directed by Nikos Foskolos in 1970; and *Evdokía*, directed by Alexis Damianos in 1971.[3]

This study follows the choices of my interlocutors and their relationship with these films in order to show that certain films and their dance scenes have become deeply familiar to Greek people (Pateraki and Zografou 2015). The two dance scenes my interlocutors used in their narratives, oral and embodied, represent the culmination of the plot of the films they appear in. These dance scenes have been famous in Greece since their first screening in the early 1970s, while both films were very popular among my informants in Korydallos. *Oratótis Midén*, in particular, belongs to a range of films that were broadcast almost weekly for several decades on public and private television channels, resulting in repeated viewings for my interlocutors. Additionally, the activity of keeping family or personal videotape archives, constructed by recordings of these films that were screened on T.V., has rendered these scenes, actors and their performances 'unforgettable' (Pateraki forthcoming). Certain films remain strikingly popular, deeply woven into our lives (see Sutton and Wogan 2009), highlighting that cinema has 'the power to move people' and enact relationships that are 'dialogic at heart' (Gray 2010: 137). Focusing on such relationships, which are imbued with people's personal experience, reveals a rich ethnographic research field (Crawford 1992: 74; Banks and Morphy 1997: 13; Pink 2001: 1).

The study of public culture in contemporary urban contexts has shifted anthropological attention towards the mediation of power and the manipulation of media, as well as practices of normalization (see Ginsburg, Abu-Lughod and Larkin 2002). With regard to the cinema of Greece as another marginalized 'minor, peripheral, popular cinema' of Europe (Iordanova 2006), several scholars have illustrated its relation with the dominant national discourses, especially during the period when it was becoming established (1950–75), arguing that this was based on the projection of selected readings, which highlighted the politics of tourism (Eleftheriotis 1995; Constantinidis 2000; Kymionis 2000; Tsitsopoulou 2000; Dermentzopoulos 2002; Papadimitriou 2006; S. Dimitriou 2011). Cinema, however, is not merely a reflection of national hegemony but, among other things, a performative space of identity formation (Butler 1993), with different groups striving for representation (Page 2009). By tracing the powerful relationship between cinema and society, therefore, the focus of this chapter turns to what the viewers say. Specifically, adopting an anthropological conception of the viewer as a political subject 'thinkable and practicable by means of mass-mediated communications' (Cody 2011: 38), it focuses on 'seeing' as a form of exploration and understanding of the world (Buck-Morss 1991), and on how it triggers a dialogue between 'viewers' and the world around them that moves beyond spectatorship. Attention, then, turns to the ways in which film viewers commented on the outside world through cinematic dance scenes and thus beyond their comments about films as isolated cinematographic artefacts.

To examine the forms of social interaction that came up through cinematic dance, this chapter draws upon the concept of 'cultural proximity' as it has been conceptualized by Michel Serres (1995) and recently discussed by Daniel Knight (2015). More specifically, the French philosopher Michel Serres has worked on the theory of cultural proximity based on the superimposition of different temporalities, arguing that 'two distant points can suddenly become close, even superimposed' (1995: 57–59). Serres discusses issues of time in terms of non-linear progress. He focuses on distances among points, moments and ideas, and underscores the fact that, even though they are distant, there are several reasons that can bring them very close. These are related to the power with which several moments in our lives are imbued and which can pull them together. Approaching the concept of cultural proximity from an anthropological perspective, Knight (2015) argues that cultural proximity depends on one or more defined historical moments where people can recognize past traits in their present lives and feel as if they are in a context where both past and present collapse into the same meaningful moment. Knight addresses the ways people explain what happens to their lives using different folds of public, domestic, conscious and unconscious spheres.

Following this lead, the present chapter focuses on certain cinematic dance scenes that have sparked social dialogue in both public and domestic settings. My interlocutors used Greek films from the 1970s, and especially from the Junta period, as examples in their effort to explain the current economic downturn. What follows will elaborate on how people tried to analyse their current circumstances by bringing different historical times closer to the present through dance and embodied memory. Cultural proximity, therefore, is not about just recalling the past, but also about bringing to the fore historical time and social memory mediated through the body (Knight 2012: 359).

My ethnographic account oscillates between the comments through which certain people foregrounded the metaphorical use of dance, and specifically cinematic dance, in their everyday narratives, and the claims of others that it was 'inconceivable' and 'irrational' to feel like dancing during the crisis. However, my informants perceived dance as a practice of self-empowerment and a form of 'fighting' against the crisis. This was relevant to the notion of viewing life in Greece as an ongoing struggle. Dancing, therefore, despite its 'irrationality', facilitated people's livelihoods in an uncertain social context. From this perspective, dance is not just about self- or community expression, or collective symbols, but additionally 'it structures and spreads cultural meaning' (Zografou 2006: 88), 'cultivating a dialogic and practical narration infused with political considerations' (Zografou and Pipyrou 2008). Although dance as an embodied social practice can become a locus for the acting out of competition and differentiation (idem 2011), it is also intrinsically related to collaboration and solidarity, as well as to the handling of difficult situations in transitional and religious celebrations (see Campbell 1964: 114–23; Danforth 1995: 197; Nitsiakos 2003: 158; Zografou 2003: 18, 70; Bareli 2013).

Yet the notions of dancing as a practice of self-empowerment and solidarity, as well the idea of life in Greece as an ongoing struggle, have been relatively sidelined in anthropological accounts of the current economic crisis.[4] Even though anthropologists have extensively discussed the agonistic dimension of life in Greece in relation to previous crises, especially in the twentieth century (e.g., Herzfeld 1985; Dubisch 1995; Knight 2012), dance as a culturally significant process pertinent to self-empowerment and solidarity is missing from the discussions on the current recession. Adding to the growing anthropological literature on the economic crisis in southern Europe (see Knight and Stewart 2016), the aim here is to contribute to the ethnographic exploration of responses to austerity.

Constituting an embodied, local critical commentary on the crisis (see Kirtsoglou 2010) and formulating a site of 'informal resistance' (idem 2004), cinematic dance became an explanatory tool and part of an informal political discourse at the local level. According to Theodossopoulos (2014a), anti-austerity local discourse can be acknowledged as indirect resistance to neoliberal economic priorities and provide an explanation of the crisis. Theodossopoulos calls for the 'de-pathologizing [of] vernacular political discourse' (ibid.: 492), and he explains that 'when applied to social processes, pathologization – the tendency to treat a condition as psychologically abnormal – usually aims at de-legitimizing the social process in question: its dismissal as either detrimental or unreasonable, or even unhealthy and potentially destructive' (idem 2014b: 419). Moving beyond their 'denigration as irrational or pathological' (idem 2014a: 492), this chapter highlights the power of both local political discourse and dance.

Reflections on Fieldwork

Conducting fieldwork on Greek cinematic dance has been the result of three different but equally strong influences on me. The cornerstone has been my father. As an electrician, he was working in cinemas during the 1960s. Through my father's narratives, I learned about the 'tough' historical circumstances in Greece in the 1960s and the conditions of cinema screenings through his time in the projection room, where he handled the screening of the film. His narratives gave breath to what I watched in *Cinema Paradiso*, a film by Jussepe Tornatore (1988). My father used to say that 'cinema is education: you can learn and craft your view of the world around you through the directors' perspectives'. Also inspirational was my relationship with Korydallos, a city with its own cinematic history. Korydallos is located between two important and influential cities – Athens and Piraeus (the central port of Greece). Firstly, Korydallos is the place where I spent my childhood. Additionally, since 2003, Korydallos has been where I live and work. As a result, I have experienced the city in several different ways. Working for the local municipal government – mainly as an administrator but also as a dance teacher – provided me with the opportunity to meet and share my thoughts with many people. Last but not least, the impetus to study the intersection of dance and cinema stemmed from a study of Zorba's cinematic dance (Zografou and Pateraki 2007), which marked the starting point of my involvement in the anthropology of dance.

I conducted my research in Korydallos from July 2011 to June 2013. During my fieldwork, I talked with people who lived, studied and worked in the area and accompanied them to different places inside and outside of the city, such as to the cinema club *Cine-Parádeisos* – named by Jussepe Tornatore himself after his film *Cinema Paradiso*. Moreover, we watched films on video together in their living rooms, attended dance performances in theatres, and went to dance clubs and taverns, socializing, drinking, eating and dancing.[5] Furthermore, I participated to a plethora of self-organized, self-funded dinner parties and dance events. People would bring some food or wine, or help in some way with the organization of the events (e.g., by cleaning or bringing chairs and tables from their homes).

Additionally, I followed people to a number of free local events. The organizers, under the notion that 'no one should be alone during the crisis', tried through solidarity networks to encourage people to participate in these collective events.

The next section of this chapter will start with a very brief exposition of the historical and cultural roots of *zeibékiko* dance, upon which the two cinematic dance performances used as case studies are based, followed by a concise discussion of the historical period in which the films were produced. Then, the storyline of each film will be presented, describing the particular dance scenes and elaborating on my interlocutors' narratives about them. Finally, one specific ethnographic dance event in which cinematic dances were performed will be examined in detail. This event was a staged Greek-traditional dance performance organized by a municipal dance troupe in Korydallos. As a result of tight economic policies, public funding was scarce and thus the members of the troupe (almost 150 people) had decided to share the cost of the event between them in order to be able to celebrate with their friends and relatives. As one of my interlocutors, who was sitting beside me that night, told me: 'Dance animates you ... it gives you strength .... It's really important for people to dance from time to time'.[6]

Zeibékiko

The dance performances that this chapter will focus on are based on *zeibékiko* motifs and draw upon an urban folk culture known as *rebétiko*.[7] *Zeibékiko* (plural *zeibékika*) is a powerful solo dance with rich masculine associations that started being performed by women only lately and mainly in urban settings. In more traditional contexts during the 1960s and 1970s, for example, the reaction to a woman dancing to a *zeibékiko* was so strong that in some places the musicians would stop playing and put their instruments aside (see Kirtsoglou 2004). As Kirtsoglou writes in her ethnography of central Greece in the early 2000s, most of the characteristics of the *zeibékiko* remain intact today, apart from two main features: many people can dance a *zeibékiko* simultaneously and some of those dancers can be women.

Zeibékiko dance refers to boldness and resilience among poor people (Damianakos 1987 61–62). Expressing significant 'cultural stuff' (Barth 1969: 16), *zeibékiko* also refers to *magkiá* (mainly meaning 'skilfulness'), which contributes to people's ability to survive. According to Damianakos and his extensive analysis of *rebétika* songs as a peculiar expression of folk tradition in urban places, *zeibékiko* dance is 'par excellence the solitary and individual expression of the new conditions governing social relations of anonymous urban society dominated by kinetic improvisation' (ibid.: 61–62). *Zeibékiko* indicates the wandering of the solitary man, the lack of permanent housing and his ongoing movement, which is related to *rebétes*' worldview of personal independence and freedom. At the core of *zeibékiko* is a contradiction between, on the one hand, relations of solidarity within a small group of people that give priority to openness and honesty among friends, as well as a sense of pride, and on the other hand the rejection and depression of the solitary man who, through his mute movements of despair, tries to be released. As Cowan (1990: 175) points out in her research in northern Greece in the late 1980s, even though *zeibékiko* performances are public, *zeibékiko* rests on the originality and talent of the dancer, who engages in an almost esoteric pursuit of the perfect, controlled, intense performance that exists only for himself.

The Production Period of the Films: Social and Political Context

The 1950s was a period of reorganization for Greece after a long time of successive disturbances – the Greco-Italian War (1940), the German Occupation (1941–44) and, finally, the Civil War (1946–49) – during which people faced division, bloody conflict and 'social and political ostracism' (Avdela 2006: 16). The economic progress during the 1950s and 1960s was based on the flow of both state and private foreign capital but could not sustain a socioeconomic balance. It was during this era of social conflict and strong arguments that centred on the question of whether Greece belonged to the West or to the East (see Herzfeld 1989) that Greek cinema was established, growing into a 'western context' (Constantinidis 2000). The Greek military dictatorship of 1967–74, which is considered by some as the culmination of the turmoil of the 1940s (see Clogg 2002), was a watershed regime for Greek political life and cinema as well. Foreign interventions, the fiscal policy at the end of the 1960s, which had worried the country's economic oligarchy, and, finally, certain military views that the country was 'exposed to communism' led to a surprise coup d'état, which initially met no resistance (ibid.: 185). However, the rest of the period until the fall of the Junta was ambiguous, as on the one hand people resisted the military regime,[8] while on the other hand U.S. policy attempted to normalize the political situation by supporting the participation of Greek politicians in it (see Svoronos 1986).

The impact of the dictatorship was felt across the country, as well as in each and every aspect of cultural and cinematic production (Papargyris 2006: 99–100). As Papargyris notes, *Evdokía* is remembered as an 'authentic and insightful portrayal of life in Greece during the Junta period; it is a film that is representative of Damianos's ability to encapsulate the harshness of the period' (ibid.: 104). *Evdokía* is the second and most successful film by Alexis Damianos. Originally entitled 'The Prostitute and the Soldier', *Evdokía* was at first censored for its politically controversial content, although the ban was eventually lifted. It was an exceptionally successful endeavour, especially if one takes into consideration the bleak conditions in Greece at the time. It sold an impressive 70,852 tickets in the year of its release and won the special award of the Cineclubs of France (ibid.: 98). *Evdokía* occupies a special position in the history of Greek cinema, not only because of its artistic properties, but also because of the politically sensitive time in which it was made. Damianos was able to remain true to the spirit of everyday life with its mundane preoccupations and characters. At the same time, he kept his work away from the trap of excessive dramatization.

In terms of filming techniques, *Evdokía* was influenced by Italian neorealism, while the film's music was composed by Manos Loizos, who was influenced by *rebétiko* and urban folk culture. At the time, significant new developments were already taking place in the Greek world of film. In 1971, several younger directors satisfied the need for a new, innovative national cinema in the tradition of the French nouvelle vague and other European cinematic movements. The 'New Greek Cinema', as it came to be called later, made its appearance during this period and *Evdokía* was among the films that constituted the foundation of this movement. However, even though this movement had political resonance, it was never truly popular mainly because of its lack of continuity and coherence (Papargyris 2006: 104).

On the other hand, Nikos Foskolos, who was the director and scriptwriter of *Oratótis Midén*, shot that film in 1970 as part of the mainstream production of the period. *Oratótis Midén* belongs to a corpus of films that were later identified by scholars as films of 'social accusation' (Kartalou 2005: 324). As Kartalou argues, films of social accusation articulate 'a rhetoric that concerns society through a personal case, [while] the solution is in the hands of someone that can make the difference' (ibid.: 161). In contrast to *Evdokía*, where the main characters were played by amateurs or novice actors, *Oratótis Midén* featured several well-known actors, such as Nikos Kourkoulos (in the role of Aggelos Kreouzis), Mary Chronopoulou, Manos Katrakis, Nikos Galanos, Spyros Kalogirou, Aggelos Antonopoulos and Vaggelis Kazan, among others. Its iconic dance scene has been the most popular and enduring scene across all films of social accusation (ibid.: 327). Following Kartalou, it could be argued that its popularity derives mainly from the fact that it brings into sharp focus what happens when someone chooses to engage in social accusation. This dance scene and its relevance to my informants' narratives will be examined below, before the *zeibékiko* dance scene in *Evdokía* is explored.

'It's Raining Fire on My Path'

According to the script of *Oratótis Midén*, Aggelos Kreouzis, the protagonist, works as an oiler for a shipping company. After a disastrous shipwreck, he is the only man to survive from the crew. He decides to expose the shipping company's wrongdoings, a process which, among other consequences, results in the death of the company's owner. The decision to expose the company leads to their intervention each time Aggelos attempts to find a new job. As a result, Aggelos and his brother cannot find a way to make a living and that forces the latter to leave school and get a job, without saying anything to Aggelos. When Aggelos eventually finds out the truth, he becomes furious with his brother and they end up fighting. As Aggelos returns home, another shock awaits him. Because of an eviction notice, his belongings have been thrown into the yard outside of his house. Aggelos has reached his lowest point. Under the pressure of ultimate desperation, he sets a fire and burns all his things. Before doing so, however, he uses his gramophone, a gift from his brother, to play a song entitled 'Vréhei Fotiá sti Stráta Mou' (It's Raining Fire on My Path), originally performed by Stratos Dionysiou (1970; music by Mimis Plessas and lyrics by Lefteris Papadopoulos).[9] The song refers to a symbolic death: a burning fire ends Aggelos's previous way of life. There is no place for this way of life any more, because his pursuit of social justice has brought about his social death. As such, he decides to make a new beginning. After his constant failures, Aggelos finally begins a love affair with the deceased company owner's daughter. By reaching an agreement with the company's representatives, he gradually rises to a management position. Unfortunately, another shipwreck occurs and, for the second time, Aggelos has to tell the truth about the cause of the shipwreck and the company's responsibilities.

The Case of Georgia and Thaleia

The film became very popular and the featured dance has been undeniably the most well-known cinematic *zeibékiko* dance in Greece. Although Aggelos, the lead actor, is not actually dancing (Kartalou 2005: 357), the camera's movement transforms his actions into choreography. In her extensive analysis of social accusation films that were made by mainstream filmmakers in Greece during the Junta era, Kartalou comments that Aggelos Kreouzis is facing a hysterical inability to find any alternative and finally finds himself at point zero. After reaching this point zero, and following his reaction to it, he finds a new way to survive and improve his social standing.

While being interviewed on cinematic dance and the 'crisis', my interlocutors recounted the film's storyline and specifically the aforementioned dance scene. Two events, seemingly far apart – the famous cinematic scene from the 1970s on the one hand and contemporary hardship on the other – were brought into proximity; a proximity facilitated by a shared notion of the crisis and common narratives about the uncertainty of survival. Along with others in Korydallos, Georgia and Thaleia, two women who were brought very close due to the circumstances, spoke to me of the scene during my fieldwork. Georgia and Thaleia were good friends and lived in different flats in the same building. Their friendship is based on an idea of solidarity that both share and which is expressed in their everyday lives. They have always helped each other when needed (e.g., sharing food, Thaleia caring for Georgia's children, and so on). Georgia was a 45-year-old, unemployed single parent with two children. Georgia has a degree in accounting, but after she got married she stayed at home, mainly taking care of her husband, children and parents. Her husband had a good income but, following his death in 2009, Georgia had to find a job. During the recession this was very difficult.

Consequently, Georgia was working sporadically in different jobs, mainly as an administrator. Thaleia was a 45-year-old, freelance visual artist, divorced with no children. She spent most of her time in a painting studio that she had set up in her flat, working on ideas for different projects. She made her living from iconography (εικονογραφία), but her income was just enough to make ends meet.

Georgia commented on the economic crisis as follows:

> What happens now concerns everyone [the Greek people]. Business activity is shrinking and that applies to all of us. Everyone has more or less contributed to this situation. Even though we didn't have lots of expenses and deposits, we have, in our way, contributed to what has happened. We all made mistakes. Of course, we're now paying for them, but to a greater extent than we should. Others have made bigger mistakes but now we all pay the same, even though it shouldn't be so. In fact, compared to those who overspent or abused their power, we're perhaps even paying more. Our parents made a fresh start after World War II. We went a step further. If I were more conservative in my spending, I would probably own a second flat now. However, I wasn't – I chose to have more fun, a better quality of life. I wouldn't change a single thing from the life I lived. See what's happening now.

Agreeing with the above comment, Thaleia concluded: '*It's raining fire on our path*. We have to reset and start from the beginning'.

Georgia and Thaleia are critical both towards their personal choices and the national discourses on the economic crisis. The national discourse mainly expresses the idea that severe austerity, as provided by external 'experts', is the only solution to the financial crisis. This is based on the moral notion that Greeks have to 'pay back' for a way of life that they did not deserve. This 'undeserved' form of life has culminated in punitive measures, ranging from extra taxes to the paying back of bank loans without any changes to their terms, although many people have lost their jobs or half of their income. By evoking the 'point zero' of the famous film, Thaleia and Georgia perceive the economic recession as the lowest point, where a change is needed in order to improve, hence the need for a turning point. Georgia perceives the economic crisis as an event that is the same for all Greeks. However, she makes a distinction based on what each one has to pay back. The recession may concern everyone, yet mistakes are not the same for everyone. She clarifies her choices and defends them by giving priority to 'a better quality of life', which she relates to having 'more fun' instead of making a fortune or providing her family with a 'second flat'. However, she also holds a 'mainstream expectation', as Theodossopoulos puts it: the idea that life becomes more comfortable over time, from generation to generation, as a rather 'naturalized perception' (2014: 493). Thaleia explicitly identifies the hard austerity of the economic crisis with the outstanding cinematic dance scene, stressing that people have reached their limits, their own point zero. She chooses to bring up this specific scene and explore the present through it. Georgia also projects the new beginnings that her parents' generation experienced in the 1950s and 1960s as internal migrants (from rural areas to urban centres) onto the contemporary predicament and the urgent need to 'reset and restart'.

The notion of a new beginning is a way to distance oneself from attitudes that brought people to this situation. Georgia and Thaleia do not reflect on economic crises as being inherent to capitalism (see Marx 1990 [1867]); instead, they focus on their personal and collective responsibility. Trying to think positively, they stress their expectation of a new beginning that will include *them* as well. They look for a beginning that can improve their own lives specifically, not only generally and anonymously. Based on their belief that there is still light at the end of the tunnel for them, they draw parallels between the disaster of the war and the economic crisis, mediating such connections through the social death of Aggelos Kreouzis. They superimpose two distant historical times through the 'point zero'.

The focus on my interlocutors' comments allows us to see how they 'understand history as well as [how] they participate in its creation' (Kirtsoglou 2010: 2). Furthermore, this is articulated, as can be seen from the above commentaries, by putting their narratives into broad historical contexts (World War II; their parents' actions), which have shaped their perception of history. Given that these 'narrations are imbued with historicity and cultural meaning' (idem 2004: 98), they bring together the power of personal and public history. Inside informal commentaries, then, there is a locus for rethinking and reforming history and social processes, where agents have the ability to act, as Kirtsoglou suggests (2010). Georgia's rhetoric, for example, reveals certain cracks in the formal national discourse about the economic crisis (i.e., the recession concerns everyone; but everyone does not pay based on his or her responsibility and capacity). Although informal, these local commentaries are popular and criticize the 'naturalness' of the crisis. As severe austerity seems to have lost its capacity as an adequate solution to the problems people face, my interlocutors point towards the possibility of a new beginning, precisely as the film suggests. In doing so, they choose a dominant discourse (i.e., social accusation means social death) as a context for understanding and critiquing the contemporary situation. Even though *Oratótis Midén* means metaphorically that things are blurred, and while individual social accusation equals social death, the two women suggest that the point zero is already here; and that, after all this, there has to be a new beginning. While this new beginning seems inevitable, as there is nothing left to lose, it does not correspond with the beginning of Aggelos Kreouzis. By contrast, it shines a light in the darkness, because it can be hopeful. My interlocutors underscore that the 'bleeding' of Greek society has to stop here. Even though they have no clear sense of what this new beginning could be, their daily practices of solidarity demonstrate what it might entail.

'Evdokia's Dance Is an Antidote to the Crisis'

Evdokía recounts an episode from the life of a beautiful young prostitute who makes a desperate effort to escape her destiny. The film follows Evdokia's affair and subsequent marriage to Yiorgos, a sergeant of the Greek army. Mainly due to Evdokia's profession, their relationship immediately faces the mockery of Yiorgos's fellow soldiers and the hostility of Evdokia's entourage. Their marriage cannot withstand the social pressure it is subjected to and comes to a dramatic end with serious consequences for both protagonists. According to Valoukos (2011), *Evdokía* is a film that expresses a notion of Greekness as it has been encapsulated in the work of the Greek poet Odysseas Elytis, which blends folk tradition, the countryside and its bright light, as well the ancient Greek and latter Byzantine-Christian culture. This film is about a love story that represents the subversion of urban stereotypes for marriage, women and morality. It is a social drama based on allegory, where love stands for happiness but also emerges as a reminder of the viewers' period of innocence. However, love can be also a medium for exercising power, authority and ultimately oppression (ibid.: 79–80). Lakis Papastathis, the assistant director of *Evdokía*, has mentioned that the soldier represents the ethos of Greece and the Greek countryside and thus is opposed to the governors of that period (ibid.: 82). The dance scene comes when Evdokia and Yiorgos, accompanied by a fellow soldier, meet for the first time in a rundown tavern. Evdokia, a frequent visitor, is with her pimp and his friends, a particularly aggressive group. As Yiorgos dances and openly courts Evdokia, a fight breaks out between him and Evdokia's pimp.[10] The two soldiers escape unharmed and return to the barracks.

The Case of Mary and Alkis

The Greek state's continuous raising of taxes and the gradual shrinkage of employment have added to people's everyday uncertainty about their work and income. This has resulted in prolonged inactivity, which has strongly affected the lower-middle classes since 2008. Mary was a 43-year-old woman, married with two children, and she works as a lawyer. She has supported her own law firm since the early 2000s. Working as a self-employed lawyer during the economic crisis makes it very hard for her to 'stand on [her] feet', as she explains to me. 'Our only future would be to become low-income employees somewhere'. Before the recession, Mary was planning to move [her] firm to the city centre, to a more comfortable place, and employ two young colleagues to work with her. Instead, she decided to stay in the same place and work on her own without any help, as sometimes she could not even afford to pay her own expenses. By using a metaphor, she highlights an aspect of handling the resulting uncertainty through dance:

I feel like I dance the *'zeibékiko* of Evdokia'. Two people are fighting against the system; they know that they probably cannot achieve their goal but still they dance, they challenge it. It seems that they're thinking: 'I'll try it, even if it's going to stop here'. They're trying, they're struggling, knowing that there's a predetermined situation that others have decided for them, but they won't allow it without a fight.

Mary uses the film *Evdokía* to elaborate on her understanding of the economic crisis. In doing so, she identifies the couple with herself and the Greek people. Moreover, Mary identifies the couple's entourage, who are against their decision to live together, as 'the system'. For her the system is the global economic system that imposes severe austerity on the Greek people through transnational institutions (i.e., the 'Troika'). Yet, even though things are dominated by the system, people still have to keep fighting. Facing the problems of the economic crisis in her everyday life, Mary feels that she is fighting against the system. Mary concedes that this fight is extremely difficult, because the opposite side is almost impossible to subdue, just as in the film (i.e., the prostitute's fate is predetermined – she is not destined for marriage and true love). However, it is a fight for life, not for money, as Mary argues.

Fighting for life until the end is an idea shared by many people in Korydallos. One of them is Alkis. I had known Alkis several years before I started my fieldwork. He was a 55-year-old secondary school teacher, married with two children, who are university students, and he has lived in Korydallos for almost thirty years. The economic crisis affected his life significantly. Even though both Alkis and his wife had jobs and their family as a whole was frugal, they still had financial problems. Exceptional expenses, as the recent loss of both of his parents within a two-year period demonstrated (i.e., hospital and funeral costs, as well as inheritance tax), were overwhelming. At the same time, Alkis had to help some of his unemployed relatives. Feeling that economic austerity had turned his life upside down, he used to say: 'I am dead'. He commented:

[Having] no money means you're still. Everything stops. For instance, my car and heating system are still without fuel. However, this dance [the *'zeibékiko* of Evdokia'] can put in motion the whole world for me, this is my feeling when I listen to it. It's an 'antidote' to the crisis. I collect every version of Evdokia's melody. Whenever I listen to it, I start moving. For example, if I'm driving, I might stop my car, get out and dance to it. The roles [in the film] characterize our life; we carry them within us. The soldier in the film is facing embarrassments and abuse. He has no power to attack the gangsters. However, because he's in the army he scares them, as well as invoking respect, and they don't go near him. This is not a dance – I feel I come out of my body, I look at myself, I like to look at myself dancing it. Even a dead man can dance it. It's psychological and physical resurrection. It feels like you're flying, your mind is flying. The body is dancing on earth and you're looking from above. That's why I don't feel tired when I dance to it. Not every *zeibékiko* dance, but this particular one. Let me explain. It was winter, before the Junta's subversion. I bought the vinyl record with the songs from the film. I had to work on an assignment that was part of a school celebration. It was a study on *zeibékiko* dance. First we had to talk about it and then someone had to dance. As I was very fond of this kind of music, my friends suggested that I should do it. Following the celebration, I became obsessed with it and I danced it everywhere, it was my dance. After several years, in 1989, I shared it again with my colleagues; it was a period when we were working on union actions and we had organized an excursion. Recently, in 2007, we met and danced it once more, celebrating again our trade union movement.

The above narrative, just like various other formal commentaries and economic analyses, addresses the financial crisis in Greece as a form of 'stillness' that has strongly affected people's lives. 'Austerity makes my life still', Alkis told me. Yet this stillness – this 'point zero' – can be challenged by its antidote, namely his favourite dance performance, which, for him, means literal and metaphorical mobility. A cinematic dance performance penetrates his life. This dance, as Alkis said, is '*not* a dance'. Actually, it is more than its choreography that is significant to him; this *zeibékiko* is an orchestration that can move 'the whole world'. Through this dance he becomes alive – it sets in motion his body, mind and soul. As Alkis explained, this cinematic dance brings together different significant moments from his life, which overlap at the current juncture. The dance has an ability to motivate him, although things seem to have come to a halt.

As one of Kirtsoglou's informants in Kallipolis, in central Greece, illustrates: 'When you dance a *zeibékiko* you feel like a king, like a God. All that is large becomes small and all that is small becomes large' (2004: 14). This comment echoes my interlocutors' statements above when they refer to a notion of self-empowerment through dancing. In the case of Georgia, Thaleia, Mary and Alkis, dance expresses the embodiment of their struggle against a way of life that becomes worse every day. As such, it constitutes a commentary about austerity, the 'Greekness' and the supposed naturalness of the economic crisis, as well as asserting their choices to fight for a better life instead of becoming resigned to their fate. On the one hand, Georgia and Thaleia want to change their lives; they want to discard the past and make a new beginning. On the other hand, Mary and Alkis want to fight for what they have lost, trying to get something out of 'the system', as the soldier in *Evdokía* tries to do. Still, as Alkis commented, 'everyone faces it alone'. Indeed, these two alternatives are guiding my interlocutors in a rather lonely path. In both cases, they try, but they do so in very small groups.

They need to extend their collaborations. They need to connect their voices with other people's voices and work together towards a better life through acting collectively and expanding their solidarity networks.

Collectively Reworking Embodied Memories

This chapter has so far examined the stories of particular individuals and the role of cinematic dance in their lives. This section, therefore, presents a distinctive moment from my fieldwork, which demonstrates the collective reflexivity enacted by the performance of cinematic dance. The municipal group for 'Greek traditional dance' in Korydallos organizes a special event in June every year to mark the end of the dance courses. The 2013 event was a particularly important occasion as the group was going to celebrate their twenty-fifth anniversary, as well as the founding teacher's twenty-fifth year of involvement. It was a glamorous event with gilded costumes, well-known musicians and skilful dancers. Arrangements had been made between the dancers and the municipality regarding lowering the costs of both the costume rental and hiring the band. This event was a collective effort and at the same time an act of solidarity, as it was free for anyone who wanted to attend. Friends and relatives of the dancers, as well as students and workers, had gathered for the dance event.

Among various melodies from well-known Greek films, the *zeibékiko* 'Vréhei Fotiá sti Stráta Mou' was given an exceptional position. A politician, who was particularly popular and beloved in Korydallos and played a central role in local political life, was sitting at the front. Suddenly, the dancing and the music stopped. Dancers went close to the politician and asked him to dance with them. He accepted the invitation and the well-known song started again: 'It's raining fire on my path, fire that burns me ...'. The audience clapped rhythmically and sang with passion. The politician danced modestly. Even though he was a political leader, he definitely was not the kind of person to take a leading role in the dance. Applauding and exclamations were opening up his path to dance. His dance was a humble, easy-going *zeibékiko*, in contrast to the fancy and skilful performance of the dancers a few minutes earlier. His dance was more familiar to the audience because it resembled how they would dance.

The connotations of this cinematic dance allowed people in the small theatre to interpret present time through things they had seen in the past, by recalling certain significant moments. Thus, the audience invoked their memories of that cinematic scene of the 1970s and brought them close to contemporary time through their passionate singing of the song's lyrics, participating in the politician's dance. A cinematic dance performance from the 1970s – which had its own historical context – was becoming part of contemporary time. Following Knight (2015), we could say that this dance emerged as an assemblage of different embodied historicities, superimposed through social memory, voice and bodily movement. Moreover, it stressed the message of the song that a certain way of life ends here by recalling the scene in which Aggelos Kreouzis ends his way of life by burning his belongings. The presence of the local political leader and the audience reaction demonstrate people's shift to community networks that local governments can support. The encouragement from the audience was both a reward for what already exists and a claim for more.

On a basic but fundamental level, this dance event highlighted another dimension, namely that, despite the economic crisis, people still manage to collaborate and transform their problems into opportunities for gathering and having fun. It also demonstrated how culturally significant dance motifs, in this case *zeibékiko*, shape embodied memory where different elements enact a hybrid process, which 'transforms static reminisces into reworking memory' (Knight 2012: 359). This process 'combines previous experiences and nationalized discourses which penetrate the private space through public channels and contribute to the conception of the symbolic meaning' (ibid.). The politician's performance was based on a well-known *zeibékiko* melody from a cinematic dance scene that was part of the previous experience of many people and had become the key symbol of social accusation in the 1970s, as well as the national symbol of 'masculine dance', as my interlocutors emphasized (see also Kartalou 2005). Additionally, the lyrics were related to disaster – the point zero. Seeing that things are getting worse, people in Korydallos highlight that, finally, Greece has reached point zero in terms of the economic crisis.

Cultural proximity allows us to see how people manage information derived from the public sphere through a 'hub formation that remains active in memory' (Knight 2012: 359). This recorded, embodied memory emerges in action. This was well-expressed during my fieldwork, conveying the strong relation between viewers and certain actors, film directors, dancers and cinematic scenes. These scenes embodied the key national and cultural narratives of a particular era. However, they also became the means to critique the current situation. As Georgia and Thaleia stressed, there is a strong need for a turning point, but not for giving up. Instead, through cinematic dance, people challenged the formal discourse that provided austerity as the only solution.

Epilogue

The use of cinematic dance in Korydallos was one of the ways in which my informants explained, criticized and responded to the economic crisis and handled the imposed harsh austerity. The hope for a new beginning and the fight for a better life were the main points that people in Korydallos argued about, revealing on the one hand the way they understood the economic crisis and on the other hand the manner in which they addressed this situation. Carrying their own historical context, cinematic scenes become part of our present time, too. Dance performances from Greek cinema were significant for people in Korydallos because they depicted culturally intimate characteristics of people's everyday life. These scenes have also fed public discussion and have become part of the national and cultural fabric by blending past, present and future. The very fact that people in Korydallos foregrounded two films from the Junta period to elaborate on their severe economic hardship forcefully underscores that cinema can be a performative space of informal but powerful political discourse.

The engagement of dance practices in social dialogue and cultural production attests to the fact that dance activities, too, can become the locus for the production of alternative discourses. Thus, dance and discussion about dance and its cinematic mediation reflected political considerations and transformed dance events into sites of collective contestation. Crucially, dance practices demonstrated that people recognized in dance events a place for the acting out of solidarity. Dance emerged as a tangible instantiation of this in Korydallos at that time, allowing people to express their thoughts on society and its history and collectively become part of its ongoing creation.

Acknowledgements

I would like to express my sincere thanks to the Municipality of Korydallos for funding my doctoral studies. Several people have provided advice, inspiration and constructive feedback on versions of this chapter. I am grateful to Magda Zografou, my Ph.D. supervisor, Stavroula Pipyrou and Daniel Knight for providing scholarly inspiration and to Ioanna Papadopoulou for her thought-provoking comments on the first draft of this chapter. I am indebted to Penelope Otapasidou for her very helpful suggestions and proofreading of the chapter. The extensive comments, advice and encouragement provided by the editors of this volume, Evangelos Chrysagis and Panas Karampampas, have been invaluable. This chapter is dedicated to my interlocutors in Korydallos and to the memory of Alinda and Sotiris Dimitriou, who stood by me with love and generosity.

Mimina Pateraki holds a Ph.D. in Anthropology of Dance from the National and Kapodistrian University of Athens. Her doctoral research focused on the anthropological analysis of cinematic dance in Korydallos, Attica. Her work suggests that dance participation can yield rich data that enhance cultural understanding when conducting research in communities where dance matters. She has published on Zorba's cinematic dance and on dance performances as forms of local commentary on nationalization processes.

Notes

1. The social engagement of dance draws upon the idea that art objects can mediate social agency, as explored by Alfred Gell in his landmark study on social relationships and art objects (1998: 6, 16–21). Pipyrou (2016) discusses the social engagement of dance in

her study on power relations within different social networks, such as kinship, friendship and patronage, in the Greek-speaking minority of Reggio Calabria in southern Italy. She argues that power emerges as a direct result of a person's 'productive movement' in action. Studying specific rituals, she reveals that dance can be seen as a symbolic actor (agent) that strengthens the dancers, as they become entities of the tradition in question (see ibid.: 158–84).
2. The 'economic crisis' or 'socioeconomic crisis' in Greece is identified as the period from late 2008 onwards owing to processes at play within wider sociopolitical spheres, such as the Eurozone. Along with other principal national economies that went into recession, the Greek economy faced extensive financial problems by the end of 2009. 'Strategies were implemented on the national and transnational level that would significantly affect the socio-economic prospects of Greeks. A vast range of austerity measures has since been introduced to cut the national deficit' (Knight 2012: 353; see also Rakopoulos 2014). Knight argues that the Greek economic crisis is part of a pan-European economic crisis, which is derived from global economic trends. Following Knight (2012), I suggest that Korydallos can be seen as a microcosm that embodies all the elements of the economic crisis.
3. Evdokia is an ancient Greek female name meaning 'good wisdom'.
4. For a recent ethnographic examination of solidarity in Greece see the Special Section 'The Other Side of the Crisis: Solidarity Networks in Greece' in *Social Anthropology* (2016).
5. However, austerity has dramatically restricted my informants' recreational activities, forcing them into a form of isolation inside their homes (see Pateraki 2014).
6. Interviews and conversations with informants were conducted in Greek. All quotations in this chapter have been translated into English by the author, and the names of informants have been changed to ensure anonymity.
7. *Rebétiko* (plural *rebétika*) reflected diversity in the process of social integration and unification of *rebétes* (*rebétiko* musicians), the inertia of the system and the resistance to marginalization of social groups and cultural traditions that were perceived as inferior. *Rebétes* were mainly related to hashish smokers and petty thieves, as well as working-class people and Greek-speaking refugees after 1922's Asia Minor Catastrophe (see Damianakos 1987; Cowan 1990). *Rebétika* songs manifested social divides and exclusions, and presented a series of 'repressed' experiences and perceptions of the 'silent' daily routine in a simple and joyful manner (Kotaridis 1997: 16).
8. Especially for women's participation in resistance movements during the military dictatorship see Alinda Dimitriou's documentary *Ta Korítsia tis Vrohís* (2011). https://www.youtube.com/watch?v=EIMHAlBfuXM. Accessed 20 March 2016.
9. https://www.youtube.com/watch?v=XcrlQXKwwWM. Accessed 8 March 2016.
10. https://www.youtube.com/watch?v=z1cfln_sV44. Accessed 8 March 2016.

References

Avdela, E. 2006. *For Reasons of Honour: Violence, Feelings and Values in Post-Civil War Greece* [*Δια Λόγους Τιμής: Βία, Συναισθήματα και Αξίες στη Μετεμφυλιακή Ελλάδα*]. Athens: Nefeli.
Banks, M., and H. Morphy. 1997. 'Introduction: Rethinking Visual Anthropology', in M. Banks and H. Morphy (eds), *Rethinking Visual Anthropology*. New Haven, CT: Yale University Press, pp. 1–35.

Bareli, M. 2013. 'Aspects of the Gift and the Commons in the Ikarian Paniyiri: Issues of Social Reproduction and Change', *23rd Biennial International Symposium of the Modern Greek Studies Association, Bloomington, 14–16 November 2013.* Bloomington: Indiana University.
Barth, F. 1969. 'Introduction', in Fredrik Barth (ed.), *Ethnic Groups and Boundaries: The Social Organization of Culture Difference.* Boston: Little, Brown and Company, pp. 9–38.
Buck-Morss, S. 1991. *The Dialectics of Seeing: Walter Benjamin and the Arcades Project.* Cambridge, MA: The MIT Press.
Butler, J. 1993. *Bodies that Matter: On the Discursive Limits of 'Sex'.* New York: Routledge.
Campbell, J.K. 1964. *Honour, Family and Patronage: A Study of Institutions and Moral Values in a Greek Mountain Community.* Oxford: Clarendon Press.
Clogg, R. 2002. *A Concise History of Greece*, 2nd edn. Cambridge: Cambridge University Press.
Cody, F. 2011. 'Publics and Politics', *Annual Review of Anthropology* 40: 37–52.
Constantinidis, S.E. 2000. 'Greek Film and the National Interest: A Brief Preface', *Journal of Modern Greek Studies* 18: 1–13.
Cowan, J.K. 1990. *Dance and the Body Politic in Northern Greece.* Princeton, NJ: Princeton University Press.
Crawford, P.I. 1992. 'Film as Discourse: The Invention of Anthropological Realities', in P.I. Crawford and D. Turton (eds), *Film as Ethnography.* Manchester: Manchester University Press, pp. 66–82.
Damianakos, S. 1987. *Tradition of Rebellion and Folk Culture* [Παράδοση Ανταρσίας, και Λαϊκός Πολιτισμός]. Athens: Plethron.
Damianos, A. 1971. *Evdokía* [Ευδοκία]. Katamor Productions/Poreia. [Film].
Danforth, L. 1995. *The Anastenaria of Saint Helen: Firewalking and Religious Healing* [Τα Αναστενάρια της Αγίας Ελένης: Πυροβασία και Θρησκευτική Θεραπεία], trans. M. Polentas. Athens: Plethron.
Dermentzopoulos, C. 2002. 'Tradition and Modernity in Greek Cinema: The Mountain Adventure Films' [Παράδοση και Νεωτερικότητα στον Ελληνικό Κινηματογράφο: Οι Ταινίες Ορεινής Περιπέτειας], in D. Leventakos (ed.), *Replaying the Old Greek Cinema* [Ξαναβλέποντας τον Παλιό Ελληνικό Κινηματογράφο]. Athens: Greek Directors/Centre of Audiovisual Studies, pp. 79–98.
Desmond, J.C. 1997. 'Introduction', in J.C. Desmond (ed.), *Meaning in Motion: New Cultural Studies of Dance.* Durham, NC: Duke University Press, pp. 1–25.
Dimitriou, A. 2011. *Ta Korítsia tis Vrohís* [Τα Κορίτσια της Βροχής]. Self-Released. [Film].
Dimitriou, S. 2011. *Cinema Today: Anthropological, Political and Semiotic Dimensions* [ΟΚινηματογράφος Σήμερα: Ανθρωπολογικές, Πολιτικές και Σημειωτικές Διαστάσεις]. Athens: Savvalas.
Dionysiou, S. 1970. *Together with Stratos* [Μαζί με τον Στράτο]. Athens: Columbia. [LP].
Dubisch, J. 1995. *In a Different Place: Pilgrimage, Gender, and Politics at a Greek Island Shrine.* Princeton, NJ: Princeton University Press.
Eleftheriotis, D. 1995. 'Questioning Totalities: Constructions of Masculinity in the Popular Greek Cinema of the 1960's', *Screen* 36: 233–42.
Farnell, B.M. 2001. 'Introduction', in B.M. Farnell (ed.), *Human Action Signs in Cultural Context: The Visible and the Invisible in Movement and Dance.* Metuchen, NJ: Scarecrow Press, pp. 1–28.

Foskolos, N. 1970. *Oratótis Midén [Ορατότης Μηδέν]*. Athens: Finos Film. [Film].
Gell, A. 1998. *Art and Agency: An Anthropological Theory*. Oxford: Clarendon Press.
Ginsburg, F.D., Abu-Lughod, L., and B. Larkin. 2002. 'Introduction', in F.D. Ginsburg, L. Abu-Lughod and B. Larkin (eds), *Media Worlds: Anthropology on New Terrain*. Berkeley: University of California Press, pp. 1–36.
Gray, G. 2010. *Cinema: A Visual Anthropology*. Oxford: Berg.
Herzfeld, M. 1985. *The Poetics of Manhood: Contest and Identity in a Cretan Mountain Village*. Princeton, NJ: Princeton University Press.
———. 1989. *Anthropology through the Looking-Glass: Critical Ethnography in the Margins of Europe*. Cambridge: Cambridge University Press.
Iordanova, D. 2006. *The Cinema of the Balkans*. London: Wallflower Press.
Kartalou, A. 2005. 'The Unfulfilled Genre: Films of Social Accusation by Finos Film' [Το Ανεκπλήρωτο Είδος: Οι Ταινίες Κοινωνικής Καταγγελίας της Φίνος Φιλμ], Ph.D. dissertation. Athens: Panteion University of Social and Political Sciences.
Kotaridis, N. 1996. 'Introduction', in N. Kotaridis (ed.), *Rebetes and Rebetiko Song [Ρεμπέτες και Ρεμπέτικο Τραγούδι]*, Athens: Plethron.
Kirtsoglou, E. 2004. *For the Love of Women: Gender, Identity and Same-Sex Relations in a Greek Provincial Town*. London: Routledge.
———. 2010. 'Introduction: Rhetoric and the Workings of Power—the Social Contract in Crisis', *Social Analysis* 54(1): 1–14.
Knight, D.M. 2012. 'Cultural Proximity: Crisis, Time and Social Memory in Central Greece', *History and Anthropology* 23: 349–74.
———. 2015. *History, Time and Economic Crisis in Central Greece*. New York: Palgrave Macmillan.
Knight, D.M., and C. Stewart. 2016. 'Ethnographies of Austerity: Temporality, Crisis and Affect in Southern Europe', *History and Anthropology* 27: 1–18.
Kymionis, S. 2000. 'The Genre of Mountain Film: The Ideological Parameters of Its Subgenres', *Journal of Modern Greek Studies* 18: 53–66.
Marx, K. 1990 [1867]. *Capital: A Critique of Political Economy, Volume One*, trans. Ben Fowkes. London: Penguin.
Nitsiakos, V. 2003. *Constructing Place and Time [Χτίζοντας τον Χώρο και τον Χρόνο]*. Athens: Odysseas.
Papadimitriou, L. 2006. *The Greek Film Musical: A Critical and Cultural History*. Jefferson, NC: McFarland.
Papargyris, J. 2006. 'Evdokia: Alexis Damianos, Greece, 1971', in D. Iordanova (ed.), *The Cinema of the Balkans*. London: Wallflower Press, pp. 97–105.
Pateraki, M. 2014. 'Cultural Proximity and Cinematic Dance: An Anthropological Analysis of Cinematic Dance with the "Viewers" in Korydallos, Attica' [Πολιτισμική Εγγύτητα και Κινηματογραφικός Χορός: Ανθρωπολογική Ανάλυση του Κινηματογραφικού Χορού με τους "Θεατές" στον Κορυδαλλό Αττικής], Ph.D. dissertation. Athens: National and Kapodistrian University of Athens.
———. Forthcoming. '"Unforgettable" Beauty in Cinematic Dance: Challenging "Economic" Crisis through Masqueraded Choreographies in Local Rhetoric in Korydallos of Attica, Greece', *Anthropological Notebooks*.

Pateraki, M., and M. Zografou. 2015. 'Avoiding Dilemmas in Film Analysis: A Proposal for Emic Perspective in Anthropological Analysis of Cinematic Dance in Greece', *Papers in Ethnology and Anthropology* 25(14): 29–48.
Page, J. 2009. *Crisis and Capitalism in Contemporary Argentine Cinema*. Durham, NC: Duke University Press.
Pink, S. 2001. *Doing Visual Ethnography: Images, Media and Representation in Research*. London: Sage.
Pipyrou, S. 2010. 'Power, Governance and Representation: An Anthropological Analysis of Kinship, the 'Ndrangheta and Dance within the Greek Linguistic Minority of Reggio Calabria, South Italy', Ph.D. dissertation. Durham: Durham University.
———. 2016. *The Grecanici of Southern Italy: Governance, Violence, and Minority Politics*. Philadelphia: University of Pennsylvania Press.
Rakopoulos, T. 2014. 'The Crisis Seen from below, within, and against: From Solidarity Economy to Food Distribution Cooperatives in Greece', *Dialectical Anthropology* 38: 189–207.
Serres, M. 1995. *Conversations on Science, Culture, and Time*, trans. R. Lapidus. Ann Arbor: The University of Michigan Press.
Sutton, D., and P. Wogan. 2009. *Hollywood Blockbusters: The Anthropology of Popular Movies*. Oxford: Berg.
Svoronos, N.G. 1986. *Overview of Modern Greek History* [Επισκόπηση της Νεοελληνικής Ιστορίας], trans. A. Asdraha. Athens: Themelio.
'The Other Side of the Crisis: Solidarity Networks in Greece'. 2016. *Social Anthropology* 24: 142–210.
Theodossopoulos, D. 2014a. 'The Ambivalence of Anti-Austerity Indignation in Greece: Resistance, Hegemony and Complicity', *History and Anthropology* 25: 488–506.
———. 2014b. 'On De-Pathologizing Resistance', *History and Anthropology* 25: 415–30.
Tornatore, G. 1988. *Cinema Paradiso* [*Nuovo Cinema Paradiso*]. Cristaldifilm/Les Films Ariane/Rai 3/TF1 Films Production/Forum Picture. [Film].
Tsitsopoulou, V. 2000. 'Greekness, Gender Stereotypes, and the Hollywood Musical in Jules Dassin's *Never on Sunday*', *Journal of Modern Greek Studies* 18: 79–93.
Valoukos, S. 2011. *New Greek Cinema [1965–1981]: History and Politics* [Νέος Ελληνικός Κινηματογράφος [1965–1981]: Ιστορία και Πολιτική]. Athens: Aigokeros.
Zografou, M. 2003. *Dance in Greek Tradition* [Ο Χορός στην Ελληνική Παράδοση]. Athens: Art Work.
———. 2006. 'Contemporary Issues in Dance Research: Anthropology of Dance or Ethno-"Chorologia" as Well?' [Σύγχρονοι Προβληματισμοί στην Έρευνα του Χορού: Ανθρωπολογία του Χορού ή και Εθνο-«Χορολογία»;], *Εθνολογία* 12: 173–91.
Zografou, M., and M. Pateraki. 2007. 'The "Invisible" Dimension of Zorba's Dance', *Yearbook for Traditional Music* 39: 117–31.
Zografou, M., and S. Pipyrou. 2008. 'Dancing in History: Socio-Political Aspects of Dance Identity of Two Distinctive Groups in Greece', *Studia Choreologica* 10: 25–41.
———. 2011. 'Dance and Difference: Toward an Individualization of the Pontian Self', *Dance Chronicle* 34: 422–46.

PART V

Motion, Irony and the Making of Lifeworlds

Chapter 9

Performing Irony on the Dance Floor
The Many Faces of Goth Irony in the Athenian Goth Scene

Panas Karampampas

Saturday night at the Darkness club. As George and I were on a sofa glancing around the dance floor, we began gossiping, starting from dance performances and jumping to other, somehow related (or not) topics, such as relations, politics, clothes, travel, sex, fitness and many others. When I asked him why he was not dancing (George spends most of his time on the dance floor), he answered that in that club he did not feel confident to dance because 'they [the other clubgoers] will *ironize* [him] because of [his] different dance style' (*tha me ironeutoúne*).

George started to participate in the goth scene the same day I began my research in 2010 and from his first day he was fascinated by the industrial dance style – it was the period when industrial dance was becoming popular in Greece. Over the years, George became very skilful in industrial dance. However, industrial dance was never accepted in the Darkness club and its patrons have shown a negative attitude towards industrial dancers. George continued: 'However, if you want, you can go and dance but you have to dance in front of Psycho,[1] because the only free space is there', and lowering his voice as if he was talking to himself, he said: 'I wonder why'. I asked him where he meant because I knew that person from Facebook but did not have the chance to be introduced to him face-to-face. George, greatly surprised, replied:

> REALLY? Don't you know him? He's the one who dances two steps forwards, two steps backwards and moves his hands up and down like holding two imaginary knives and endlessly stabbing a poor victim. You can recognize him just from his psychotic gaze. That's why I told you to dance only by facing towards him and not show him your back; that's the reason why there is free dance space in front of him [*laughs*]. Only

Apollo stands a chance against him because his dance is like some kind of alien martial art and John is like a giant who crushes people under each trampling [dance] step.[2]

Although George's comments were humorous, as well as sarcastic, after a long discussion George said that he believed that Psycho was 'not really' psychotic but also 'not totally all right' and that it was better for me to stay away from him. We continued discussing different topics until we returned to dancing. As he recalled certain instances when patrons of Darkness had been looking at him with a condescending gaze, he said with disappointment:

Why is it that when Lilith and Selene go to Darkness, nobody criticizes them, although they [Lilith and Selene] do not dance like Darkness' patrons and are always dressed differently? Even when they wear their [decorative] horns [nobody criticizes them]. Is that because, unlike me, they are regulars at the club?

It was an interesting night. We discussed a lot about dancing, although we did not dance at all.

The goth scene is a musical scene and goth clubs occupy a central role in it because clubs are the main places where goths meet, discuss and have the opportunity to perform their identity. Dance has a central role in the lives of goths. During the performance of goth dance, style and goth practices are intertwined (see Karampampas 2016), individuals exchange ideas and make judgements about and evaluations of others. Goth nights are held weekly in clubs in different cities around the world, thus providing a platform for information exchange among participants in the goth scene. Goth has been influenced by numerous ideas and scenes.[3] From its first appearance and over the last thirty years or so of its development these influences have changed many times, giving birth to new goth styles that coexist and sometimes clash with preceding ones. Irony is the main trope in these internal clashes and it is also used to challenge stereotypes, exclusion and the peripheralization that they face from 'outsiders'.

This chapter examines how Athenian goths[4] use irony when they talk about dance and dancers and how they perform irony in dance, in order to show the centrality of irony in goth. However, the reader should take into account an important factor that Herzfeld has highlighted, namely that in Greece irony (*ironía*) is mostly (but not exclusively) used as an insult or mockery (2001: 73), as well as being a synonym for sarcasm (*sarkasmós*). Due to this complex peculiarity, in each instance here, the overlapping meanings of irony will be provided. In what follows, audiovisual material from social media and the Internet, as well as dance performances in clubs and houses, are scrutinized. This benefits a multilevel and multisensory analysis appropriate for the goth scene, where people very often use or make reference to videos, pictures, songs and dances in their ironic statements.

Focusing mainly on dance and moving bodies, this study analyses how dance and the goth scene are articulated through different types of irony and how these become verbal, somatic and aesthetic statements for goths. Corporeal and verbal performances of irony are used to comment on uncomfortable situations, sociopolitical changes and paradoxes that cannot be fully fathomed, which provide fruitful ethnographic material to be unpacked (Haugerud 2013: 32–36; Pipyrou 2014). This analysis builds on existing ethnographic research on irony in Greece (e.g., Herzfeld 2001; Knight 2015b), which has focused mainly on the political aspect of irony. In addition to these approaches to irony, following the strands of Nigel Rapport (2014) and Ronald Stade (2014), irony is understood here as the human capacity for self-distancing in order to critically reflect on oneself and on the Other. From the various types of irony that Stade analyses, the focus in this chapter is on those that are widely used in goth: nihilistic and liberal ironies.

Nihilism is an important aspect of goth irony. '*Nihilistic* irony dismisses all notions of order and knowledge in a human life … except the knowledge that life is brief, death inevitable, and all interim projects and claims are "therefore" meaningless' (Rapport and Stade 2014: 471; italics in the original). Nevertheless, nihilism is also connected to the second aspect of goth irony, the liberal irony, which is 'an awareness of the contingent, relative nature of any discursive claim, whether to scientific knowledge or moral … . Hence, the liberal ironist hopes to eschew ethnocentrism in a society whose normative arrangements predispose towards tolerance and diversity' (ibid.). This is based on the reasoning that, because life is meaningless, humans are free to live it as they want, as long as they do not interfere with the lives of other individuals. Yet the common destination of all beings, death, creates a common characteristic that brings individuals together and puts their differences aside. It is here that the greatest irony of goth is found, which partially passes unnoticed by outsiders: goth is not about death, but about acknowledging and accepting death in order to celebrate life and what it means to be human.

The next section discusses anthropological theories of irony and relates them to ethnographies that directly or indirectly examine irony in Greece. The following section then aims to contextualize the research and provide an initial understanding of goth based on the existing literature. The third section presents the irony of gothic bodies and dance. Based on three ethnographic examples, it provides a detailed analysis of how and why Athenian goths perform nihilistic and liberal irony in their dance. In the final section, the performance of irony in goth dance and the use of irony in discussions about dance and dancers are explored. In this way, the narratives and performances of my research participants and how they relate themselves and their dance performances to a variety of dances, which they categorize as 'Greek dances', are examined. At the same time, many of them disassociate themselves from, and devalue, 'Greek dances', thus creating additional ironic contradictions. Athenian goths, it will be suggested here, employ irony, self-irony and sarcasm in order to cope with everyday ironic situations. This chapter, therefore, grapples with multiple layers of irony, which are applied in a variety of dance examples in order to illuminate goth dance and identity performance.

Which Irony?

Irony demonstrates a willingness to take a risk and creates a high degree of uncertainty (Malaby 1999; Herzfeld 2001: 63). An ironist challenges another person, an authority or an institution, usually one with higher power or status, with the intention to subvert the established order or become self-critical. Irony is usually a critical reflection on a situation and reveals absurdities and inequalities; it can be linguistic and somatic and can even take the form of an artistic object, while a situation that is challenged through irony becomes clearer and precarious (Herzfeld 2001: 64). However, at times, irony may be so delicate that nobody can be sure whether it was imagined or whether it was an intended action (Comaroff 1985; Scott 1985), thus creating a high degree of uncertainty. This is especially true for nonlinguistic irony (for example, a piece of art or bodily actions), where a gesture can be an ironic comment, while verbally the ironist is offering polite words that contradict the performing body. This may be seen when someone says 'nice to meet you', while his or her facial expressions contradict the verbal statement and show signs of dissatisfaction (as is elaborated below with examples from goth dance). Therefore, in a delicate irony, the ironized cannot take offence because the ironist can easily deny any intention. The accusation of being ironic is then a double-edged sword: it assumes ill intentions, yet then reveals that the accuser perceives the ironist as malicious. Being accused as ill-intentioned can be offensive to the ironist, while also showing that the ironized is projecting their mischievous reasoning to others and that there is some validity in the words of the ironist (Herzfeld 2001). In the introductory vignette, George, being afraid that the patrons of Darkness would ironize him, projected his mischievous reasoning to them, which is verified by the fact that, as our discussion unfolded, he became ironic towards some of his potential ironists as well.

Research focused on the use of irony can provide a deeper understanding of a seemingly straightforward ethnographic scene, analysing its contradictions and complexities (Pipyrou 2014: 533). However, the researcher needs linguistic fluency, attention to every small detail and familiarity with research participants and their bodily and linguistic idioms to understand these slight hints. As Herzfeld notes, the prosodic feature of irony in Greek language can provide further suggestions to the ethnographer (2001: 66), which I also found helpful, although not every irony is prosodic. Prosody can take the form of emphasizing a word in an exaggerated manner, posing a statement as a question, altering the accent of a word or phrase, or other innovative forms depending on the context and the skill of the ironist.

Over six years of fieldwork, I became familiar enough with my research participants to be able to identify even the subtlest forms of irony, regardless of whether the ironist made use of any prosody in their voice. This was because I gradually became efficient in identifying contradictions on topics that we had already discussed and comments that were not in line with the lives of my research participants. Therefore, my long-term fieldwork, along with my background as one who grew up and was educated in Greece and was fluent in Greek, provided me with a sense of 'cultural intimacy' (Herzfeld 1997) and the linguistic and performative awareness to recognize contextual irony (idem 2001: 63; Pipyrou 2014: 538).

Irony can be more than subversion and resistance: 'Irony is to be understood as a human capacity for self-distancing: for reflecting on the self, its social position, its world-views, values and designs on life, and for standing intellectually and emotionally apart from these – for moments at least' (Rapport 2014: 445; see also Stade 2014). Ironists detach themselves in order to critically examine their roles and practices. They try to see themselves and others as role-players who have been asked to play a role of a specific ethnicity, class or nationality. They place themselves in the position of an Other and explore how they *could* be, envisioning themselves with different relationships and lifestyles. They also deconstruct how their communities are presented to them and to the outside world, that is, as essentialistic, singular and homogenous (Rapport 2014: 451–52; see also Amit and Rapport 2002). If the ironist does all this, all the differences will have been placed aside. Then, one can see the others and oneself as individuals, as human beings who recognize one another as being alike in their chosen individual differences; the ironist can become 'Anyone' (Rapport 2003, 2012).

This does not mean that ironists disband any membership or affiliation, but that irony can work as 'a mode of vision' (idem 2014: 449) or as a means to self-alienate and reflect (Stade 2014), which the ironists temporarily use as a device at their own convenience. However, it is a device that provides the freedom to have multiple affiliations; to be cosmopolitan, a citizen (*polítis*) of the world (*cósmos*), not being identified with only one city (*pólis*),[5] and, therefore, to see every person on equal ground; to see every individual as different, while sharing the same cosmos; to see the sameness-in-difference in every human (Rapport 2014). Similar to the human cosmos, the goth scene is articulated by many goth factions (such as trad goths, cybergoths, industrials, Victorian goths), some of which have no obvious connection – stylistic or musical – to each other. However, goths embrace their differences, focusing on the things that they share. This process, mediated by irony, can be traced in the ways that goths try to avoid self-labelling and in how they talk about their body and its extension, that is, their clothes and their dance movements.

Ethnographies in Greece have documented how Greeks use irony as a political commentary (Knight 2015b), have explored the role of irony in everyday language (Herzfeld 2001) and have demonstrated its importance at the nexus between gender, sexuality and dance (Cowan 1990). More specifically, Daniel Knight (2015b) shows how ironic and satirical slogans provide a way for Trikalinoi (people of Trikala city) to express their political agency against austerity measures and the reshaping of social relations resulting from the current economic crisis (see also Chapter 8; Kallianos 2012, 2013; Knight 2013, 2015a; Rakopoulos 2013, 2014a, 2014b; Theodossopoulos 2013, 2014). Slogans are mostly metaphorically related to food, such as: 'For five days you eat cucumber, but on Saturday you are someone' and 'Antoni leave the Wi-Fi and give food to the people'.[6] These slogans highlight everyday difficulties vis à vis people's struggle to keep their values and social status (the former) and the irrationality of the decisions of political leaders (the latter). These ironic and satirical comments do not always target individuals but mostly are addressed to government institutions and politicians in general (see also Muehlebach 2009; Haugerud 2013). Through them, Greeks blame political figures (in Greece and abroad) for the decrease in living standards to resemble those of World War II (Knight 2012). Trikalinoi write ironic slogans on the walls and when they use them in everyday speech they express their fear of returning to a past perceived (by the rest of Europe) as being 'premodern' or 'pre-European' (idem 2015b: 242). They also underscore their collective victimhood and solidarity against the Other, either a politician or an impersonal institution. Irony, in this case, is an act of resistance and hope.

Michel Herzfeld (2001), who mostly focuses on the Greek language, also discusses resistance and hope in the use of irony. Greek 'complex language history in which heightened awareness of the politics of syntax and lexicon offers innumerable opportunities for ironic word play [and] the ambiguous status of Greece itself as both the hearth of Western civilization and the exotic margin of Europe' (ibid.: 66) provide a first understanding of the regular use of irony in Greece. Uses of it range from distinguishing and separating the insider from the outsider and providing a critical political comment showing how the ironist is helpless but ethically superior to the wrongdoings of a politician or an institution (ibid.: 74, 76–77), to creating a feeling of solidarity based on the Greek presumption that human beings are flawed, divided and sinful. Yet acknowledging these human characteristics allows ironists to position themselves in the place of the ironized, thus affording a degree of understanding (ibid.: 77).

If irony in Greece is somewhat under-examined by anthropologists, then irony in Greek dance is rarely mentioned. Jane Cowan provides the only example in the literature of the use of irony in Greek dance. Cowan focuses on dance performances of *zeibékiko* in a formal ball. She explains that, while *zeibékiko* was considered inappropriate for that specific event, the dancer parodied his performance and was thus able 'to transform the meaning of the act by reframing it' (1990: 21). Cowan asserts that: 'Not only [are] the meanings of zeibekiko ... manipulated in performance ... but the performance itself may on occasion constitute a critical multilayered commentary on the unfolding social interaction' (ibid.: 179). In contrast to the above ethnographic examples where irony is a strategy for the oppressed to subvert the order of the powerful, in Cowan's case, an ironic *zeibékiko* dance was performed by the vice-president of the association that organized the ball. Framing his dance, which takes place outside of the formal dance floor (Pateraki and Karampampas 2014: 164; see also Chapter 8), as a 'choreographic joke', he is parodying the 'serious' performances on the central dance floor. Here, a member of the ruling faction reflects on the intense and overly serious atmosphere of the ball and his self-mockery is a strategy to distance himself from the other dancers and their performances. Even in this case, although a person in power performs ironic dance, he still reassesses and subverts existing power relations (Cowan 1990: 179).

Goth and Goth Irony

It is often the case that the term 'goth' is used to categorize a 'youth culture' (Van Elferen 2011: 89). However, the goth scene began in the early 1980s in England and, therefore, some of the early participants who are still members are over forty years old. For these goths, participation in the scene is not a continuation of their youth but a collective experience that accompanies the development of their adult lives (Hodkinson 2011: 262). Goth has been presented as an expression of a participant's feelings (often disappointment) through music, in order to escape a pessimistic reality (Van Elferen 2011: 93) of an unsatisfactory society (Young 1999: 76, 89). Meanwhile, others agree that goth is about self-expression and acceptance (Miklas and Arnold 1999; Hodkinson 2002; Sweet 2005) or the transformation of depression into semi-ironic aesthetics (Brottman 2007; Goulding and Saren 2009: 28; Van Elferen 2011: 100). For others, goth is a scene in which music and style are intimately intertwined through a notion of 'dark' or 'darkness' (Gunn 2007: 43–44, 48). 'Darkness' can possess the simple meaning of being dark in colour, but it can take on alternative meanings, such as 'obscurity' or 'depth', as well as various other more personal interpretations (ibid.: 44). However, for all goths, darkness is an important characteristic of their identities that distinguishes them from the 'mainstream' (ibid.: 45).

Goths are liminal people inspired by Gothic fiction, according to Isabella van Elferen (2009). Gothic creatures are ambiguous beings, between life and death (e.g., vampires, ghosts) or human and machine (e.g., Frankenstein's monster) (ibid.: 100). Gothic time reflects another era while gothic places are distorted, hidden and/or labyrinths. Though historical Gothic differs from the 'subcultural', 'in goth parties you may encounter modern vampires, and at cybergothic parties you meet cyborgs' (ibid: 101). In other words, goths and cybergoths[7] embody a gothic narrative, mediating it through their appearance.

Thus, goths (and cybergoths), according to Van Elferen, 'criticise cultural dichotomies through acceptance and radical incorporation of ambivalence' (ibid.). However, the above statements are replete with (ironic) contradictions between goth narratives and representations and the movement and lifestyle of goths because goths do not live in distorted places or labyrinths and neither are they hybrids of machinery and flesh or undeads, living in another era.

Goths have many different and complex ways of self-labelling, sometimes resisting any sort of labelling (Jasper 2004; Schilt 2007: 77) or using the idea self-ironically (Young 1999: 79, 84; Brottman 2007; Goulding and Saren 2009: 28). Nearly all of my research participants avoided identifying themselves as goths but very often they used self-ironic stereotypes, imposed on goths and their scene by outsiders, to reflect on goth practices and identities. The black colour and clothes are some of them, which Alex and Luna pondered about on Facebook (Illustration 9.1). Both of them have been participants in the scene for over a decade. Alex, a 25-year-old fashion designer, often makes his own club clothes, which combine goth characteristics with historical trends, while 27-year-old Luna is inspired by gothic and sci-fi literature, horror films and punk.

In their comments, both Alex and Luna stand back and reflect on how they follow some of the imposed stereotypes. Another time, in a goth club, Luna was asked by a mutual friend: 'Are you sick or something? Today you are dressed up in red and white and nothing in black! Is that *you*?' And she replied: 'Sorry,

Πας για ψώνια περνας βιτρίνες μαγαζιά κοιτας κοιτας κοιτας...
Καταλήγεις παλι σε 1 σωρό μαυρα ρουχα!
Τι χαρα λες ανανέωσα την μαυρη καρνταρομπα μου!

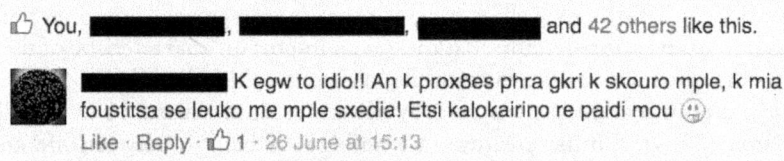

K egw to idio!! An k prox8es phra gkri k skouro mple, k mia foustitsa se leuko me mple sxedia! Etsi kalokairino re paidi mou :)

Illustration 9.1 Alex and Luna's Facebook discussion. Screenshot from the Facebook profile used by the author for research purposes. Alex: 'You go shopping, you do some window shopping, you look, look and look ... you end up again with a pile of black clothes! "What a joy", you say, "I renewed my black wardrobe!"'. Luna: 'Me too!! Though the day before yesterday I bought grey and dark blue [clothes], and a white skirt with blue patterns! You know, something for the summer :p [ironic].

I forgot that I am a goth and I have to wear only black'. Both comments were equally ironic, being critical towards the stereotypes, their identities and the goth scene in general.

Stereotypes are oversimplified conceptions of a group of people and, regardless if they are true or not, they may have some usefulness. Goths often personalize stereotypes, discard or ridicule parts of stereotypes that do not apply to them, and give them diverse interpretations within the context of their own lives. Participating in the 'common and conventional' goth stereotypes becomes another device for them to feel more connected with other goths and enhance the scene's solidarity (Rapport 1995: 269). Flexibility and nonfixation are fundamental characteristics of the goth ironist. A goth may or may not wear black, because certain goth styles are not based on the colour black, while being goth does not mean that one cannot be affiliated with and stylistically influenced by other scenes. Crucially, one may or may not dress up as a goth, because goth is not about style but it is a lifestyle.

Irony of Gothic Bodies and Dancing the Irony

As I was catching up on the phone with Dave, one of my research participants, who the previous year (2014) had relocated in a village in Yorkshire because of his job, he became homesick:

> I hope that we meet again soon in Athens. I miss our nights out. Do you remember the night that the fucking drunken bastard crashed my car? I still wonder how I walked away unscathed. However, I came to the club, and do you remember? I entered, still shocked by the accident, and I came directly to you to request 'Plague' [I was DJ'ing that night] by Mens..., you know what I mean [he cannot pronounce 'Menschdefekt']! You noticed that I was not all right and you asked me what had happened to me. Oh my God! I was so freaked out that I told you 'Fuck you! Just play the song and I will tell you after I dance!' [*laughs*]. After that I felt much better, but now that I think about it that is so ironic. I always liked that song but at that moment was so fitting and relevant. However, even now, the noise of the machines in the factory [where he works] sometimes reminds me the sound of metal during that car crash. And it is in these moments that I miss our nights out the most. I will die anyway. At least, until then I want to listen and dance to my music and be around my friends and not die in this freaking village in the middle of nowhere by an industrial accident.

On Nihilistic Irony

A Victorian goth dresses up similar to Bela Lugosi in *Dracula* (Browning 1931); a cybergoth wears latex clothes with fluorescent colours, a gas mask, accessories made from metal, microchips and plastic, and cyberlocks (plastic hair extensions) that hide the hair and give an impression of a half-mechanical body. Both cases refer to liminal creatures: a vampire, in the first case, and a cyborg in the second – an android, that is, a machine resembling a human or a human whose body parts have been replaced by mechanical ones (see Illustration 9.2).

Although vampires and cyborgs are liminal creatures, in between life and death and in between human and machine respectively, this attire on bodies that are clearly alive is an ironic statement. I suggest that goths detach from themselves to critically examine their human nature and thus their mortality. Ronald Stade notes that the more we learn about the functioning of the human brain the more the science argues against the autonomy and rationality of the human subject (2014: 475). Thus, cognitive science uses terms that echo artificial intelligence and tries to understand the mechanical functions of the brain and human cognition, while medicine endorses how easy is to 'change' (transplant) a human heart or get a 'new mask' (plastic surgery). Goth irony, on the other hand, questions what makes us humans. It is critical to the aforementioned technologies, which are geared towards prolonging life, because even fictive creatures that are considered immortal, such as vampires, cannot escape death.

Two years ago, I met Hellboy in the Unlife club. Very soon, he told me that he had stopped going out because he was totally broke, being unemployed for several months. However, that night he had decided to go out and dance because two days later his father would undergo triple coronary bypass surgery and, therefore, he had decided that he needed to go out and dance. He told me that the surgeon was trying to convince him that the operation would be successful but the way that the surgeon was talking about his father – like he was a malfunctioning machine that should be fixed, 'as if they will add a pipe to bypass the blockage' – annoyed him a lot. Eventually, the operation was successful and Hellboy got a new job three months later. Recently, Hellboy stopped going out because he is again unemployed. He was also informed that his father has cancer. When I met him again, I decided not to ask him if the new surgeon also talks about his father as if he was a malfunctioning machine.

As goths dance, they often recite the lyrics of the music that inspires them and to which they can relate – like Dave, mentioned above, who was reciting the lyrics of 'Plague (The Human Parasite)' by Menschdefekt (2010),[8] which comments on the greed and destructiveness of humanity. Singing and dancing are employed to express their everyday problems, their disappointment with humanity and society, and their belief that humanity is misguided and that the more scientific knowledge advances the more machines are used for what most people consider 'evil and obscene purposes' (Rapport and Stade 2014: 475). During the car crash, Dave came close to death by misused technology. By dancing to Menschdefekt's (literally 'Human Defect') song he was able to express his

Illustration 9.2 Cybergoth. Photo and editing by Abdel Bentroudi. Model and design Melanie V. Xort. Photo used with permission.

anger (with his powerful stomping and strong movement). Moreover, towards the end of his monologue, he shared his reflections on how close to death he feels and in his own way expressed that this makes him want to celebrate his remaining life by dancing with his friends. This is Dave's, Hellboy's and other goths' simplified but practical way to talk about and perform nihilistic irony via dance.

On (or against?) Liberal Irony

There is an online video that has been recurrently shared by goths over the past three years and has triggered discussion about dance and how goths dance in Greece. This highly (self-)ironic video entitled 'How to Dance Goth'[9] is a basic tutorial for learning goth dance. The video demonstrates four basic moves: 'so many, many webs', 'have a cappuccino – you're not cool enough for cappuccino', 'step over your dead friend' and 'look out for the bee', and requests the viewer to follow the dance moves of the tutors. The voices of the narrator and the actors are overly serious (as goth is perceived to be by outsiders), while the titles of the moves are humorous and ironic (as goth is for insiders). The context is also self-ironic and humorous: these moves are performed by trad goths (the first goth style that developed in the early 1980s) and the final piece demonstrates how the moves look when many goths dance together to 'This Corrosion' (The Sisters of Mercy 1987), which also provides a good reference for trad goth dancing. However, the focus of the camera on the facial expressions of the actors 'observing' the viewer's practice is a reflective and critical comment on how goths usually face outsiders and newbies.

Thanos was the third person that rediscovered and shared this video to his Facebook profile in January 2015, just commenting 'hahahahahahaha'. Thanos is heavily influenced by postpunk and trad goth style, although he is relatively young for those styles (twenty-seven years old), which are mainly appreciated by goths introduced to the scene when they were in their teens during the 1980s. He received numerous replies, which created a long discussion about goth dance in general and prompted comments with additional ironic videos on goth dance and specific dance performances of Athenian goths.

Two comments from that discussion should be highlighted. Lilith commented: 'that's the way to learn to dance!!!!' (*etsi na ma8ainoume na xorevoume!!!!*), and many comments later, George (with whom I was chatting in the Darkness club) wrote: 'after the milking of the cow we have the spiderweb move' (*meta to armegma ageladas exoume ton isto araxnhs*).[10] Lilith is well-known and admired in the scene for her personalized, flamboyant style and dance. Her words have a double meaning. The first meaning is that of an act of modesty, while the second criticizes unskilled dancers. Her comment does not subvert any power relations because it comes from a person who is an established and admired figure in the goth scene. Unlike Cowan's ethnographic example, Lilith's comment is neither self-ironic nor reflective, but mocks the weak and solidifies the established order. By contrast, George's comment about 'milking of the cow' refers to Psycho, the 'psychotic dancer' of the opening vignette. Irony here is a discreet and polite way to critically comment on someone's dancing without offending them and is understood only by George's close friends, who gossip about the person ironized. Moreover, when George, an aficionado of industrial dance, a relevantly new goth dance style (see Karampampas 2016), ironizes the 'spiderweb move', he provides a subversive comment targeting a goth dance style that was established in the early 1980s. At the same time, it is also an indirect comment on how patrons of Darkness exclude other goths who do not match their style, as it was expressed in the introductory vignette.

Therefore, although the creators of 'How to Dance Goth' intended to humorously explain goth dance to outsiders and at the same time to be self-ironic and critical towards goth and goths, Athenian goths, in order to embrace diversity and practise the inclusion that goth promotes, responded to it negatively. They used irony as a polite and discreet way to express their dissatisfaction towards exclusive power structures (as George did), while simultaneously keeping their own power structures that are beneficial for them (as Lilith did). The liberal irony that goth promotes can engender ambivalent reactions and is sometimes lost in the midst of the local micro-politics of the Athenian scene. However, this does not diminish the importance of liberal irony in goth, which may be practised in varying degrees as is shown by the creators of 'How to Dance Goth' and the responses to the video.

However, is it not ironic that goth promotes inclusion, when some goths exclude other goths, similarly to how nongoths peripheralize goths?

Performing Irony on the Dance Floor: Industrial, *Zeibékiko* and *Tsiftetéli* Dances

Greek goths constantly relate and compare their or another's performance of industrial dance to dances they characterize as 'Greek' (such as *zeibékiko* and *tsiftetéli*). The comment that Jess received from one of her friends on a picture she uploaded is a telling example: 'Do you dance zeimpekicore?' In the picture, Jess was dancing industrial and the caption reads: 'xD industrial dance at the [... club] :p'. She uploaded it on Facebook on 11 December 2014 and received more than one hundred likes in less than a week.

The word 'zeimpekicore' invented by the commenter combines the words '*zeibékiko*' (dance) and 'core' (music)[11] and it is one of the many cases in which my research participants use neologisms to describe dance performances. The most frequently used are the words '*industrialozeibékiko*' and '*tsifteteloindústrial*', which combine the words '*zeibékiko*' and '*tsiftetéli*' with the term 'industrial' respectively. *Zeibékiko* is an improvisation dance that embodies *magkiá*,[12] *egoismós*[13] and masculinity and is traditionally danced in the centre of the dance floor by an individual who 'owns' that performance, the song and the dance floor, as has been discussed by other anthropologists (Herzfeld 1985; Cowan 1990; Loutzaki 2001; Kirtsoglou 2004; Koutsougera 2012, 2013). *Tsifteteli* is an individual, couples' or group dance that is very popular in many clubs (*bouzoukia* or *skiladika*),[14] formal balls and house parties (see Cowan 1990; Kirtsoglou 2004; Koutsougera 2012, 2013). Most of the time, comparisons to *tsifteteli* and *zeibekiko* come in the form of sarcasm, like the video that Nikos shared on his Facebook profile (Illustration 9.3), or in the form of self-irony, as in some replies to the post. The title of the video was 'Greek Industrial Video'[15] and Nikos's caption to the post was 'Holy Mary and Jesus Christ!!!! The ultimate dance video!!! XD'.

The video depicts male and female non-Greek goths dancing industrial synchronized to Vasilis Karras's[16] song 'Tha Mou Kleíseis to Spíti' (You Will Destroy My Family (1997)), which is danced as *tsifteteli*. The creator of the video combined different industrial dance videos, muted the sound and replaced it with Karras's song. The comments on the Facebook post are either sarcastic ('That was great!!! Congratulations to the one who created it!!! Finally it will help some guys and gals at the clubs to behave better …')[17] or self-ironic ('Aren't we all dancing like that?', 'Mmmm yes suddenly everyone is so serious about it xD just like me at [Unlife] dancing *tsifteteli* or something similar xD' and 'Do you want [to go to] *bouzoukia* club? Let's go!!!').[18]

The self-ironic, reflexive comments demonstrate that my research participants are used to criticizing behaviours of exclusion by goths who mock people whose movements may remind them of 'Greek dances' (first comment), and promoting inclusion by focusing on the commonalities between their (nonideal) dance performances (second comment). The third comment: 'Do you want [to go to] *bouzoukia* club? Let's go!!!' has a double meaning. First, it refers to a stanza of a familiar Greek song and, second, it implies that some goths are also visiting Greek nongoth clubs (*bouzoukia* or *skiladika*) or at least that they dance *tsifteteli* and *zeibekiko* in family gatherings and celebrations. Therefore, the second and third comments demonstrate how goths argue for tolerance and how they privilege nonhomogenized preferences and diversity, all of which are central aspects of liberal irony.

At nearly every club night, especially in semi-joking cases but also in serious performances of industrial dance, 'Greek dances' are present in goth performances. This may be in the form of dancing industrial on the table, similar to *tsifteteli* dancers (Illustration 9.4), or dancing *zeibekiko* on the goth dance floor in between others who dance industrial, just to annoy a friend or show a dislike for a song. In other cases when Greek goths dance industrial, they may make fun of parts of a song that reminds them of *tsifteteli* music, like Infected Mushroom's song 'Becoming Insane' (2007).[19]

Illustration 9.3 Screenshot of Nikos's Facebook post, 1 April 2015.

Illustration 9.4 Female goth dances industrial on a table and one of her male friends dramatizes 'the usual reaction of a kágoura'. Photo by the author, December 2011.

Another example is when certain goth clubs play *tsiftetéli* and *zeibékiko* music (and the goths dance to it accordingly). During *Apókries* (Greek Carnival), for example, many goths dress up in different costumes that do not resemble their usual goth attire, while others are dressed as usual (Illustration 9.5). Often they are inspired by Greek fashions and trends that they dislike, embodied by stereotypical figures such as *kágoures*, *skiládes*[20] and others, or anything else (for example, sheep costumes and Greek gods). The music in goth clubs during *Apókries* parties is diverse and combines goth music with other songs, usually classified under the broad categories of 'disco' and 'Greek music' (*skiládika* and 'folk music'). The dancing is also diverse and the attendees engage in different dances that frequently do not correspond with the music. My first *Apókries* in a goth club was in March 2011 and I was surprised by the random fluctuation of the music styles. At certain points during the night, goths were dancing industrial, while at other times they were dancing *tsifteteli* and *zeibékiko* to industrial music. Some time later, others were dancing industrial, *tsifteteli* and *zeibékiko*, but this time to *tsifteteli* music. Finally, the DJ also played some *sirtó* and *hassapiá* dances (the two most common folk dances in Greece), which were danced accordingly.

*Illustration 9.5 Greek Carnival (*Apókries*) at Seven Sins club. Photo by the author, March 2011.*

Apart from *Apókries*, in two goth clubs in Athens 'Greek music' is also often played during the last songs before the end of the night. Those songs are usually *tsifietéli* music or other 'Greek music' that is often categorized by many goths as 'trash music'. Many of the remaining clubbers dance accordingly. However, these are the preparations for the 'after-party', as well as a way for the club owners to persuade the remaining clients to leave. Goth clubs in Greece close between 6am and 9am and some of these clubbers then go together to a *trashádiko* (a club that plays 'Greek trash music'). Many goths argue that any kind of 'Greek music' is of lower quality, others exclude from this category *rebétiko* and folk music, while very few even state that they enjoy going to a *skiládiko* a few times per year. Nonetheless, they are competent (on various levels) *zeibékiko* and *tsifietéli* dancers, many can also recite the lyrics of the songs while they dance and a few have some competency in folk dances as well.

For Athenian goths, dancing *zeibékiko* and *tsifietéli* constitute performances of Greekness. As discussed previously, 'Greek dance' in goth spaces is performed to ironize nongoth Greeks, their ideologies and their practices (see also Cowan 1990: 179). Simultaneously, it is an opportunity to enjoy dancing the same dances they denigrate. Their irony and sarcasm is thus another mechanism to relate to nongoth Greeks and to incorporate practices, which they believe to be incompatible with theirs.

Conclusion

This chapter has examined how goths in Athens perform nihilistic and liberal irony when they dance or when they reflect on dance. In doing so, goths question established categories of inclusion and exclusion (see, for example, Fernandez and Taylor Huber 2001). One of the tropes employed by goths is to repeat stereotypical phrases that outsiders use, identifying some truth in them. Through hyperbole, they show how they have been victimized and pigeonholed by non-goths (see, for example, Garland and Hodkinson 2014; Pipyrou 2014: 539; cf. Pipyrou 2012). These forms of irony and self-irony, although they seek to subvert existing power structures, in the end achieve nothing. Instead, they provide a critical commentary, showing how the ironist is helpless but ethically superior to the wrongdoings of outsiders, people or institutions that hold more power than the ironist. However, their lack of power over society is no different than that of most of humanity (see Fernandez and Taylor Huber 2001; Haugerud 2013). In ironizing their own powerlessness, irony becomes a tool to engage with others (Rapport 2014) and show tolerance towards difference. This is the liberal irony. Additionally, their powerlessness over society seems insignificant compared to their powerlessness over death. As the narrations of my research participants have shown, they understand how close they and their loved ones are to death, and because they are incapable of avoiding it they decide to celebrate their remaining life. This is the nihilistic irony. Dance is a method to perform both types of irony. Therefore, goth emerges as a celebration of life and of individuality, while irony and dance are the cornerstones for goths to fulfil that.

Although this chapter is focused on dance performances, examples of how goths use self-irony on social media have also been provided. As they do when they dance, goths use irony as a reflexive device on social media and face-to-face encounters. By using irony, they step back from their lives and attempt to interrogate them impartially. Reflecting on stereotypes, they find common threads to connect with other goths and the scene, enhancing their solidarity. Additionally, goths question, negotiate and redefine Greek stereotypes, question what Greekness is and elaborate reflexively (and ironically) on their own social positionings. Reflecting on death, they use the idea of mortality to connect with every other human and, helped by ironic goth styles and concepts (that of the vampire and cyborg), explore the idea of what is to be human. Therefore, although the theoretical framework of liberal irony suggests that ironists remove themselves from all their existing social relations, goth practice goes one step further: goth ironists remove themselves from their social relations in order to move back and re-establish them under new terms.

Focusing on irony has also highlighted a discrepancy between theoretical elaborations of irony and native categories because the words 'irony' and 'sarcasm' in Modern Greek are mostly used interchangeably. Therefore, while goth practices and narratives – even when Athenian goths use the word irony (*ironía*) to mean sarcasm (*sarkasmós*) – can be analysed under the theoretical prism of irony (Rapport and Stade 2014), they can, in turn, enrich our theoretical models and broaden our understanding of irony and how it is employed in different ethnographic contexts. For example, these semantic particularities highlight additional ways in which Greek irony creates boundaries in the goth scene, similar to the ones imposed by stereotypes, but also enhances feelings of solidarity among goths and nongoths, based on the Greek presumption that human beings are flawed, divided and sinful.

Finally, this chapter has also demonstrated that irony is useful for the researcher's understanding of contradictory verbal and somatic statements, because irony cuts across the mind–body dualism. Without focusing on irony, goth lifestyle and ideology, and by extension, dance, cannot be fathomed. Therefore, irony can be seen as an index of local understanding pertaining to anthropological research methods. Michel Herzfeld (2001) contends that only when the researcher can understand verbal and somatic irony has he or she attained the 'cultural intimacy' that is required for an anthropological project.

Acknowledgements

I am particularly grateful to Dr Stavroula Pipyrou with whom I had long conversations about the subject of this chapter and Professor Nigel Rapport for his theoretical insights. Additionally, I thank Dr Evangelos Chrysagis for his feedback on an earlier version of this chapter, as well as the third-year students of the Reading Ethnography module (2015–16) at the University of St Andrews and the module convener, Dr Paloma Gay y Blasco, for their enthusiastic comments. I would also like to thank the anonymous reviewers for their valuable suggestions. Most of all, I want to thank my research participants, without whom this research would never have been realized. The writing of this chapter was supported by an Anastasios Tsioris scholarship for academic excellence from the Anastasios Tsioris Trust and the Ministry of Culture, Education and Religious Affairs, Greece.

Panas Karampampas is a post-doctoral researcher at the Institut Interdisciplinaire d'Anthropologie du Contemporain (IIAC), École des Hautes Études en Sciences Sociales (EHESS). He currently works on Intangible Cultural Heritage policies and global governance. Previously he was a guest lecturer in the Department of Social Anthropology at the University of St Andrews, where he also completed his Ph.D. His doctoral research focused on the goth scene, digital anthropology, dance and cosmopolitanism. He has also conducted ethnographic research on Roma education as a scientific associate in the Centre for Intercultural Studies at the University of Athens.

Notes

1. Most of my research participants use pseudonyms in the scene and on Facebook. In many cases, they also use their pseudonyms in interpersonal relations outside of the scene. However, all names and pseudonyms have been replaced in order to preserve the anonymity of my informants. The 'Darkness' and 'Unlife' clubs are also pseudonyms for two Athenian goth clubs.
2. Apollo and John, as well as Lilith and Selene, are regulars at the Darkness club. They have participated in the Athenian goth scene for many years and they have exerted considerable influence within the scene, the first two as DJs and the latter with their idiosyncratic dancing and elaborate DiY dress styles.
3. Each scene is seen as constituting a 'lifestyle' or a coherent social world and, therefore, a compact action system. It is possible for the participants of these formations to belong to more than one scene at the same time. In every participating scene, someone has to adopt and perform different values and practices, like taking a theatrical role, so that 'life is becoming like theater' (Irwin 2005: 76; see also Chapter 4).
4. In my Ph.D. research, I discuss concepts of cosmopolitanism and peripherality in the Greek and wider European goth scene. This research, multisited in its conceptualization (Marcus 1995), took place in three different locations: Greece, Britain and Germany, as well as in cyberspace, where I closely followed the development of goth scenes. Because the focus of this chapter is the Athenian goth scene, only data from my research in Greece are used, in addition to data acquired online.

5. As first used by Diogenis of Sinopi (see Stade 2014).
6. In Greek, the slogans are as follows: '*5 μέρες τρως αγγούρι μα το Σαββάτο είσαι μούρη*' and '*Αντώνη άσε το Wi-Fi και δώσε στον λαό να φάει*'. For a detailed analysis see Knight (2015b). 'Antonis' here refers to the Greek ex-Prime Minister Antonis Samaras (2012–15).
7. The mixing of idioms and specifically the influence from the trance/rave scene led to the creation of the cybergoth style. Even though it was first reported in 1999 (Steele and Park 2008: 49–50), in Greece cybergoth has only been evolving for the past few years, while the changes that it brought to the goth scene are plentiful (Karampampas 2016). The first change to be observed is that the use of black, which was almost exclusively the only colour of dress across different goth styles, is rejected by cybergoths (*saiberádes*, neologism for cybergoths), who adorn themselves in mostly neon colours. Cybergothic outfits represent and sometimes constitute a highly technological aesthetic, accessorized with goggles, microchips, fluorescent make-up, cyberlocks (plastic hair extensions), gas masks, fluorescent PVC clothes (sometimes only lingerie), fishnets and corsets. Almost every part of this ambiguous techno-body is visible, expressing eroticism (Van Elferen 2009: 106–7). Men's and women's outfits are barely distinguishable, because cyborgs believe in being androgynous.
8. Music track available here: https://www.youtube.com/watch?v=cg3tcOSTWQ8. Accessed 8 April 2016.
9. The video was shown at the Hubba Hubba Revue Goth Show (22 March 2012) and can be found here: https://vimeo.com/39084398. Accessed 8 April 2016.
10. Original written in Greeklish. 'Greeklish' is a neologism, which combines the words Greek and English and mainly refers to writing Greek by using Latin characters. Unlike the official system of Romanization of Greek, which is used internationally for official documents and name transliteration, Greeklish uses varied and inconsistent formats. These are based on phonetic similarity, visual equivalence (including numerical characters) and corresponding keyboard keys.
11. Core music does not relate to goth, but Jess, as well as a few other goths, likes this music and participates in the local core scene.
12. *Magkiá* has been traditionally considered 'a tough, swaggering yet also introspective style of masculinity' (Cowan 1990: 173). In recent decades, however, the term has acquired a more negative connotation and is connected to showing off a fake toughness or being cunning (*ponirós*).
13. *Egoismós* is translated as self-regard. However, in Greece, it can be understood as a social value and not as an individual trait. This value can be attributed to people who do not care only for themselves, but also try to demonstrate their individuality through being part of a particular group, such as a kin group, village, region or country. A good performance of *egoismós* (one who acts with *egoismós*) is considered the action that proves to the group how the *egoistís* exceeds the rest of the group in one or more qualities (such as in dancing) and shows his or her idiosyncrasy, but without exceeding too much the norms of the group (Herzfeld 1985: 11–26).
14. *Bouzoúkia* are nightclubs with live music. The name comes from the musical instrument *bouzoúki*, which is the singular form of *bouzoúkia*. See also Cowan (1990). On one side of the club is the dance floor where the singer is at the centre of attention, having the

orchestra in the background. The patrons, on the other side, are seated around tables and very often they dance on them. *Skiládika* (literally 'dog houses') sometimes is used interchangeably with *bouzoúkia* but more often it is used to distinguish such places from *bouzoúkia*, because the former are believed to attract working-class patrons or singers who sing like 'dogs'. See also Koutsougera (2012, 2013).
15. Video available here: https://www.youtube.com/watch?v=_gLGyIjLoYg. Accessed 8 April 2016.
16. Vasilis Karras is a Greek *laiká* (literally 'folk', but considered a distinct genre from Greek folk songs) singer born in 1953 in Kavala, Greece. He first appeared in 1963 in a small club in Thessaloniki and made an impact because of his distinct voice. Despite his young age he started a promising career, writing his own songs, and in 1980 released his first album. Since then, he has often collaborated with other famous *laiká* singers and in recent years has often performed abroad in places where there is a large Greek diaspora. For the *laiká* genre see Koutsougera (2012: 11, 15).
17. Original: '*Korufh htan!!! Mpravo se opoion to eftia3e!!! Epitelous na arxisoun na 3ekavalan to kalami merikoi k merikes sta club …*'.
18. Originals: '*Κάπως έτσι δεν χορεύουμε όλοι μας;*', '*Mmm nai nai oloi sovara to eidate xD opos egw pou sto [club name] xorevw kai ta tsiftetelia mou kati tetoio xD*' and '*Θελεις μπουζουκια, παμε!!!*'.
19. Although it is not a goth but a psy-trance/electronic song, it is popular in Greek goth clubs. Music video available here: https://youtu.be/Z6hL6fkJ1_k. Accessed 8 April 2016.
20. *Kágoures* are working-class youths akin to British 'chavs'. *Skiládes* are the patrons of *skiládika*.

References

Amit, V., and N. Rapport. 2002. *The Trouble with Community: Anthropological Reflections on Movement, Identity and Collectivity*. London: Pluto Press.
Brottman, M. 2007. 'Goth's Wan Stamina', *The Chronicle of Higher Education*, 15 June.
Browning, T. 1931. *Dracula*. New York: Universal Pictures. [Film].
Comaroff, J. 1985. *Body of Power, Spirit of Resistance: The Culture of History of a South African People*. Chicago, IL: The University of Chicago Press.
Cowan, J.K. 1990. *Dance and the Body Politic in Northern Greece*. Princeton, NJ: Princeton University Press.
Fernandez, J.W., and M. Taylor Huber (eds). 2001. *Irony in Action: Anthropology, Practice and the Moral Imagination*. Chicago, IL: The University of Chicago Press.
Garland, J., and P. Hodkinson. 2014. '"F**king Freak! What the Hell Do You Think You Look Like?": Experiences of Targeted Victimization among Goths and Developing Notions of Hate Crime', *The British Journal of Criminology* 54: 613–31.
Goulding, C., and M. Saren. 2009. 'Performing Identity: An Analysis of Gender Expressions at the Whitby Goth Festival', *Consumption Markets & Culture* 12: 27–46.
Gunn, J. 2007. 'Dark Admissions: Gothic Subculture and the Ambivalence of Misogyny and Resistance', in L.M.E. Goodlad and M. Bibby (eds), *Goth: Undead Subculture*. Durham, NC: Duke University Press, pp. 41–64.
Haugerud, A. 2013. *No Billionaire Left Behind: Satirical Activism in America*. Stanford, CA: Stanford University Press.

Herzfeld, M. 1985. *The Poetics of Manhood: Contest and Identity in a Cretan Mountain Village*. Princeton, NJ: Princeton University Press.
———. 1997. *Cultural Intimacy: Social Poetics in the Nation-State*. New York: Routledge.
———. 2001. 'Irony and Power: Toward a Politics of Mockery in Greece', in J.W. Fernandez and M. Taylor Huber (eds), *Irony in Action: Anthropology, Practice and the Moral Imagination*. Chicago, IL: The University of Chicago Press, pp. 63–83.
Hodkinson, P. 2002. *Goth: Identity, Style and Subculture*. Oxford: Berg.
———. 2011. 'Ageing in a Spectacular "Youth Culture": Continuity, Change and Community amongst Older Goths', *The British Journal of Sociology* 62: 262–82.
Infected Mushroom. 2007. *Vicious Delicious*. Holon: BNE. [CD].
Irwin, J. 2005. 'Notes on the Status of the Concept Subculture', in K. Gelder (ed.), *The Subcultures Reader*. London: Routledge, pp. 73–77.
Jasper, A. 2004. '"I Am Not a Goth!": The Unspoken Morale of Authenticity within the Dutch Gothic Subculture', *Etnofoor* 17(1/2): 90–115.
Kallianos, Y. 2012. 'The Fall of the "Purified" Community: Crisis, Transformation and Collective Action in Greece', *The Unfamiliar* 2(2): 28–34.
———. 2013. 'Agency of the Street: Crisis, Radical Politics and the Production of Public Space in Athens 2008–12', *City* 17: 548–57.
Karampampas, P. 2016. 'Dancing into Darkness: Cosmopolitanism and "Peripherality" in the Greek Goth Scene', Ph.D. dissertation. St Andrews: University of St Andrews.
Karras, V. 1997. *M'Echis Kani Aliti* [Μ'έχεις Κάνει Αλήτη]. Athens: Minos EMI. [LP].
Kirtsoglou, E. 2004. *For the Love of Women: Gender, Identity and Same-Sex Relations in a Greek Provincial Town*. London: Routledge.
Knight, D.M. 2012. 'Cultural Proximity: Crisis, Time and Social Memory in Central Greece', *History and Anthropology* 23: 349–74.
———. 2013. 'The Greek Economic Crisis as Trope', *Focaal* 65: 147–59.
———. 2015a. *History, Time, and Economic Crisis in Central Greece*. New York: Palgrave Macmillan.
———. 2015b. 'Wit and Greece's Economic Crisis: Ironic Slogans, Food, and Antiausterity Sentiments', *American Ethnologist* 42: 230–46.
Koutsougera, N. 2012. 'From Street Dances and "Breaking" to Night Clubbing: Popular Entertainment as Cultural and Symbolic Capital in Contemporary Athens', *The Unfamiliar* 2(2): 10–17.
———. 2013. '"Laiki" Night Life of Youth: An Anthropological Perspective' [Νυχτερινή «Λαϊκή» Διασκέδαση Των Νέων: Μία Ανθρωπολογική Προσέγγιση], Ph.D. dissertation. Athens: Panteion University of Social and Political Sciences.
Loutzaki, I. 2001. 'Folk Dance in Political Rhythms', *Yearbook for Traditional Music* 33: 127–37.
Malaby, T.M. 1999. 'Fateful Misconceptions: Rethinking Paradigms of Chance among Gamblers in Crete', *Social Analysis* 43(1): 141–64.
Marcus, G.E. 1995. 'Ethnography in/of the World System: The Emergence of Multi-sited Ethnography', *Annual Review of Anthropology* 24: 95–117.
Menschdefekt. 2010. *The Human Parasite*. Stockstadt am Main: Infacted Recordings. [CD].
Miklas, S., and S.J. Arnold. 1999. '"The Extraordinary Self": Gothic Culture and the Construction of the Self', *Journal of Marketing Management* 15: 563–576.

Muehlebach, A. 2009. '*Compexio Oppositorum*: Notes on the Left in Neoliberal Italy', *Public Culture* 21: 495–515.

Pateraki, M., and P. Karampampas. 2014. 'Methodological Insights in Dance Anthropology: Embodying Identities in Dance Celebrations in the Context of Metamorphosis of Sotiros in Sotira, South Albania', in V. Nitsiakos, I. Manos, G. Agelopoulos, A. Angelidou and V. Dalkavoukis (eds), *Balkan Border Crossings: Third Annual of the Konitsa Summer School*. Berlin: LIT, pp. 149–74.

Pipyrou, S. 2012. 'Commensurable Language and Incommensurable Claims among the Greek Linguistic Minority of Southern Italy', *Journal of Modern Italian Studies* 17(1): 70–91.

———. 2014. 'Cutting *Bella Figura*: Irony, Crisis, and Secondhand Clothes in South Italy', *American Ethnologist* 41: 532–46.

Rakopoulos, T. 2013. 'Responding to the Crisis: Food Co-operatives and the Solidarity Economy in Greece', *Anthropology Southern Africa* 36: 102–7.

———. 2014a. 'Resonance of Solidarity: Meanings of a Local Concept in Anti-austerity Greece', *Journal of Modern Greek Studies* 32: 313–37.

———. 2014b. 'The Crisis Seen from Below, Within, and Against: From Solidarity Economy to Food Distribution Cooperatives in Greece', *Dialectical Anthropology* 38: 189–207.

Rapport, N. 1995. 'Migrant Selves and Stereotypes: Personal Context in a Postmodern World', in S. Pile and N. Thrift (eds), *Mapping the Subject: Geographies of Cultural Transformation*. London: Routledge, pp. 267–82.

———. 2003. *I Am Dynamite: An Alternative Anthropology of Power*. Abingdon: Routledge.

———. 2012. *Anyone: The Cosmopolitan Subject of Anthropology*. Oxford: Berghahn.

———. 2014. 'Whim of Iron? Irony as Collective Virtue and Defence against Essentialism', *Social Anthropology* 22: 445–56.

Rapport, N., and R. Stade. 2014. 'Debating Irony and the Ironic as a Social Phenomenon and a Human Capacity', *Social Anthropology* 22: 443–78.

Schilt, K. 2007. 'Queens of the Damned: Women and Girls' Participation in Two Gothic Subcultures', in L.M.E. Goodlad and M. Bibby (eds), *Goth: Undead Subculture*. Durham, NC: Duke University Press, pp. 65–78.

Scott, J. 1985. *Weapons of the Weak: Everyday Forms of Peasant Resistance*. New Haven, CT: Yale University Press.

Stade, R. 2014. 'Two Anthropologies, One Anthropos: Towards an Emancipation of Dissonance', *Social Anthropology* 22: 457–69.

Steele, V., and J. Park. 2008. *Gothic: Dark Glamour*. New Haven, CT: Yale University Press.

Sweet, D.R. 2005. 'More than Goth: The Rhetorical Reclamation of the Subcultural Self', *Popular Communication* 3: 239–64.

Theodossopoulos, D. 2013. 'Infuriated with the Infuriated? Blaming Tactics and Discontent about the Greek Financial Crisis', *Current Anthropology* 54: 200–21.

———. 2014. 'The Ambivalence of Anti-austerity Indignation in Greece: Resistance, Hegemony and Complicity', *History and Anthropology* 25: 488–506.

The Sisters of Mercy. 1987. *Floodland*. London: WEA Records. [LP].

Van Elferen, I. 2009. 'Dances with Spectres: Theorising the Cybergothic', *Gothic Studies* 11(1): 99–112.
———. 2011. 'East German Goth and the Spectres of Marx', *Popular Music* 30: 89–103.
Young, T.H. 1999. 'Dancing on Bela Lugosi's Grave: The Politics and Aesthetics of Gothic Club Dancing', *Dance Research* 17(1): 75–97.

Chapter 10

The Intoxicating Intimacy of Drum Strokes, Sung Verses and Dancing Steps in the All-Night Ceremonies of Ambonwari (Papua New Guinea)

Borut Telban

The polymath and literary critic George Steiner puts music, especially classical music, at the top of his list of human achievements. Though he has never learned to play any instrument, he repeatedly claims that it is music that helps humans to come as close as possible to their deepest metaphysical or philosophical-theological experiences. He writes, for example: 'It is music which can invade and rule the human psyche with a penetrative strength comparable, it may be, only to narcotics or to the trance reported by shamans, saints, and ecstatics. Music can madden and it can help heal the broken mind. It can be "the food of love," it can also trigger the feasts of hatred' (Steiner 1998: 81). In his book *Real Presences*, he writes about poetical language: 'The meanings of poetry and the music of those meanings, which we call metrics, are also of the human body. The echoes of sensibility which they elicit are visceral and tactile' (idem 1989: 9). Steiner, like many others (see, for example, Storr 1992), mainly focused on a solitary listener and the tunes of classical music (but see Chapter 2 in this volume).

However, the above-mentioned characteristics of music are present also in the works of those who have conducted long-term ethnographic fieldwork among small-scale societies around the world. In the anthropology of Papua New Guinea, few people have written so passionately and in such detail about language, songs and senses as did Steven Feld (1981, 1984, 1990, 1996).[1] Focusing on acoustic ethnography and with extraordinary musical and cultural sensitivity he explores how places are poetically evoked and how senses are emplaced among the Kaluli of Bosavi:

> [S]inging a sequence of named places takes listeners on a journey that flows along local waterways and through local lands. The flow of these

poetic song paths is emotionally and physically linked to the sensual flow of the singing voice .... Because motion can draw upon the kinaesthetic interplay of tactile, sonic, and visual senses, emplacement always implicates the intertwined nature of sensual bodily presence and perceptual engagement. (Feld 1996: 91, 94)

Feld's discussion of the flow of poetic song paths through the landscape associated with sensual bodily presence among the Kaluli soundly captures the ceremonial life of the Karawari-speaking people of Ambonwari village, East Sepik Province, Papua New Guinea. While circling inside the house during an all-night singing and dancing event, the singing dancers follow ancient paths to and from their village; by revisiting a series of named places they recreate their landscape. The house in which the event is staged thus becomes a miniature cosmos where different places, times and people intermingle. A combination of drum strokes, sung verses and dancing steps creates an intoxicating relationship between the rhythmic and melodic patterns of the all-night singing and dancing event. It is intoxicating because rhythm and melody enhance the lived experience of the moving bodies, stepping while singing, which, after releasing the impeding emotions of embarrassment and shame, become gripped by the song-dance and ready to move for twelve or more hours.

This chapter will focus on an event, which needs to be drummed, sung and danced, and which is, as Ambonwari say, through multiple senses experienced on the skin (i.e., body) of the dancers. Feld's focus on the local sociology of sound led him to conclude that 'sound and an ear- and voice-centred sensorium are central to Kaluli experience and expression in the tropical rainforest' (1996: 91). I would say that Ambonwari, who also live in the tropical rainforest, do not place such priority on any particular sensory experience but rather engage in multisensual perception and expression of their lifeworld. This pertains equally to everyday life and their celebrations. The following sections first present how Ambonwari talk about their senses and how specific sounds, images and movements of the dancers' decorated bodies are associated with their environment. The study then focuses on one of their most popular events, *yamin siria* (song-dance of the house).[2] The next section interweaves my own experience of dancing with an account of Ambonwari's visual, auditory and tactile perception of a song-dance. Although having all characteristics of a ritual, the all-night song-dance is also an entertaining ceremony that offers ample opportunities for flirting and seduction. The actual sexual encounters are hidden from the eyes of fellow villagers and it is only through stories and sung verses that they come, as people say, to an 'open place'. The following section then considers a variety of socially shaped gender dynamics as they are captured in the sung verses. Through rhythmic drum strokes, sung verses in predominantly figurative language, the movements of dancers and their body decoration, an all-night song-dance brings together a plurality of visual, auditory, tactile and kinaesthetic sensory experiences. Facilitated by betel nut and aromatic-bark chewing, smoking and dancers' harmonious movement forward, this highly structured event provides the villagers with powerful feelings of belonging and a sense of 'mutuality of being' (Sahlins 2013).

The Ambonwari and Their Song-Dances

For the Ambonwari, the saying *arim sambis ngandikim kwandikas ngandikim* (skin has eyes and ears) emphasizes the importance of seeing and hearing in people's experience of the world (Telban 1998a: 173; Vávrová 2014). They do not downplay the importance of smell and taste, but by using the verb *andi-* (hear) for the former (i.e., 'hearing the smell') and the verb *sanggwa-* (see, look) for the latter (in a compound with the verb 'eat'), they see them rather as variations of hearing and seeing. Body movements in terms of *kay* (way of doing things) (Telban 1998a, 1998b) are not only auditory, visual and tactile expressions of someone's intentions, but are simultaneously creators of their lifeworld. Similarly, acoustic expressions in terms of playing a flute, beating a drum, calling a name, singing a song or weeping a dirge are not only auditory performances but necessary for the creation and transformation of specific relationships. The Ambonwari, like many other Sepik and Papua New Guinean groups, attribute the origin of their music, both flute music and song-dances, to the ancestral spirits (Telban 2008; see also a chapter in Hoenigman 2015 for the neighbouring village of Kanjimei and their all-night song-dance called *Kaunjambi*).[3] Therefore, it is appropriate to say that 'the ancestors have not only sung, but also danced the world into existence' (Telban and Vávrová 2010: 22). Their descendants, together with the spirits of the land and spirits of the dead, continue to do so.

In Karawari language, in which 'skin' is the only term used to refer to one's whole body, it is skin – with eyes and ears – that is also the outer encasement of the body. Skin connects interior with exterior, oneself with another, beings with their environment; and during intentional acts such as dance, skin chooses what touches it and gets under it (in the transformation of a being) and what comes out from under it (in the transformation of the external world). It is a permeable, sensuous membrane on and through which inductive and creative acts are made. As Yamada (2001: 104) writes: 'It often happens that we feel sounds through skin sensation or the visual image through sounds. It is essentially impossible to separate the aural sense from other such sensations … [S]ound is felt on the horizon of the body not only through the aural sense but also through skin sensation, or as visual image, rhythm, and spatial expanse'.

In Ambonwari, *siria* (singing and dancing) is a homonym of *sirias* (flowers, a cluster of flowers) that appear on trees and other plants. For people who spend all of their lives on the rivers and creeks and on the paths of the rainforest, images of blooming palms, trees and vines (some of the latter having blood-coloured flowers) are continually experienced on the skin, internalized and talked about. While paddling in their canoes people often say that flowering *pitpit* (wild sugar cane, *Saccharum* sp.) dances backwards and forwards in the stream. They use all kinds of expressions to depict the beauty of a decorated dancer, just as they perceive flowering creeks to be beautiful. They say that a man has to decorate himself to become beautiful, in order to be attractive to women. Women will praise and desire him, the story goes, and after sexual intercourse will reproduce him, his lineage and clan through their son.

Flowering *pitpit* defines two main periods or seasons: (1) *yuwayn maray* (water of the flowering *pitpit*) or *manambin pisinim* (period/time of rain), lasting from December to May with budding occurring in March, and (2) *yuwayn kangim* (dryness of the flowering *pitpit*), lasting from May till the middle of September (Telban 1998a: 50; 2015). There are many types of *pitpit*, each with its own name. Their flowers and indeed the whole flowering plant are called not only *yuway* but also *yuwayn simbiak*, which can be translated as 'grass skirt of *pitpit*' (another allusion to body decoration and dancing). *Pitpit* is known for its movement in wind and water. Many other important plants, such as sago palm for instance, have individual names for their flowers. However, the term *sirias* covers all of them.

Sirias is also a term that refers to one of the most common of children games: cat's cradle, the moving strings of which produce images that resemble dancing. It is understood that body decoration, as an expression of beauty and attractiveness, and dance (movement of the body and decoration), as an expression of seductiveness and sexuality, are fundamental features of every Ambonwari celebration. The times when plants blossom and those when people dance are the times of abundance, splendour and reproduction. To state that the connection between decorated dancers engaged in singing and dancing (*siria*) and flowers (*sirias*) is merely metaphorical would be to ignore the fundamental relationship between people and their environment; between thoughts and practices; between perception and embodiment. We would fail to notice the connection between being (*kay*) and understanding (*wambung*) that produces lived images.

Yamin Siria

The all-night dance held in private houses is called *yamin siria* or *yamin sia* (song-dance of the house).[4] It is a spectacular and extremely popular event involving the participation of the whole village – men, women and children. It can be held for a number of reasons: a celebration of the restoration of harmonious relations following a dispute; to celebrate the opening of a new house; or as a celebration for the parents of a boy who is about to be initiated in the men's house (see Telban 1998a: 207–21).[5]

There are three song-cycles of *yamin siria*, only one of which is chosen some days before organizing the all-night celebration in a private house. When more successive all-night singing and dancing events are planned, the leading singer, together with other senior men, decides which of the three song-cycles will be sung on the first night, which on the second and which on the third. The spatial specificity of the three song-cycles is such that they follow different paths through the surrounding landscape. Every place name covers different parts of a landscape, such as a hill, forest, creek, grassland and so on. For the Ambonwari song-dances 'it is the relationship between movement (i.e., routes) and stasis (i.e., roots) that continually reconstructs places, the whole landscape and their ongoing sociality. New movements give rise to new places and new relationships and, vice versa, new places and new relationships require new movements' (Telban and Vávrová 2010: 22). Among the Kaluli, explains Feld, the idea of *tok* (path) is 'one of the key devices of song composition and performance' and Feld's Kaluli friends made him 'well aware of how much the emotional power of songs depended on their placename sequences' (1996: 104–5). The forms of landscape, places and paths are experienced in a multisensual way by the coordination of walking, seeing and hearing (ibid.: 105). This is very similar to how the Ambonwari express their experience of the song-dances through their own terms of *arim* (skin), *konggong* (path) and *kuray-* (walk around, move around). While for the Kaluli and the Waxei the central metaphor for movement in song-dances, and for the relationship between sound and body, is the flow of water (idem 1984: 93–94; 1996: 91; Yamada 2001: 105), for the Ambonwari it is moving around. Thus, beside *siria-* (sing and dance), associated with the flowering plants that 'sing and dance' in wind or water, the verb *kuray-* (move around) captures the movements on specific land and water paths of Ambonwari ancestors and the present-day dancers. The verb *kuray-* also refers to the movements of water, while *maray min konggong* (path of water) refers to a waterfall.

The song-cycles are further divided into sub-cycles, each of them attached to a specific, named place (serving also as a mnemonic device).[6] There are additional stanzas, which are sung while the dancers are still outside approaching and circling the house they will dance in. Each stanza has a leading line sung by the lead singer and subsequent lines sung by the chorus – that is, by all those dancers who know (at least approximately) the short and cryptic verses describing events and practices of the precolonial past. It is then that the distinction between music and dance is abolished in a deafening movement of the dancers. The ending of each stanza is accompanied by exclamations and vigorous stepping of the dancers while they move forward. This can be seen also from the musical notation in Illustration 10.1.

The first five stanzas of the first song-cycle of *yamin siria* go as follows:

1. *Maynjimansaun aprang kambra kina wapar amindukuri wandakar kapuk-o Wandapisir-a*
   Kisangrimari aprang kambra kina wapar amindukuri wandakar kapuk-o

Song of the House

Illustration 10.1 *The first stanza of the first song-cycle of* yamin siria *(song-dance of the house) (recorded in Ambonwari with Francis Kwandikan Andari and Samson Kamungay Marakawi, 14 May 2011). The claves – that is, two sticks used by Francis at the time of recording of the Ambonwari songs – stand for the drumming of a slit-drum (*yimbung*).*

> *Amindukuri wandakar kapuk-o*
> *Wandapisir-a, a-a-a-a-a*
> Maynjimansaun [name of the bush-spirit] went up to the fishing place and did not catch anything; his chin was wagging while he walked with a stick
> He made noise [hitting the floor of a house with a stick] while walking slowly

Kisangrimari [another name of the same bush-spirit] went up to the fishing place and did not catch anything; his chin was wagging while he walked with a stick

His chin was wagging while he walked with a stick

He made noise while walking slowly

2. *Maynjimansaun aprang kambra kina wapar yawunma wasa pupunggina kanga sanggwaykiamba-o*
   Anggin pupunggina kanga
   Kisangrimari aprang kambra kina wapar yawunma wasa pupunggina kanga sanggwaykiamba-o
   Yawunma wasa pupunggina kanga sanggwaykiamba-o
   Anggin pupunggina kanga a-a-a-a-a

   Maynjimansaun went up to the fishing place and did not catch anything; his mistress watched him at night through a narrow fissure [in the wall]

   She [watched] him through the fissure where light comes through

   Kisangrimari went up to the fishing place and did not catch anything; his mistress watched him at night through a narrow fissure [in the wall]

   His mistress watched him at night through a narrow fissure [in the wall]

   She [watched] him through the fissure where light comes through

3. *Akiring wusir kay manggwar ika ambikan yanda sambin yuwan waria yaka sikira yanggri yakama krarkapingor*
   Amban yakama apan
   Wanakasir kay manggwar ika ambikan yanda imbunan yuwan waria yaka sikira yanggri yakama krarkapingor
   Yanggri yakama krarkapingor
   Amban yakama apan a-a-a-a-a

   [A woman says:] My canoe from which I put fishing string into the water is on the other side of the creek; What will I do to this oily tree [penis]? Will I only wave my hands to him?

   Will I make a plan and wave [my hands] to him?

   [A woman says:] My canoe from which I put a hook into the water is on the other side of the creek; What will I do to this stick [penis] from the platform above the fireplace? Will I only wave my hands to him?

   Wave my hands to him?

   Will I make a plan and wave [my hands] to him?

4. *Kambis akim kuraparimanga mikir wasika yamban wandar pambandambin apir mikir wasika yan minggayngor-o*
   Mikir wasika yana

Marin akim kuraparimanga mikir wasika yamban wandar pambandambin apir mikir wasika yan minggayngor-o
Mikir wasika yarimboran mikir-o
Mikir wasika sambar a-a-a-a-a-a
At the grassland you are a woman who makes noise while lying on the grass; I open the grass [vagina], put the rattan [penis] inside and you are afraid of it
This rattan inside you
At the old grassland you are a woman who makes noise while lying on the grass; I open the grass, put the rattan inside and you are afraid of it
This rattan from the uncle's forest, rattan
This rattan [which you fear] is not from the big forest

5. *Arimbas saun sikimindia kawi akwiyambina wasanarin yanan isa angar-o*
 Arapayn yana
 Arimbas maman sikimindia samindi akwiyambina wasanarin yanan isa angar-o
 Apia sangut paninggri kambra imbi sangara kawi akwiyambina wasanarin yanan isa angar-o
 Arapayn yana a-a-a-a-a-a
 You, the light-skinned women, are slowly catching fish, sharing [only] among yourselves
 [You give only to each other] those few [fish]
 You, the very dark-skinned women, are slowly catching 'big mouth' fish, sharing [only] among yourselves
 We are two lines of decorated men and we watch how you are slowly catching fish, sharing among yourselves [you do not give us any fish]
 [You give only to each other] those few [fish]

The Ambonwari's practice of singing and dancing is semantically, syntactically and semiotically interwoven with their landscape (and the spirits of the land), mythology, social organization, kinship and so forth. Ambonwari song poetry talks about their allies and enemies from a wider region, some speaking the same Karawari language. Song poetry is important for preserving cultural memory and for providing, enacting and circulating critical cultural knowledge, particularly of places, clan histories and relationships with neighbouring groups. Through a dialogic construction of verses, where the first- or second-person pronoun (usually singular but also dual and plural) is used (words are often put into the mouths of people in the verses), the following main topics are addressed: beauty and decoration, food-obtaining practices, sharing and exchange, fights and killings, sexual encounters, love affairs and adultery. The majority of events and practices evoked in the verses, however, did not take a 'proper' or expected course. Repeatedly questioning people's skill, generosity and morality, the verses entertain. Ambonwari song poetry shows how their society is not closed, autonomous and isolated, but has since the beginning existed in relationship with others who have actively participated in the construction of their microcosm.

Dancing with the Ambonwari

I arrived in Ambonwari for the first time on 8 October 1990. The village comprised one main men's house with many carved spirit-things hidden in it (posts, flutes, slit-drums and spirit-crocodiles, each of them with an ancestral personal name), six smaller men's houses with only few spirit-things and fifty-seven family houses with 422 people in total. Although each of the twelve village clans possessed the name of one or more men's houses, not all of the houses were built. The members of smaller clans who did not have a men's house of their own simply joined discussions and celebrations in the men's houses of those clans with whom they were historically closely associated. I still remember how during my very first days in the village the monotonous drumming on slit-drum and hand-drums (*wanggin*, from *wang* [large hole]), followed by a kind of mumbling of verses, echoed through the darkness every evening late into the night. While I lived at one end of the village, the sounds were reaching me from the other end, though the two places were more than a kilometre apart (see Map 3 in Telban 1998a: 69). The sounds were coming from the Cassowary clan's Yanjanman men's house. I soon learned that Ambonwari men were rehearsing for a forthcoming *yamin siria*, an all-night singing and dancing event in the neighbouring village of Imanmeri. I was told that the people of Imanmeri, who speak a different language, had organized the ceremony to settle an old dispute between the two villages. They had already hunted down seven pigs in order to feed their singing and dancing guests. Bob Kanjik, a brilliant interpreter of sung verses, who in the following months became my 'father', led the rehearsals. He had been for many years *siriar pam* (leader of the song-dance) (lit. 'stump of the song-dance') or *siria yaparar* (man who starts the song-dance). He was the man who knew *kanapanggin siria* (the headlines of the song), which were followed by the verses sung by the chorus made up of all participants. I joined the small group of men in the men's house, enjoying the sound and rhythm while not understanding a word of what they were singing about.

Although over the following twenty-five years I sang and danced with the Ambonwari many times, I still remember the night of 19 October 1990, only eleven days after my arrival in the village. It was the first singing and dancing event that I joined as both participant and observer. At 1.30pm we packed ourselves into canoes carrying kerosene lamps (they would be used first for soot, to be applied on faces and bodies, and later to provide light), bed sheets (it could be a cold night on Imanmeri's hill), mats (on which children would sleep) and of course everything imaginable for decoration: red, black and white ochre, sooty pieces of burned firewood, plumes and feathers of birds of paradise and cassowaries, headbands made of possum's fur or young coconut sprouts, armbands, dyed skirts made of tender leaflets of sago palm, dried skins of flying foxes, decoration made from young palm sprouts, bracelets, anklets and necklaces made of shells and dried seeds (they would add to the sound during the dance), cassowary-bone daggers and other ornaments. The waters were dry and we formed a procession of few large war canoes surrounded by many small ones.

We landed near Kurumbat Primary School, tied up our canoes and began to walk uphill towards Imanmeri. Near the last creek, we washed and began to decorate. The village healer Boniface painted specific parts of my forehead, nose and cheeks with black soot, then white-rimmed them with white ochre and later coloured the empty spaces with reddish ochre. The design was called *akuriak* (type of bird). After I tied a headband made of a coconut sprout, a long bird of paradise feather was stuck behind it. I regretted not having thick curly hair, as it would have been much easier to wear different ornaments in it. This decorating pause lasted quite a long time. Women tied their grass skirts and coloured their faces. They were much faster than the men, who endlessly checked themselves in the mirrors and adjusted their plumes. The men took care to ensure that a dried skin of a flying fox was properly stuck into the front of their belts, while a large bundle of newly collected red or green *kambukwi* (*Cordyline* leaves) were stuck in the back. But most of all, they paid special attention to their painted faces.[7]

Although there are eight standard facial painting designs in Ambonwari (see Illustrations 10.2, 10.3 and 10.4), they are generally open to improvisation. Sometimes white edges are omitted or one may add dots to certain designs. The details of facial paintings are like details of verses in the all-night songs. Some can be left out, applied in a different order, or even changed slightly or improvised. However, the main visual and auditory frameworks remain the same. By painting their faces with designs called pig, scorpion, type of bird, bananas, spirit of a dead woman and so on, these beings are 'called up' to join the singing and dancing ceremony. Painting of body and face not only means adornment; it also means remaking of the cosmos from which these same designs originate (see Telban 1998a, 2008, 2014b). Decorated dancers become a link between people and spirits, between the interior of a house and exterior of the landscape, between the present and the past. I would argue that body decoration and face painting bring the singing dancers into a multitemporal, multispatial mode of existence, when they exist as both humans and mythical beings. Phenomenology of the present is therefore informed by and coexistent with the ontology of the past. While circling the house, the dancers 'move' on paths through the forest from one named place to another. While their movements generate the sounds (rhythmic pattern of dancing steps, rattling of shells, seeds and lime containers, echoing of hand-drums, the musical pitch of their voices), these same sounds generate their movements.[8]

Illustration 10.2 The leading dancers with their specific decoration impersonate the first ancestors of Crocodile-1 and Bird of Paradise clans. Photo by the author, 1991.

Finally, we moved uphill. Just before reaching Imanmeri village, we stopped. We arranged ourselves in pairs with our *warimbinmas* (dancing partners) and formed two parallel lines. At the front of each line were men and behind them women and children. The principal male dancers had special roles; they wore special decorations representing the particular ancestors of each Ambonwari clan (see Illustration 10.2). Then, someone started to beat a hand-drum, some coughed to clear their throats, others murmured the words of the warming up verses. The procession moved forward, accepting betel nuts, piper betel and lime offered by our hosts. We approached the house allocated for the dancing event. Someone in the house started beating a slit-drum, inviting us to move on the spot. Bob sang the leading line of the first stanza and the chorus joined in. We circled the house three times so that sound and music would awaken the spirits of the house. We then entered it and the singing and dancing officially started. Men, moving in an anticlockwise direction and slightly bent forward, marched resolutely while swaying their headdresses and other body decorations up and down. The women's steps were gentler. They moved their hips left and right, swinging their grass skirts horizontally. Seven dancing men held and beat the hand-drums following the rhythm of a slit-drum. One could sense the palpable enjoyment of the closed circle of dancers, as if the world beyond the house did

Illustration 10.3 Painted faces of the dancers. Clockwise from top left: imbian *(pig),* ambrikukumbinma *(type of scorpion),* akuriak *(type of bird),* kindim *(design, pattern).*

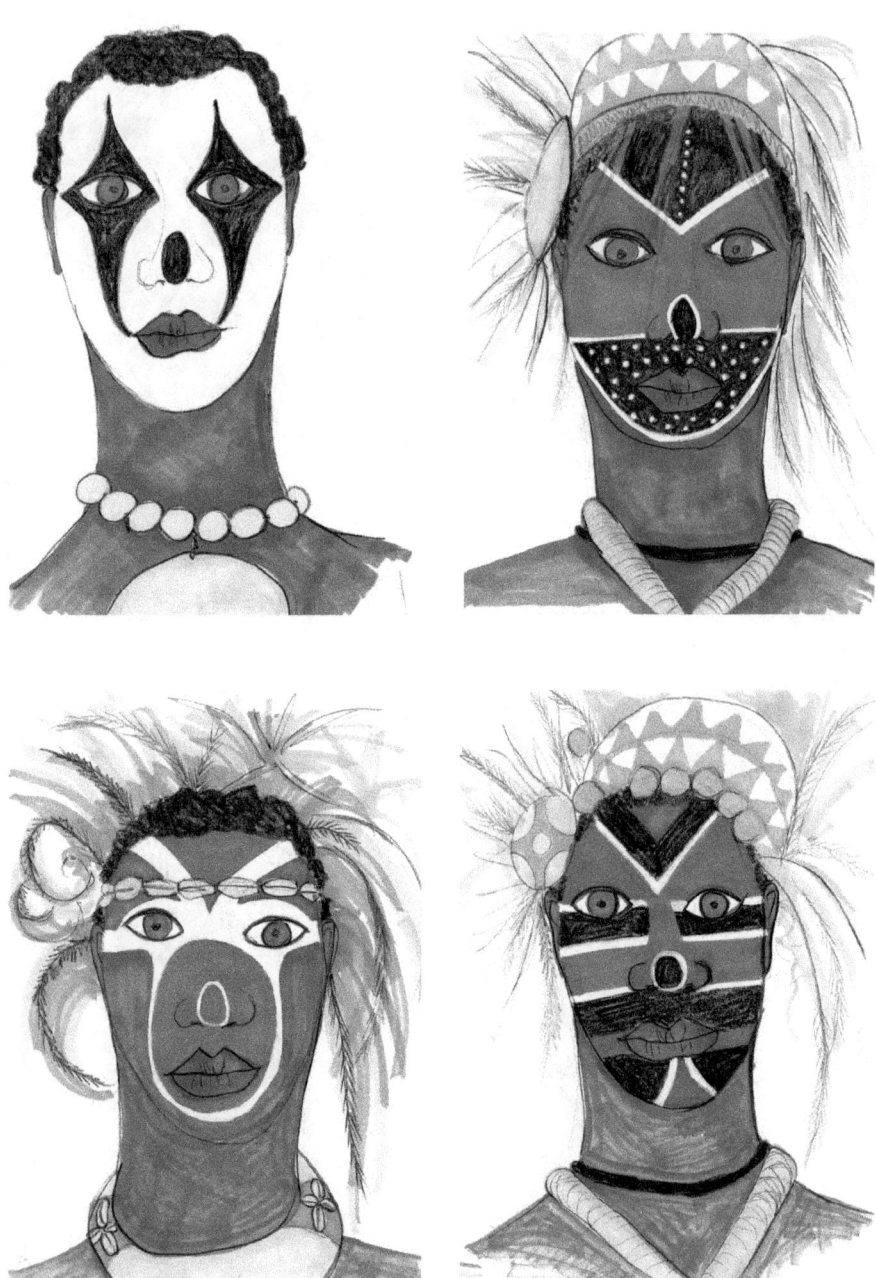

Illustration 10.4 Painted faces of the dancers. Clockwise from top left: yas *(tears),* marama *(big face),* mambaynggi *(bananas),* kambunggun wunduma *(pattern of a female spirit of the dead).*

not exist. Their singing and dancing brought a plurality of relationships into a single whole.

The sounds of music and drumming and the design of their body decoration – familiar also from the carved spirit-things – made the invisible world of spirits and people's relationships with them visible. Such association is reminiscent of the Walbiri of Central Australia, of whom Nancy Munn wrote:

> Indeed, it seems that in positing the close association of songs and designs in their cosmological assumptions about the nature of the world Walbiri are expressing symbolically the relation for them of verbal language and graphic or, more generally, nonverbal communication as a whole. Songs are in a sense symbols of oral language, and ancestral designs are symbols of visual and graphic 'language.' The ancestors are in effect 'talking about' the things that happen to them in both visual-graphic and verbal ways, and such 'talking' objectivates the world around them, giving it social, communicable reality. (1986: 148–49)

For the Ambonwari the images and sounds of humans during a song-dance are those of spirits, the former calling the latter to join them.[9] Both spirits and humans move together and merge. The dancers become spirits and the spirits become dancers. Images become sounds and sounds become images. Although the Imanmeri did not understand the language of their singing and dancing guests, through image, music and sound they were nevertheless able to identify and appreciate the synchronicity of senses and synaesthetic experience of those who sang and danced while circling the house. Moreover, Imanmeri's own singing and dancing practices were very similar, if not the same. This is what Severi writes about the music of the Wayampi and other groups of the Upper Orinoco region of Venezuela and Brazil, describing the transmutation of narratives into visual images and visual images into sounds:

> In both visual and acoustic images, the passage from verbal to iconic signs (or from one nonverbal code to another) mobilized by transmutation never limits itself to the description of the appearance of the beings it represents. On the contrary, the process of transmutation of words in images (be they visual or acoustic) makes the presence of supernatural beings indirectly perceivable through the appearances of *other* beings.... Music makes audible implicit relationships that collectively designate special (nonhuman and invisible) beings, which are thus 'called for' and made ritually present. (2014: 59, *emphasis* in the original)

Gender Relations and Sexual Encounters Captured in the Verses

In what follows, neither the individual positions and roles of the dancers, food breaks, who can eat and who cannot, nor the social organization of the dance will be discussed (but see Telban 1998a: 207–21). This section will focus instead on one specificity. Although the song-dance of a house incorporates many elements of initiation rituals, which take place in a men's house, it is still predominantly a very public event. There are no secrets involved. For many, the main purpose of the song-dance of the house is celebration. However, the visual, auditory and tactile relationships between the dancers and their ancestors, between human and nonhuman realms generally, enacted in a coordinated action, make the ceremony a highly ritualized event. The festivity reaches its peak whenever it is performed as the final stage of a *kurang* ceremony, when a young man (rarely a girl) who achieves something important (finishes school, catches his first pig or builds his first house) is carried around on the shoulders of his uncles and honoured by his 'mothers', who dance directly in front of him (ibid.: 212).[10] This happens also during an ordinary song-dance of the house, as there is always a purpose behind its organization. Such occasions create the opportunity for young people to exchange small gifts of betel nuts and tobacco and to sneak away from the dancing house into the forest. Many verses sung during all-night song-dances of a house – as one can see from the five verses presented above – describe such situations and refer more or less explicitly to sexual intercourse.

The verses in all-night songs are about fishing, gathering, hunting, accidents, amusing events, fighting and killing. Roughly a third of them, however, are about beauty and decoration, the exchange of small gifts of food, tobacco or betel nut between lovers, their longing for each other, their secret meetings, their sexual encounters and their embarrassment. Filled with allusions to sexuality, they are very much men's talk. It is as if the verses were verbal enigmas, wrapped in the poetic language of figurative transpositions (*wapaysur mariawk* [climbing talk]), with only a fragment of the story told and only a partial explanation of what is going on (idem 2008, 2014b). The verses are often deliberately obscene, so the young men who sing them appear to be pompous, boasting and showing off. Bob Kanjik once commented, when young men felt slightly embarrassed about singing these verses: 'Don't be ashamed. Just sing. It is not you that made them. The ancestors composed them'.

The all-night dances present perfect opportunities to recreate gender relations and conduct love affairs. On the one hand, the blend of drum strokes, sung verses and dancing steps generates the embodiment of village morality. On the other hand, however, it provides ample opportunities for old liaisons to be renewed and new ones initiated. Hoenigman (2015: 203) writes that all-night singing and dancing events in neighbouring Kanjimei are an aphrodisiac resulting in several sexual engagements and future marriages.

In a community such as Ambonwari, sexual encounters, discussions and disputes arising from them, resulting in village court cases, constitute an important part of daily life. Many people have secret relationships with women or men who are not their spouses. Young people continually search for partners;

there are many clandestine relationships, 'broken hearts', unfulfilled longings and undisclosed memories. In the gloom of a rainforest lovers meet, exchange small gifts and make love. In the darkness of a moonless night young men crawl under particular houses, remove the bark floor and sneak under the mosquito nets of their mistresses. There is always the possibility of discovery and consequently of trouble. If a partner does not respond in the expected way, if someone sees or overhears the lovers or if relatives disapprove of the relationship there can be trouble, even if they agree to get married and even if they are from lineages and clans that have intermarried in the past. There is the need to win the support of relatives and to confirm the relationship in public.

But without covert courtship and seduction there would be only prearranged marriages, something that both men and women would rather avoid. This is especially so in more recent times when the young favour and 'fight' for 'like marriage' based on sexual attraction and love. Young men are sometimes seduced by older women, especially those who are single, while girls often have to take the initiative to overcome the shyness and embarrassment of young men. Older men who were never married are the least desirable partners; more so than widowers or widows. Young men do not admit their innocence, especially in the presence of their friends. They boast about their sexual knowledge, invent liaisons with different girls and sing mildly obscene songs, putting words into the mouths of women. They only do this, of course, when in a group. When walking by a recreational house where several young women sit to gossip, smoke and chew betel nut, they feel quite uncomfortable. To overcome their embarrassment they may ask in a seemingly authoritative voice for a betel nut, lime, pepper betel or a cigarette. Young women, on the other hand, aware of their attractiveness, push their chests out and walk around as confident as if they had already experienced life to the full. A girl may be caught alone by a group of young, unmarried men in a canoe while she is putting fish-traps into the river and she may be harassed in a way that is not always pleasant. She will usually look away and try to ignore the young men, who risk admonishment from their elders.

All the incidents mentioned here very much depend on kin relationships of those involved. Women may later speak out about their experiences or keep them to themselves. If the boys or young men are from some other village, such events can lead to angry arguments. A woman's brothers and fathers, especially classificatory ones, can get angry trying by all means to protect her. This can lead to a serious fight.

While we were dancing in Imanmeri, the dancers were singing the verses from the first song-cycle of *yamin siria*. In one of the more gentle verses (1/34, i.e., the thirty-fourth stanza of the first song-cycle) about two lovers hiding, the lyrics are as follows: 'My partner, we must talk to each other only with the mime of our faces. We must talk to each other only with our eyes. Let's leave your vagina as it is. Let's leave your buttocks as they are'. The lovers fear they were being observed. They are careful not to be overheard and to communicate only with their eyes. At the moment it is too dangerous to make love. In another verse (1/48), the leading singer puts words into the mouth of a woman who calls to her lover: 'Sapisikay, Sakurisikay, move your leg away'. Sexual intercourse is then alluded to in the chorus line through the words of a boasting lover: 'I am firm. I push you down and break your backbone. You, widow, you jump like a little fish; you jump like a "long mouth" fish'.

In the verses 1/134 to 1/136, Ambonwari sing about Imaynja, an older woman who stayed in her cooking area, and the young men who wanted to have sex with her ('they wanted to turn her around'). The men sing: 'You, Imaynja, you are a fat [nice] woman from Imanmeri'. They go on to say that cane flowers fell off her when they copulated with her. Verse 1/136 is even more explicit and obscene: 'Imaynja, your vagina is not covered, it is open like a men's house, waiting for men to go inside'. They call her by another name (common for the parallelism of verses), Apiakirima, and repeat that she is a nice fat woman who, however, does not know how to paddle a canoe. They say her vagina is uncovered and an entire men's house – that is, all the men of that clan – could enter her vagina.

Verses 1/157–159 and 161–162 begin with a tree (a metaphor for a woman) at Mikyanmarin grassland, saying that someone made a hole in it. The chorus lines specify that it was her future husband who made that hole (i.e., had sex with her). Bob explained how her sisters and grandmothers gathered round and teased her: 'You, a young girl, you go around by yourself, you did it'. She replied that she would marry this man. The sisters went on, saying: 'Yes, our tree from the grassland has a hole, the tree is already old, it is already firewood [old tree, old woman], the hole has been made'. In the next verse we learn that a flying fox is in this hole and then: 'Flying foxes do not really stay in the holes all the time'. Bob again explained that her sisters are not angry with the girl. Indeed, they praise her. 'She is not nobody; she has a hole; there is food inside'. However, in verse 159 the men become vulgar (when men sing this verse, women scream that they should stop). They call the woman by her name and sing how a big sago omelette (a metaphor for vagina) opens and closes; and how young men from Yanbonman (the men's house of Crocodile-1 clan) 'put their eyes inside her' (i.e., saw her private parts) as she did not cover her vagina properly. In verse 161 they repeat that her real husband made a hole in a tree; he carved her (i.e., had sex with her). Then he covered himself with the dry skin of a flying fox at the front and *Cordyline* leaves at the back. In verse 1/162 the words are put into a woman's mouth when she asks her brothers from Yanbonman men's house to bring her the man, to hold her 'bird' (lover) from Mikyanmarin, saying that he is hers, that she will marry him.

In a recent article (Telban 2014b), I have shown how the Ambonwari's figurative speech, *wapaysur mariawk* (climbing talk), as exemplified in the above verses, makes ordinary speech more potent. How? Ambonwari say that it climbs on one's skin and grips a person, like illness, ritual and custom do (Telban 2014b: 93–94). Because 'skin has eyes and ears', one not only feels and hears what is expressed in a trope but also sees it. Tropes place things before people's eyes and make things visible. It is through tropes that verses in all-night songs appear to the senses and enliven one's existence (cf. Ricœur 2003 [1977]: 48). Whenever such tropes are used in joking or playful relationships, they make people excited, cheerful, embarrassed and so on. In any case, they do not leave them untouched or indifferent. Just as body decoration, song, music and movement of the dancers are not simply reflections of a specific lifeworld but are rather creators of it, so 'tropes [are] not merely figures of speech playing with similarities and resemblances for the sake of verbal effect, but are active, change-producing transpositions.... They are not just symbolic, but also inductive' (Telban 2014b: 93; see also Telban 2008).[11]

Conclusion

During my first dancing experience with the Ambonwari, about eight big men (including Bob Kanjik) and some younger ones knew the majority of the verses. The rest were only able to join the chorus, especially the repetitions. Some verses were general knowledge and whenever it was their turn to be sung the drumming and singing grew louder. When people were excited about a particular verse the drummer kept beating the slit-drum without a pause and the same verses were repeated two, three or more times. Every two hours or so we stopped, sat down and ate. Then the singing and dancing continued. Silhouettes of the dancers moved in the pale light of kerosene lamps as if they had lives of their own. These *anggindarkwi* (shadows, spirits of living beings) spread in all directions. Soon after midnight I could not feel the pain in my legs any more. My movements became automatic. I was given more betel nuts and aromatic bark to chew than I wanted. Children soon slept on the mats spread out against the walls of the house. The bark floor was creaking and cracking and people said that the spirits of the house were dancing with us. At 8am we moved outside and circled the house for the last time. After shaking hands with our hosts, we descended towards Ambonwari throwing away our leaves and other temporary decorations.

The all-night singing and dancing event is characterized by the seemingly endless repetition of specific prosody – that is, rhythmic pattern, intonation, volume and pitch of sung verses – and by the constant bodily movement, either up and down (men) or left and right (women). Facilitated by chewing of betel nut mixed with small pieces of aromatic bark, the rhythm creates an intoxicating intimacy between the dancers. A singing and dancing ceremony creates a setting where mutuality of being permeates the participants' bodies; that is, when people participate intrinsically in each other's identity and existence, when intersubjective belonging of kinfolk means that persons are members of one another (Sahlins

2013: ix, 2). Interestingly, Ambonwari would express this kind of mutuality of being with the term *wambung*, the mindful and affective insideness of a being. *Wambung* in the state of becoming (*si-* [become, feel, do], as in *ama wambung ama sikan* [I feel insideness]) makes a person compassionate and caring – that is, favourably disposed towards others. Predecessors, consociates and those not yet born, as well as the spirits of the land and spirits of the dead, their deeds and movements, are all called up and brought together in an event that epitomizes the primordial migrations, the process of their relational becoming. '[W]here being is mutual, experience itself is transpersonal' (Sahlins 2013: 44).

Because ancestors and spirits are also part of this mutuality of being in Ambonwari, the singing and dancing ceremony expands ordinary kinship into the political-religious domain of the whole society (see Godelier 2011). Moreover, when dancing in another village, this political-religious domain encompasses an even wider area, bringing together groups, who recall ancient kinship ties with the Ambonwari, even if these no longer exist. As I have written elsewhere (Telban 1998a: 220–21), the sentimentality of belonging to familiar places, paths and people is evoked by a line of song, a footstep, the sound of a drum, the colours of painted bodies and the heat, the rhythm and the tempo of the moving dancers. Intimate sociality, which settles old disputes and suppresses momentary disagreements (those with stronger grudges anyway abstain from participation in the all-night singing and dancing event), merges the members of different clans and lineages into a single whole. The dancers experience their existence in terms of 'we', with all the strength of what Schütz called a 'mutual tuning-in relationship' (1977: 108, 115). Additionally, the dances become excellent occasions for the creation of new relationships between young men and women.

The feeling of mutuality of being in song-dances is created by bringing together visual, auditory, tactile and kinaesthetic sensory experiences, transmuting into each other. Even if the sung words were unintelligible, the singing, drumming and dancing, spread over twelve to fourteen hours and enhanced by betel nut chewing and smoking, generated a powerful feeling of being one, of having one 'insideness' and one skin (i.e., body), with the people with whom I lived and danced.

During the next few years after my initial fieldwork all the big men died and it was Francis Kwandikan Andari, Bob Kanjik's brother's son, who kept enough interest in the songs and became the lead singer. The situation changed again following the arrival of the Catholic charismatic movement in December 1994 and its rejection of traditional rituals and other customary practices controlled by senior men (Telban 2009, 2013). Two aspects of people's lives, however, were less affected: those practices related to birth and death. As the charismatic leaders explained, they did not want to challenge the birth-giving and mourning practices of their mothers. *Yamin siria* continued to play a major role in the celebrations of young people's achievements. But for several years after 2001 I was the only one who had access to all the verses of *yamin siria*. A couple of times I was dancing behind Francis Kwandikan Andari with my typed verses, prompting him with the first few words whenever he felt unsure about how to continue. I then gave copies of all the songs I had recorded to Francis. Once 'disco' became popular in the village, however, the younger generation preferred to dance to the tunes of Papua New Guinea string bands, regardless of whether the singing and dancing celebration was part of a *kurang* ceremony. Nowadays, a proper *yamin siria* takes place every few years, but nobody knows whether it will be abandoned like those song-dances associated with the men's house.

Acknowledgements

Many discussions held during my first fieldwork in Ambonwari between 1990 and 1992 with Bob Kanjik Anjapi (now deceased) about the people, places, names, tropes and verses were extremely important for my elucidation of their songs. Subsequent information was gathered over the following years when talking to different people, most recently in 2011 with Francis Kwandikan Andari, the eldest son of Bob Kanjik's younger brother, with whom all the songs were recorded. The elementary-school teacher Julias Sungulmari has from the very beginning of my research assisted with transcriptions and translations from Karawari language into Tok Pisin. I am grateful to the Firebird Foundation for Anthropological Research, where the recordings, transcriptions and translations of all Ambonwari songs are now stored, for a supplemental grant in 2011. I also thank The Royal Society of Edinburgh for the Caledonian Research Fund / RSE European visiting research fellowship at the University of St Andrews between 25 October 2014 and 24 February 2015 and Evangelos Chrysagis, Panas Karampampas and especially Michael Young for their careful reading of an earlier version of this chapter. For the drawings of Ambonwari painted faces I would like to thank Jill Skulina of Newport, St Andrews in Scotland. Jill used my photographs of some painted faces and sketches of faces I drew in my notebook during my first fieldwork in Ambonwari.

Borut Telban received his Ph.D. in Anthropology from The Australian National University in 1994. He is currently Research Advisor and Professor at the Research Centre of the Slovenian Academy of Sciences and Arts. He held several visiting positions, such as Leach/RAI Fellow at the University of Manchester (1995–96), Fulbright Scholar at the University of California, San Diego (2006–07) and The Royal Society of Edinburgh Visiting Research Fellow at the University of St Andrews (2014–15). His anthropological research among the Karawari-speaking people of the East Sepik Province, Papua New Guinea, has spanned more than twenty-five years. In his published books, articles and chapters he has explored in detail Ambonwari cosmology, kinship and social organization, ritual, death, poetics, language, cultural space and time and socio-cultural change pertaining to the impact of the Catholic charismatic movement. He is the author of *Dancing through Time: A Sepik Cosmology* (Clarendon Press, 1998) and *Andaypa: Essays on Death in a New Guinea Community* (in Slovenian, Obzorja, 2001).

Notes

1. An impressive corpus of works in ethnomusicology and sung poetry has been published by The Institute of Papua New Guinea Studies in a series called Apwitihire: Studies in Papua New Guinea Musics, under the editorship of Don Niles (see, for example, Wassmann 1991; Yamada 1997; Drüppel 2009). Reviews of works about ethnomusicology in Papua New Guinea can be found in Niles (1992, 2001). On sung tales in the New Guinea highlands see Rumsey and Niles (2011) and on poetic imagery of songs among the Foi, the Kaluli neighbours, see Weiner (1991).
2. The phoneme /i/, used throughout this chapter, is heard as the vowel in 'sir'.
3. Amazonian peoples also acquired music from nonhumans (Severi 2014: 45).
4. While *sia-* (singing and dancing) is also a verb, the Ambonwari use *siria* more than they use *sia* for different kinds of singing and dancing celebrations, be they in a men's house, private house or outside. It could be that the term *sia* was imported from the northern coast of New Guinea. Don Niles writes: 'Whatever the origin *sia* has spread well beyond the Siassi region [in Morobe Province, west of West New Britain] and the reputation of the Siassi as expert dancers as well as traders, has undoubtedly contributed to this distribution ... *sia* has retained its name throughout the area of its distribution' (2009: xix, xxi). While many performers who have bought *sia* dances do not understand the song texts, the Ambonwari have their own. Also, the drumming of a slit-drum, which is very important for the Ambonwari, is absent in the Siassi region (ibid.: xxvii). There is some similarity, however, in that *sia* drummers, both in northern parts of New Guinea and in Ambonwari, dance as they play their hand-drums. However, the ways in which the Ambonwari sing and dance are different from *sia* performances among the Kaulong, for example (Drüppel 2009: 212–23).
5. Besides *yamin siria*, the Ambonwari held several other song-dances in the past: *masungun siria* (song-dance of the enemy) was performed at the front of the men's house, while *kambin siria* (song-dance of the shield), *sanggut siria* (song-dance of the flute) (Telban 2014b) and *manbon siria* (song-dance of the crocodile) (Telban 2008) were performed in the men's house.
6. The first song-cycle of *yamin siria* comprises nineteen sub-cycles with 370 stanzas; the second one, eight sub-cycles with 158 stanzas (while additional three sub-cycles with seventy-seven stanzas are taken from the beginning of the first song-cycle); and the third one, eleven sub-cycles with 237 stanzas. I use 'stanza' interchangeably with 'verse' to refer to a set of lines that make up a singing whole.
7. The verb *kakayapi-* explicitly refers to painting a face and joining the dancers. Thus, a man who has painted his face for a dance is called *kakayapikin* and a woman *kakayapikinma*.

Two other verbs, *karing-* (carve, shape, hew, point, sharpen, make with an axe, build, work, draw) and *kara-* (incise, make incisions, cut skin as a part of initiation), are used for the process of making carvings, as well as cutting or tattooing of skin. Both refer to the shaping of skin and thus making a being.

8. Like many other terms, *kapuk* is a polysemic word meaning sound, noise, thunder, crack, call, cry, drumming signal, bird's call and sound of an animal. *Kapuk* can be used with several verbs but most often with the verb *sukwa-* (beat, trash, kill; bite, sting). When *sukwa-* is used with *mariawk* (talk, speech, story, thought) it refers to 'speak out, tell, divulge, gossip' (Telban 2014a: 264–66); when used with *kapuk* (sound, noise) it refers to 'call, sing (bird), speak out, talk out'. The sound of a hand-drum (*wanggin*, from *wang* [large hole]) is called *kapuk*. The sound of a slit-drum (*yimbung*) and the totemic signals of each clan (idem 1998a: 190–93) are also called *kapuk*. Every sound is a call. Every call is directed towards somebody and is therefore relational from its inception.

9. It should be no surprise to learn that the villagers often interpreted the voices in mobile phones as those of the spirits of their dead (Telban and Vávrová 2014).

10. This ceremony is known as *naven* among the Iatmul (see Bateson 1980 [1958]; Houseman and Severi 1998; Silverman 2001).

11. Many different tropes are used in songs referring to both people and their sexual organs. For an attractive young man or a nicely decorated dancer, Ambonwari use metaphors such as *saun* (egret), *yambari* (eagle), *saki* (bush spirit), *sanggur* (flute), *wambunggay* (type of bird), *koni* (type of bird), *kaminggran* (large *Octomeles sumatrana* tree) and *kawi* (small fish). Metaphorical expressions for young, lively and attractive women are: *yakwayma* (hen), *andima* (cockatoo), *yarikrak* (type of red parrot), *yarkwarang* (type of red and green parrot), *warmakay* (night heron), *awanma* (female cassowary), *mikisinma* (female lizard), *imbiyayma* (swine), *apirma* (fish-catching woman), *wurumayma* (type of fish), *yuwambak(ayma)* (turtle), *sanggurma* (flute) and *amin andi* (black ochre). For both young women and young men they use terms such as *pian* (fish with a long mouth), *andanban* (type of tree growing on grassland), *kwarima* (wild duck) and *yamara/yamakara* (bird of paradise). A lover is referred to as *yawun mayn* (outside husband) and a mistress as *yawun yarima* (outside wife).

References

Bateson, G. 1980 [1958]. *Naven*, 2nd edn. London: Wildwood House.

Drüppel, B. 2009. *Re-counting Knowledge in Song: Change Reflected in Kaulong Music*. Boroko: Institute of Papua New Guinea Studies.

Feld, S. 1981. '"Flow Like a Waterfall": The Metaphors of Kaluli Musical Theory', *Yearbook for Traditional Music* 13: 22–47.

———. 1984. 'Sound Structure as Social Structure', *Ethnomusicology* 28: 383–409.

———. 1990. *Sound and Sentiment: Birds, Weeping, Poetics, and Song in Kaluli Expression*, 2nd edn. Philadelphia: University of Pennsylvania Press.

———. 1996. 'Waterfalls of Song: An Acoustemology of Place Resounding in Bosavi, Papua New Guinea', in S. Feld and K. Basso (eds), *Senses of Place*. Santa Fe, NM: School of American Research Press, pp. 91–135.

Godelier, M. 2011. *The Metamorphoses of Kinship*, trans. N. Scott. London: Verso.

Hoenigman, D. 2015. '"The Talk Goes Many Ways": Registers of Language and Modes of Performance in Kanjimei, East Sepik Province, Papua New Guinea', Ph.D. dissertation. Canberra: Australian National University.

Houseman, M., and C. Severi. 1998. *Naven or the Other Self: A Relational Approach to Ritual Action*, trans. M. Fineberg. Leiden: Brill.

Munn, N. 1986. *Walbiri Iconography: Graphic Representation and Cultural Symbolism in a Central Australian Society*, 2nd edn. Chicago, IL: The University of Chicago Press.

Niles, D. 1992. 'Collection, Preservation, and Dissemination: The Institute of Papua New Guinea Studies as the Centre for the Study of all Papua New Guinea Music', in A.M. Moyle (ed.), *Music and Dance of Aboriginal Australia and the South Pacific: The Effects of Documentation on the Living Tradition*, Oceania Monograph 41. Sydney: University of Sydney, pp. 59–74.

———. 2001. '"Local" and "Foreign" Ethnomusicological Writings in Papua New Guinea', in H.R. Lawrence (ed.), *Traditionalism and Modernity in the Music and Dance of Oceania: Essays in Honour of Barbara B. Smith*, Oceania Monograph 52. Sydney: University of Sydney, pp. 121–37.

———. 2009. 'Editor's Introduction', in B. Drüppel, *Re-counting Knowledge in Song: Change Reflected in Kaulong Music*. Boroko: Institute of Papua New Guinea Studies, pp. xv–xl.

Ricœur, P. 2003 [1977]. *The Rule of Metaphor: The Creation of Meaning in Language*, trans. R. Czerny with K. McLaughlin and J. Costello, SJ. London: Routledge.

Rumsey, A., and D. Niles (eds). 2011. *Sung Tales from the Papua New Guinea Highlands: Studies in Form, Meaning, and Sociocultural Context*. Canberra: The Australian National University Press.

Sahlins, M. 2013. *What Kinship Is—and Is Not*. Chicago, IL: The University of Chicago Press.

Schütz, A. 1977. 'Making Music Together: A Study in Social Relationship', in J.L. Dolgin, D.S. Kemnitzer and D.M. Schneider (eds), *Symbolic Anthropology: A Reader in the Study of Symbols and Meanings*. New York: Columbia University Press, pp. 106–19.

Severi, C. 2014. 'Transmutating Beings: A Proposal for an Anthropology of Thought', *HAU: Journal of Ethnographic Theory* 4(2): 41–71.

Silverman, E.K. 2001. *Masculinity, Motherhood, and Mockery: Psychoanalyzing Culture and the Iatmul Naven Rite in New Guinea*. Ann Arbor: The University of Michigan Press.

Steiner, G. 1989. *Real Presences*. Chicago, IL: The University of Chicago Press.

———. 1998. *Errata: An Examined Life*. New Haven, CT: Yale University Press.

Storr, A. 1992. *Music and the Mind*. London: HarperCollins.

Telban, B. 1998a. *Dancing through Time: A Sepik Cosmology*. Oxford: Clarendon Press.

———. 1998b. 'Body, Being and Identity in Ambonwari, Papua New Guinea', in V. Keck (ed.), *Common Worlds and Single Lives: Constituting Knowledge in Pacific Societies*. Oxford: Berg, pp. 55–70.

———. 2008. 'The Poetics of the Crocodile: Changing Cultural Perspectives in Ambonwari', *Oceania* 78: 217–35.

———. 2009. 'A Struggle with Spirits: Hierarchy, Rituals and Charismatic Movement in a Sepik Community', in P.J. Stewart and A. Strathern (eds), *Religious and Ritual Change: Cosmologies and Histories*, Ritual Studies Monograph Series. Durham, NC: Carolina Academic Press, pp. 133–58.

———. 2013. 'The Power of Place: Spatio-Temporality of a Melanesian Religious Movement', *Anthropological Notebooks* 19(3): 81–100.
———. 2014a. 'Saying, Seeing and Knowing among the Karawari of Papua New Guinea', in A.Y. Aikhenvald and R.M.W. Dixon (eds), *The Grammar of Knowledge: A Cross-Linguistic Typology*. Oxford: Oxford University Press, pp. 260–77.
———. 2014b. 'The Poetics of the Flute: Fading Imagery in a Sepik Society', *Folklore* 125: 92–112.
———. 2015. 'Seeing and Holding Time: Karawari Perceptions of Temporalities, Calendars and Clocks', *Time and Society*. DOI: 10.1177/0961463X15577273.
Telban, B., and D. Vávrová. 2010. 'Places and Spirits in a Sepik Society', *The Asia Pacific Journal of Anthropology* 11: 17–33.
———. 2014. 'Ringing the Living and the Dead: Mobile Phones in a Sepik Society', *The Australian Journal of Anthropology* 25: 223–38.
Vávrová, D. 2014. '"Skin Has Eyes and Ears": Audio-Visual Ethnography in a Sepik Society', Ph.D. dissertation. Cairns: James Cook University.
Wassmann, J. 1991. *The Song to the Flying Fox: The Public and Esoteric Knowledge of the Important Men of Kandingei about Totemic Songs, Names and Knotted Cords (Middle Sepik, Papua New Guinea)*, trans. D.Q. Stephenson. Boroko: National Research Institute, Cultural Studies Division.
Weiner, J.F. 1991. *The Empty Place: Poetry, Space, and Being among the Foi of Papua New Guinea*. Bloomington: Indiana University Press.
Yamada, Y. 1997. *Songs of Spirits: An Ethnography of Sounds in a Papua New Guinea Society*, trans. J. Ohno. Boroko: Institute of Papua New Guinea Studies.
———. 2001. 'Acoustic Body: Voice Resounding through the Waxei People, Papua New Guinea', in H.R. Lawrence (ed.), *Traditionalism and Modernity in the Music and Dance of Oceania: Essays in Honour of Barbara B. Smith*, Oceania Monograph 52. Sydney: University of Sydney, pp. 103–12.

Index

ability, 38, 52–53, 76, 80, 132, 134, 191–92, 196, 199
  athletic, 75
  dance, 102, 104, 108, 112–13
  musical, 8
  disability, 101, 110
absence, 11, 14, 56, 87, 146, 154
accent, 71, 122, 180–81, 212
accumulation, 142, 144, 147, 170, 176
accusation, 212. *See also* social accusation
acoustemology, 2, 29
acoustic, 29, 51, 236, 247
  ethnography, 234
action, 18, 73–74, 83, 96, 99, 102, 111–112, 124, 135n8, 153, 196, 199, 202n1, 212, 229n13, 248
  centre of, 173
  chants, 69
  creative, 19, 79, 236
  embodied, 65
  ethical, 7, 79 (*see also* ethical)
  field of, 91n4
  flow of, 81
  reaction, 56, 110, 191, 194, 201, 224illustration9.4
  reflective, 15
  signs, 103
  system, 228n4
activity, 1, 5, 28, 30, 35–36, 70, 85, 87, 93n24, 107, 111, 149, 171, 187, 203n5
  artistic, 65
  business, 195
  communal, 129
  dance, 6, 8, 98–100, 104–5, 113, 202

DiY, 142–45, 151–52 (*see also* DiY)
DJ'ing, 142 (*see also* DJ'ing)
  extramusical, 16
  inactivity, 197
  individualistic, 130
  music, 8
  promotional, 16, 139–40
  recreational, 203n5
  sexual, 66
  visceral, 75
actor, 148, 157
  stage, 92n16, 187, 193–94, 201, 220
  ethical, 7, 140, 151, 153
  social, 4, 8, 12, 34–35, 91n4, 152, 166, 175, 202n1
aesthesis, 9
aesthetics, 39, 97, 132
  Buddhist, 58
  histories of, 29
  ironic, 215
  of differentiation, 9
aesthetic, 68
  elements, 32
  intimacy, 66
  of simplicity, 150
  practice, 97
  principles of Zen, 56
  rules, 174
  sensibilities, 69
  statement, 150, 210
affect, 2, 7, 9, 14–16, 39–40, 66, 78–79, 91n8, 126–27, 131, 134, 252. *See also* emotion; feeling
African
  traditions, 166
  descent, 171

age, 44–45, 48–49, 58, 70, 101–102, 108, 128, 180–181, 230n16
agency, 28, 71, 80, 124, 202n1
  political, 214
alcohol, 17, 25, 137, 140–44. See also drinking
amateur
  musician, 58
  dancer, 104, 106
  actor, 203
Ambonwari music. See music styles
America (Latin), 130, 135n4, 138, 170, 186
American (Latin)
  dance, 167, 175, 183n2
American (North), 176
  choreographer, 65, 81, 92, 95
  dance, 67, 70–71, 91n9
  dancer, 69
  formations, 70
  sociologist, 99
ancestors, 55, 235, 238, 244, 247–248, 252
ancestral, 69, 82, 89, 236, 242, 247
Andean folklore. See music styles
anethical, 148
animador, 4, 7, 15, 121–24, 127–29, 134, 135n5
anonymity, 104, 128, 158, 183, 203, 228
anyone, 41, 92, 213. See also Rapport, Nigel
appearance, 100, 107, 178, 193, 211, 247
Apókries, 222–26
appropriation, 7, 14, 56–59, 87
art, 1, 28–29, 47, 70, 74, 84–85, 90n1, 92n9, 99, 105, 170–72, 202n1, 212
  (see also martial arts)
artist, 15, 65, 67, 70, 75, 87, 90n1, 128, 132, 172, 195
Asian
  musicians, 49, 59
  Other, 57
  dancers 67
askēsis, 140, 153–155. See also ethical: work
Athens (city), 12, 17–18, 190, 210, 212, 217, 220–21, 225, 227
attendees, 108, 128, 130, 225
audible, 29, 31–32, 247
audiovisual, 210

audience, 141–142, 145–49, 152–53
auditory, 108, 235–36, 242, 248, 252
  knowledge, 38
aural, 9, 13, 29–30, 34, 78, 236
austerity, 189–190, 195–96, 198–99, 201, 203n2, 203n5, 214
authenticity, 13, 16–17, 58, 108, 163–69, 172, 175–79, 182, 192
awareness
  bodily, 10, 33, 35, 40, 74
  kinaesthetic, 14, 74–75
  linguistic, 213–14
  of any discursive claim, 211
  performative, 213
  self–, 12–14, 85
  sensory, 27, 34, 75, 80, 82
  shifting of, 37
  sonic, 30, 144
  zanshin (martial awareness), 33

back stage. See Goffman, Erving
balance, 68, 74, 145
ballet. See dance styles
ballroom dance. See dance styles
band (music), 47, 139–58, 165, 171, 200, 253
beauty, 18, 27, 241, 248
body. See corporeal; embodiment; visceral
boundaries, 3, 5, 48, 100, 113, 127, 141, 227
bouzouki. See musical instruments
bouzoúkia (nightclub), 222, 229n14
brain, 73, 78, 89, 218
Buddhist, 32, 35, 38–39, 58, 59, 67
butoh, 14, 67, 70, 81, 92n16

capacity, 2, 9, 13, 17, 44, 53, 126, 140, 142, 196, 211, 213
capital, 71, 151
  economic, 16, 48
  foreign, 170, 172, 182, 192
carnival. See *Apókries*
casino. See dance styles
celebration, 5, 9, 32, 127–28, 189, 191, 198, 200, 211, 220, 222, 226, 234, 237, 242, 248, 253, 254n4
child, 44, 47, 53, 55, 70–71, 78, 96, 104,

106–7, 111, 113, 181, 190, 194–95, 197–98, 237, 242, 244, 251
chorus, 238, 241, 244, 250, 251
cinema
    dialogic, 188–89
    Italian neorealism, 192–93
    mainstream production, 193
    new Greek, 191, 193, 196, 201–2
    See also film
clans, 242, 244, 249, 252
class
    dance, 15, 33, 48–49, 88, 96, 99, 101–14, 122, 131, 133, 149, 163, 165, 178, 183n1, 197, 203n7, 213, 229n14, 230n20
    social, 15, 131, 139, 167–68, 170–72, 174
classical music. *See* music styles
classification, 4, 183n1, 225, 240
club
    cinema, 190
    goth, 15, 96, 101–4, 108, 110, 114, 142–43, 151, 190, 192, 209–10, 216–18, 225–26, 230
    nightclub, 96, 142, 151, 222, 226, 229n14
    salsa, 15, 101–4, 108, 110, 114
collaboration, 14–15, 66, 74, 98, 102, 152–53, 200
    artistic, 74
    with capital, 151
    and dance, 189
    democratic, 73
    in fieldwork, 3, 48–49, 65, 104–5, 108, 113, 157, 183n5
    and intimacy, 40, 48–49, 65 (*see also* intimacy)
    participation and, 10–12
colonial, 91n7, 131, 177, 238
commercial, 16, 122, 128, 139, 145, 149, 154–55, 178
communitas, 9
community, 9, 31, 67, 82, 92n14, 99, 132, 174, 176, 179, 181, 189, 201, 248
competitive dance. *See* dance styles
concert, 30, 49, 55, 59, 67, 71, 87, 91n9, 122–23, 129–33, 139, 150, 164, 167

concert promoter. *See* music promoter
conscious, 10, 37, 100, 109–10, 127, 148, 153, 189
    less-than-, 75
    not, 31
    self-, 56, 83
    subconscious, 54
    unconscious, 36, 89, 109–10, 189
consciousness, 34, 37, 47, 75
conservatory (music), 48, 54
consumption, 15, 130, 177
contact improvisation. *See* dance styles
contemporary dance. *See* dance styles
corporeal, 2, 7–10, 12, 16, 28, 74–75, 82
cosmopolitanism, 47, 67, 82, 213, 228n3
cosmos, 39, 213, 235, 243
costume, 91n10, 122, 200, 222, 225
craft, 13–14, 32, 67, 72, 190
creative
    appropriation, 151
    art, 90n1
    artist and practitioner, 75
    force, 144
    ideas, 12, 85, 92n16, 152, 155
    industries, 16
    movement, 71, 78, 106
    procedures, 65
    projects, 29
creation, 32, 40, 68, 183n1, 196, 202, 229n7, 236, 249, 252
creativity, 14, 110, 149, 157
crisis, 71, 214
    a scene of, 148–49
    global financial, 154
    in Greece, 187, 189–91, 194–99, 201, 203n2
critical commentary, 189, 199, 214–15, 226
cultural intimacy, 67, 85, 87, 213, 227. *See also* intimacy
cultural proximity, 188–89, 201
critique, 14, 15, 29, 98–99, 102, 187, 201
crowd, 121–23, 128–29, 132, 147, 152. *See also* audience
Cubanness, 16–17, 167, 175, 178, 183n1
cyborg, 215, 218, 227, 229n7
cybergoth, 213, 215, 217, 219illustration9.2, 229n7

dance
  as antidote to the crisis, 17, 197–99
  cinematic, 13, 17, 187–89, 190–91, 194, 196, 199–202
  as embodied commentary, 187, 189, 201
  event. *See* event
  floor, 209, 215, 221–6
  improvisation, 191, 221
  metaphorical use of, 180, 189, 196
  participatory, 98–99, 105, 113
  partner, 66, 72, 85, 108, 110, 224
  performance. *See* performance
  public, 14, 121, 164, 172–73, 179, 187–89, 191–92, 196, 201–2, 248–49
  as resistance, 5, 189–90, 190, 203n7, 214
  and self-empowerment, 189, 199
  social engagement of, 5, 121, 187, 202, 235
dance anthropology, 3, 9, 97–98. *See also* ethnochoreology
dance ethnography, 15, 105
dance studies, 97–98, 113
dance styles
  ballet, 71, 78, 81, 84, 90n1, 91n9, 96, 99, 100–114, 172
  ballroom, 90n1, 163–64, 174, 183n4
  butoh (*see* butoh)
  casino, 178–79, 184n11
  competitive, 163–64, 167, 175, 177, 186
  contact improvisation, 73, 103, 110
  contemporary, 65–67, 81, 87, 91n5, 91n9
  'Greek dances', 211–12, 221–22, 225–26
  folk, 90n1, 172, 178, 191, 225–6
  industrial, 209, 221–25
  rumba, 16–17, 163–75, 177–84
  line dancing, 96, 99, 101–4, 111–12, 114
  salsa, 15, 96, 108, 110, 122, 164, 169, 177–78, 182, 183n1
  tsiftetéli, 221–22, 225–26
  zeibékiko, 17, 191–94, 198–201, 214–15, 221–22, 225–26
dance videos, 173–4, 177, 210, 220, 222
dancer, 1, 4, 8, 12, 14–15, 65–71, 77–89, 96, 101, 108, 111, 113, 220, 235–38, 243–49, 251–52, 254n4
  contemporary, 66–7

ballet, 101, 104, 106
highland, 109, 112
contact improvisation, 110
ballroom, 90n1, 163–64, 174, 183n4
zeibékiko, 191–92, 200–201, 214, 221–22, 225–26
industrial (goth), 209–11
tsiftetéli, 221–22, 225–26
darkness, 70, 196, 215, 242, 249
dead, 198–99, 216, 220, 236
  spirits of the, 236, 243, 252, 254n9
  undead, 216
  See also death
death, 211, 215, 218, 226–27, 252
  in Zen Buddhist philosophies, 38
  social, 194, 196
  symbolic, 194
  See also dead
desire, 45, 82, 96, 101, 108, 126, 131, 135n3, 237
dialogic, 29, 30, 188–89, 241
dictatorship, 81, 192
digital, 13, 28, 31, 36
director
  artistic, 73, 78, 102, 113
  of Afro Cuba, 165, 171
  film, 190, 193, 197, 201
discipline, 10, 14–15, 31–32, 38, 53, 57, 73, 78–9, 84–85
discrimination, 134, 170–71, 182
dissatisfaction, 143, 212, 221
distinctions, 12, 30, 34, 53, 135n8, 158n3, 195, 238
diverse
  cultures, 50
  ethnically, 67
  forms of 'Japaneseness', 53
  interpretations, 217
  perspectives, 166
diversity
  ethnographic, 2
  musical, 145, 225
  of genres, 177, 225
  of narratives, 182
  social, 203n7, 211, 221–22, 225
DiY, 16, 228n2
ethics, 149–50

music promoter, 143, 146–48
  vs. independent, 149–51
  and stigma, 149–50
  See also do-it-yourself
DJ'ing, 12, 142, 146, 153, 217, 225, 228n2
do-it-yourself, 141, 157. See also DiY
dōjō, 28, 31–34, 39–40
dramaturgical loyalty. See Goffman, Erving
dramaturgical model. See Goffman, Erving
drinking, 15, 121–24, 127–28, 134, 142, 163, 190
  as a technology of the self, 129–32
  See also alcohol
drums. See musical instruments

economy, 170–72, 182, 203n2
  and music, 154 (see also live music)
  and dance, 168, 170–72
education, 31, 52, 58, 88, 190
  and discipline, 14, 53
  dance, 15, 172
  music, 6, 41, 53–55
  outdoor, 97
  primary, 96, 114
  system, 55, 89
embodiment, 9, 32, 56, 65, 103, 108, 133, 135n8, 203n2, 237
  'embodied sounding', 30
  and collaboration, 11
  disembodied, 31
  and disposition, 8
  and governance, 5
  of identity, 130, 225
  of irony, 18
  and knowledge, 10, 15, 67, 71, 74, 80, 85, 88–89, 90n2, 180
  and memory, 13, 17, 178, 187, 189, 200–201
  and music learning, 36
  and narrative, 215
  of gendered moral norms, 7, 221, 248
  of social hierarchies, 7, 199, 221
  of social values, 7, 134, 199, 221, 248
  of sound, 30, 36–40, 50, 59
  and poetics, 66, 87
  of social practice, 189

and subject formation, 124, 127
and understanding, 14, 93n29
emotion, 2, 7, 9, 15–16, 28–31, 38, 50, 52, 53–58, 66, 72, 78–79, 91n8, 100, 106, 126–127, 130–34, 151, 174, 178, 213, 235, 238. See also affect; feeling
ethnochoreology, 3, 9. See also dance anthropology
ethnographic
  data, 3, 6, 98, 105, 113
  encounter, 13, 29, 100, 131, 228n3
ethnomusicology, 3, 254n1
Enlightenment, 42, 45–46, 48–49
environment
  acoustic, 29
  dance, 74, 77–78, 81–83, 85, 100
  digital, 4
  ethical, 152
  learning, 39, 163
  meaningful, 30
  musical, 51
  natural, 18, 51, 236 (see also landscape)
  public, 28
  social, 67, 104, 123, 139, 152, 236–7
  sonic, 18, 28–31, 35, 40
  urban, 30, 71
ethnicity, 46–47, 50, 52, 57, 67, 101, 122, 124, 131, 134, 213
ethical, 1–2, 6–8, 15–16, 123–24, 126–27, 131–33
  ambivalence, 7, 127, 131, 133
  complexity, 140–41, 151–53, 157
  context, 134
  conversion, 16, 141, 148–50
  criteria, 132, 149
  dilemma, 149, 151–52
  discourse, 8, 149–50
  imagination, 126
  evaluation, 132
  exercise, 7, 141, 145–46, 149, 154 (see also technologies of the self)
  field, 123
  innovation, 153
  issues in research methods, 11
  judgement, 7, 16, 139–41, 149, 151
  life, 133–34
  mediator, 121, 124

ethical (*cont.*)
  pedagogue, 140, 143
  pluralism, 7
  practice, 3, 8, 16, 126–27, 134
  project, 2
  reflection, 145, 148 (*see also* problematization)
  rule, 174
  space, 6
  subject, 122–24, 127, 132, 134, 139–40, 144, 148, 151–52, 154, 157, 158n2 (*see also* subject position)
  subjectivation, 140, 144–45, 148, 151, 153–54, 157 (*see also* subjectification)
  substance, 131–32, 140–41, 153–54, 158n6
  superiority, 214, 226
  telos, 140–41, 153–54
  value(s), 8, 13, 140, 143, 153
  tools, 144
  work, 133, 140, 154–55 (see also *askēsis*)
  See also ethics
  See also morality
ethics, 4, 6–8, 16, 24, 114, 122, 124–27, 129, 132, 160
  and aesthetics, 136n12, 174
  anthropology of, 6–7, 124–26, 140, 157
  and cultural policy, 16
  and disposition, 153
  and hospitality, 158n5
  intersubjective, 140
  and morality, 6–8, 16, 127, 134, 135n8, 151, 158n3
  and routinization, 153
  and the self, 3, 6, 7, 13, 15–16, 123–27, 132–33, 140, 144–45 (*see also* self-fashioning)
  sonic, 6
  See also ethical
  See also morality
ethos, 6, 8, 14, 16, 140, 145, 197
  as telos, 141
etiquette, 15, 96, 100–101, 104–6, 108, 129
Europe, 45–46, 48–51, 53–56, 58, 67, 90n5, 91n9, 97, 165, 167, 174–75, 177–78, 183 188–89, 193, 203n2, 214

European
  audiences, 50
  cinematic movements, 193
  culture, 50
  dance, 67, 91n9, 92n16, 174–75, 177
  economic crisis, 203n2
  languages, 50
  music, 55–56
  music education, 53
  pre-, 214
  sound, 51
  style of approaching classical music, 50, 51
  tradition, 56
Evdokia (film) 17, 187, 192–93, 197–99
event, 7, 10, 88, 93n24, 123, 129, 133–34, 164–65, 183n1, 191, 194–95, 214
  dance, 3–5, 9, 167–78, 184n11, 190–91, 200–202
  ethical, 122, 134
  music, 10, 12–13, 15–16, 141–48, 152–53, 155
  song-dance, 235–38, 242, 244, 248, 251–52
  sonic, 3, 30
example
  ethical, 140, 151, 155
  as exemplar, 7, 140, 143, 151
exchange, 11, 87, 89, 133, 210, 241, 248–49
exercise, 33, 99, 107, 109, 111–12, 141, 145–46, 149, 154. *See also* ethical: exercise
exclusion, 5, 18, 50, 203n7, 211, 222, 226
exotic, 170, 176–77, 179, 214
experience, 5, 15, 17, 66, 71–72, 80, 93n24, 96, 106, 122, 134, 142, 144, 151–54, 188, 203
  authentic, 167, 182
  aesthetic, 9
  audience, 123, 132
  bodily, 13, 36, 126, 178
  categories of, 124, 132
  collective, 215, 252
  dance, 83–85, 102–5, 108–9, 112, 182, 184n11, 201, 238, 251–52
  and discipline, 53
  emotion, 55, 77–78, 127

fieldwork, 10–11, 29, 98, 190, 235
  and identity, 46, 131, 176, 201
  kinetic, 6, 77, 103, 252
  learning, 165
  migration, 14, 49, 51, 133, 196 (*see also* migrant)
  musical, 8, 50
  of philosophical ideas, 38, 234
  performance, 69–70
  sensory, 13, 103, 235–36, 238, 247, 252
  shared, 11, 111, 133
  social, 58
  sonic, 6, 8–9, 13, 27–32, 34, 36–37, 39–40, 46, 50–51, 238
  tourist, 165–66, 175, 177
  visceral, 3, 8–9, 78
experiential, 4, 5, 29, 51, 83
experimental, 67, 69, 77, 91n9
expression, 6, 9, 15, 38, 48, 51, 54–55, 58, 97, 106, 110–11, 127, 142, 145, 178, 189, 191, 212, 215, 218, 220–21, 229n7, 235–38, 247, 255n11
expressiveness, 38, 71
exterior, 5, 68, 79, 236, 243

Facebook, 173, 209, 216, 220–23, 228n1. *See also* media
familiarity, 56, 111–12, 212
fanzine, 142, 152
Farnell, Brenda, 8, 14, 90n3
fashion, 13, 16, 216, 255
Faubion, James D., 16, 136n12, 140, 148, 153, 157, 158n2
fear, 110, 125, 150, 214, 241, 249
feeling, 5, 29, 32–40, 46, 54–55, 66, 75, 78–79, 97, 104, 109–10, 112–14, 124, 126–27, 132–33, 135n8, 141, 153–54, 174, 178, 198, 214–15, 227, 236, 252. *See also* affect; emotion
Feld, Steven, 29–30, 46, 234–35, 238
festival, 70, 145, 152, 155
fieldwork, 10–11, 13, 18, 46, 96, 103, 122, 134, 139, 143–44, 146–47, 152, 157, 168, 170, 174, 183n1, 190, 194, 198, 200–202, 213, 234, 252–53
  'yo-yo fieldwork', 98
  See also collaboration

film, 17, 69–70, 84, 142, 150, 177, 187–202, 216. *See also* cinema
flute. *See* musical instruments
folk, 163, 174, 178, 191, 193, 197, 230n16
  music (*see* music styles)
  song, 50, 123, 230n16
  dance (*see* dance styles)
  folkloric events, 123
food, 139, 144, 146, 181, 190, 194, 214, 234, 241, 247–48, 250
forms
  of art, 47, 70
  of discipline and education, 14
  of ethnographic knowledge, 11
  of ethnographic participation, 3, 12
  of human activity, 8, 87
  of irony, 212, 222
  of movement, 17, 31–32, 91n9, 109–13, 166, 199, 222
  of sociality, 3, 87, 188
  of understanding, 188
  sensory, 10
Foucault, Michel
  on aesthetics, 136n12
  on the care of the self, 125–26, 133
  on discourse, 124, 150
  on docile bodies, 97
  on ethics, 123–26, 131, 140, 153–54
  on problematization, 126, 148
freedom, 55, 71, 191, 213
friends, 46, 49, 129, 141, 144, 146, 168, 174, 191–92, 194, 197, 199–200
friendship, 92n14, 174, 194, 202n1
front stage. *See* Goffman, Erving
function
  dance, 17
  of dance, 167–68, 180
  human, 68, 73, 92n20, 218
  social, 2, 99

gaze, 177, 209, 210
gender, 7, 13, 18, 58, 101, 124, 128, 131, 167, 169–70, 214, 235, 347, 251
generosity, 153–154, 157, 158n6, 202, 241
genre
  dance, 18, 90n1, 166, 170–71, 173, 177–79

genre (*cont.*)
  music, 18, 59, 122, 133, 230n16
  performance, 2, 29
gesture, 69–71, 82–85, 101, 103, 107, 109, 127, 132–33, 212
gossip, 209, 221, 249, 255n8
Glasgow (city), 15–16, 96, 98, 141, 143, 145, 152, 155–57
globalization, 17, 126, 178
Goffman, Erving
  on back stage, 100, 105, 107–8, 110, 113
  on discrepant role, 102
  on dramaturgical loyalty 101, 113
  on dramaturgical model 15, 96–98, 100, 113
  on front, 100–102, 105–6
  on front stage, 88, 100, 104, 106, 108, 111
  on inside secret, 106
  on intimate cooperation, 101, 108, 111
  on personal front, 100–101, 105
  on stigma, 149–50
  on team collusion, 107
  on unmeant gestures, 101
  on vocabulary of fronts, 101–2, 105–6, 109, 112–13
Gothic, 211, 215–16
government, 47, 166, 172, 190, 201, 214
governance. *See under* embodiment
'Greek dances'. *See* dance styles

habitus, 7, 40, 47, 111
hardship (economic), 17, 174, 194, 202
health, 27, 99
hearing, 33–34, 38–39, 92n20, 112, 168, 236, 238.
heritage, 16, 24, 52, 163, 165, 167, 170–71, 175–76, 178, 180, 182, 186, 232
  'heritage agnosticism', 175
Herzfeld, Michael, 66, 85, 210, 212, 214
hierarchies, 7, 12, 60n4, 131, 133, 144,
historical, 7, 28, 31, 47, 54–55, 60n2, 65, 70–71, 82, 89, 99, 123, 127, 130, 158n2, 175, 187–91, 196, 200–201, 215–16, 242
home, 33, 61, 128, 132–33, 135n10, 143, 151, 165, 172, 181, 190, 194, 203n5, 210, 217, 227
honour, 248
hope, 157, 196, 201, 211, 214, 217
huayno. *See* music styles
hybrid, 59, 91n9, 105, 166, 201, 216

identity, 5, 8, 14–15, 45–47, 49, 53, 57–59, 61, 71, 88, 126, 129–132, 134, 157, 167, 170, 176, 178, 180, 188, 210, 212, 228n3, 251
imagery, 73, 77, 79, 254n1
imagination, 1, 4, 13, 18–19, 36, 39, 46, 65, 68, 72–73, 77–79, 82, 85, 89, 92n16, 126, 131, 135n9, 174, 176–77, 184n10, 209, 212, 242
impression management, 100, 113
improvisation. *See* dance styles: contact improvisation; dance: improvisation; jazz improvisation
immoral, 140. *See also* unethical
incident, 99, 101, 109, 111, 113, 148, 170, 249
inclusion, 18, 66, 78, 96, 99, 101–4, 110–11, 114, 149, 178, 221–22, 226
inclusive dance 96, 99, 101–4, 110–11, 114
incommensurability, 17, 227
incorporation, 36, 56–7, 89, 165–66, 175, 216, 226, 248
independent promotion, 141, 148–51. *See also* DiY
individual, 1, 4, 7, 9–10, 14, 16, 30, 35, 37, 40, 46, 52–54, 56, 59, 66, 74, 83, 89, 90n1, 98–102, 104, 106, 113, 124–25, 130, 132, 134, 140, 143, 145, 149, 157, 170, 191, 196, 200, 210–14, 221–22, 229n13, 237, 247
industrial dance. *See* dance styles
industry
  tourist, 17, 176–77
  classical music 59
  commercial folkloric music, 122,
  See also live music: industry
inequality, 107, 166, 168, 171, 212
intangible cultural heritage, 170, 176
intention, 74, 99, 111, 125, 155, 169, 187, 212, 236

interpellation, 122, 124, 132, 135n7
interpersonal, 38, 73, 75, 123, 151, 228n1
intersubjectivity, 74, 124, 126–27, 134
intimacy, 2–9, 16, 85, 87–88, 90n4, 91n8, 101, 108, 111, 121, 128, 131, 141, 147, 153, 157, 201, 213, 215, 227, 252
    collaborative, 48–49, 153 (*see also* collaboration)
    intoxicating, 234
    kinaesthetic, 3, 14, 65, 67, 74–77
    physical, 9, 66, 78, 126, 133
    public, 132
    See also cultural intimacy
intoxicating, 235. *See also* intimacy
intoxication, 127, 129, 131, 134
irony, 13, 17–18, 60n5, 71, 209–15, 217–18, 220–22, 226–27
    liberal, 17–18, 211, 220–22, 226–27
    nihilistic, 17–18, 211, 217–20, 226
isolation, 166, 176, 188, 203n5, 242

Japaneseness, 13, 46–47, 51, 53, 56, 58–59
Jazz. *See* music styles
Jazz improvisation, 6.
judgement, 7, 16, 50, 124, 127, 135n8, 139, 140, 141, 149, 151, 210. *See also* ethical: judgement
Junta, 187, 189, 192, 194, 199, 202

kinaesthesia, 8–9, 67, 71, 74, 78, 92n20, 112–13
kinaesthetic, 9–10, 14, 65–67, 74–77, 79–80, 85, 87–88, 92n20, 103, 110, 112, 135, 236, 252
kinship, 202n1, 241, 252, 257
knowledge, 3, 10–13, 15, 18, 30–32, 36, 39, 49, 56, 66–67, 69, 72–75, 77, 79–80, 82, 84–85, 87–89, 90n2, 91n4, 101–6, 108–9, 148, 163–64, 174, 179–81, 211, 218, 241, 249, 251

landscape, 14, 18, 51, 68, 70, 235, 238, 241, 243
language, 14, 17, 46–47, 50–53, 57, 59, 69, 88, 106, 111, 132, 155, 214, 234–36, 241–42, 247–48

Latin popular music. *See* music styles
learning, 28, 32, 34–37, 40, 48, 53–54, 60n3, 68, 72, 74, 80, 83, 85, 88, 92n13, 103, 107, 110–13, 128, 165–68, 174, 180, 181, 190, 218, 220
leisure, 1, 27, 32, 97, 178
liberal irony. *See under* irony
lifestyle (goth), 14, 213, 216–17, 227, 228n4
lifeworld, 13, 17–18, 235–36, 251
line dancing. *See* dance styles
linguistic
    anthropology, 28, 65
    relativity, 50
    irony, 212
listening, 8–11, 13, 28–31, 34–40, 51–52, 123, 128, 131–33, 145, 147, 234
    passive, 13–4, 28, 37, 50, 123, 132
live music, 123, 128, 139
    ecology, 157
    economy of, 154
    industry, 145, 152, 157
    and cultural policy, 157
    and devolution in Scotland, 157
    See also music promoter
discourse, 46, 50, 53, 56, 58, 85, 87–88, 91n6, 93nn28–29, 124–25, 127, 131, 136n13
    ethical, 8
    local political, 190, 201
    martial, 33
    musical, 46
    nationalist, 13
    on suffering, 132
love, 18, 111, 123, 130–34, 197–98, 226, 234, 241, 248–50

machine, 71, 122, 215–18
mainstream, 130, 193, 194–95, 215
marriage, 197–98, 248–49
martial arts, 28, 31–35, 79, 210
material, 8, 14, 16, 29, 70, 78–9, 82, 126, 144, 211, 228n3
media, 58–59, 175–78
    mass, 49, 188, 227
    social, 17, 146, 147, 210, 227
membership, 105–6, 108–10, 113, 213

metaphor, 38, 97, 180, 189, 196–99, 214, 237–38, 250, 255n11
methods (research), 1–4, 10–13, 17, 27, 31, 36, 39, 47, 49, 72, 88, 97–98, 105, 110, 157, 227
migrant, 14–15, 53, 122, 124, 128, 130–34, 196
mind, 9, 32–33, 37, 46, 57, 75, 77, 79, 88, 112, 199, 227, 234
   mushin ('no mind'), 32
mind–body dualism, 9, 46, 57, 79–80, 88, 112, 199, 227
mockery, 17, 197, 210, 215
money, 48, 87, 144, 146–48, 150, 154–55, 172, 198
moral, 195, 211,
   agent, 144
   codes, 125, 140
   definition of, 135n8
   expectations, 129, 134
   good, 8, 127
   ideas, 136n11
   norms, 7, 125
   obligation, 82, 140
   philosophy, 124
   pressure, 130
   rules, 125, 140
   torment, 149
   virtue, 7
morality, 6–8, 16, 18, 135n8, 140, 151, 158n3, 197, 241, 248
   and the city, 144
   as society, 7
   See also ethics
   See also ethical
muga (nonself), 57
music
   equipment, 141, 146, 155
   event (*see* event)
   performances (*see* performance)
   pop, 69, 131
   popular, 128, 131, 135
   spectacle, 15–16, 122–23, 127
   See also live music
music promoter
   and collaboration, 144–45, 151–53, 157
   commercial, 139, 145, 149, 154–55,

   and ego, 145–46
   as entrepreneur 139, 147, 155
   as ethical subject, 140
   ethics of, 140
   and funding, 146, 152, 154–55
   and fundraising, 146, 155
   and generosity, 153–54; 158n6
   and hospitality, 146, 158n5
   and laziness, 150
   and money, 141, 144, 146–48, 150, 154–55
   and musical taste, 145
   and organizational aspects of music promotion, 145–48
   and pay-to-play, 143, 158n4
   and publicity of music events, 146
   and routines, 148
   and sense of vocation, 155
   and tickets, 141–42, 145, 147, 158n4
   and trust, 153
music styles
   Ambonwari music, 236, 238, 244
   Andean folklore, 128
   classical, 13–14, 44, 46–50, 54–55, 57–59, 234
   folk, 128, 169, 225–26, 230n16 (*see also* folk: song)
   huayno, 15, 121–34, 135n2, 135n5, 138
   Jazz, 6, 9, 56 (*see also* jazz improvisation)
   Latin popular, 128
   postpunk, 220
   punk, 150, 216
   rebétiko, 136n13, 191, 193, 203n7, 226
   rumba, 16–17, 163–75, 177–84
   trad goth, 220
   'trash music', 226
Musical instruments
   bouzoúki, 229n14
   drums, 178, 180–81, 242–44, 254n4
   flute, 236, 242, 254n5
   ney, 6
   piano, 44–45, 48, 57
   shakuhachi, 13, 27–28, 31, 35–40
   violin, 45–46, 48–56
musicology, 30
muscle, 74, 75
   memory, 109

nationalism, 47, 59, 60n5
native, 67, 95, 142
   categories, 2, 17, 227
   language, 47, 49
   anthropologist, 49,
neighbourhood, 122, 128, 172–74, 181
neoliberal, 89, 177, 190
network, 144, 149, 152–53, 177, 191, 200–201, 202n1, 228n3
New York (city), 14, 30, 65, 67, 69–71, 88
ney. *See* musical instruments
nihilistic irony. *See under* irony
noise, 28–31, 34, 217, 239–41, 255n8
notation
   movement and dance, 10, 12
   music, 36, 238

object, 3, 30–32, 35, 38, 71–72, 82, 126–27, 144, 202n1, 212
observer, 11, 30, 75, 100–101, 103–8, 112–13, 242
online, 31, 146, 220, 228n3
oral
   symbols, 9, 247
   narratives, 14, 66, 187
Oratótis Midén (film) 17, 187, 192–93, 197–99

pain, 70, 130–31, 133, 251
paradise, 10, 243, 255n11
participant observation, 11, 15, 102–5. *See also* methods (research)
participation. *See under* collaboration
participatory performance, 12
passion, 55, 66, 144, 164, 177, 200, 234
past, 80, 131, 188–89, 199–202, 214, 220, 238, 243, 249
pathways, 4–6, 18, 89
patrons, 88, 209–10, 212, 221, 229n14
pedagogy, 7, 14–15, 16, 66, 99, 106, 133, 145, 147, 152
perception, 28, 30, 38, 40, 50, 67, 70, 75, 93n24, 98, 100, 111, 166, 175–76, 195–96, 203n7, 235, 237
performance, 11–13, 17, 30, 37–38, 46, 48, 57, 75, 89, 97, 99, 101, 134, 142, 144, 200–201, 211–12, 226, 229, 254
   dance, 4–5, 17, 73, 84, 87, 106, 108–11, 165, 167, 169, 171–74, 176–79, 181–82, 190–92, 199, 209–10, 214–15, 220–22, 227
   music, 8, 49, 50–52, 55–59, 123, 133–39, 188, 236, 238
   See also staged performances
performative, 188, 202, 213
peripheral, 75, 122, 143, 188, 211, 221, 228n1
peripheralization, 15, 108, 143, 188, 211, 228n3
personal front. *See* Goffman, Erving
personhood, 39, 67, 73, 81–84, 89
physical, 5, 8–9, 11, 14, 27–28, 32, 39, 51, 57, 66–78, 85, 88, 100, 106–13, 126, 133, 199, 235
piano. *See* musical instruments
poetics, 66, 87, 235, 248
policy, 16, 143, 147, 157, 192
politics, 5, 16–17, 28, 36, 57, 89, 130–31, 135n3, 139, 167, 171, 176, 187–90, 192–93, 200–202, 203n2, 209, 211, 214, 221, 252
postmodern, 67, 70–71, 89, 91n9
postpunk. *See* music styles
power structures, 221, 226
powerlessness, 226
presentation of self in everyday life, 8, 97
primacy of movement, 2, 18
problematization, 126, 151.
   and thought, 148, 149
   See also ethical: reflection
professional, 96, 106
   ballet class, 96–97, 103–4, 106, 113–14
   dancer, 67, 75, 90n1, 106, 163, 165, 172, 174, 183n1
   identity, 157
   musician, 46–48, 52–53, 165, 183n1
   promoter, 145 (*see also* music promoter)
prosody, 212–13, 251
punk. *See* music styles

qualities, 3, 5, 8, 13, 29, 37, 39, 49, 55, 72, 74, 82–83, 150, 176, 229n13

racial, 16–17, 46, 131, 166–68, 170, 172, 174–75, 182, 184n6
radical, 90n1, 91n9, 97, 170, 216
Rapport, Nigel, 12, 211, 213. *See also* anyone; cosmopolitanism
raw, 164, 173, 178–79
rebétiko. See music styles
recession, 17, 189, 194–97, 203n2. *See also* crisis: in Greece
reflexivity, 10, 13, 15, 30–32, 34–35, 39, 49, 59, 88, 96, 98, 103, 113, 200, 222, 227
rehearsal, 51–52, 89, 90n3, 111, 169, 171, 242
religion, 8, 17, 57, 168, 170, 174, 180–81, 184nn6–7
remembering, 35–6, 66, 68, 180–81, 192, 217, 242
repertoire, 37, 39, 52, 58
reproduction, 131, 151, 153, 237
resistance, 5, 124, 189–90, 192, 203nn7–8, 213–14
resonance, 34, 37–38, 51, 66, 157, 193, 232
respect, 53, 56, 66, 84, 90n2, 103–5, 110, 112–13, 129, 145, 198
revolution, 91n9, 166–67
rhetoric, 59, 170, 177, 193, 196
rhythm, 8, 37, 51, 74, 108, 122, 128, 178–180, 184n11, 200, 235–36, 242–44, 251–52
ridicule, 217
risk, 84–85, 110, 147, 154–55, 212, 249
ritual, 1, 18, 33, 57, 59, 168, 202n1, 235, 247–48, 251–52
rules, 92n16, 125, 140, 154, 174, 179, 181, 234
rumba. *See* dance styles; music styles
rural, 4, 123, 130, 135n3, 196

salsa. *See* dance styles
sarcasm, 17, 210, 212, 222, 226–27
satire, 214
seduction, 89, 169, 235, 249
self-fashioning, 3, 6, 7, 16, 123–24, 127, 132, 140, 144. *See also* ethics: and the self
selfhood, 7, 15, 46

sensation, 14, 27, 29, 34, 38–40, 45, 66, 74–78, 83, 109–10, 112, 126, 236
senses, 14, 28–29, 32–34, 68, 74, 77, 79–80, 85, 91n8, 123, 234–35, 247, 251
sensitivity, 14, 51, 74, 157, 234
sensory, 6, 10, 13, 15, 27, 29–35, 40, 66, 74, 75, 77–79, 82, 131, 235–36, 252
  multi-/pluro-, 3, 9, 78, 85, 88, 123, 210
sensual, 9, 34, 41n1, 72, 75, 77–78, 80, 121, 177–78, 235, 238
sentiment, 15, 44, 59, 107, 111, 124, 130–34, 252
sentimental subject, 132–34
sex, 209, 250
sexual, 18, 66, 78, 91n16, 128, 133, 179, 214, 235, 237, 241, 247–51, 255n11
shakuhachi. *See* musical instruments
shared anthropology, 3
sign vehicles, 100
silence, 28
singer, 122, 124, 127, 132–33, 229n14, 238, 250, 252
singing, 9, 18, 50, 132, 179, 200, 218, 234–38, 241–44, 247–49, 251–53, 254n4
skiládika (nightclub), 222, 225, 229n14, 230n20
skills, 213, 241
  body, 35, 88
  dance, 10, 71, 74–75, 79, 82, 90n1, 102, 108, 180, 220
  organizational, 180
  research 3
  sensory, 6
  technical (music), 53
skin, 8, 172, 235–38, 241, 243, 250–52, 254n7
sleep, 141, 144, 242
  anthropology of, 43
slogans, 214, 228
smell, 92n20, 236
social accusation, 196, 201
  films of, 193–94 (*see also* film)
social interaction, 5, 9, 13, 28, 30, 58, 84, 96–98, 100, 103, 105–6, 113, 188, 215

social media. *See* Facebook; media
sociology of dance, 98
solidarity, 1, 9, 17, 189, 195, 197, 203n4, 214, 217, 227
　networks, 191, 200, 202
somatic, 2, 10, 13, 18, 40, 91n8, 92n20, 127, 134, 210, 212, 227
sonic ethnography, 29, 31
sound recording, 13, 27–34, 36–39, 41n6, 128, 187, 91n6, 128, 239Illustration10.1, 253
sounded anthropology, 2, 31
soundscape, 28–29, 31–32, 47
space, 2–6, 9, 11–13, 15–16, 27–35, 40, 56, 65, 68, 72, 74–75, 77–82, 87–88, 92n14, 98, 100, 104–13, 123, 141, 144, 147, 168, 172–74, 178, 182, 188, 201–2, 209, 226, 228, 243
spatial, 1–2, 5–6, 14, 28, 74, 103, 236–38, 243
spirits, 131, 136, 241, 243–44, 247, 251–52, 255n9
sport, 53, 60n4, 87, 92n20, 97, 111, 164
　rugby football, 68
staged performances
　dance, 73, 84, 191
　music, 59, 123, 128, 133, 142, 165
status, 12, 14, 87, 98, 108, 113, 135n5, 157, 165, 167–68, 171, 212, 214
story, 38, 46, 73, 97, 133, 155, 197, 237, 248, 255n8
strategy, 57–58, 71, 107–8, 111–12, 139, 154, 167, 176, 182, 203n2, 215
strength, 68, 75, 92n16, 191, 234, 252
stereotype, 18, 54, 105, 112, 131, 150, 197, 211, 216–17, 225, 226–27
structuralism, 100
struggle, 5, 34, 37, 150, 174, 189, 199, 214
studio (dance), 71, 73, 75, 84, 88, 98, 100, 104, 106, 109–10
style 32, 35, 41n6, 50–52, 56, 59, 91n9, 164, 175, 178–79, 182, 183n2, 209–17, 220–21, 225, 227, 228n2, 229n7, 229n12
subject formation, 3, 15–16, 122, 124, 127, 134, 188

subject position, 8, 16, 123–27, 130–34, 139, 140, 145, 151–52, 158n2
　alteration of, 153
　reproduction of, 153
　and identity, 157
　See also ethical: subject
subjectification, 15, 125–26, 130, 140, 144–45, 148, 153–54. *See also* ethical: subjectivation
subjectivation. *See under* ethical
subvert, 212, 215, 220, 226
superior, 52, 112, 214, 226
symbol, 9, 35, 47, 57, 71–72, 100, 107, 170, 176–78, 189, 194, 201, 202n1, 247, 251
symbolic interactionism, 100

tact, 101
tactile, 234–36, 248, 252
taste, 52, 92n20, 145, 236
teacher
　aikido, 32–35
　dance, 4, 12, 15, 101–2, 106–7, 109–13, 163, 169, 174, 181, 190, 198, 200
　music, 48, 50, 53–54
　piano, 44
　school, 48, 68, 253
　shakuhachi, 35–40
　violin, 45
team collusion. *See* Goffman, Erving
technique, 14, 32–33, 49, 54, 71, 92n20, 101, 106, 179, 181–82, 193
technologies of the self, 6, 15, 18, 124–26, 129–32, 140, 145, 147, 149. *See also* ethical: exercise
telos. *See under* ethical
temple, 28, 33, 173
temporal, 5–6, 14, 17, 157, 188, 243
theatre, 88, 92n13, 97, 190, 200. *See also* butoh
theatrical, 68–69, 72, 82, 99, 228n4
tolerance, 211, 222, 226
touch, 35, 78, 92n20, 147, 154, 180, 236, 251
tourism, 167, 170–72, 175–77, 188
trad goth. *See* music styles

traditional, 35–37, 50, 53, 60n4, 65, 74, 105, 109, 180–81, 191, 200, 252
training
   dance, 3, 12, 15, 69, 71, 75, 78–79, 83–84, 88, 90n1, 91n9, 104, 106, 108–10, 172, 175, 179–81, 183n1
   music, 13, 38–39, 48, 54, 69
   somatic, 10, 13, 28, 31–35, 41n6
'trash music'. *See* music styles
transnational, 49, 58, 167, 170, 198, 203n2
trust, 66, 74, 78, 84, 96, 103, 106, 109–10, 153, 168
tsiftetéli. *See* dance styles

uncertainty, 27, 194, 197, 212
UNESCO, 170
unethical, 8. *See also* immoral
unfamiliar, 67, 164
urban, 4, 7, 28, 30, 47, 71, 122, 135n3, 188, 191, 193, 196–97
unmeant gestures. *See* Goffman, Erving

vampire, 215, 218, 227
verbal, 6, 14, 18, 30, 36, 46, 50, 99, 123, 128, 134, 210, 212, 227, 247–48, 251
   nonverbal, 14, 50, 99, 247
victimhood, 214
video recording, 10, 187
viewer, 38, 80, 82, 188, 197, 201, 220
violence, 70, 135n3

violin. *See* musical instruments
virtual, 4–5
virtue, 7, 10, 87, 98, 124–25, 132–33
visceral, 3, 8–9, 14, 67–8, 73, 75–83, 88–9, 91n6, 234
vision, 14, 65, 67, 70, 75, 89, 92n20, 213
visual, 9, 29, 32, 66, 71, 73, 75, 77–79, 83, 91n9, 103, 112, 141, 175, 177–78, 195, 210, 235–36, 243, 247–48, 252
vocabulary of fronts. *See* Goffman, Erving
vocal, 2, 15, 39, 41n2, 65, 79, 85, 87, 103, 132, 134
voice, 14, 30, 39, 50, 66, 71, 87, 121, 127, 132–33, 200, 209, 213, 230n16, 235, 243, 249, 255n9
volunteer, 101, 110–11
vulnerability, 74, 78, 82, 84, 132

walking, 30, 37, 71, 96, 174, 238, 249
wellbeing, 28, 152
Western, 14, 30, 44–50, 52, 56–59, 60n5, 70, 74, 79, 82, 88, 90, 92n16, 97, 163, 166, 176, 178, 192, 214

youth, 18, 215, 230n20
YouTube, 176, 221

zeibékiko. *See* dance styles
Zen, 14, 32, 35, 38–39, 56–59, 60n5, 67, 81

www.ingramcontent.com/pod-product-compliance
Lightning Source LLC
Chambersburg PA
CBHW070914030426
42336CB00014BA/2408